1984

MASTERPIECES O   E

A NINE VOLUME SE.

CENTRAL EUROPEAN THEATRE / *The Game of Love* and
La Ronde Schnitzler / *Electra* Hofmannsthal / *R.U.R.* Čapek /
The Play's the Thing Molnár

ENGLISH THEATRE / *The Importance of Being Earnest* Wilde /
Major Barbara Shaw / *Loyalties* Galsworthy / *Dear Brutus* Bar-
rie / *Enter Solly Gold* Kops

FRENCH THEATRE / *The Parisian Woman* Becque / *Christo-
pher Columbus* de Ghelderode / *Electra* Giraudoux / *Eurydice
(Legend of Lovers)* Anouilh / *Queen After Death* Montherlant /
Improvisation or The Shepherd's Chameleon Ionesco

GERMAN THEATRE / *Woyzeck* Buechner / *Maria Magdalena*
Hebbel / *The Weavers* Hauptmann / *The Marquis of Keith*
Wedekind / *The Caucasian Chalk Circle* Brecht

IRISH THEATRE / *The Countess Cathleen* Yeats / *The Playboy
of the Western World* and *Riders to the Sea* Synge / *The Silver
Tassie* and *Cock-a-Doodle Dandy* O'Casey

ITALIAN THEATRE / *Six Characters in Search of an Author*
and *The Pleasure of Honesty* Pirandello / *Crime on Goat Island*
Betti / *Filumena Marturano* Filippo / *The Academy* and *The
Return* Fratti

RUSSIAN THEATRE / *A Month in the Country* Turgenev /
Uncle Vanya and *The Cherry Orchard* Chekhov / *The Lower
Depths* Gorky / *The Bedbug* Mayakovsky

SCANDINAVIAN THEATRE / *Hedda Gabler* Ibsen / *Miss
Julie* and *The Ghost Sonata* Strindberg / *The Difficult Hour*
Lagerkvist / *The Defeat* Grieg / *Anna Sophie Hedvig* Abell

SPANISH THEATRE / *The Witches' Sabbath* Benavente / *The
Cradle Song* Martínez-Sierra / *The Love of Don Perlimplín and
Belisa in the Garden* Lorca / *The Dream Weaver* Vallejo Buero /
Death Thrust Sastre

MASTERPIECES OF THE MODERN RUSSIAN THEATRE

Edited by ROBERT W. CORRIGAN

FIVE PLAYS

A MONTH IN THE COUNTRY

UNCLE VANYA

THE CHERRY ORCHARD

THE LOWER DEPTHS

THE BEDBUG

COLLIER BOOKS, *NEW YORK*

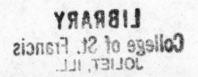

CONTENTS

CONTENTS

THE RUSSIAN THEATRE: CZARIST AND AFTER

by Robert W. Corrigan

HAMLET, in giving advice to the players, pointed out that the purpose of the theatre was to hold "the mirror up to nature." A little earlier he had commented that the players were "the abstract and brief chronicles of the time." If Shakespeare was right about this, then it is clear that the political, economic, and artistic programs of Soviet Socialism have not been very hospitable to the artistic spirit, nor have they provided very fertile ground in which the arts might take root. Nowhere is this barrenness more apparent than in the Russian theatre. Russia is certainly one of the chief participants in the mid-twentieth century drama of the not-so-cold war, but its theatre failed to survive the Revolution. In fact, it has not even entered the twentieth century. Whenever one speaks of the modern Russian theatre, he is referring—almost without exception—to plays which are essentially nineteenth century in tone, style, theme and technique, if not in actual date of composition.

Most critics maintain that the "modern" Russian drama begins with Nikolai Gogol (1809–52) whose famous play, *The Inspector General*, was first produced in 1836. But it was not until 1849, when Turgenev's *A Month in the Country* was published, that the new Russian theatre was firmly established. Two things are crucial to know about Turgenev: 1) Like Gogol, he was more a novelist than a playwright, and since their work established the dominant pattern of the Russian theatre until the Revolution all of the plays written for the serious theatre during the second half of the century tended to be influenced as much by fictional techniques as they were by theatrical conventions. 2) Although Westernized and

[7]

liberal, Turgenev was a czarist until he died in 1883. His is the drama of czarist Russia in full bloom. There are no revolutionary tendencies, no tearing apart of the social fabric, no profound questions about life's meaning. In all of Turgenev's work we find an expansive and tolerant spirit exposing the frailty of human beings when they are submitted to certain pressures. But Turgenev, as Richard Schechner has pointed out, never really concerns himself with the *angst* of society itself.

Chekhov did, but always within the context of the crumbling world of the landed gentry which he knew so well. Chekhov has been touted in recent years as one of the parents of the "Theatre of the Absurd." In a sense this is true: his epiphanic structures, his gentle irony, and his disbelief in the possibility of people doing anything of positive consequence do seem to be the prototypes of much that has been written in the years since World War II. But Chekhov was always a nineteenth-century writer. He wrote of a world in collapse, but he was of that world, in that world. Some of his characters talked of bright new days to come, but it is clear—in spite of Stanislavsky's interpretations—that Chekhov did not identify himself with them. He revealed the plight of his world, but he did not judge it. He spent his lifetime trying to improve the quality of life in his land, but he never repudiated it.

Even Maxim Gorky, the great rebel, who lived well into our century (he died in 1936), never succeeded as a twentieth-century playwright. There is a tendency, even among knowledgeable teachers of the drama, to think of Gorky as a writer of numerous significant plays. However, when we look more closely at the body of his theatre, only *The Lower Depths*, which was completed, first produced, and published in 1902, comes up to such a standard. Gorky, always in revolt, went on to be one of the most articulate spokesmen for Soviet realism, but he never again spoke to the world through his plays.

Indeed, what we think of as modern Russian drama stopped in 1904 with the death of Chekhov. But this did not mean the Russian theatre itself went into decline. On the contrary, the reverse was true: this has been the *great* century for the Russian theatre. Stanislavsky emerged as probably the most influential single figure in twentieth-century theatre; the experiments and innovations of Meyerhold, Tairov, and Vakhtanghov have still not been assimilated by most theatre practitioners in the rest of the world, and the Russian theatre of today is imbued with a spirit of craftsmanship equaled by no other theatre. But for all of this experimentation in theatrical technique, and in spite of the unmatched standards of performance which are maintained by her actors, the Soviet Union has not produced a single new drama of international significance. The reasons for this are numerous, and all of them are ironic. Since the beginning of the century, the leaders of the Russian theatre have been more concerned with technique than they have been with meaning. This tendency was already noticeable in the many arguments between Stanislavsky and Chekhov over the interpretation of the latter's plays. Stanislavsky was undoubtedly a great performer, but he didn't understand Chekhov's plays (Chekhov accused him of "ruining" his plays), and some of his later writings make one question whether the famous actor-director understood most plays very well. Despite lip service (undoubtedly sincere) to the primacy of the playwright's intention, Stanislavsky was always far more concerned with technique and style than he was with content or meaning. This became the dominant trait of all who followed him, including those, like Meyerhold, who revolted against his methods. By the early 1920s, the great Russian directors had publicly announced that their first responsibility was not to the playwright's script; indeed, they took great pride in their revisions of the classics, both ancient and modern, to conform to the principles of Soviet realism *and* their new production techniques. The result: a formalism more sterile than anything conceived by the decadent practitioners of bourgeois capitalism.

I once tried to persuade several publishers to put out a volume of Soviet plays in English translation. I was not successful. Each of them agreed that it was a good idea to know what had been written for the Russian theatre during the past quarter of a century, but when we read the manuscripts, all of us had to admit that they were pretty bad and certainly not worth the effort and expense of publishing them. The best of the lot was Mayakovsky's *The Bedbug* (1928), and this renowned poet-playwright has been dead for thirty-five years. *The Bedbug* has some good moments in it, and is undoubtedly interesting to stage, but how meager it seems when compared to even the slightest of Chekhov's works. The play has a superficial effectiveness and an ersatz vitality which is momentarily engaging, but it is, in the last analysis, theatricality for its own sake.

The contemporary Russian theatre is schizoid in nature: its plays are, for the most part, propagandistic; and its techniques have no function except self-perpetuation. Until this condition changes, Russian theatre will continue in its moribund state.

MASTERS OF THE MODERN THEATRE

by Robert W. Corrigan

AFTER VISITING the United States in 1835, Alexis de Tocqueville described the kind of literature he believed an industrialized democratic society would produce. "I am persuaded," he wrote in *Democracy in America*, "that in the end democracy diverts the imagination from all that is external to man and fixes it on man alone.... It may be foreseen in like manner that poets living in democratic times will prefer the delineation of passions and ideas to that of persons and achievements. The language, the dress, and the daily actions of men in democracies are repugnant to conceptions of the ideal.... This forces the poet constantly to search below the external surface which is palpable to the senses, in order to read the inner soul.... The destinies of mankind, man himself taken aloof from his country, and his age, and standing in the presence of Nature and of God, with his passions, his doubts, his rare prosperities and inconceivable wretchedness, will become the chief, if not the sole theme of poetry." Any examination of the arts of the past century would seem to indicate that Tocqueville's prophecy has been fulfilled, and it is certainly clear that the theatre's general pattern of development during this time can be best described as a gradual but steady shift away from universal philosophical and social concerns toward the crises and conflicts of man's inner and private life. It is possible to discover foreshadowings of this change in direction and emphasis in the plays of the early nineteenth-century romantics—Buechner, Hebbel, Kleist, Gogol, Musset—but it was not until Ibsen that the theatre's revolutionary break with the past became clearly discernible. In fact, Ibsen's career as a playwright to a large extent parallels both in form and in theme the modern drama's increasing tendency to be concerned more with the conflicts of the individual's interior world than with the significance of his public deeds.

The causes of any revolution are always as difficult to untangle as its consequences are to assess, and any attempt on the part of the critic to describe them will inevitably result in oversimplification. But it is possible to discover certain basic changes in attitude which had been evolving in Europe since the time of Luther and which had begun to crystallize in Continental thought by the second half of the nineteenth century. And the works of the revolutionary playwrights—Ibsen, Strindberg, Chekhov, Shaw, and Hauptmann —were the first to express in the theatre certain of these radical shifts in the way man had come to think of nature, society, and himself. What follows is an attempt to set forth briefly some of the more important aspects of this revolution in the drama which Ibsen referred to as "a war to the knife with the past."

One of the dominant ideas of the modern *Weltanschauung* is the belief that it is impossible to know what the world is really like. Beginning with Luther's refusal to accept that there was any intelligible relationship between faith and works, the sacramental view of experience gradually disappeared. In rejecting the phenomenal world as an outward and visible manifestation of man's spiritual condition, Luther began a revolution in thought which, because of the achievenents of science and technology in the past two hundred years, now makes it impossible for man to attach any objective value to the observations of his senses. This insistence on such a clear-cut division between the physical and the spiritual aspects of reality had a profound effect on the modern dramatist. Inevitably, it made him increasingly distrustful of his sensory responses to the "outside" world, and at the same time it tended to negate whatever belief he might have had in the objective validity of his subjective feelings and sensations. The modern artist no longer holds a mirror up to nature, at least not with any confidence; he can only stare at his own image. He becomes a voyeur to his own existence.

Probably no force in the nineteenth century did more to destroy man's belief in an established norm of human nature, and hence begin this process of internalization in the theatre, than the advent of psychology as a systematized field of study. In his book *"Modernism" in The Modern Drama*, Joseph Wood Krutch argued that the basic issue confronting all the dramatists of the past hundred years was the problem of "modernism." Briefly, modernism involves both the conviction and the practice that to be modern is to be, in many important ways, different from anyone who lived before. This does not mean that man has changed; human nature is the same, but man's way of looking at himself has changed significantly. It is this new view of man that creates the problem for the dramatist.

Good examples of this changed perception can be found in Ibsen's *Hedda Gabler* (1890) and Strindberg's *Miss Julie* (1888). Hedda and Julie have the distinction of being the first fully and consciously developed neurotic heroines in dramatic literature. By neurotic we mean that they are neither logical nor insane (in the sense of being random and unaccountable) but that the aims and motives of each has a secret personal logic of their own. The significant thing about both characters is that they are motivated by the premise that there is a secret, and sometimes unconscious, world of aims and methods, a secret system of values which is more important in human experience than rational ones. This approach to character is not, however, the same as the Romantic attitude which affirms the superior validity of the nonrational. We need only read Strindberg's famous Preface to *Miss Julie* or Ibsen's working notes for *Hedda Gabler* to discover that they did not believe, as did the nineteenth-century Romantic poets, that the irrational was a supernatural and unknowable force; rather, in giving detailed account of why their heroines behaved as they did, Ibsen and Strindberg insisted that neurotic behavior and mysterious events are always explainable in terms of natural causes. The significant difference is that neither of these characters can be explained or judged by a common standard; the actions of each character (and by extension, of each human being) are explicable only in terms of that peculiar combination of forces, frustrations, and desires which is unique to himself.

For us living in the middle of the twentieth century there is nothing very new in these psychological ideas; but, coming when they did, they were quite revolutionary, and they have created problems for the playwright which have not yet been solved. By convincingly demonstrating that normal people are not as rational as they seem, and that abnormal people do not act in a random and unintelligible way, psychology has made it difficult, if not impossible, for the dramatist to present his characters in a direct way. In earlier times when it was believed that there was a sharp distinction between the sane and the insane, the irrational "aberrations" of human behavior were dramatically significant because they could be defined in terms of a commonly accepted standard of sane conduct. It seems clear, for instance, that Shakespeare believed Lear on the heath to be insane, while it is equally clear that Macbeth at the witches' cauldron was not. But for the modern dramatist deeds do not necessarily mean what they appear to mean, and in themselves they are not directly revelatory of the characters who commit them. Miss Julie, Hedda Gabler, and Kostya Treplev of Chekhov's *The Sea Gull* are all suicides; but, unlike Othello's suicide, the meaning of each of their deaths cannot be clearly ascertained from the actions that preceded it. The plight of the modern dramatist in this regard becomes apparent when we realize that without Strindberg's Preface or Ibsen's Notebook we could never know for certain what the significance of each heroine's death really was. And the ambiguity of almost every interpretation of *The Sea Gull* is largely due to the fact that Chekhov never made the meaning of Treplev's suicide explicit.

All drama of the past is based upon the axiom "By their deeds shall ye know them." The significance of the dramatic hero was revealed by his deeds, and there was a direct relationship between the hero's overt acts and his inner spiritual condition. The significance of Oedipus, for instance, is revealed by his deeds, not by some explanation that he is suffering from an Oedipus complex; and there is a direct relationship between the act of tearing out his own eyes and his solving the riddle of the Sphinx. Even when a character commits a dissembling deed, it is to deceive the other characters in the play, not the spectators. Certainly one of the chief functions of the soliloquy in Elizabethan drama was to keep the audience informed as to what was going on. Hamlet may put on an antic disposition, but not before he tells the audience he is going to do so. However, beginning in the nineteenth century, the drama began to reflect man's growing distrust in the ability of his senses to comprehend the true nature of reality. Appearances are no longer believed to be direct reflections of ideal reality, like the shadows on the wall of Plato's cave; rather they are thought of as a mask which hides or distorts reality. And by the time of Pirandello, particularly in such plays as *Right You Are, If You Think You Are*

(1916), *Six Characters in Search of an Author* (1921), and *The Mock Emperor Enrico IV* (1922), appearances not only do not express reality, they contradict it, and the meaning of these plays is not to be found in appearance or reality but in the contradiction itself.

One of the great achievements of the Elizabethan dramatic form was its ability to express several levels of experience simultaneously. The world of Hamlet is both public and private, a world in which personal and familial relationships, fantasy and mystery, and political and psychological conflict coexist in a state of constant dramatic tension. One of the main reasons why the Elizabethan dramatic form works so successfully is that appearances can be taken at face value. But when the dramatist begins to distrust the validity of his sensory perceptions, it becomes difficult, if not impossible, for him to dramatize the complex totality of experience in a single form. Reality must be broken down into its component parts, and each part can be expressed only in a form peculiar to itself. Admitting individual differences in the works of each dramatist's writing of any given period, it is nonetheless possible to describe with some accuracy the dramatic form employed by the playwrights of the fifth-century Greek theatre, the Elizabethan and Restoration theatres of England, and the French neo-classic theatre of the seventeenth century. But in discussing the modern theatre we must always speak of forms, for there is no single, dominant form in the serious theatre of the past hundred years. It is for this reason that the evolution of the drama since the time of Shakespeare has been so aptly described as a process of fragmentation.

It is likely that every serious dramatist believes it his artistic duty to be true to his presuppositions about the real nature of the world in which he lives. However, once a playwright believes that the meaning of every human action is relative and intelligible only in terms of a unique and subsurface combination of forces, the dramatic events of the plot cease to have meaning in themselves, and they take on significance only as the secret motivations of the characters who participate in them are revealed. (The technique of earlier drama is just the reverse: the motivations of the characters are revealed by the events of the plot.) But how does the dramatist objectify the hidden and unconscious, and what happens to the theatre when he feels obligated to explain and probe into his characters' hidden lives? Explanation is always a dangerous business in the theatre (since the time of the ancient Greeks, exposition has always been the dramatist's most difficult problem), but the moment a playwright assumes that if he explains his characters he has written a play, that danger becomes mortal. All too often the writers of the modern theatre have forgotten that a dramatic situation requires not that we *understand* a character but simply that we *believe* in him. Dramatic action always leads to a judgment; it requires that something shall happen to and through the characters; something that is embodied in the events of which the characters are a part. Whenever the personality of the character, rather than the action of which the character should be a part, becomes the playwright's chief concern, dramatic process dissolves into explanation, and when that occurs, the range of the theatre is drastically reduced, if not unalterably damaged.

One has only to compare the plays of the mid-twentieth century to those of Ibsen, Shaw, or Strindberg to realize just how much the scope of the theatre has been narrowed. However, early evidence of the gradual loss of belief in dramatic heroes, who needed no explaining, can be found in the sentimental bourgeois drama of the eighteenth century. For the first time a character was no longer noble, responsible, or morally significant, and therefore dramatically interesting just because of his birth, position, power, or wealth. As a result, the dramatist was obliged to justify both his choice of characters and the situations in which they are engaged. The Romantic drama of the eighteenth and nineteenth centuries resisted a break with the past and attempted unsuccessfully to perpetuate the forms and figures of earlier times. Certainly the revolt of Ibsen and his contemporaries in the last quarter of the nineteenth century was in some measure due to their conviction that the dramatic conflicts of the Romantic drama were inflated and without significance, and that the nobility of its characters was artificial and contrived. In rejecting the artificialities of Romanticism, the modernists changed the theatre in many ways; but for all their dissatisfaction with their predecessors they were unable to forestall disbelief in the possibility of heroic characters who needed no explaining.

This was largely because as a literary movement nineteenth-century naturalism was so closely related to nineteenth-century biology. Darwin's theories of evolution (*Origin of Species,* 1859) and the discovery of new genetic laws had convinced many writers that man's existence, including his personality, was a phenomenon that could be explained in terms of scientific laws. As a result, increasingly, man's complex biological needs rather than his capacity to make moral choices were thought to be his most significant characteristic. Once such a view was accepted, however, the exceptional man, who because of his position and power had the greatest freedom of choice, ceased to be the fullest embodiment, and therefore the best representative, of those conflicts and choices that most clearly define the human condition. Instead, the lives of the poor—where the role of natural necessity is most readily observable— became the playwright's most suitable subjects. The drama of the common man, then, did not happen by accident, nor did it evolve because some dramatist or group of dramatists wanted it to. Given the problem of creating in a world in which all human actions tend to be explained in terms of psychological or sociological cause and effect, a world in which the possibility of deliberative and moral choice is doubted if not rejected outright, it is difficult, if not impossible, for the playwright to fashion a character of traditional heroic stature.

There is an old saw about no man being a hero to his valet. Neither is he one to his psychoanalyst. Nor can he be one to a playwright who views his actions as behavioral phenomena explicable in terms of some kind of laws—scientific or otherwise. Oedipus, for example, remains a hero of great stature so long as he is not suffering from an Oedipus complex. But once we learn to explain him in terms of repressed hopes and fears, traumatic childhood experience, or a vitamin deficiency in infancy, although he may remain interesting—in fact he may gain a new kind of interest, as Cocteau's *The Infernal Machine* attests—he loses stature. Even if we are able, temporarily to accept the Elizabethan attitude toward heroes, which of us can understand a Hamlet or a Lear? And which of us can forgive an Othello or a Macbeth? But it is precisely because they seem mysteriously beyond our powers of understanding that they remain heroes for us. And it is a belief in a mysterious, unknowable quality in men that substantiates man's sense of his own importance in the universe. However, if a playwright comes to believe that all human actions are in reality predictable behavioral responses, and his moral judgments of these actions can be dissolved by psychological understanding, how can he pattern a tragedy or create characters with stature? If there can be no possibility for an appraisal of personality as such, why should Hamlet's death be any more significant than that of Rosencrantz and Guildenstern?

But the problem does not end here. For once the dramatist dismisses the possibility of passing moral judgments on his characters' actions, he comes face to face with an even more frightening spectre—guilt that has no form of expiation and thus turns into anxiety. It has long been known that art must ultimately fail in its attempt to come to grips with the facts of death. Perhaps this is also true of anxiety. How can there be drama in an Age of Anxiety? What kind of play will be produced when the central conflict is between something and nothing? Many of the arts may be able to express the condition of anxiety; but the theatre, because of the objective reality and irremovable presence of the living actor, and because the drama is essentially an embodiment of the conflict between at least two opposing recognizable and nameable forces, is incapable of dealing with anxiety, or it does so to its own great peril. Beginning with the Watchman in the opening scene of the *Orestia* right on through the ghosts of Elsinore and the tormented heroes of Schiller and Kleist, the theatre has always found a way to transform anxiety into fear; that is, give it a definite object. But when we come to such plays as Ibsen's *Ghosts* and *The Master Builder* and Strindberg's *There Are Crimes and Crimes,* and *The Ghost Sonata,* we discover that although this process of objectification is attempted, it is not totally successful. And when the transformation does not take place, the form and content of drama begin to change in uncontrollable ways, as some of the plays of Beckett and Ionesco, Pinter and Albee will attest. It is difficult enough to find a meaning for man in a world that views a return to nothingness as the ultimate reality, but it is next to impossible to create a dramatic "action" which can encompass the terror of being on the edge of the abyss. Kierkegaard, and more recently Paul Tillich, have declared that this threat of nothingness is the central anxiety of modern man. Many modern playwrights have sought to overcome the despair of this situation by maintaining that the only meaning of life is to be found in that death which is inevitable. But this is not an assertion that gives meaning to any of the particularities of life; in fact, it drains them of meaning. At best, it is a method of redeeming existence from meaningless anarchy by showing that the pattern of life is simple and imperturbable. But such a pattern, though it may appear to conquer chaos, is too abstract to live successfully in the theatre.

In life as we experience it, we are conscious of our physical natures, our social situation, and our unique psychic existence; and we live on all three of these levels simultaneously. For this reason it is impossible for us to act or make a choice without some element of human behavior— what we do out of physical necessity or because of social habit—playing a significant role in our decision. At the same time, because of the simultaneity of our being, it is impossible for us to understand completely the individuality of our actions. But in the theatre we see life as pure deed, that is, life in which the arbitrariness of human behavior has been eliminated and in which the mysterious transformations of individuality have been fixed. Thus, in contrast to a person in life, who is recognized by the continuity of his being and finally can only be known through intuition, a character in a play is an identity who is defined by the coherence of his acts. For this reason the deeds of a dramatic action are always public, and the characters best suited to drama are men and women who, either by fate or choice, lead a public life and whose deeds are of public concern. This explains why kings, princes, and nobility have traditionally been the most suitable subjects for drama. But as the increasing dominance of the machine in modern life has gradually destroyed the direct relation between a man's intention and his deeds, public figures have ceased to be our most appropriate heroes because, as W. H. Auden points out, "the good and evil they do depends less upon their characters and intentions than upon the quantity of impersonal force at their disposal."

Our world, it would seem, has become almost too big for the playwright. Power is too impersonal, great deeds are collective achievements, and the great man is one who is capable of withstanding some of the pressures of a mass society and manages, somehow, to maintain a face and stance more or less his own. Compare, for example, the achievement of a Lindbergh (our last "lone" hero) to that of a Colonel Glenn, who was interchangeable with five other astronauts. Or, how can the power of a Napoleon be envisioned today? In our times power is so enormous that it is barely visible and those who govern are little more than incidental and easily replaceable expressions of that power. Power is like an iceberg; the largest part is submerged—in abstraction, anonymity, and bureaucracy. Government, like modern physics, has lost its physical reality and can be expressed only in statistics and formulae. Indeed, the true men of action in our time, those who transform the world, are not the statesmen and politicians but the scientists. Unfortunately, their most significant actions are not suitable subjects for the theatre, because their deeds are concerned with things, not people, and are, therefore, speechless.

But what are the implications of this for the theatre? Who are the true representatives of a world whose heroes are nameless? As the Swiss playwright Duerrenmatt put it: "Any small-time crook, petty government official, or policeman better represents our world than a senator or president. Today art can only embrace victims if it can reach men at all; it can no longer come close to the mighty. Creon's secretaries close Antigone's case."

That there has been a shift in attitude toward the heroic is easily seen when we examine any one of the many modern adaptations of the Greek tragedies. For example, today most people find Anouilh's *Antigone* much more a reflection of their attitudes and thus more immediately interesting than Sophocles' tragic working of the theme. The characters and the dilemma of their situation seem more human. Antigone is not a hard and almost inhuman girl, with such a monomaniacal fixity of purpose that she rejects all other feelings and desires. In the modern version she is, humanly, both weak and strong. She has a lover in Haemon, whom she rejects; but she is also a helpless little girl who runs to "Nanny" for comfort and strength; as she approaches death, she is afraid and seeks the consolations of even the most callous of guards. Creon is not a blind and power-mad tyrant; he is a businessman king who is caught in the complex web of compromise and expediency which will not allow abstract moral principles to upset the business of government.

However, what the play gains in humanity it loses in tragic force. The sense of Antigone's aloneness and Creon's moral blindness, and of the inevitable destruction implicit in their conflict, has been softened. Anouilh's Antigone is not alone and unloved, and his Creon is not blind. We pity their situation because they are two quite attractive people caught up in a situation which neither of them likes but which they cannot control. They are victims in a disordered world which they have not created and which they have no moral obligation to correct. As the play ends, we are left with an ambiguity that allows for no reconciliation.

One of the most important functions of the hero, both in art and life, is to supply those images, values, and ethical standards which people aspire to and which they would like, if possible, to incorporate into their own lives. It would seem, however, that increasingly our modern industrialized society not only does not need heroes, but it actually suppresses or perverts our need of them. In their important book *Industrialism and Industrial Man*, Kerr, Dunlop, Harbison, and Myers convincingly demonstrate that "like ideologies, the great personality—the one great figure around whom historians so frequently weave their story—began to seem less important. Instead of ideologies and dominant personalities, we became increasingly attentive to the inherent nature of the particular industrializing system and the basic strategy and forces at work within it." Only the system, then, is important, and it fills men's remaining need for heroes by promoting celebrities, those heroes of the surface who play well their constantly shifting roles.

Furthermore, specialization—the key operative principle of an industrial society—produces not only pluralism in our economic system but also a pluralistic deviation of heroic types. However, when there are and can be so many heroic types—one cannot even begin to count all the heroes of the popular imagination—you begin to get a leveling; and with that leveling not only is the stature of heroism diminished, but the individual's sense of his own identity is actually invalidated.

Traditionally, the hero is always best described in terms of those forces that urge him to spiritual redemption. Maxwell Anderson once wrote that "from the point of view of the playwright, the essence of a tragedy, or even a serious play, is the spiritual awakening, or regeneration, of his hero." But the one thing that characterizes the hero of surfaces—and this is certainly in large measure due to industrialization and bureaucracy—is precisely the fact that he lacks the dimensions of spiritual awareness, personal morality, and social responsibility. Paul Tillich wrote in his *The Religious Situation* that "the fundamental value in ethics of a capitalistic society is economic efficiency—developed to the utmost degree of ruthless activity." Such an ethical standard is hardly conducive to the creation of great heroes in the drama.

That we live in an antiheroic age is a commonplace. Carlyle proclaimed its coming in the nineteenth century when he said: "We shall either learn to know a hero . . . when we see him, or else go on to be forever governed by the unheroic." This transformation has occurred; we have accepted it; we are even used to it. Whatever nostalgia we may still occasionally feel is more than adequately taken care of by television. In the place of the hero we have the celebrity, that triumph of the ordinary. In our time, hero worship has become horizontal; indeed, we even look down to a "man like myself."

While the advent of psychology as a systematized field of study may have been the most powerful single force to shape the modern theatre, actually the process of internalization had begun much earlier. For instance, it is clear from Hebbel's essays on the drama that the despair of old Anton's "I don't understand the world any more" in the final scene of *Maria Magdalena* is much more than an expression of the age-old frustration of the parent who does not understand the behavior of his children. It also reflects his dimly understood but tremendously painful realization that it is no longer possible for him to comprehend what the world has become or to imagine what the future will be like. Until the Industrial Revolution, patterns of life were passed on from father to son with the confidence that these patterns would satisfy the needs and desires of each new generation. Such confidence was justified, for life changed so gradually and imperceptibly that when changes did occur they were easily assimilated into the shared life of the community. But by the middle of the nineteenth century the effects of the Industrial Revolution had begun to be felt on all levels of society. Technology, with its ever increasing capacity to transform man's way of living, not only made the future so unpredictable that it soon became impossible for him to imagine what his life would be like twenty years hence, but in its singular concern with the individual's functional qualities technology tended to isolate him from his fellows and invalidate his spiritual values and metaphysical concerns. At the same time, the discoveries of the nineteenth-century archeologists, and the ensuing interest in anthropology, tended to break down provincial and absolutist attitudes concerning human nature. Early anthropologists like Mannhardt, Robertson-Smith, Tylor, and the great James Frazer made it clear that human nature was not something fixed and unchanging but only that kind of behavior exhibited in each culture. In fact, as early as 1860 scholars were demonstrating that human nature is so plastic that it can, as Frazer was later to point out in the Preface to the first edition of *The Golden Bough* (1890), "exhibit varieties of behavior which, in the animal Kingdom could only be exhibited by different species." Furthermore, by the middle of the century, democracy was finally beginning to be established both as a way of life and as a form of government. Today we tend to forget what a revolutionary idea democracy is and the shattering effects that it had upon the values of eighteenth- and nineteenth-century Europe. Alexis de Tocqueville told us long ago: "Not only does democracy make every man forget his ancestors, but it hides his descendants and separates his contemporaries from him, it throws him back forever upon himself alone and threatens in the end to confine him entirely within the solitude of his own heart." In short, by the middle of the nineteenth century every established view of God, human nature, social organization, and the physical universe was beginning to be seriously challenged if not invalidated. And this revolutionary climate had a profound effect on the theatre.

Of all the arts, theatre is the only art that has always concerned itself with human destinies. Dramatic action is historical in the sense that the perpetual present of each moment on the stage is created out of past events and is directed toward a definite, if yet unknown, future. In previous ages the destiny of any dramatic action was significant because the ever-changing events in the lives of dramatic heroes could be meaningfully related to eternity, that is, to some permanent value or idea such as Fate, the Gods, or Heaven and Hell, which transcends the human condition and which is believed in by the dramatist and/or his audience.

In the plays of Buechner and Hebbel we discover the first indications in the theatre of that sense of alienation from both God and Society which underscores the fact that man's belief in eternity had been shaken. And one of the most significant aspects of Ibsen's work (at least after *Peer Gynt,* 1867) is the fact that the realm of ultimate value has either disappeared or has become so mysterious that it has ceased to have dramatic relevance. In its place we find instead a belief in some form of social ideal or societal structure;

first, as the agent of some unknown Destiny, and then as Destiny itself. But when society begins to assume the role of Destiny, that is, is thought of as the determining force for good or evil in the lives of men, man cannot help but feel eventually that the meaning of his Destiny has been drastically reduced. For Society, as Robert Bolt writes in the Preface to his *A Man for All Seasons*, "can only have as much idea as we have what we are about, for it has only our brains to think with. And the individual who tries to plot his position by reference to our society finds no fixed points, but only the vaunted absence of them, 'freedom' and 'opportunity'; freedom for what, opportunity to do what, is nowhere indicated. The only positive he is given is 'get and spend' . . . and he did not need society to tell him that. In other words we are thrown back by our society upon ourselves, which of course sends us flying back to society with all the force of rebound."

And mind capable of spiritual aspiration seeks in the actions of the dramatic hero that which affirms the vitality of the free will in any given situation. Man's free will may be defeated by the forces of Destiny—in fact, the great plays have always testified that the destroying forces of Destiny are as much a part of the hero's character as his free will; it may be paralyzed and thus incapable of action; it may be submerged by the battle in such a way as to become part of that Destiny; it may even turn out to be an illusion; but it must always be an active force if we are to believe that we are partaking in human greatness. Such a Destiny must be greater than an aggregate of human beings or an expression of social patterns.

Ironically, the revolt of Ibsen and Shaw against the conventional nineteenth-century drama was motivated by a desire to enlarge the range of Destiny in the theatre. In their attempts to present man in his total historical and social setting, they were rebelling against the narrow and private worlds that had been dominating the stage since the Restoration. But in spite of their efforts, nothing could change the fact that in the two hundred years since Shakespeare the world of the spirit had greatly diminished. The Ekdals' attic and Mrs. Warren's drawing room were not—and never could be—the same as Elsinore or Cleopatra's barge.

Nonetheless, the pioneers of the modern drama had revitalized the theatre precisely because they believed that significant social issues should be dealt with in the theatre. Thus for nearly three decades the theatre had a vitality of spirit and a forcefulness of manner which it had lacked for more than a century for the very reason that its context had been reduced. To the playwright writing at that time the human and social problems, which were the source materials of the naturalistic play, appeared capable of solution if only man and society would learn to use their common sense; which usually meant one of two things—the acceptance of a less rigid standard of social morality or the espousal of some form of socialism. But with the collapse of the established social order in the first World War, the validity of these too-easy solutions was impugned, and beginning with the plays of the early German Expressionists (written 1912–1916) the positive optimism of the Edwardian era gave way to a sense of bewilderment, exasperation, and defeatism, only occasionally tempered by the slim hope that the war had brought man to the threshold of a "New Age." The theatre reflects these changes from confidence to doubting and despair, from complacent faith in cherished values to an anxious questioning, from a rigorous but rigid morality to the mystic evangelism, the fanatical polemics, and the frivolous apathy of a disintegrating world. These changes are most apparent in the Jekyll and Hyde theatre of the German Expressionists whose nerve-shattered playwrights alternated between a militant idealism and grotesque nightmares. But one need only compare Shaw's *Heartbreak House* to *Major Barbara*, Pirandello's *Right You Are, If You Think You Are* to *Liolá*, or Hauptmann's *Winter Ballad* to *The Weavers* to realize that the effects of the collapse of the old order were widespread and were reflected in the works of established writers as well as those of the new generation. Immediately after the war the theatre on the continent was dominated by attitudes of emotionalism and cynicism, but these gradually gave way to feelings of frustration, futility, and despair, and by the middle of the 1920's the serious drama of Europe had become almost totally introspective and psychological in its orientation.[1]

---

[1] Because they were essentially isolated from the main currents of European history in the first two decades of the century, the Irish and American theatres were not immediately effected by the spreading paralysis which was transforming the rest of modern drama. But it is clear from O'Casey's *The Plow and the Stars* (1926) and *The Silver Tassie* (1927) that the Abbey Theatre could not withstand for long the theatre's introspective tendencies,

Obviously, this tendency toward paralyzing introspection has by no means been accepted by everyone writing for the theatre. In fact, a large segment of the modern theatre might be best described as a reaction against the despair and dehumanizing implications of the modernist position. These "resistance movements" have sought to discover the means, both formal and substantive, whereby the possibility and validity of selfhood and human integrity, personal responsibility, and morally significant judgments could be reasserted in the theatre. Some playwrights—especially Eliot, Fry, Betti, and Claudel—have turned to orthodox Christian belief to provide a metaphysical structure for their drama. Others, like Lorca and Synge, have written out of the traditions and value systems of premodern hieratic societies. Probably the largest group of all is composed of those dramatists who have sought to escape the deadly strictures of modernism by turning to classical mythology.

All of these writers shared one common and fundamental attitude: each of them was in some way rebelling against the conditions of the modern world. They were not only conscious of that lack of a sense of community which inevitably occurs in an increasingly democratic society; more important, they were aware of man's growing sense of his own isolation. The modern world, with its growing collectivism, paradoxically tends to throw man back upon himself, while at the same time it increasingly tends to destroy the individual's sense of his own selfhood. This creates an impasse which the modern dramatist, for the most part, has been unable to overcome.

Joseph Warren Beach, in analyzing the problems of modern fiction, describes the reaction of many writers to this condition in this way: "One of the hardest things for man to bear is spiritual isolation. The sense that he stands alone in the universe goes terribly against his gregarious instincts. He has an over-powering impulse to construct a system which will enable him to feel that he does not stand alone but is intimately associated with some force or group infinitely

---

and there was no serious American drama until O'Neill's plays were first produced right after the war. In the twenty years between O'Neill's *Beyond the Horizon* (1920) and *The Iceman Cometh* (1941) the American theatre repeated the Continental cycle in its own terms, and by the beginning of the Second World War all of the Western theatre had reached that No Man's Land between comedy and tragedy, between pathetic aspirations and ridiculous bewilderment, between never-beginning action and never-ending talk.

more powerful and significant than himself." It is clearly evident in the work of all those playwrights who have rebelled against modernism that they too are seeking to construct a system that will restore meaning to life and validity to art. In the end, however, they have not been completely successful, because they have all too often had to deny the realities of the modern world in the process. Furthermore, they have not accepted the wisdom of Brecht's statement that "when one sees that our world of today no longer fits into the drama, then it is merely that the drama no longer fits into the world." By insisting upon values that we may once have cherished but which no longer in actuality exist, the playwrights of the resistance have not been able to revitalize the theatre or its audiences. And most important, they have not succeeded in stretching the imaginations of men in order that they might conquer that sense of isolation and despair that pervades the modern world. And this brings us to the playwrights of the mid-twentieth century.

In an age dominated by space orbits and telestars, the fear of nuclear war, the tension of cold war diplomacy, and the insecurity of a defense economy, our greatest uncertainty is whether or not in the midst of epochal disorder man has any good chance, to borrow Faulkner's phrase, of prevailing; and if he does, what kind of man will prevail?

This uncertainty has had a profound effect on our theatre, and if there is one thing that characterizes the work of almost all of our serious playwrights of the last two decades it is that their plays express the contemporary theatre's tremendous concern to find a metaphor for universal modern man as he lives on the brink of disaster—a metaphor that expresses the inalienable part of every man, that irreducible part of each of us that exists after all the differences have been stripped away and which is beyond and beneath all that is social, political, economic, religious, and ideological. In short, they are searching for a metaphor of man left face to face with himself.

Such an idea of the theatre has tremendous implications for the drama, and we are just now becoming aware of them. First of all, it abolishes the traditional linear plot because our contemporary playwrights are not interested in presenting an action in any Aristotelian sense but are, rather, dramatizing a condition. Whenever one asks what the central action of a Beckett, Ionesco, or Pinter play is, he comes a cropper; "action" for the contemporary playwright is an artificial concept. He is concerned with showing life as it is, and in life there is no central action, there are only people, and the only thing that is basic to each individual is the ontological solitude of his being. The dramatist's only concern is to create in his plays a situation which will reveal the private drama that each man has inside himself and which is enacted every day in the random, apparently meaningless, and undramatic events of our common routine. "History," said James Joyce's Stephen Daedalus, "is a nightmare from which I must awake." Therapidity of historical change and the apparent powerlessness of the individual to affect Collective History has led in the theatre to a retreat from history. Instead of tracing the history of an individual who is born, grows old, and dies, many modern playwrights have devoted their attention to the timeless passionate moments of life, to states of being. They want to express the paradox, the contradiction, and the incompleteness of experience. They are attempting to suggest the raggedness, the confusion, the complexity of motivation, the "discontinuous continuity," and the basic ambiguity of all human behavior. They are, in short, pursuing the premises of modernism to their fullest and most logical conclusions. The writers of the contemporary theatre are facing the "facts of life." If the dramatic meaning of their plays is that drama is no longer possible, they would contend that any other meaning would be artificial, illusory, false; if the dialogue in their plays consists of meaningless clichés and stereotyped phrases, they would insist that this is the way we talk; if their characters are constantly changing their personalities, these playwrights would point out that no one today is really consistent or truly integrated. If the people in their plays seem to be helpless puppets without any will of their own, they would argue that we are all passively at the mercy of blind fate and meaningless circumstance. They call their theatre "Anti-Theatre," and this they insist is the true theatre of our times. If they are correct, so be it! Then history has again followed its own inexorable laws. The very forces that gave life and strength to the modern theatre have caused its decline and death.

But the theatre is always dying, and with equal regularity, like the phoenix, it is resurrected. No one can say with certainty what its new form will be, but that there will be a future seems certain. First, largely because of the development of college and university theatre programs in this country and the large increase in the number of professional repertory theatres here and abroad, there are more people who have experienced good theatre than ever before. And this enlarged audience wants and needs theatre, and it will not be satisfied for long with the maimed rites of psychological and moral cliché, or impassioned jeremiads from prophets of doom, or the meandering contemplations of writers who are morbidly consumed in introspection and self-analysis. Fortunately, there are audiences who want and need the theatre, and they go to the theatre in the hopeful anticipation that the stage will be capable of accommodating all of the terrible-wonderful emotions and insoluble dilemmas of our shared life together. This demand or insistence by audiences on a drama that deals with the significant issues and concerns of our public life will, I believe, force our playwrights to open up new frontiers in the drama and thus extend the boundaries of the theatre. The second great hope of the theatre is that, in spite of the overriding temper of despair and the dominance of antitheatricality in current drama, our playwrights still find human action significant, still find it necessary to write plays, and, in the very act of writing, attest to the miracle of life. We live in one of the most dramatic ages in the history of mankind, and if the past is any kind of reliable guide to what the future of the theatre will be, we have good reason to believe that the theatre of tomorrow can be as dramatic as the world in which we live today.

MASTERPIECES OF THE

MODERN RUSSIAN THEATRE

IVAN TURGENEV

1818–1883

IVAN TURGENEV was Russia's first internationally famous writer. Born of the aristocracy, wealthy, he lived most of his mature life in western Europe, particularly in France. As a liberal, westernized aristocrat, Turgenev believed in reform (he wrote eloquently and often about freeing the serfs), but he was opposed to the radical spirit of social change which was rapidly moving eastward from the continent where he lived in self-imposed exile. Turgenev was a part of the naturalist movement in fiction which was sweeping Europe. He was a close friend of Gustave Flaubert, and was on intimate terms with the Goncourts, DeMaupassant, George Sand and Henry James. None of these writers bring to mind the theatre and, like his friends, Turgenev was essentially a novelist and not a playwright.

He wrote a half-dozen plays, but only his masterpiece, *A Month in the Country* (1849) is remembered. The play has had several important productions, but it is not a great theatre piece. In theme and technique it is closely akin to the fiction which brought him his fame. Turgenev was a master stylist and he always wrote exquisitely—much too precisely for effective dramatic dialogue. He was always much more interested in character development than in plot, and his plays are not so much dramatic actions as they are a series of duo scenes leading up to a full revelation of his central character —usually a woman. Although he was meticulous in filling in the dramatic background, he was really only concerned with what his heroines thought and felt.

A Month in the Country is an autobiographical play. It dramatizes many aspects of his complex relationship with the well known nineteenth-century French singer, Pauline Viardot; and although the play is set in Russia, the real-life setting of the play is Madame Viardot's château outside of Paris, where Turgenev lived much of his adult life and where he died of cancer in 1883.

Always a superb craftsman, Turgenev lacked a well developed histrionic sensibility. In creating Natalya Petrovna, he has given the theatre one of its finest characters, but his chief contribution to the theatre was the fact that he prepared the way for Chekhov by making the drama a respectable literary form for serious Russian writers.

[34]

HAMLET AND DON QUIXOTE[1]

by *Ivan Turgenev*

(1860)

THE FIRST EDITION of Shakespeare's tragedy, *Hamlet*, and the first part of Cervantes' *Don Quixote* appeared in the same year at the very beginning of the seventeenth century.

This coincidence seems to me significant . . . It seems to me that in these two types are embodied two opposite fundamental peculiarities of man's nature—the two ends of the axis about which it turns. I think that all people belong, more or less, to one of these two types; that nearly every one of us resembles either Don Quixote or Hamlet. In our day, it is true, the Hamlets have become far more numerous than the Don Quixotes, but the Don Quixotes have not become extinct.

Let me explain.

All people live—consciously or unconsciously—on the strength of their principles, their ideals; that is, by virtue of what they regard as truth, beauty, and goodness. Many get their ideal all ready-made, in definite, historically developed forms. They live trying to square their lives with this ideal, deviating from it at times, under the influence of passions or incidents, but neither reasoning about it nor questioning it. Others, on the contrary, subject it to the analysis of their own reason. Be this as it may, I think I shall not err too much in saying that for all people this ideal—this basis and aim of their existence—is to be found either outside of them or within them; in other words, for every one of us it is either his own *I* that forms the primary consideration or something else which he considers superior. I may be told that reality does not

[1] Translated by David Modell.

permit of such sharp demarcations; that in the very same living being both considerations may alternate, even becoming fused to a certain extent. But I do not mean to affirm the impossibility of change and contradiction in human nature; I wish merely to point out two different attitudes of man to his ideal. And now I will endeavor to show in what way, to my mind, these two different relations are embodied in the two types I have selected.

Let us begin with Don Quixote. . . .

What does Don Quixote represent? We shall not look at him with the cursory glance that stops at superficialities and trifles. We shall not see in Don Quixote merely "the Knight of the sorrowful figure"—a figure created for the purpose of ridiculing the old-time romances of knighthood. It is known that the meaning of this character had expanded under its immortal creator's own hand, and that the Don Quixote of the second part of the romance is an amiable companion to dukes and duchesses, a wise preceptor to the squire-governor —no longer the Don Quixote he appears in the first part, especially at the beginning of the work; not the odd and comical crank, who is constantly belabored by a rain of blows. I will endeavor, therefore, to go to the very heart of the matter. I repeat: What does Don Quixote represent?

Faith, in the first place; faith in something eternal, immutable; faith in the truth, in short, existing *outside* of the individual, which cannot easily be attained by him, but which is attainable only by constant devotion and the power of self-abnegation. Don Quixote is entirely consumed with devotion to his ideal, for the sake of which he is ready to suffer every possible privation and to sacrifice his life; his life itself he values only insofar as it can become a means for the incarnation of the ideal, for the establishment of truth and justice on earth. I may be told that this ideal is borrowed by his disordered imagination from the fanciful world of knightly romance. Granted—and this makes up the comical side of Don Quixote; but the ideal itself remains in all its immaculate purity. To live for one's self, to care for one's self, Don Quixote would consider shameful. He lives—if I may so express myself—outside of himself, entirely for others, for his brethren, in order to abolish evil, to counteract the forces hostile to mankind—wizards, giants, in a word, the oppressors. There is no trace of egotism in him; he is not concerned with himself, he is wholly a self-sacrifice—appreciate this word;

he believes, believes firmly and without circumspection. Therefore is he fearless, patient, content with the humblest fare,
with the poorest clothes—what cares he for such things! Timid
of heart, he is in spirit great and brave; his touching piety
does not restrict his freedom; a stranger to variety, he doubts
not himself, his vocation, or even his physical prowess; his
will is indomitable. The constant aiming after the same end
imparts a certain monotonousness to his thoughts and one-
sidedness to his mind. He knows little, but need not know
much; he knows what he is about, why he exists on earth—
and this is the chief sort of knowledge. Don Quixote may
seem to be either a perfect madman, since the most indubitable
materialism vanishes before his eyes, melts like tallow before
the fire of his enthusiasm (he really does see living Moors in
the wooden puppets, and knights in the sheep); or shallow
minded, because he is unable lightly to sympathize or lightly
to enjoy; but, like an ancient tree, he sends his roots deep
into the soil, and can neither change his convictions nor pass
from one subject to another. The stronghold of his moral con-
stitution (note that this demented, wandering knight is everywhere and on all occasions the moral being) lends especial
weight and dignity to all his judgments and speeches, to his
whole figure, despite the ludicrous and humiliating situations
into which he endlessly falls. Don Quixote is an enthusiast, a
servant of an idea, and therefore is illuminated by its radiance.

Now what does Hamlet represent?

Analysis, first of all, and egotism, and therefore incredulity.
He lives entirely for himself; he is an egotist. But even an
egotist cannot believe in himself. We can only believe in that
which is outside of and above ourselves. But this *I*, in which he
does not believe, is dear to Hamlet. This is the point of departure, to which he constantly returns, because he finds
nothing in the whole universe to which he can cling with all
his heart. He is a skeptic, and always pothers about himself;
he is ever busy, not with his duty, but with his condition.
Doubting everything, Hamlet, of course, spares not himself;
his mind is too much developed to be satisfied with what he
finds within himself. He is conscious of his weakness; but even
this self-consciousness is power: from it comes his irony, in
contrast with the enthusiasm of Don Quixote. Hamlet delights
in excessive self-depreciation. Constantly concerned with
himself, always a creature of introspection, he knows minutely
all his faults, scorns himself, and at the same time lives, so

to speak, nourished by this scorn. He has no faith in himself, yet is vainglorious; he knows not what he wants nor why he lives, yet is attached to life. He exclaims:

> O that the Everlasting had not fix'd
> His canon 'gainst self-slaughter . . .
> Most weary, stale, flat, and unprofitable
> Seem to me all the uses of this world.

But he will not sacrifice this flat and unprofitable life. He contemplates suicide even before he sees his father's ghost, and receives the awful commission which breaks down completely his already weakened will—but he does not take his life. The love of life is expressed in the very thought of terminating it. Every youth of eighteen is familiar with such feelings as this: "When the blood boils, how prodigal the soul!"

I will not be too severe with Hamlet. He suffers, and his sufferings are more painful and galling than those of Don Quixote. The latter is pummeled by rough shepherds and convicts whom he has liberated; Hamlet inflicts his own wounds —teases himself. In his hands, too, is a lance—the two-edged lance of self-analysis.

Don Quixote, I must confess, is positively funny. His figure is perhaps the most comical that ever poet has drawn. His name has become a mocking nickname even on the lips of Russian peasants. Of this our own ears could convince us. The mere memory of him raises in our imagination a figure gaunt, angular, rugged-nosed, clad in a caricature armor, and mounted on the withered skeleton of the pitiable Rosinante, a poor, starved and beaten nag, to whom we cannot deny a semi-amusing and semi-pathetic co-operation. Don Quixote makes us laugh, but there is a conciliatory and redeeming power in this laughter; and if the adage be true, "You may come to worship what you now deride," then I may add: Whom you have ridiculed, you have already forgiven—are even ready to love.

Hamlet's appearance, on the contrary, is attractive. His melancholia; his pale though not lean aspect (his mother remarks that he is stout, saying, "Our son is fat"); his black velvet clothes, the feather crowning his hat; his elegant manners; the unmistakable poetry of his speeches; his steady feeling of complete superiority over others, alongside of the biting humor of his self-denunciation—everything about him pleases, everything captivates. Everybody flatters himself on passing for a Hamlet. None would like to acquire the appellation of "Don Quixote." "Hamlet Baratynski,"[2] wrote Pushkin to his friend. No one ever thought of laughing at Hamlet, and herein lies his condemnation. To love him is almost impossible; only people like Horatio become attached to Hamlet. Of these I will speak later. Everyone sympathizes with Hamlet, and the reason is obvious: nearly everyone finds in Hamlet his own traits; but to love him is, I repeat, impossible, because he himself does not love anyone.

Let us continue our comparison.

Hamlet is the son of a king, murdered by his own brother, the usurper of the throne; his father comes forth from the grave—from "the jaws of Hades"—to charge Hamlet to avenge him; but the latter hesitates, keeps on quibbling with himself, finds consolation in self-depredation, and finally kills his stepfather by chance. A deep psychological feature, for which many wise but short-sighted persons have ventured to censure Shakespeare! And Don Quixote, a poor man, almost destitute, without means or connections, old and lonely, undertakes the task of destroying evil and protecting the oppressed (total strangers to him) all over the world. It matters not that his first attempt to free innocence from the oppressor brings redoubled suffering upon the head of innocence. (I have in mind that scene in which Don Quixote saves an apprentice from a drubbing by his master, who, as soon as the deliverer is gone, punishes the poor boy with tenfold severity.) It matters not that, in his crusades against harmful giants, Don Quixote attacks useful windmills. The comical setting of these pictures should not distract our eyes from their hidden meaning. The man who sets out to sacrifice himself with careful forethought and consideration of all the consequences—balancing all the probabilities of his acts proving beneficial—is hardly capable of self-sacrifice. Nothing of the kind can happen to Hamlet; it is not for him, with his penetrative, keen and skeptical mind, to fall into so gross an error. No, he will not wage war on windmills; he does not believe in giants, and would not attack them if they did exist. We cannot imagine Hamlet exhibiting to each and all a barber's bowl, and maintaining, as Don Quixote does, that it is the real magic helmet of Mambrin. I suppose that, were truth itself

---

[2] Baratynski was a Russian lyric poet, a contemporary and successful follower of Pushkin, whom contemplation of "the riddles of the universe" had made very disconsolate.—TRANSLATOR.

to appear incarnate before his eyes, Hamlet would still have misgivings as to whether it really was the truth. For who knows but that truth, too, is perhaps non-existent, like giants? We laugh at Don Quixote, but, my dear sirs, which of us, after having conscientiously interrogated himself, and taken into account his past and present convictions, will make bold to say that he always, under all circumstances, can distinguish a barber's pewter bowl from a magic golden helmet? It seems to me, therefore, that the principal thing in life is the sincerity and strength of our convictions—the result lies in the hands of fate. This alone can show us whether we have been contending with phantoms or real foes, and with what armor we covered our heads. Our business is to arm ourselves and fight.

Remarkable are the attitudes of the mob, the so-called mass of the people, toward Hamlet and Don Quixote. In *Hamlet* Polonius, in *Don Quixote* Sancho Panza, symbolize the populace.

Polonius is an old man—active, practical, sensible, but at the same time narrow-minded and garrulous. He is an excellent chamberlain and an exemplary father. (Recollect his instructions to his son, Laertes, when going abroad—instructions which vie in wisdom with certain orders issued by Governor Sancho Panza on the Island of Barataria.) To Polonius, Hamlet is not so much a madman as a child. Were he not a king's son, Polonius would despise him because of his utter uselessness and the impossibility of making a positive and practical application of his ideas. The famous cloud scene, the scene where Hamlet imagines he is mocking the old man, has an obvious significance, confirming this theory. I take the liberty of recalling it to you:

POLONIUS: My lord, the queen would speak with you, and presently.
HAMLET: Do you see yonder cloud, that's almost in shape of a camel?
POLONIUS: By the mass, and 'tis like a camel, indeed.
HAMLET: Methinks it is like a weasel.
POLONIUS: It is backed like a weasel.
HAMLET: Or, like a whale?
POLONIUS: Very like a whale.
HAMLET: Then will I come to my mother by and by.

Is it not evident that in this scene Polonius is at the same time a courtier who humors the prince and an adult who would not cross a sickly, capricious boy? Polonius does not in the least believe Hamlet, and he is right. With all his natural, narrow presumptiveness, he ascribes Hamlet's capriciousness to his love for Ophelia, in which he is, of course, mistaken, but he makes no mistake in understanding Hamlet's character. The Hamlets are really useless to the people; they give it nothing, they cannot lead it anywhere, since they themselves are bound for nowhere. And, besides, how can one lead when he doubts the very ground he treads upon? Moreover, the Hamlets detest the masses. How can a man who does not respect himself respect anyone or anything else? Besides, is it really worth while to bother about the masses? They are so rude and filthy! And much more than birth alone goes to make Hamlet an aristocrat.

An entirely different spectacle is presented by Sancho Panza. He laughs at Don Quixote, knows full well that he is demented; yet thrice forsakes the land of his birth, his home, wife and daughter, that he may follow this crazy man; follows him everywhere, undergoes all sorts of hardships, is devoted to him to his very death, believes him and is proud of him, then weeps, kneeling at the humble pallet where his master breathes his last. Hope of gain or ultimate advantage cannot account for this devotion. Sancho Panza has too much good sense. He knows very well that the page of a wandering knight has nothing save beatings to expect. The cause of his devotion must be sought deeper. It finds its root (if I may so put it) in what is perhaps the cardinal virtue of the people—in its capability of a blissful and honest blindness (alas! it is familiar with other forms of blindness), the capability of a disinterested enthusiasm, the disregard of direct personal advantages, which to a poor man is almost equivalent to scorn for his daily bread. A great, universally historic virtue!

The masses of the people invariably end by following, in blind confidence, the very persons they themselves have mocked, or even cursed and persecuted. They give allegiance to those who fear neither curses nor persecution—nor even ridicule—but who go straight ahead, their spiritual gaze directed toward the goal which they alone see—who seek, fall and rise, and ultimately find. And rightly so; only he who is led by the heart reaches the ultimate goal. "Les grandes pensées viennent du cœur," said Vovenarg. And the Hamlets find nothing, invent nothing, and leave no trace behind them, save that of their own personality—no achievements whatsoever. They neither love nor believe, and what can they find? Even

in chemistry—not to speak of organic nature—in order that
a third substance may be obtained, there must be a combination of two others; but the Hamlets are concerned with themselves alone—they are lonely, and therefore barren.

"But," you will interpose, "how about Ophelia—does not
Hamlet love her?"

I shall speak of her, and, incidentally, of Dulcinea.

In their relations to woman, too, our two types present much
that is noteworthy.

Don Quixote loves Dulcinea, a woman who exists only in
his own imagination, and is ready to die for her. (Recall his
words when, vanquished and bruised, he says to the conqueror,
who stands over him with a spear: "Stab me, Sir Knight . . .
Dulcinea del Tobosco is the most beautiful woman in the
world, and I the most unfortunate knight on earth. It is not
fit that my weakness should lessen the glory of Dulcinea.")
He loves purely, ideally; so ideally that he does not even
suspect that the object of his passion does not exist at all;
so purely that, when Dulcinea appears before him in the
guise of a rough and dirty peasant woman, he trusts not the
testimony of his eyes, and regards her as transformed by
some evil wizard.

I myself have seen in my life, on my wanderings, people
who laid down their lives for equally non-existent Dulcineas
or for a vulgar and oftentimes filthy something or other, in
which they saw the realization of their ideal, and whose
transformation they likewise attributed to evil—I almost said
bewitching—events and persons: I have seen them, and when
their like shall cease to exist, then let the book of history be
closed forever: there will be nothing in it to read about. Of
sensuality there is not even a trace in Don Quixote. All his
thoughts are chaste and innocent, and in the secret depths of
his heart he hardly hopes for an ultimate union with Dulcinea
—indeed, he almost dreads such a union.

And does Hamlet really love? Has his ironic creator, a most
profound judge of the human heart, really determined to give
this egotist, this skeptic, saturated with every decomposing
poison of self-analysis, a loving and devout heart? Shakespeare
did not fall into this contradiction; and it does not cost the
attentive reader much pains to convince himself that Hamlet
is a sensual man, and even secretly voluptuous. (It is not for
nothing that the courtier Rosencrantz smiles slily when Hamlet says in his hearing that he is tired of women.) Hamlet does

not love, I say, but only pretends—and mawkishly—that he
loves. On this we have the testimony of Shakespeare himself.
In the first scene of the third act Hamlet says to Ophelia: "I
did love you once." Then ensues the colloquy:

OPHELIA: Indeed, my lord, you made me believe so.
HAMLET: You should not have believed me . . . I loved you not.

And having uttered this last word, Hamlet is much nearer
the truth than he supposed. His feelings for Ophelia—an
innocent creature, pure as a saint—are either cynical (recollect
his words, his equivocal allusions, when, in the scene representing the theatre, he asks her permission to lie . . . in her lap),
or else hollow (direct your attention to the scene between
him and Laertes, when Hamlet jumps into Ophelia's grave and
says, in language worthy of Bramarbas or of Captain Pistol:
"Forty thousand brothers could not, with all their quality of
love, make up my sum. . . . Let them throw millions of acres
on us," etc.).

All his relations with Ophelia are for Hamlet only the
occasions for preoccupation with his own self, and in his
exclamation, "O, Nymph! in thy orisons be all my sins remembered!" we see but the deep consciousness of his own
sickly inanition, a lack of strength to love, on the part of the
almost superstitious worshiper before "the Saint of Chastity."

But enough has been said of the dark sides of the Hamlet
type, of those phases which irritate us most because they are
nearer and more familiar to us. I will endeavor to appreciate
whatever may be legitimate in him, and therefore enduring.
Hamlet embodies the doctrine of negation, that same doctrine
which another great poet has divested of everything human
and presented in the form of Mephistopheles. Hamlet is the
selfsame Mephistopheles, but a Mephistopheles embraced by
the living circle of human nature: hence his negation is not
an evil, but is itself directed against evil. Hamlet casts doubt
upon goodness, but does not question the existence of evil;
in fact, he wages relentless war upon it. He entertains suspicions concerning the genuineness and sincerity of good; yet
his attacks are made not upon goodness, but upon a counterfeit
goodness, beneath whose mask are secreted evil and falsehood,
its immemorial enemies. He does not laugh the diabolic, impersonal laughter of Mephistopheles; in his bitterest smile there
is pathos, which tells of his sufferings and therefore reconciles
us to him. Hamlet's skepticism, moreover, is not indifference

and in this consists his significance and merit. In his makeup good and evil, truth and falsehood, beauty and ugliness, are not blurred into an accidental, dumb and vague something or other. The skepticism of Hamlet, which leads him to distrust things contemporaneous—the realization of truth, so to speak—is irreconcilably at war with falsehood, and through this very quality he becomes one of the foremost champions of a truth in which he himself cannot fully believe. But in negation, as in fire, there is a destructive force, and how can we keep it within bounds or show exactly where it is to stop, when that which it must destroy and that which it should spare are frequently blended and bound up together inseparably? This is where the oft-observed tragedy of human life comes into evidence: doing presupposes thinking, but thought and the will have separated, and are separating daily more and more. "And thus the native hue of resolution is sicklied o'er with the pale cast of thought," Shakespeare tells us in the words of Hamlet.

And so, on the one side stand the Hamlets—reflective, conscientious, often all-comprehensive, but as often also useless and doomed to immobility; and on the other the half-crazy Don Quixotes, who help and influence mankind only to the extent that they see but a single point—often non-existent in the form they see it. Unwillingly the questions arise: Must one really be a lunatic to believe in the truth? And, must the mind that has obtained control of itself lose, therefore, all its power?

We should be led very far indeed even by a superficial consideration of these questions.

I shall confine myself to the remark that in this separation, in this dualism which I have mentioned, we should recognize a fundamental law of all human life. This life is nothing else than an eternal struggle and everlasting reconcilement of two ceaselessly diverging and continually uniting elements. If I did not fear startling your ears with philosophical terms, I would venture to say that the Hamlets are an expression of the fundamental centripetal force of nature, in accordance with which every living thing considers itself the center of creation and looks down upon everything else as existing for its sake. Thus the mosquito that settled on the forehead of Alexander the Great, in calm confidence of its right, fed on his blood as food which belonged to it; just so Hamlet, though he scorns himself—a thing the mosquito does not do, not having risen to this level—always takes everything on his own account.

Without this centripetal force—the force of egotism—nature could no more exist than without the other, the centrifugal force, according to whose law everything exists only for something else. This force, the principle of devotion and self-sacrifice, illuminated, as I have already stated, by a comic light, is represented by the Don Quixotes. These two forces of inertia and motion, of conservatism and progress, are the fundamental forces of all existing things. They explain to us the growth of a little flower; they give us a key to the understanding of the development of the most powerful peoples.

I hasten to pass from these perhaps irrelevant speculations to other considerations more familiar to us.

I know that, of all Shakespeare's works, *Hamlet* is perhaps the most popular. This tragedy belongs to the list of plays that never fail to crowd the theatre. In view of the modern attitude of our public and its aspiration toward self-consciousness and reflection, its scruples about itself and its buoyancy of spirit, this phenomenon is clear. But, to say nothing of the beauties in which this most excellent expression of the modern spirit abounds, one cannot help marveling at the master genius who, though himself in many respects akin to his Hamlet, cleft him from himself by a free sweep of creative force, and set up his model for the lasting study of posterity. The spirit which created this model is that of a northern man, a spirit of meditation and analysis, a spirit heavy and gloomy, devoid of harmony and bright color, not rounded into exquisite, oftentimes shallow, forms; but deep, strong, varied, independent and guiding. Out of his very bosom he has plucked the type of Hamlet; and in so doing has shown that, in the realm of poetry, as in other spheres of human life, he stands above his child, because he fully understands it.

The spirit of a southerner went into the creation of Don Quixote, a spirit light and merry, naïve and impressionable— one that does not enter into the mysteries of life, that reflects phenomena rather than comprehends them.

At this point I cannot resist the desire, not to draw a parallel between Shakespeare and Cervantes, but simply to indicate a few points of likeness and of difference. Shakespeare and Cervantes—how can there be any comparison? some will ask. Shakespeare, that giant, that demigod! . . . Yes, but Cervantes is not a pygmy beside the giant who created King Lear. He is a man—a man to the full; and a man has the right to stand on his feet even before a demigod. Undoubtedly Shakespeare

presses hard upon Cervantes—and not him alone—by the
wealth and power of his imagination, by the brilliancy of his
greatest poetry, by the depth and breadth of a colossal mind.
But then you will not find in Cervantes' romance any strained
witticisms or unnatural comparisons or feigned concepts; nor
will you meet in his pages with decapitations, picked eyes
and those streams of blood, that dull and iron cruelty, which
are the terrible heirloom of the Middle Ages, and are disappearing less rapidly in obstinate northern natures. And yet
Cervantes, like Shakespeare, lived in the epoch that witnessed
St. Bartholomew's night; and long after that time heretics
were burned and blood continued to flow—shall it ever cease
to flow? *Don Quixote* reflects the Middle Ages, if only in the
provincial poetry and narrative grace of those romances which
Cervantes so good-humoredly derided, and to which he himself
paid the last tribute in *Persiles and Sigismunda*. Shakespeare
takes his models from everywhere—heaven and earth—he
knows no limitations; nothing can escape his all-pervading
glance. He seizes his subjects with irresistible power, like
an eagle pouncing upon its prey. Cervantes presents his not
over-numerous characters to his readers gently, as a father
his children. He takes only what is close to him, but with
that how familiar he is! Everything human seems subservient
to the mighty English poet; Cervantes draws his wealth from
his own heart only—a heart sunny, kind, and rich in life's
experience, but not hardened by it. It was not in vain that
during seven years of hard bondage[3] Cervantes was learning,
as he himself said, the science of patience. The circle of his
experience is narrower than Shakespeare's, but in that, as
in every separate living person, is reflected all that is human.
Cervantes does not dazzle you with thundering words; he
does not shock you with the titanic force of triumphant
inspiration; his poetry—sometimes turbid, and by no means
Shakespearean—is like a deep river, rolling calmly between
variegated banks; and the reader, gradually allured, then
hemmed in on every side by its transparent waves, cheerfully
resigns himself to the truly epic calm and fluidity of its course.

The imagination gladly evokes the figures of these two
contemporary poets, who died on the very same day, the
26th of April, 1616.[3] Cervantes probably knew nothing of
Shakespeare, but the great tragedian in the quietude of his

---

[3] Recent biographies of Cervantes give the period of his captivity as *five*
years, and the date of his death *April 23*.—TRANSLATOR.

Stratford home, whither he had retired for the three years preceding his death, could have read through the famous novel, which had already been translated into English. A picture worthy of the brush of a contemplative artist—Shakespeare reading *Don Quixote*! Fortunate are the countries where such men arise, teachers of their generation and of posterity. The unfading wreath with which a great man is crowned rests also upon the brow of his people.

A certain English lord—a good judge in the matter—once spoke in my hearing of Don Quixote as a model of a real gentleman. Surely, if simplicity and a quiet demeanor are the distinguishing marks of what we call a thorough gentleman, Don Quixote has a good claim to his title. He is a veritable hidalgo—a hidalgo even when the jeering servants of the prince are lathering his whole face. The simplicity of his manners proceeds from the absence of what I would venture to call his self-love, and not his *self-conceit*. Don Quixote is not busied with himself, and, respecting himself and others, does not think of showing off. But Hamlet, with all his exquisite setting, is, it seems to me—excuse the French expression— *ayant des airs de parvenu*; he is troublesome—at times even rude—and he poses and scoffs. To make up for this, he was given the power of original and apt expression, a power inherent in every being in whom is implanted the habit of reflection and self-development—and therefore utterly unattainable so far as Don Quixote is concerned. The depth and keenness of analysis in Hamlet, his many-sided education (we must not forget that he studied at the Wittenburg University), have developed in him a taste almost unerring. He is an excellent critic; his advice to the actors is strikingly true and judicious. The sense of the beautiful is as strong in him as the sense of duty in Don Quixote.

Don Quixote deeply respects all existing orders—religions, monarchs and dukes—and is at the same time free himself and recognizes the freedom of others. Hamlet rebukes kings and courtiers, but is in reality oppressive and intolerant.

Don Quixote is hardly literate; Hamlet probably kept a diary. Don Quixote, with all his ignorance, has a definite way of thinking about matters of government and administration; Hamlet has neither time nor need to think of such matters.

Many have objected to the endless blows with which Cervantes burdens Don Quixote. I have already remarked that in the second part of the romance the poor knight is almost unmolested. But I will add that, without these beatings, he would be less pleasing to children, who read his adventures with such avidity; and to us grownups he would not appear in his true light, but rather in a cold and haughty aspect, which would be incompatible with his character. Another interesting point is involved here. At the very end of the romance, after Don Quixote's complete discomfiture by the Knight of the White Moon, the disguised college bachelor, and following his renunciation of knight-errantry, shortly before his death, a herd of swine trample him under foot. I once happened to hear Cervantes critized for writing this, on the ground that he was repeating the old tricks already abandoned; but herein Cervantes was guided by the instinct of genius, and this very ugly incident has a deep meaning. The trampling under pigs' feet is always encountered in the lives of Don Quixotes, and just before their close. This is the last tribute they must pay to rough chance, to indifference and cruel misunderstanding; it is the slap in the face from the Pharisees. Then they can die. They have passed through all the fire of the furnace, have won immortality for themselves, and it opens before them.

Hamlet is occasionally double-faced and heartless. Think of how he planned the deaths of the two courtiers sent to England by the king. Recall his speech on Polonius, whom he murdered. In this, however, we see, as already observed, a reflection of the medieval spirit recently outgrown. On the other hand, we must note in the honest, veracious Don Quixote the disposition to a half-conscious, half-innocent deception, to self-delusion—a disposition almost always present in the fancy of an enthusiast. His account of what he saw in the cave of Montesinos was obviously invented by him, and did not deceive the smart commoner, Sancho Panza.

Hamlet, on the slightest ill success, loses heart and complains; but Don Quixote, pummelled senseless by galley slaves, has not the least doubt as to the success of his undertaking. In the same spirit Fourier is said to have gone to his office every day, for many years, to meet an Englishman he had invited, through the newspapers, to furnish him with a million francs to carry out his plans; but, of course, the benefactor of his dreams never appeared. This was certainly a very ridiculous proceeding, and it calls to mind this thought: The ancients considered their gods jealous, and, in case of need, deemed it useful to appease them by voluntary offerings (recollect the ring cast into the sea by Polycrates); why, then, should we not believe that some share of the ludicrous must inevitably be mingled with the acts, with the very character, of people moved unto great and novel deeds—as a bribe, as a soothing offering, to the jealous gods? Without these comical crank-pioneers, mankind could not progress, and there would not be anything for the Hamlets to reflect upon.

The Don Quixotes discover; the Hamlets develop. But how, I shall be asked, can the Hamlets evolve anything when they doubt all things and believe in nothing? My rejoinder is that, by a wise dispensation of nature, there are neither thorough Hamlets nor complete Don Quixotes; these are but extreme manifestations of two tendencies—guide posts set up by the poets on two different roads. Life tends toward them, but never reaches the goal. We must not forget that, just as the principle of analysis is carried in Hamlet to tragedy, so the element of enthusiasm runs in Don Quixote to comedy; but in life, the purely comic and the purely tragic are seldom encountered.

Hamlet gains much in our estimation from Horatio's attachment for him. This character is excellent, and is frequently met with in our day, to the credit of the times. In Horatio I recognize the type of disciple, the pupil, in the best sense of the word. With a stoical and direct nature, a warm heart and a somewhat limited understanding, he is aware of his short-comings and is modest—something rare in people of limited intellect. He thirsts for learning, for instruction, and therefore venerates the wise Hamlet and is devoted to him with all the might of his honest heart, not demanding even reciprocation. He defers to Hamlet, not as to a prince but as to a chief. One of the most important services of the Hamlets consists in forming and developing persons like Horatio; persons who, having received from them the seeds of thought, fertilize them in their hearts, and then scatter them broadcast through the world. The words in which Hamlet acknowledges Horatio's worth, honor himself. In them is expressed his own conception of the great worth of man, his noble aspirations, which no skepticism is strong enough to weaken.

> Give me that man
> That is not passion's slave, and I will wear him
> In my heart's core, ay, in my heart of hearts,
> As I do thee.

The honest skeptic always respects a stoic. When the ancient world had crumbled away—and in every epoch like unto that—the best people took refuge in stoicism as the only creed in which it was still possible to preserve man's dignity. The skeptics, if they lacked the strength to die—to betake themselves to the "undiscovered country from whose bourn no traveler returns"—turned epicureans; a plain, sad phenomenon, with which we are but too familiar.

Both Hamlet and Don Quixote die a touching death; and yet how different are their ends! Hamlet's last words are sublime. He resigns himself, grows calm, bids Horatio live, and raises his dying voice in behalf of young Fortinbras, the unstained representative of the right of succession. Hamlet's eyes are not turned forward. "The rest is silence," says the dying skeptic, as he actually becomes silent forever. The death of Don Quixote sends an inexpressible emotion through one's heart. In that instant the full significance of this personality is accessible to all. When his former page, trying to comfort Don Quixote, tells him that they shall soon again start out on an expedition of knight-errantry, the expiring knight replies: "No, all is now over forever, and I ask everyone's forgiveness; I am no longer Don Quixote, I am again Alonzo the Good, as I was once called—Alonso el Bueno."

This word is remarkable. The mention of this nickname for the first and last time makes the reader tremble. Yes, only this single word still has a meaning, in the face of death. All things shall pass away, everything shall vanish—the highest station, power, the all-inclusive genius—all to dust shall crumble. "All earthly greatness vanishes like smoke." But noble deeds are more enduring than resplendent beauty. "Everything shall pass," the apostle said, "love alone shall endure."

A MONTH IN THE COUNTRY

by IVAN TURGENEV

1924

A MONTH IN THE COUNTRY[4]

Translated by Richard Newnham

CHARACTERS

ARKADY SERGEYICH ISLAYEV, *a rich landowner, aged 36*

NATALYA PETROVNA (NATASHA), *his wife, aged 29*

KOLYA, *their son, aged 10*

VERA ALEXANDROVNA (VEROCHKA), *their adopted daughter, aged 17*

ANNA SEMYENOVNA ISLAYEVA, ISLAYEV'S *mother, aged 58*

LIZAVETA BOGDANOVNA, *a lady companion, aged 37*

ADAM IVANICH SCHAAF, *a German tutor, aged 45*

MIKHAIL ALEXANDROVICH RAKITIN, *a friend of the family, aged 30*

ALEXEI NIKOLAYICH BELIAYEV, *a student, Kolya's tutor, aged 21*

AFANASY IVANOVICH BOLSHINTSOV, *a neighbor, aged 48*

IGNATY ILYICH SHPIGELSKI, *a doctor, aged 40*

MATVEY, *a servant, aged 40*

KATYA, *a maidservant, aged 20*

The action takes place on Islayev's estate in the early 1840's. One day passes between Acts I and II, one day between Acts II and III, and one day between Acts IV and V.

[4] *A Month in the Country*, by Ivan Turgenev, translated by Richard Newnham, is reprinted here by permission of the translator and his agent. First published by Chandler Editions Publishing Company. Copyright © 1962 by Richard Newnham.

All rights whatsoever in this translation are strictly reserved and applications for performances etc. should be made to Margaret Ramsay Limited, 14a Goodwin's Court, London W.C.2, England. No performance may be given unless a license has been obtained prior to rehearsal.

ACT ONE

[*A drawing room. On the right is a card table and a door leading to a study. In the center is a door into the hall. On the left are two windows and a round table. Two sofas are in the corners of the room. At the card table* ANNA, LIZA *and* SCHAAF *are playing.* RAKITIN *and* NATALYA *are at the round table, he with a book, she embroidering on canvas. It is early afternoon.*]

SCHAAF. Hearts.

ANNA. What, again? Come come, old friend, you'll play us right off the table like this.

SCHAAF [*calmly*]. Eight hearts.

ANNA [*to* LIZA]. What a man! It's no good trying to play against him.

[LIZA *smiles.*]

NATALYA [*to* RAKITIN]. Why have you stopped? Keep reading.

RAKITIN [*slowly, lifting his book*]. "*Monte Cristo se redressa haletant . . .*" Natalya Petrovna, are you really interested in this?

NATALYA. Not in the least.

RAKITIN. Then why are we reading it?

NATALYA. I'll tell you why. The other day a lady said to me "Do you really mean you haven't read *Monte Cristo*? Oh but you *must*—it's wonderful." I didn't answer her at the time, but now I can tell her that I read it and found absolutely nothing wonderful in it at all.

RAKITIN. Well of course, if you've had enough of it to convince yourself . . .

NATALYA. You're just being lazy.

RAKITIN. Oh please—I'm quite willing to go on. [*Finds place where he stopped.*] "*Monte Cristo se redressa . . .*"

NATALYA [*interrupts*]. Have you seen Arkady today?

RAKITIN. I met him down at the dam—they're repairing it. He was telling something to the men, and went into the sand right up to his knees to explain it to them.

NATALYA. He always throws himself into everything he does, and goes at it too hard. It's a fault, don't you think?

[53]

RAKITIN. I quite agree.

NATALYA. How monotonous! You always agree with me. Go on with the book, please.

RAKITIN. Ah, I suppose that means you want me to quarrel with you, does it? Very well.

NATALYA. I want . . . I want . . . I want *you* to want it. But I've already asked you to go on reading.

RAKITIN. Madam, your obedient servant. [*Picks up book again.*]

SCHAAF. Hearts.

ANNA. What, not again? This is too much! [*To* NATALYA] Natasha, Natasha . . .

NATALYA. What is it?

ANNA. Just imagine, Schaaf's beaten us hollow. First he gets seven hearts, then eight of them.

SCHAAF. And now again we have seven.

ANNA. Listen to him—it's terrible.

NATALYA. Yes, terrible.

ANNA. Well, come along then. [*To* NATALYA.] But where's Kolya?

NATALYA. He's gone for a walk with the new tutor.

ANNA. Ah, I see. Lizaveta Bogdanovna, I call you.

RAKITIN. What tutor's this?

NATALYA. Oh of course—I forgot to tell you. We've taken on a new tutor since you were last here.

RAKITIN. To take Doufour's place?

NATALYA. No, he's a Russian. The princess is getting hold of another Frenchman for us in Moscow.

RAKITIN. What sort of fellow is he, this Russian—old?

NATALYA. No, young. We've only taken him on for the summer months, by the way.

RAKITIN. Oh, as a vacation job.

NATALYA. Yes, that's apparently the phrase they have for it. Now here's an idea, Rakitin: You love to watch other people, analyze them, delve into them. . . .

RAKITIN. Excuse me, but what makes you think . . . ?

NATALYA. Oh, yes, yes. . . . You take a look at him. He pleases me—thin, well knit, a cheerful face with something fearless about it. You'll see for yourself. He's pretty uncouth, one must admit, and of course that damns him in your eyes.

RAKITIN. You're certainly being terribly hard on me today, Natalya Petrovna.

NATALYA. Am I really? [*Thoughtfully.*] Go on reading.

RAKITIN. *"Se redressa haletant . . ."*

NATALYA [*turning suddenly*]. Where's Vera? I haven't seen her since this morning. [*Smiling at* RAKITIN.] Shut that silly book. . . . I can see that we won't get any reading done today. I'd rather you told us a story or something . . .

RAKITIN. All right then. . . . What ever shall I tell you, though? . . . You remember that I've been spending a few days with the Krinitsins?—Just imagine, our young friends are bored to death already.

NATALYA. How could you tell that?

RAKITIN. Is it possible to hide boredom? Everything else, perhaps, but not boredom.

NATALYA [*glancing at him*]. *Is* it possible to hide everything else?

RAKITIN [*pausing*]. Yes, I think so.

NATALYA [*lowering her eyes*]. Well, and what did you do with yourselves, you and the Krinitsins?

RAKITIN. Oh, nothing. To be bored with one's friends is awful. You feel at home, you're not embarrassed, you like the people you're with and you've got nothing to put you into a bad temper, but all the same boredom hangs over you and fills you with a dull, hungry ache.

NATALYA. By the sound of it you're often bored with friends.

RAKITIN. But surely you too know what it's like to be with someone you love but whom you're sick and tired of!

NATALYA [*slowly*]. Someone whom you love . . . that's saying a lot. You're being very mysterious today.

RAKITIN. Mysterious? Why mysterious?

NATALYA. Yes, that's your biggest fault. You know, Rakitin, you're terribly clever, of course, but . . . sometimes when we talk together it's exactly as though . . . as though we were making lace. . . . Have you ever seen how they make lace? Well, they make it in stuffy rooms, sitting absolutely still. Lace is a fine enough thing, but a glass of water on a hot summer's day is much better.

RAKITIN. Natalya Petrovna, today you're . . .

NATALYA. I'm what?

RAKITIN. Today you're annoyed with me about something.

NATALYA. Oh you clever people, how little you really understand for all your cleverness. . . . No, I'm not annoyed with you.

ANNA. At last he's collapsed! He's defeated! Natasha, the villain has lost!

SCHAAF [*acidly*]. The fault was Lizaveta Bogdanova's.

LIZA [*angrily*]. I beg your pardon, but how was I to know that Anna Semyenovna didn't have any hearts?

SCHAAF. In the future I'll never ask Lizaveta Bogdanovna to be my partner.

ANNA [*to* SCHAAF]. But what has she done?

SCHAAF [*as before*]. In the future I'll never ask Lizaveta Bogdanovna.

LIZA. But why should I care? What next! . . .

RAKITIN. You know, Natalya Petrovna, the more I look at you today, the less I can recognize you.

NATALYA [*half curious*]. Really?

RAKITIN. Yes, I mean it. There's something that's changed about you.

NATALYA. Well, if that's the case, do me a favor. If you know me as well as that, then make a guess at what the change is—what can have happened to me.

RAKITIN. Now wait just a moment . . .

[*Suddenly* KOLYA *rushes noisily into the room, going straight to* ANNA.]

KOLYA. Grandma, look what I've got! [*Shows her a bow and arrows.*] Look!

ANNA. Show me, dear. . . . Oh, what a fine bow! Who made it for you?

KOLYA. He did. . . .

[*Pointing to* BELIAYEV, *who stands in the hall doorway.*]

ANNA. Oh, but how beautifully it is made! . . .

KOLYA. I've been shooting at a tree with it, grandma—and I hit it twice! [*Jumps with excitement.*]

NATALYA. Show me, Kolya.

KOLYA [*runs to her, while she examines bow*]. Oh mommy, but you should see how Alexei Nikolayich climbs trees! He says he'll teach me, and how to swim as well—he'll teach me everything! [*Skips from one foot to the other.*]

NATALYA [*to* BELIAYEV]. It's very good of you to look after him so well.

KOLYA [*interrupts her*]. I like him very much, mommy—very much.

NATALYA [*stroking* KOLYA'S *head*]. I think I've been spoiling him a little. I hope you'll make a strong and active boy out of him for me.

[BELIAYEV *bows.*]

KOLYA. Alexei Nikolayich, let's go to the stables and take Favorite some bread, shall we?

BELIAYEV. Come on.

ANNA [*to* KOLYA]. Come and give your grandmother a kiss first.

KOLYA. Oh later, later! [*Runs out to hall.*]

[BELIAYEV *exits after him.*]

ANNA [*watching* KOLYA]. What a sweet boy! [*To* SCHAAF *and* LIZA.] Isn't he?

LIZA. Yes, indeed.

SCHAAF [*pausing*]. I pass.

NATALYA [*eagerly, to* RAKITIN]. Well, how did he strike you?

RAKITIN. Who?

NATALYA [*pausing*]. The . . . Russian tutor.

RAKITIN. Oh, I'm sorry—I forgot to notice him. I was so busy thinking about the question you asked me.

[NATALYA *looks at him with a faintly mocking smile.*]

. . . Well now, his face is . . . er . . . really . . . Yes, he has a fine face. I like him. But he seems to be very shy.

NATALYA. Yes, he is.

RAKITIN [*looking at her*]. But of course I can't really say.

NATALYA. How would it be, Rakitin, if we were to take charge of him? Would you like to? Let's finish his education. Here's a splendid opportunity for dull, sensible people like you and me to do something useful. Well, we are dull and sensible, aren't we?

RAKITIN. You're really taken with that young man, aren't you? If he were to find out, he'd probably be flattered.

NATALYA. Oh, goodness me no! You mustn't judge him by what a brother of ours or someone might do in his position. He's quite different from our sort, Rakitin. That's where we go wrong: we study ourselves with great care and then take it into our heads that we understand people.

RAKITIN. Each of us is a closed book, that's true. But why these hints? Why do you keep tormenting me?

NATALYA. Whom should we torment, if not our friends? You *are* my friend—and you know it. [*Presses his hand.*]

[RAKITIN *smiles and his face brightens.*]

A very old friend. [*Laughs.*] But it's only the nicest things that make you sick.

RAKITIN. Maybe, but that doesn't make it any easier for them.

NATALYA. Come now, that's enough. [*Lowering her voice.*] As though you didn't know how much you mean to me.

RAKITIN. You're playing with me like a cat with a mouse. But the mouse has no objections.

NATALYA. Oh, poor little mouse!

ANNA. That's twenty from you, Adam Ivanich! Ha! Ha!

SCHAAF. In the future I'll never ask Lizaveta Bogdanovna.

MATVEY [*enters from hall*]. Doctor Shpigelski, madam.

SHPIGELSKI [*enters after him*]. Doctors are never announced, you know.

[*Exit MATVEY.*]

Greetings to the whole family. [*Approaches ANNA.*] Good afternoon, grandmother. Winning, I hope?

ANNA. Let's have no talk of winning! It's only through sheer good luck that I'm managing to keep my head above water. It's all the fault of this villain here. [*Pointing to SCHAAF.*]

SHPIGELSKI. Adam Ivanich, and with ladies, too! That's not right—I'm ashamed of you.

SCHAAF [*through his teeth*]. Mit ladies . . . mit ladies . . .

SHPIGELSKI [*goes to round table*]. Good afternoon, Natalya Petrovna, and to you, Mikhail Alexandrovich.

NATALYA. Good afternoon, doctor. And how are you?

SHPIGELSKI. That's a very pleasing question, because it means that *you* are well. What could ever be wrong with me? A doctor worth his salt is never ill, or at least, if he does catch anything, he just ups and dies without wasting any time. Ha! Ha!

NATALYA. Do sit down. Yes, I'm well enough, but in rather a bad mood. I suppose that's a disease of a kind.

SHPIGELSKI [*sits next to her*]. Let me take your pulse. [*Does so.*] Oh dear, what nerves we've got! You don't take enough exercise, Natalya Petrovna, and you don't laugh enough, that's the trouble. Mikhail Alexandrovich, I make you responsible for the patient. But some of my little white pills will help—I'll prescribe some for you.

NATALYA. I'm quite prepared to laugh. [*With liveliness.*] Now you, doctor, you've got a malicious tongue in your head, and I like it—I respect you very much for it. Tell me something amusing. Mikhail Alexandrovich has been so serious all day.

SHPIGELSKI [*looking at* RAKITIN *out of the corner of his eye*]. It's clear that it's not only your nerves that are out of order—your bile has been giving you a little trouble, too, if I'm not mistaken.

NATALYA. But please don't you add to it, doctor! Make all the diagnoses you want, but kindly not out loud. Everyone knows how shrewd you are—how shrewd you both are.

SHPIGELSKI. As you wish, madam.

NATALYA. Tell us something amusing.

SHPIGELSKI. Very well. Though I never dreamt for a moment —I never imagined—"one, two, tell us a story," just like that! It's difficult. Let's see if a bit of snuff will help. [*Takes snuff*.]

NATALYA. What preliminaries!

SHPIGELSKI. But my dear Natalya Petrovna, just think for a moment. Not everyone has the same sense of humor. It's a question of who wants what. For example, as far as your neighbor Khlopushkin's concerned, it's enough to raise your little finger and he's in peals of laughter. But in your case . . . However, with your permission, I'll start. Do you know Verenitsin?

NATALYA. I believe we've met, but maybe I've only heard the name.

SHPIGELSKI. He's got a mad sister. It's my opinion that they're either both mad or else both normal, for there's nothing to choose between them. But that's not the point. There's a divinity doth shape our ends, rough-hew them how we may. Well, Verenitsin has a daughter, a sweet young thing, you know, with little pale eyes and a little nose and little white teeth—quite a nice girl, in short. Plays the piano, got a lisp, you know—the usual sort of thing. She stands to inherit two hundred serfs, plus another hundred and fifty from her aunt, even though the old woman's still alive and will last a long time yet. All lunatics live to a ripe old age, but there's always hope, of course. . . . She's signed everything over to her niece, and the night before she made her will I personally bathed her forehead with cold water— a pointless thing to do, as a matter of fact, for there's no hope of bringing her to her senses. Well now, Verenitsin's daughter obviously has a pretty high rating on the marriage market. He begins to take her out—suitors start appearing, among others a certain Perekuzov, a washed-out young man, and timid too, but of excellent behavior. The father takes to him, and the daughter as well. It seems as though marriage bells are imminent, everything goes so well—Verenitsin's begun nudging Perekuzov in the ribs and clapping him on the shoulder, you know—when suddenly out of the blue comes an officer, Ardallion Protobekassov. He sees the Verenitsin girl at the governor's ball, dances three polkas with her, tells her how miserable he is or some such rubbish, very likely, rolling his eyes to heaven, and my young lady loses her head at once. Tears follow, and sighs, and "oh's." Perekuzov doesn't get another look or another word, and even the very mention of marriage sends the girl into hysterics . . . God almighty, what a fuss! "Well," thinks Papa Verenitsin, "if it's to be Protobekassov, all right then, it's Protobekassov. Good thing he's a man of means." They invite the officer round, saying "do us the honor," and do it he does. He flirts with the girl, falls in love with her and eventually offers his hand and heart. Now what do you think happens—that the Verenitsin girl joyfully accepts on the spot? Not a bit of it—God forbid! More tears and sighs and fainting fits. The father's in a fix. What does it all mean? What more does she want? And what do you think is the answer?—"Oh goodness, I don't know which one I'm in love with, daddy." "What's that you say?" "I'm sure I don't know—I'd better not marry at all, but just be in love with them." Of course, this sends Verenitsin into a towering rage. The suitors end up wondering what it's all about, and the girl has her way. There you are—that's the sort of thing that happens round here.

NATALYA. I don't see anything surprising about that: why shouldn't one love two people at once?

RAKITIN. Ah, you think . . . ?

NATALYA [*slowly*]. I think . . . but no, I really don't know . . . perhaps it simply means that one isn't in love with either. . . .

SHPIGELSKI [*taking snuff and looking at them both*]. Yes, yes . . .

NATALYA [*quickly, to* SHPIGELSKI]. Your story was very good, but all the same you haven't made me laugh yet.

SHPIGELSKI. Perhaps not, my good lady, but I ask you, who could manage to do that today? You don't really want to laugh at present.

NATALYA. What do I want, then?

SHPIGELSKI [*affectedly humble*]. The Lord alone knows!

NATALYA. Oh how boring you are!—you're really worse than Rakitin.

SHPIGELSKI. You honor me with the comparison.

[NATALYA *makes a gesture of disgust.*]

ANNA [*rising*]. Well, at last. [*Sighs.*] My foot's fallen asleep.

[LIZA *and* SCHAAF *also rise.*]

Oh, oh . . .

NATALYA [*goes to them*]. Do you really enjoy sitting still for so long?

[SHPIGELSKI *and* RAKITIN *rise.*]

ANNA [*to* SCHAAF]. You owe me seventy kopeks, my friend.

[SCHAAF *bows coldly.*]

You can't expect to thrash us every time. [*To* NATALYA.] My dear, you're looking pale today. Are you well? Shpigelski, is she well?

SHPIGELSKI [*who is whispering to* RAKITIN]. Oh yes, she's quite well, madam.

ANNA. All the same, though . . . Well, I'm going to have a little rest before dinner—I'm ready to drop from exhaustion. And my legs . . . Liza, let us be going.

[*Exits with* LIZA *to hall.* NATALYA *accompanies her to the door. The others stay in the foreground.*]

SHPIGELSKI [*offering snuff to* SCHAAF]. Well, Adam Ivanich, *wie befinden Sie sich?*

SCHAAF [*taking snuff importantly*]. Vell, thank you. And you?

SHPIGELSKI. Thank you, not so bad. [*Aside to* RAKITIN.] Do you *really* not know what's the matter with Natalya today?

RAKITIN. I haven't the slightest idea.

SHPIGELSKI. Well, if *you've* no idea . . . [*Turns to meet* NATALYA, *who is coming back from the door.*] I've got a little matter to discuss with you, Natalya Petrovna.

NATALYA [*going to the window*]. Indeed, and what might that be?

SHPIGELSKI. I'll have to discuss it with you in private. . . .

NATALYA. Good heavens, how you alarm me!

[*In the meantime* RAKITIN *has taken* SCHAAF *by the arm and is walking him up and down, whispering to him in German.* SCHAAF *smiles and speaks quietly:* "Ja, ja, ja! Jawohl, sehr gut!"]

SHPIGELSKI [*lowering his voice*]. Actually, the matter doesn't concern you alone.

NATALYA [*looking out into garden*]. What are you trying to say?

SHPIGELSKI. Well, I'll tell you. A very close friend of mine asked me to find out your . . . your intentions regarding your adopted daughter Vera.

NATALYA. My intentions?

SHPIGELSKI. Yes. Not to beat about the bush, my friend . . .

NATALYA. You don't mean to say he wants to marry her?

SHPIGELSKI. Exactly.

NATALYA. You're joking.

SHPIGELSKI. Not in the least.

NATALYA [*laughing*]. But for goodness sake, she's still a child. What an extraordinary commission to be given.

SHPIGELSKI. Why so extraordinary, Natalya Petrovna? My friend . . .

NATALYA. You're a great one for getting things done, aren't you, Shpigelski. What sort of man is this friend?

SHPIGELSKI [*smiling*]. Pardon me, but you haven't yet told me anything definite about . . .

NATALYA. That will do, doctor. Vera is still a child, you know that yourself, you arch-diplomat. [*Turning.*] And here she comes.

[VERA *and* KOLYA *run in from the hall.*]

KOLYA [*runs to* RAKITIN]. Rakitin, we must have glue—tell them to give us some glue.

NATALYA [*to* VERA]. Where have you been? [*Strokes her cheeks.*] How flushed you look.

VERA. We've been out in the garden.

[SHPIGELSKI *bows to her.*]

Good afternoon, doctor.

RAKITIN [*to* KOLYA]. What's the glue for?

KOLYA. Oh, we need it. . . . Alexei Nikolayich is making us a kite. Tell them to get us some.

RAKITIN [*about to ring*]. Wait a moment . . .

SCHAAF. *Erlauben Sie*, but Master Kolya hasn't learnt his lesson for today. [*Takes* KOLYA *by the hand.*] Come now.

KOLYA [*grumpily*]. I'll do it in the morning, Herr Schaaf.

SCHAAF. Procrastination is the thief of time. Come along.

[KOLYA *resists.*]

NATALYA [*to* VERA]. Who have you been outside with for so long? I haven't seen you since this morning.

VERA. With Alexei Nikolayich . . . and Kolya. . . .

NATALYA. Ah! [*Turning.*] Kolya, whatever are you doing?

KOLYA [*lowering his voice*]. Herr Schaaf . . . Oh, mother . . .

RAKITIN [*to* NATALYA]. They're making a kite outside, but inside it seems to be time for lessons.

SCHAAF [*with dignity*]. *Gnädige Frau.* . . .

NATALYA [*sternly to* KOLYA]. Do as you're told, Kolya—you've had quite enough running about for one day. Go with Herr Schaaf.

SCHAAF [*leading* KOLYA *out*]. *Es ist unerhört!*

KOLYA [*passing by* RAKITIN, *in a whisper*]. You'll still see about the glue, won't you?

[RAKITIN *nods.*]

SCHAAF [*pulling* KOLYA]. *Kommen Sie, mein Herr.* . . . [*Exits with him to hall.*]

[RAKITIN *follows them.*]

NATALYA [*to* VERA]. Sit down, dear—you must be tired. [*Sits down herself.*]

VERA [*sitting down*]. Oh no, Natalya Petrovna, I'm not the least bit tired, thank you.

NATALYA [*smiling to* SHPIGELSKI]. Shpigelski, you look at her: she *is* tired, isn't she?

SHPIGELSKI. Ah, but it's a good kind.

NATALYA. All right, I won't argue. . . . [*To* VERA.] Well, and what did you do in the garden?

VERA. Oh, we played and ran about. First of all we watched them repairing the dam, and then Alexei Nikolayich climbed after a squirrel—right up a tree until the top began swaying. We were all terribly frightened. Then in the end the squirrel fell down and one of the dogs almost caught her, but she got away.

NATALYA [*smiling to* SHPIGELSKI]. And after that?

VERA. Then Alexei Nikolayich made a bow for Kolya—it hardly took him a moment—and then he crawled up behind our cow in the meadow and suddenly jumped on her back. The cow got frightened and ran and bucked, but he just laughed [*Laughs herself.*]—and then Alexei Nikolayich decided to make us a kite, so we came indoors.

NATALYA [*pats her on the cheek*]. You baby, you're such a child, a complete child, aren't you. What do you think, Shpigelski?

SHPIGELSKI [*slowly, looking at* NATALYA]. I quite agree with you.

NATALYA. Such a child.

SHPIGELSKI. But really, that's no obstacle. . . . On the contrary.

NATALYA. Do you think not? [*To* VERA.] Well, and did you have a wonderful time?

VERA. Oh yes, thank you . . . Alexei Nikolayich is such fun.

NATALYA. Is he now? [*Pauses a moment.*] Vera dear, how old are you?

[VERA *looks at her in surprise.*]

You're so young. . . .

[RAKITIN *enters from the hall.*]

SHPIGELSKI [*concerned*]. Oh, and I forgot . . . Your coachman is ill, and I haven't seen him yet. . . .

NATALYA. What's wrong with him?

SHPIGELSKI. Oh . . . a slight fever—nothing to worry about.

NATALYA [*as he goes*]. You'll be staying for dinner, doctor?

SHPIGELSKI. I'd be happy to, thank you. [*Exits to hall.*]

NATALYA. *Mon enfant, vous feriez bien de mettre une autre robe pour le diner.* . . .

[VERA *rises.*]

Come here to me. . . . [*Kissing her on the forehead.*] You child!

[VERA *kisses her hand and goes towards the study.*]

RAKITIN [*quietly to* VERA, *with a wink*]. I've sent everything you need to Alexei Nikolayich.

VERA [*aside*]. Thank you very much, Mikhail Alexandrovich. [*Exits.*]

RAKITIN [*goes to* NATALYA]. At last we're alone. . . .

[*She stretches a hand to him, which he immediately presses.*]

Tell me, Natalya Petrovna, what's the matter with you?

NATALYA. Nothing, Mikhail, nothing. And if there ever was, then it's gone now. Come and sit down.

[RAKITIN *sits next to her.*]

This sort of thing happens to all of us. The sun can't always be shining. Why are you looking at me like that?

RAKITIN. Because I'm happy.

NATALYA [*smiling at him in reply*]. Open the window, would you, Mikhail? How lovely it is in the garden!

[RAKITIN *rises and opens window.*]

And the breeze . . . so cool . . . [*Laughs.*] It was waiting for the chance to come drifting in here. . . . [*Turns.*] Look how it's taken hold of the whole room—we'll never be able to turn it out now.

RAKITIN. Now you're as quiet as the evening after a thunderstorm.

NATALYA [*thoughtfully*]. After a thunderstorm? Has there really been one?

RAKITIN [*nodding*]. There was one just round the corner.

NATALYA. Really? [*Looking at him and pausing.*] Do you know, Mikhail, I can't imagine anyone more kind than you. No, I really can't.

[RAKITIN *tries to stop her.*]

Let me have my say. You're understanding, affectionate, always the same—you don't change. I owe so much to you.

RAKITIN. Natalya, why have you chosen just now to say this?

NATALYA. I don't know—I'm feeling happy and relaxed. Don't stop me chattering.

RAKITIN [*pressing her hand*]. You're an angel . . .

NATALYA [*laughing*]. This morning you wouldn't have called me that. . . . But listen Mikhail, you know me—you mustn't be hard on me. Our relationship is so honest, so frank,—and yet, all the same, not quite natural. We can look everyone in the face about it, not just Arkady, it's true, but . . . [*Pauses.*] It's because of this that I sometimes get cross and depressed, and lose my temper and feel like a child who wants to get rid of its crossness on someone else—onto you in particular. Doesn't that preference for you make you angry?

RAKITIN [*with feeling*]. On the contrary . . .

NATALYA. Yes, it's sometimes fun to torment the one you love. . . . you love? . . . Well, why not be like Tatiana and say, "Why try to conceal things?"

RAKITIN. Natalya Petrovna, you . . .

NATALYA [*interrupts*]. Yes, I love you, but let me tell you something, Rakitin. I sometimes feel very strange: I love you, my knowledge of that is clear and peaceful. It never upsets me, I'm warmed by it, but . . . You've never made me cry, and I feel that I should have done . . . [*Breaks off.*] What does that mean?

RAKITIN [*hurt*]. Such a question hardly needs answering.

NATALYA [*thoughtfully*]. We've known each other so long.

RAKITIN. Four years now. Yes, we're old friends.

NATALYA. Friends . . . no, you're more to me than a friend.

RAKITIN. Natalya Petrovna, don't let's start on that. . . . I'm afraid for my happiness—that it will be destroyed if you touch it.

NATALYA. No . . . no . . . no . . . The whole point is, you're too kind. You're too tolerant with me. . . . You've spoilt me. . . . You're too kind, do you hear?

RAKITIN [*smiling*]. Yes, I hear.

NATALYA [*looking at him*]. I don't know how you feel, but I don't want anything more than this. Many women would envy me. [*Stretches out both hands to him.*] Don't you think?

RAKITIN. I'm like wax in your hands—make what you want out of me.

[*In the hall* ISLAYEV's *voice is heard:* "So you've sent for him?"]

NATALYA [*rising quickly*]. My husband! I can't see him now—good-bye! [*Exits to study.*]

RAKITIN [*watching her go*]. What does all this mean? Is it the beginning of the end, or the end itself? [*Pauses.*] Or is it the beginning, perhaps?

ISLAYEV [*enters worried, takes off his hat*]. How are you Mikhail?

RAKITIN. But we've already seen each other today.

ISLAYEV. I'm sorry—it's all this work I've got on my hands.

[*Paces up and down.*] You know, it's an extraordinary thing. The Russian peasant is very intelligent, very quick to understand what you want—I've a great respect for him—and yet, sometimes, you tell him something, repeat it over and over again till you'd have thought it had got through to him, and nothing gets done. The trouble is, he lacks, he . . .

RAKITIN. You're still at work on the dam, are you?

ISLAYEV. . . . the, er . . . *love* for his job—that's it, the love for his job. He won't let you explain things clearly. "I understand, sir," he says, but that "I understand" simply means that it's gone in one ear and out the other. Take the German: now that's another story. The Russian hasn't got patience, still I respect him. Where's Natasha, do you know?

RAKITIN. She was here a moment ago.

ISLAYEV. What time is it?—It must be time to eat. Been on my feet all morning, stacks of work to do yet and I've still not been to the building site. Time just flies by without your noticing it—it's impossible to get round to everything.

[RAKITIN *smiles.*]

Now you're laughing at me . . . but what can one do, my friend? It's not as though we were all alike. I'm a practical sort of person—I was born to run an estate and I'm good for nothing else. There was a time when I had dreams of something else, but they went wrong, my friend, and I just got my fingers burnt. . . . Where's Beliayev?

RAKITIN. Who is this Beliayev?

ISLAYEV. He's the new tutor, the Russian. He's still a bit shy, but he'll soon get used to us here—he's no fool. I asked him to have a look at the building today.

[*Enter* BELIAYEV.]

Ah, here he is. Well, how are they getting on? Nothing's been done, I suppose?

BELIAYEV. No sir—they're working.

ISLAYEV. Have they finished the second frame?

BELIAYEV. They're already onto the third.

ISLAYEV. And did you mention the beams to them?

BELIAYEV. Yes, sir.

ISLAYEV. And what did they say?

BELIAYEV. They said they've never done it any other way.

ISLAYEV. Hm . . . Is Yermil the carpenter there?

BELIAYEV. Yes, he is.

ISLAYEV. Good. Well, many thanks.

[*Enter* NATALYA.]

Ah, good afternoon, Natasha.

RAKITIN. Why is it you're greeting everyone a dozen times over today?

ISLAYEV. I've already told you—I'm overworked. Oh, that reminds me, I haven't shown you the new winnowing fan yet. Let's go and see it, it's fascinating. Like a miniature tornado when it's going, it really is. We've got time before dinner—would you like to see it?

RAKITIN. Certainly.

ISLAYEV. Natasha, are you coming with us?

NATALYA. What would I understand about winnowing fans? You two go on, but be sure to be back in time for dinner.

ISLAYEV. We won't be five minutes.

[*Exits with* RAKITIN. BELIAYEV *is about to join them.*]

NATALYA [*to* BELIAYEV]. Where are you off to, Alexei Nikolayich?

BELIAYEV. Oh, I . . . I just thought . . .

NATALYA. Of course, if you'd like to go for a walk . . .

BELIAYEV. Oh no, ma'am, I've been outdoors all morning.

NATALYA. Well then, in that case sit down. [*Pointing to a chair.*] Sit here. We haven't had a good conversation yet, have we, Alexei Nikolayich? We still don't know each other.

[BELIAYEV *bows and sits down.*]

And I want to get to know you.

BELIAYEV. That's . . . very kind of you, ma'am.

NATALYA [*smiling*]. You're afraid of me, I can see, but wait a little and when you've got to know me, you'll stop being frightened. Tell me . . . tell me, how old are you?

BELIAYEV. Twenty-one.

NATALYA. Are your parents living?

BELIAYEV. Only my father.

NATALYA. Did your mother die a long time ago?

BELIAYEV. Yes, ma'am, a long time ago.

NATALYA. But you remember her?

BELIAYEV. Of course, ma'am.

NATALYA. And your father lives in Moscow?

BELIAYEV. Oh no, ma'am, he lives in the country.

NATALYA. Have you brothers and sisters?

BELIAYEV. One sister.

NATALYA. And you're very fond of her?

BELIAYEV. Yes, ma'am. She's very much younger than I am.

NATALYA. What's her name?

BELIAYEV. Natalya.

NATALYA [*eagerly*]. Natalya, that's a coincidence—it's my name too. [*Stands up.*] And you love her very much?

BELIAYEV. Yes, ma'am.

NATALYA. Tell me, what do you think of Kolya?

BELIAYEV. He's a very nice boy.

NATALYA. Isn't he? And so affectionate! He's already become very fond of you.

BELIAYEV. I'll do everything I can for him. . . . I'm glad . . .

NATALYA. There's just one thing, Alexei Nikolayich. You realize that naturally I'd like to see him become a capable sort of person, but however that may turn out, I want him always to think of his childhood as having been a happy one. The main thing for him is to grow up in freedom. I was brought up very differently myself, Alexei Nikolayich— my father wasn't unkind so much as moody and strict. Everyone in the house, from mother on down, was afraid of him. My brother and I even used to cross ourselves if he called us to him. Occasionally father would cuddle me, but even in his arms I felt scared. My brother grew up— perhaps you've heard of the row he had with father . . . I shall never forget that terrible day. . . . Right up to his death I remained the faithful daughter to him. He called me his consolation, his Antigone—he was blind for the last years of his life, but however affectionate he was, he couldn't wipe out the earliest memories of my childhood. I was frightened of him, the old blind man, and always felt awkward in his presence. The effects of this shyness, of those years of repression may still be visible in me, perhaps. I know that at first sight I appear—how shall I put it?— cold, maybe. . . . But I'm talking to you about myself instead of about Kolya. I only wanted to say that I'm speaking from personal experience in telling you that it's a fine thing for a child to grow up in freedom. . . . I should imagine you never knew repression as a child, did you?

BELIAYEV. I don't know, madam. . . . I was never repressed, of course . . . no one really bothered about me.

NATALYA [*shyly*]. But surely your father . . .

BELIAYEV. He was always too busy. He was always away visiting the neighbors on business, or if not exactly on business, then . . . You see, that's the way he earned his living . . . by working for them.

NATALYA. Oh, so nobody bothered themselves about bringing you up?

BELIAYEV. Well, as a matter of fact, nobody did. And I expect it shows. I'm only too aware of my shortcomings.

NATALYA. Perhaps . . . but on the other hand . . . [*Stops, then goes on in embarrassment.*] Oh by the way, Alexei Niko-layich, was it you who was singing in the garden last night?

BELIAYEV. When?

NATALYA. In the evening, by the lake. Was it you?

BELIAYEV [*hurriedly*]. Yes, madam. I never dreamt . . . the lake is so far away . . . I never dreamt that it could be heard from such a distance. . . .

NATALYA. But you're apologizing! You have a pleasant voice, and you sing very well. Have you studied music?

BELIAYEV. Oh no, ma'am. I sing by ear . . . only easy songs.

NATALYA. Well, you sing them splendidly. I shall ask you to sing sometime . . . not now, but later when we've got to know each other better and have become friends. . . . We will be friends, won't we, Alexei? I feel that I can trust you, as my chattering like this shows. . . .

[*She stretches out a hand for him to shake.* BELIAYEV *takes it hesitatingly, and after some bewilderment, wondering what to do with it, kisses it.* NATALYA *blushes and draws back her hand. At that instant* SHPIGELSKI *enters from the hall, stops, and takes a step backwards.* NATALYA *quickly rises, as does* BELIAYEV.]

NATALYA [*embarrassed*]. Oh it's you, doctor . . . Alexei and I were just . . . [*Stops.*]

SHPIGELSKI [*loudly and easily*]. The things that go on in your house, Natalya Petrovna. I walk into the servants' hall and ask for the sick coachman. I look round, and there he sits at the table, stuffing himself with pancakes and onions as though he were half-starved. It's no use being a doctor and hoping to earn an honest living from illness.

NATALYA [*with a forced smile*]. Oh that's too bad. . . .

[BELIAYEV *tries to go.*]

Alexei Nikolayich, I forgot to tell you . . .

VERA [*running in from the hall*]. Alexei Nikolayich, Alexei Nikolayich . . . [*She stops on seeing* NATALYA.]

NATALYA [*surprised*]. What's this? What do you want?

VERA [*blushing and lowering her eyes*]. They're calling him. [*Points to* BELIAYEV.]

NATALYA. Who?

VERA. Kolya . . . I mean . . . Kolya asked me, about the kite . . .

NATALYA. I see . . . [*Aside to* VERA.] *On n'entre pas comme cela dans une chambre . . . cela ne convient pas.* [*Turning to* SHPIGELSKI.] Oh doctor, what time is it? Your watch is always right. . . . It must be time for dinner.

SHPIGELSKI. Please, allow me. [*Takes out watch.*] I have the honor to inform you, madam, that it's twenty past four.

NATALYA. There you are, it's dinnertime.

[*Goes to mirror and straightens her hair. Meanwhile* VERA *whispers something to* BELIAYEV. *Both laugh.* NATALYA *watches them in the mirror.* SHPIGELSKI *looks at them askance.*]

BELIAYEV [*laughing, aside*]. Did she really?

VERA [*nods*]. Yes, she tumbled off. . . .

NATALYA [*with assumed indifference, turning to* VERA]. What's that you say? Who tumbled off?

VERA [*embarrassed*]. No, no—Alexei Nikolayich built a swing in the garden, and, you see, the nurse decided to try it out . . .

NATALYA [*not waiting for the end, to* SHPIGELSKI]. Oh incidentally, doctor, come here a moment, would you? [*Leads him to one side, then speaks to* VERA *again.*] She wasn't hurt, I hope?

VERA. Oh no!

NATALYA. Yes . . . but all the same, Alexei Nikolayich, I really think you ought not . . .

MATVEY [*enters from the hall*]. Dinner is served.

NATALYA. Ah! But where's Arkady Sergeyich? You see, he and Mikhail Alexandrovich are late again.

MATVEY. The gentlemen are both in the dining room, madam.

NATALYA. And mother?

MATVEY. Also there, madam.

NATALYA. Oh well, let's join them. [*Pointing to* BELIAYEV.] Vera, *allez en avant avec monsieur.*

[*Exit* MATVEY, *after him* BELIAYEV *and* VERA.]

SHPIGELSKI [*to* NATALYA]. Did you want to tell me something . . . ?

NATALYA. Yes, I did. . . . You see . . . we'll have to talk about your . . . proposal.

SHPIGELSKI. You mean in regard to . . . Vera?

NATALYA. Yes . . . I'll think it over. . . . I'll think it over.

[*Both exit to the hall.*]

ACT TWO

[*The garden. On the right and left, benches under the trees. Center, raspberry bushes. Enter* KATYA *and* MATVEY *from the right.* KATYA *carries a basket.*]

MATVEY. Come now, Katerina Vassilyevna, what am I to think? For goodness' sake give me an answer, I beg of you.

KATYA. Matvey Yegorich, I really can't say.

MATVEY. Katerina, you know only too well how I feel about you. Of course, I'm older than you are—there's no denying that. But all the same I can still hold my own: I'm in the prime of life and I've got a gentle disposition—what more can you want?

KATYA. Believe me, I feel very proud that you should ask me, Matvey Yegorich, very proud and grateful. It's just that . . . I think we should wait just a little.

MATVEY. But what's the point of waiting, Katerina Vassilyevna? Tell me that! You didn't used to speak like that, let me remind you. And as far as respect goes, I can promise you you'll get such respect from me, Katerina, that it'll be impossible for you to want more. And besides, I don't drink and I've never had a bad word said of me by either the master or the mistress.

KATYA. I know that. Really, I don't know what to say, Matvey Yegorich.

MATVEY. Lately you've seemed so different somehow. . . .

KATYA [*blushing*]. How do you mean—"lately?" Why do you say that?

MATVEY. Oh, how should I know . . . it's just that earlier you never used to act like this with me. . . .

KATYA [*glancing sideways*]. Watch out—here comes the German. . . .

MATVEY [*crestfallen*]. Who cares about that interfering old pest . . . But we can talk about this later, can't we?

SCHAAF [*enters left, with fishing rod*]. Vere are you going, Katerina?

KATYA [*stops*]. I've got to pick some raspberries, Adam Ivanich.

[73]

SCHAAF. Raspberries? *Ach*, they are a wonderful *frucht*. Do you like raspberries?

KATYA. Oh yes, I like them. . . .

SCHAAF. Hee-hee. And so do I. I love *alles*, that you love. [*Seeing that she wants to go.*] Oh Katerina, one moment please wait.

KATYA. Oh but I've not time. The housekeeper will be angry with me.

SCHAAF. Vell, it does not matter. I'm going . . . [*Points to rod.*] How do you say? . . . to catch the fish, you understand, to catch the fish. Do you love them, the fish?

KATYA. Oh yes, sir.

SCHAAF. Hee-hee-hee. So do I. Do you know vot I'm going to tell you Katerina—in German there is a *Volkslied*: "Kathrinchen, Kathrinchen, wie lieb' ich dich so sehr." That means: "Oh Katerina, Katerina, how much I love you." [*Tries to put an arm round her.*]

KATYA. That's enough, now—you ought to be ashamed of yourself. People are coming! [*Taking refuge in the bushes.*]

SCHAAF [*sulkily*]. *Das ist dumm!* . . .

[*Enter right* NATALYA, *arm in arm with* RAKITIN.]

NATALYA. Ah, Adam Ivanich—are you going fishing?

SCHAAF. Yes, madam, that is my plan.

NATALYA. Where's Kolya?

SCHAAF. With Lizaveta Bogdanovna at the piano lesson.

NATALYA. Ah, of course. [*Looks round.*] Are you alone here?

SCHAAF. Yes, alone.

NATALYA. You haven't seen Alexei Nikolayich?

SCHAAF. No, madam.

NATALYA [*pausing*]. May we come with you, Adam Ivanich, and see what luck you have with the fish?

SCHAAF. That would be very nice.

RAKITIN [*aside to* NATALYA]. What are you saying!

NATALYA [*to* RAKITIN]. Come along, *beau ténébreux!*

[*All three exit right.*]

KATYA [*cautiously peering over bushes*]. They've gone . . . [*Emerges.*] Ugh, that German! . . . [*Sighs, and starts picking raspberries again, singing quietly.*]

> No fire burns, no spark glows
> Save for my heart alone . . .

Yes, Matvey was quite right. . . .

> My heart alone is burning, glowing
> Not for mother, nor for father . . .

Oh, what a large raspberry!

> Not for mother, nor for father . . .

Isn't it hot out here—and stuffy too.

> Not for mother, nor for father:
> It burns and glows for . . .

[*Suddenly turns, stops singing, and partly hides in the bushes.*]

[*Enter left* BELIAYEV *and* VERA. BELIAYEV *carries the kite.*]

BELIAYEV. Why don't you go on, Katya?

> It burns and glows for a pretty girl . . .

KATYA [*blushing*]. That's not how a woman would end it.
BELIAYEV. How would you sing it, then?

[KATYA *laughs, and doesn't answer.*]

What are you up to—picking raspberries? Let's have a taste.
KATYA [*passing him the basket*]. Have them all. . . .
BELIAYEV. Why all of them? Vera Alexandrovna, wouldn't you like some? [*Both take raspberries.*] That's plenty, thank you. [*Tries to return basket.*]
KATYA. No, take all of them. [*Pushes away his arm.*]
BELIAYEV. Thank you, Katya, we've had enough. [*Gives her the basket.*] Thank you. [*To* VERA.] Vera, let's sit down here for a bit. Here—[*Pointing to kite.*]—we need to put a tail on it. Will you help? [*Both sit down,* BELIAYEV *gives her the kite.*] That's the way, but be sure to hold it up straight. [*Starts to fix tail.*] What's the matter?
VERA. Oh but I can't see you like this.
BELIAYEV. But what do you want to see me for?
VERA. I mean, I can't watch you put on the tail.
BELIAYEV. Oh—well then, wait a moment. [*Moves the kite so that she can see.*] Katya, why have you stopped singing? Please sing for us.

[*After a moment* KATYA *starts to sing quietly.*]

VERA. Tell me, Alexei Nikolayich, do you ever go kite-flying in Moscow?

BELIAYEV. We've no time for kites in Moscow!—Hold this string—that's right. Do you think we've nothing better to do with our time?

VERA. Well then, what *do* you do?

BELIAYEV. What do we do? Why, we study, and go to classes.

VERA. What sort of things do they teach you?

BELIAYEV. Everything under the sun.

VERA. I'll bet you're a good student, the best of all.

BELIAYEV. No, I'm not much good. What nonsense—the best of all! I'm too lazy.

VERA. Why are you lazy?

BELIAYEV. Oh, Lord knows. I think I was born that way.

VERA [*after pausing*]. Do you have many friends in Moscow?

BELIAYEV. Oh, yes. Oh, this string isn't strong enough.

VERA. And are you fond of them?

BELIAYEV. Of course, very. Surely you're fond of your friends?

VERA. My friends? . . . I haven't got any.

BELIAYEV. Oh, but I meant your girl friends.

VERA [*slowly*]. Yes.

BELIAYEV. Surely you must have those?

VERA. Yes, but . . . I don't know why, but lately I don't seem to have been thinking very much about them. . . . I didn't even answer Liza Moshnin, although in her last letter she begged me to write.

BELIAYEV. What do you mean by saying you haven't any friends? What do you think I am?

VERA [*smiling*]. Oh you—you're different. [*Pausing.*] Alexei Nikolayich. . .

BELIAYEV. Yes?

VERA. Do you ever write poetry?

BELIAYEV. No, I don't. But why do you ask?

VERA. Oh, nothing. [*Pauses.*] One of the girls at school used to.

BELIAYEV [*tightening a knot with his teeth*]. Well, well! Was it good poetry?

VERA. I can't say. She read it to us and we cried.

BELIAYEV. What did you do that for?

VERA. Because we pitied her—we felt so sorry for her!

BELIAYEV. Did you go to school in Moscow?

VERA. Yes, at Madame Beauluce's. Natalya Petrovna took me away last year.

BELIAYEV. Are you fond of Natalya Petrovna?

VERA. Yes, she's so kind. I'm very fond of her.

BELIAYEV [*smiling*]. And perhaps a little scared of her?

VERA [*also smiling*]. A little.

BELIAYEV [*pausing*]. Who was it sent you to the school?

VERA. It was Natalya Petrovna's mother—she's dead now. I grew up in her home. You see, I'm an orphan.

BELIAYEV [*letting his hands fall*]. An orphan? Don't you remember either your father or your mother?

VERA. No. I don't remember either of them.

BELIAYEV. My mother's dead, too. So we're both alone. What can we do about it?—there's no use letting it depress us.

VERA. They say that orphans make friends with each other very quickly.

BELIAYEV [*looking into her face*]. Do they?—and do you believe them?

VERA [*looks back, smiling*]. I think I do.

BELIAYEV [*laughs, turns to kite again*]. I wonder how long it's been since I came here.

VERA. Today makes it just four weeks.

BELIAYEV. What a memory you've got! Well, that's it, the kite's ready. Look at that splendid tail—we must go and get Kolya.

KATYA [*comes up with the basket*]. Wouldn't you like some more raspberries?

BELIAYEV. No thank you, Katya.

[KATYA *exits in silence.*]

VERA. Kolya's with Lizaveta Bogdanovna.

BELIAYEV. Imagine keeping a boy indoors in weather like this!

VERA. Lizaveta Bogdanovna would only get in the way. . . .

BELIAYEV. But I'm not talking about her. . . .

VERA [*hastily*]. Kolya couldn't come with us without her. . . . Do you know that yesterday she spoke very highly of you.

BELIAYEV. Really?

VERA. Don't you like her?

BELIAYEV. Oh, she's all right—she and her snuff! What are you sighing about?

VERA. Oh, nothing . . . How clear the sky is!

BELIAYEV. I don't imagine you were sighing because of that. . . . [*Pause.*] Perhaps you're bored?

VERA. Bored? Oh no! I don't even know myself why I'm sighing. I'm not the slightest bit bored—on the contrary . . .

[*Pausing.*] I don't know—perhaps I'm not quite well. Yesterday I went upstairs for a book, and suddenly on the staircase I sat down and burst out crying—just imagine! Goodness knows why. And for a long time after tears kept coming into my eyes. Whatever can that mean, do you think? Still, all the same I'm very happy.

BELIAYEV. It's just your age—you're growing up—it's often like that. Your eyes looked a little red last night.

VERA. You noticed?

BELIAYEV. Yes.

VERA. You notice everything.

BELIAYEV. What?

VERA [*pausing*]. Whatever was it I wanted to ask you? I've completely forgotten what I was going to say.

BELIAYEV. Are you that absent-minded?

VERA. No, but . . . oh yes, I remember now. I think you've told me once already—have you a sister?

BELIAYEV. Yes.

VERA. Tell me, am I like her?

BELIAYEV. Oh no—you're much prettier than she.

VERA. That's impossible. . . . Your sister—I should like to be in her shoes.

BELIAYEV. What, would you like to be in our stuffy little house?

VERA. I didn't mean that. . . . Is your house really so small?

BELIAYEV. Very small—not at all like this place.

VERA. Well anyway, what's the use of so many rooms?

BELIAYEV. What's the use of them? Oh, in time you'll find out well enough what to do with them.

VERA. In time . . . when?

BELIAYEV. When you've got your own house to run.

VERA [*thoughtfully*]. Do you think I shall?

BELIAYEV. You wait and see. [*Pausing.*] Well, come on—let's go and get Kolya, shall we, Vera Alexandrovna?

VERA. Why don't you call me Verochka?

BELIAYEV. But do you think you should call me Alexei?

VERA. Why not? [*Starts.*] Oh!

BELIAYEV. What is it?

VERA [*lowering her voice*]. Natalya Petrovna's coming.

BELIAYEV [*also lowering his voice*]. Where?

VERA. Over there [*Nodding right.*]—along the path. With Mikhail Alexandrovich.

BELIAYEV [*rising*]. Let's go and find Kolya—he must have finished his lesson by now.

VERA. Come on then . . . I'm scared that she'll scold me.

[*Both exit left.* KATYA *hides again in the bush. Enter right* NATALYA *and* RAKITIN.]

NATALYA [*stopping*]. Isn't that Beliayev over there—with Vera?

RAKITIN. Yes.

NATALYA. They seem almost to be running away from us.

RAKITIN. Perhaps they are.

NATALYA [*pausing*]. You know, I don't think that it's quite right for Vera . . . for Vera to be alone with a young man in the garden. . . . Of course, she's still a child, but just the same, it's not right. I'll speak to her about it.

RAKITIN. How old is Vera now?

NATALYA. Seventeen! She's seventeen already. . . . Goodness, it's warm today. I'm tired—let's sit down.

[*They sit down where* VERA *and* BELIAYEV *had sat previously.*]

Has Shpigelski gone yet?

RAKITIN. Yes, he's gone.

NATALYA. It's a shame you didn't get him to stay. I can't imagine what made that man decide to become a country doctor. . . . He's very amusing, and makes me laugh.

RAKITIN. But I thought that you weren't in a laughing mood today.

NATALYA. What made you think that?

RAKITIN. Oh, I don't know.

NATALYA. Was it because I'm against anything remotely sentimental today? Well, that's true enough—I must warn you that there's absolutely nothing that could move me. But that needn't prevent me from laughing—quite the contrary, in fact. And anyway, I wanted a talk with Shpigelski.

RAKITIN. May I ask, what about?

NATALYA. No, you may not. Anyway, you know everything I think or do as it is. It's very boring.

RAKITIN. I beg your pardon . . . I wasn't suggesting . . .

NATALYA. It would be nice if I could keep at least something secret from you.

RAKITIN. Oh come now—from what you're saying one would imagine that I know everything. . . .

NATALYA [*interrupts*]. But don't you?

RAKITIN. You have such fun laughing at me.

NATALYA. And so you really don't know everything that goes

on in me? In that case I'm not very impressed with your powers of observation. For someone who watches me from morning till night . . .

RAKITIN. Does this mean you're reproaching me?

NATALYA. Reproaching you? [*Pause.*] No, but I'm convinced now that you don't really understand me.

RAKITIN. Possibly not . . . but since I watch you from morning till night, let me tell you one thing . . .

NATALYA. About myself? Please do.

RAKITIN. You won't be angry?

NATALYA. Oh no! I'd like to be, but I won't.

RAKITIN. Well, lately, Natalya Petrovna, you've been constantly irritated. This irritation is quite unconscious and internal; you're having a battle with yourself—it's as though you were confused about something. Before I went to the Krinitsins I hadn't noticed it—it's quite a recent thing in you . . .

[NATALYA *draws on the ground in front of her with her umbrella.*]

Sometimes you sigh so deeply, like a very tired person does, who can never rest properly.

NATALYA. What do you deduce from this, Mr. Detective?

RAKITIN. Nothing. But it worries me.

NATALYA. Heartfelt thanks for your sympathy.

RAKITIN. And then . . .

NATALYA [*with impatience*]. Oh please—change the subject.

[*Pause.*]

RAKITIN. You're not going out anywhere today, then?

NATALYA. No.

RAKITIN. Why not? It's lovely weather.

NATALYA. I'm feeling too lazy. [*Pause.*] Tell me . . . you know Bolshintsov, don't you?

RAKITIN. Afanasy Ivanovich, our neighbor?

NATALYA. Yes.

RAKITIN. How can you ask? Why, only the day before yesterday we were playing cards together in this very house.

NATALYA. Tell me, what sort of man is he?

RAKITIN. Bolshintsov?

NATALYA. Yes, yes—Bolshintsov.

RAKITIN. Well, I must confess, I never expected that!

NATALYA [*impatiently*]. What didn't you expect?

RAKITIN. That you would ever start asking questions about Bolshintsov! That stupid, fat, lumbering man . . . not that there's anything bad about him, of course.

NATALYA. He's not nearly as stupid and lumbering as you think.

RAKITIN. Maybe not. I must admit I haven't really paid much attention to him.

NATALYA [*sarcastically*]. You didn't watch him, then?

RAKITIN [*with a forced smile*]. But why do you mention him . . . ?

NATALYA. Oh, nothing

[*Another pause.*]

RAKITIN. How beautiful that dark green oak is against the blue sky, Natalya Petrovna! It's completely flooded with sunlight—what magnificent colors! How much indestructible life and vigor is in it, compared with that young birch tree, which looks as though it were fainting from the radiance, with its tiny leaves gleaming, almost melting in the liquid glitter. But all the same, the birch tree is beautiful, too. . . .

NATALYA. Shall I tell you something, Rakitin? I've noticed more than once: you are very alive to what are called the beauties of nature, and you talk about them most colorfully and cleverly—with such color and cleverness that I should think nature would be eternally indebted to you for your exquisite turns of phrase. You pay court to her like a perfumed duke with red-heeled boots running after a pretty little peasant girl. But the trouble is that sometimes it seems to me that she will never understand and appreciate your subtle observations, exactly as the peasant girl can't make head or tail of the duke's courtly compliments. Nature is much more simple, much more crude than you imagine, because, thank goodness, she's healthy. . . . Birch trees don't molt and faint like neurotic women . . .

RAKITIN. *Quelle tirade!* Nature is healthy . . . in other words, you're saying that I'm sickly.

NATALYA. You're not the only one—we're neither of us exactly brimming with health.

RAKITIN. Please don't imagine I don't know this way of saying the most unpleasant things to people in a completely inoffensive manner. . . . Instead of telling someone straight out that he's stupid, you just say, smiling kindly, "We're really each of us as stupid as the other."

NATALYA. Surely you're not offended? Oh come—I only wanted to say that both of us are . . . you don't like the word "sickly" . . . that both of us are old, very old.

RAKITIN. Why are we old? For my part I don't consider myself so.

NATALYA. Well then, listen: here we are on perhaps the very same seat that two really young people were sitting on a quarter of an hour ago.

RAKITIN. Beliayev and Verochka? Of course they're younger than us—there are a few years difference between us, that's all—but we aren't old merely because of that.

NATALYA. The difference between us isn't just one of years.

RAKITIN. Ah, I understand: you envy them their naïveté, their freshness and innocence—in short, their stupidity.

NATALYA. Do you think so? Do you think they're stupid? I'm beginning to realize that today everyone's stupid as far as you're concerned. No, you don't understand me. And anyway, if they are stupid, what then? What good is there in the intellect if it doesn't amuse? . . . There's nothing more depressing than gloomy cleverness.

RAKITIN. Hm, why don't you say straight out that I bore you? That's what you really mean. Why do you accuse intellect in general of what are just my own particular faults?

NATALYA. You still don't see . . .

[KATYA *comes out from the bushes.*]

Hello, Katya—have you been picking raspberries?

KATYA. Yes, ma'am.

NATALYA. Show me.

[KATYA *goes up to her.*]

What a wonderful raspberry—such a splendid red . . . just like your cheeks.

[KATYA *smiles and lowers her eyes.*]

Very well—you may go.

[*Exit* KATYA.]

RAKITIN. Another young creature who appeals to you.

NATALYA. Of course. [*Rising.*]

RAKITIN. Where are you going?

NATALYA. First, to see what Vera's doing—it's time she went indoors. And second, I must admit there's something I don't like about our conversation. We'd better stop talking about nature and youth for a while I think.

RAKITIN. Perhaps you'd like to go for a walk alone?

NATALYA. To be honest I would. We'll meet again very soon. And we're parting friends, aren't we? [*Gives him her hand.*]

RAKITIN. Of course! [*Rising and pressing her hand.*]

NATALYA. *Au revoir* then. [*She opens her umbrella and exits.*]

RAKITIN [*walking up and down*]. What's the matter with her? [*Pauses.*] Oh, just a mood. A mood? I've never noticed it in her before. On the contrary, I don't know any woman more consistent in her behavior. Then what can be the reason? [*Walks up and down again, then suddenly stops.*] Oh, how ridiculous people are who've only got one thought in their heads, one aim, one preoccupation in life . . . people like me, for example. She was quite right when she said "watch trivialities from morning to night and you become trivial yourself." . . . That's all very true, but I can't live without her—yet what I feel when I'm with her can't be called happiness. I belong completely to her—to part from her would be the same as parting from life—that's no exaggeration. What is the matter with her? What does this inner conflict mean, and this involuntary bitterness whenever she speaks? Is it just that she's started to get tired of me? Hm. [*Sits down.*] I've never deceived myself—I know very well how much she loves me—but I hoped that in time this quiet feeling . . . I hoped! Do I have the right to hope?—dare I hope? I admit that my position is rather absurd, almost contemptible. [*Pausing.*] Why go on thinking about it? She's an honest woman and I'm no young Lochinvar. [*With a bitter smile.*] More's the pity. [*Rises quickly.*] Well, that's enough—I must get all this nonsense out of my head. [*Walks up and down.*] What a wonderful day! [*Pause.*] How cleverly she went about hurting me! My exquisite turns of phrase. She's very clever, particularly when she's in a bad mood. And then that sudden fondness for simplicity and innocence—what does that mean? This Russian tutor . . . She talks to me often about him, though I must confess I don't see anything particularly unusual in him: just a student, like any other. Surely she can't . . . ? No, it's impossible. She's just in a mood, she herself doesn't know what she wants, and so she plays the cat with me a little. Children fight with their nurse, after all. That's a flattering metaphor! But there's no need to try and stop her. When this fit of restlessness and depression has gone, she'll be the first to laugh at that gangling boy, that green youth. . . . That's quite a good explanation you've got there, Mikhail old friend, but is it the right one? God knows —we shall see! It's happened more than once, old man, that after a long struggle with yourself, you've suddenly thrown up all your suppositions and conjectures, folded your hands, and waited to see what would happen. But meanwhile you must accept the fact that it's pretty awkward and unpleasant for you. . . . That seems to be your job in life. [*Looks round.*] Ah, here he is in person, our unspoiled youth! He's come just at the right moment. I still haven't had a good talk with him. Let's see what kind of person he is.

[*Enter left* BELIAYEV.]

Ah, Alexei Nikolayich!—so you've come out for some fresh air, too?

BELIAYEV. Yes.

RAKITIN. Although I must say the air today isn't exactly fresh. It's so hot. But here it's quite bearable—under these lime trees in the shade. [*Pause.*] Have you seen Natalya Petrovna?

BELIAYEV. I met her a moment ago—she and Vera Alexandrovna went indoors together.

RAKITIN. Wasn't it you and Vera I saw here half an hour ago?

BELIAYEV. Yes—we were having a walk together.

RAKITIN. Ah! [*Takes his arm.*] Well, how do you like life in the country?

BELIAYEV. Oh, I love it. There's only one drawback: the shooting's bad here.

RAKITIN. You shoot, do you?

BELIAYEV. Yes—do you?

RAKITIN. I? Oh no—I'm a poor shot, I don't bother to deny it. I'm too lazy.

BELIAYEV. Yes, I'm lazy too . . . except where exercise is concerned.

RAKITIN. Does that mean you're lazy at reading?

BELIAYEV. No—I'm fond of reading. I'm lazy when I have to work for a long time on the same subject.

RAKITIN [*smiling*]. How about when you're talking with ladies?

BELIAYEV. Now you're making fun of me. . . . It would be more right to say that I'm frightened of ladies.

RAKITIN [*somewhat embarrassed*]. What makes you think . . . what reason could I have for laughing at you?

BELIAYEV. Oh, I don't know—it doesn't matter. [*Pause.*] Tell me, can one buy gunpowder here?

RAKITIN. Well, in the town there's a shop that sells it. But do you want very good powder?

BELIAYEV. Oh no—it's not for my rifle; I want to make some fireworks.

RAKITIN. So you know how to do that?

BELIAYEV. Yes . . . I've already chosen a perfect place to shoot them off—behind the lake. I heard that it's Natalya Petrovna's birthday next week, so I'd like to have them for the party.

RAKITIN. She'll be pleased at such thoughtfulness from you— she likes you, Alexei Nikolayich, let me tell you.

BELIAYEV. I'm very flattered to hear it. . . . Oh by the way, Mikhail Alexandrovich, I believe you get a newspaper sent out to you. Could I borrow it to read sometime?

RAKITIN. Of course, by all means. There is some good poetry in it.

BELIAYEV. I'm not very fond of poetry.

RAKITIN. Why's that?

BELIAYEV. Well, funny poems strike me as being contrived, and besides, there aren't many of them. And sentimental poems . . . I don't know . . . there's something about them that I mistrust.

RAKITIN. You prefer short stories, perhaps?

BELIAYEV. Yes, I'm fond of good stories . . . but critical articles are what really appeal to me.

RAKITIN. Why?

BELIAYEV. They're written by understanding people. . . .

RAKITIN. But you yourself aren't a writer?

BELIAYEV. Oh goodness, no! What's the point of writing if you weren't born with the talent for it?—people will only laugh at you. And apart from that—it's very strange, perhaps you can explain it to me—even an otherwise clever man seems to become completely stupid when he takes a pen in his hand. No, it's no use writing—let's be thankful if we can understand what's already been written.

RAKITIN. Shall I tell you something, Alexei Nikolayich? Not many young people have as much common sense as you.

BELIAYEV. Thank you for the compliment. [*Pause.*] I chose the spot for the fireworks beyond the lake because I can make Roman candles, and they'll make such a beautiful reflection in the water. . . .

RAKITIN. That will be very pleasant. . . . Tell me, Alexei Nikolayich, may I ask if you speak French?

BELIAYEV. No, I don't. I translated Paul de Kock's novel *The Milkmaid of Montfermel*—perhaps you've heard of it —for an advance of fifty roubles, without knowing a single word of French. Just imagine: for *"quatre-vingt-dix"* I put "four-twenty-two" . . . It was a case of necessity being the mother of invention. But it's a shame—I would like to know French, it's this cursed laziness again. I'd like to read George Sand in the original. It's the pronunciation: how can you cope with the pronunciation—*en, in, on* . . . it's terrible.

RAKITIN. Oh that needn't really be so difficult. . . .

BELIAYEV. Do you have the right time?

RAKITIN [*looks at watch*]. It's half past one.

BELIAYEV. Why is Lizaveta Bogdanovna keeping Kolya at the piano so long? He must be dying to come outside.

RAKITIN [*kindly*]. Oh, but one must study, you know, Alexei Nikolayich. . . .

BELIAYEV. You shouldn't have to tell me that, and I shouldn't need to be listening, Mikhail Alexandrovich. Of course, not everyone is a undependable as I am.

RAKITIN. Come now . . .

BELIAYEV. Oh, but here I do know what I'm talking about. . . .

RAKITIN. And I know, on the contrary, that it's just what you regard in yourself as a fault—your ease of manner, your freedom—that is most charming to others.

BELIAYEV. To whom, for example?

RAKITIN. Well, to Natalya Petrovna for one.

BELIAYEV. Natalya Petrovna? Why, it's precisely with her that I don't feel easy and free, to use your expression.

RAKITIN. Is that so?

BELIAYEV. And anyway, don't you think that education is the most important thing in a person, Mikhail Alexandrovich? It's easy for you to talk . . . in fact, I don't quite understand you. . . . [*Suddenly stopping.*] What was that? Wasn't that a corncrake[5] calling in the garden? [*About to go.*]

RAKITIN. Perhaps, but where are you going?

BELIAYEV. To get my gun. [*Goes left.*]

---

[5] A bird that is a nuisance around grain fields.

[NATALYA *enters to meet him.*]

NATALYA [*smiles on seeing him*]. Where are you off to, Alexei
  Nikolayich?

BELIAYEV. Well, ma'am, I was . . .

RAKITIN. He's going for his gun. He heard a corncrake in the
  garden.

NATALYA. No, please don't shoot in the garden. . . . Let the
  poor bird live a little longer. . . . And anyway, you might
  upset grandmother.

BELIAYEV. Yes, ma'am.

NATALYA [*laughing*]. You ought to be ashamed of yourself,
  Alexei Nikolayich! "Yes ma'am"—how can you talk like
  that? Just wait: Mikhail Alexandrovich and I will teach you.
  . . . Yes we will. . . . We've already talked about you more
  than once. . . . There's a conspiracy against you, I must
  warn you. Will you let us do that?

BELIAYEV. Oh please—I . . .

NATALYA. First of all, don't be so shy—it doesn't suit you.
  Yes, we must really get to work on you. [*Points to* RAKITIN.]
  After all, we're old people and you're young, aren't you?
  See how well everything will go. You will work with Kolya,
  and I . . . that is, we . . . will work with you.

BELIAYEV. I would be very grateful.

NATALYA. That's better. What have you two been talking about
  here?

RAKITIN [*smiling*]. He was telling me how he translated a
  French book without knowing a word of French.

NATALYA. Was he? Oh well, we'll teach you French, too. By
  the way, what did you do with your kite?

BELIAYEV. I took it indoors. I felt that you didn't approve. . . .

NATALYA [*embarrassed*]. Why did you feel that? Because I
  told Vera . . . because I took Vera indoors? No, that . . .
  No, you're mistaken. [*Animatedly.*] Incidentally, you know
  Kolya must have finished his lesson by now. Go and get
  him and Vera and the kite—would you like to?—and we'll
  all go down to the meadow. How about that?

BELIAYEV. That would be very nice, Natalya Petrovna.

NATALYA. Good, then. Well, come on, let's go! [*Gives him her
  hand.*] Come on, clumsy—take my hand. Hurry up. [*Both
  exit quickly left.*]

RAKITIN [*watches them go*]. What enthusiasm, what cheerful-
  ness! I've never seen such an expression on her face before.

. . . And what a sudden change! [*Pauses.*] *Souvent femme varie* . . . But she's certainly got no time for me today, that's obvious. [*Pauses.*] Oh well, let's wait and see what happens. [*Slowly.*] Surely she . . . [*Waves his hand in dismissal.*] No, it's impossible! But that smile, that warm, tender, happy glance . . . God save me from the tortures of jealousy, especially senseless jealousy. . . . [*Looks round suddenly.*] Where did they come from?

[*Enter left* SHPIGELSKI *and* BOLSHINTSOV. RAKITIN *goes to meet them.*]

Good day to you, gentlemen. Shpigelski, I must admit, I'm surprised to see you again so soon. [*Shakes hands.*]

SHPIGELSKI. I didn't expect to be here, either. . . . I never imagined I'd come, but I went round to see him, [*Points to* BOLSHINTSOV.] and he was just climbing into his carriage to come over here, so I did an about-turn and came back with him.

RAKITIN. Welcome to you, sir. . . .

BOLSHINTSOV. I was just about to . . .

SHPIGELSKI [*changing the subject for him*]. The servants told us that you were all in the garden, and so, as there was no one in the drawing room, we came straight out here.

RAKITIN. But surely you must have met Natalya Petrovna?

SHPIGELSKI. When?

RAKITIN. Just now.

SHPIGELSKI. No. We didn't actually come straight out from the house. Afanasy Ivanovich wanted to look for mushrooms in the garden.

BOLSHINTSOV [*bewildered*]. I . . .

SHPIGELSKI. Come now, we all know what a passion you have for them. So Natalya Petrovna's gone indoors, has she? Well, we can go back too.

BOLSHINTSOV. Of course.

RAKITIN. Yes, she went indoors to get the others to go for a walk. Apparently they're going to fly a kite.

SHPIGELSKI. Oh splendid. It's perfect weather for a walk.

RAKITIN. You stay here, then, and I'll go and tell her you've arrived.

SHPIGELSKI. Oh, don't put yourself to any trouble . . . please, Mikhail Alexandrovich.

RAKITIN. It's quite all right—I was going anyway.

SHPIGELSKI. In that case we won't stop you. . . . But tell her we've just dropped in—it's all very informal.

RAKITIN. *Au revoir*, gentlemen. [*Exits left.*]

SHPIGELSKI. *An revoir*. [*To* BOLSHINTSOV.] Well, Afanasy Ivanovich?

BOLSHINTSOV [*interrupts*]. Whatever did you mean about the mushrooms, Ignaty Ilyich? I don't understand—what mushrooms?

SHPIGELSKI. But surely, man, you didn't want me to say that my Afanasy Ivanovich felt shy—that he didn't want to see anyone right away—that he wanted to get out of sight?

BOLSHINTSOV. Of course not . . . but all the same, mushrooms . . . I don't know, perhaps I'm wrong, but . . .

SHPIGELSKI. You're wrong all right, my friend. There are other things you ought to be worrying about at present. You and I have come here because you wanted it, so it's up to you not to go and spoil everything.

BOLSHINTSOV. Yes, Ignaty, but you . . . but you told me, that is to say . . . I would like to know for certain what answer to expect. . . .

SHPIGELSKI. My dear Afanasy Ivanovich! From your village to here it's at least fifteen miles, and at least three times per mile you asked me that same question, and I told you the same thing. . . . Isn't that enough for you? Well, listen to me, then, this is the last time I'll open my mouth. Here's what Natalya Petrovna told me. "I . . ."

BOLSHINTSOV [*nods*]. I knew it.

SHPIGELSKI [*annoyed*]. "I knew it"—what do you mean, "I knew it"? I haven't yet told you anything. . . . "I don't know your friend Bolshintsov very well," she says, "but he strikes me as a fine man. On the other hand, I don't in the least intend to force Vera, so let him come and visit us, and if he wins . . ."

BOLSHINTSOV. "Wins?" Did she use the word "wins"?

SHPIGELSKI. ". . . if he wins her approval, Anna Semyenovna and I won't stand in their way."

BOLSHINTSOV. "Won't stand in their way." Did she really say that—"We won't stand in their way"?

SHPIGELSKI. Oh, yes, yes, yes. What an extraordinary fellow you are! "We won't stand in the way of their happiness."

BOLSHINTSOV. Hm.

SHPIGELSKI. *H*appiness, *h*appiness. But look, Afanasy Ivanovich, this is what your next objective must be. You've got to convince Vera herself that marriage to you would be sheer paradise—you've got to win her approval.

BOLSHINTSOV [*blinking*]. Yes, yes—win her approval . . . I quite agree with you.

SHPIGELSKI. It was you who insisted I should bring you here today so let's hear your plan of campaign.

BOLSHINTSOV. Plan of campaign? Yes, yes, I suppose I've got to act, I've got to win her approval, you're perfectly right there. Only the point is, Ignaty Ilyich . . . let me confess to you, as my closest friend, one fault of mine. You're quite right in saying that it was my idea to come here today. . . .

SHPIGELSKI. It wasn't just an idea, you insisted, absolutely insisted. . . .

BOLSHINTSOV. Well, all right then, I agree I insisted. Well, you see, at home . . . I really . . . at home I seemed to be ready for anything, but now, you see, I'm overcome with shyness.

SHPIGELSKI. But whatever have you got to be shy about?

BOLSHINTSOV [*looking at him earnestly*]. It's the risk.

SHPIGELSKI. What?

BOLSHINTSOV. The risk, there's a great risk. Ignaty Ilyich, I must confess to you, as . . .

SHPIGELSKI. "as my closest friend"—I know, I know . . . go on.

BOLSHINTSOV. That's right, I agree with you. I should confess to you, Ignaty Ilyich, that I . . . in general, with the ladies, with the female sex in general, I haven't really had much acquaintance. I confess openly to you, Ignaty Ilyich, that I've simply no idea of what it's permissible to talk about with one of the female sex . . . especially alone . . . especially with a young girl.

SHPIGELSKI. You surprise me—I don't know what it's *not* permissible to talk about with one of the female sex, especially with a young girl and especially alone.

BOLSHINTSOV. Oh, but you . . . Forgive me, but I can't be compared with you. In this matter I really must throw myself on your mercy, Ignaty Ilyich, and beg for advice. They do say that in such affairs it's the first step that counts, so couldn't you perhaps give me a phrase for getting a conversation going—you know, something pleasant to say, or something, like, er . . . like . . . well something just to get things going, and then I'll take over somehow or other myself. . . .

SHPIGELSKI. I won't give you a start on any account, Afanasy

Ivanovich, because no start I could give you would be any
help at all. I could give you some advice, if you like.

BOLSHINTSOV. Oh yes, please do, old friend. And as far as my
gratitude is concerned . . . you know . . .

SHPIGELSKI. That's enough, that's enough—What do you think
this is, a business deal, or something?

BOLSHINTSOV [*quietly*]. You don't have to worry about the
horses. . . .

SHPIGELSKI. Oh, for goodness' sake! Look, listen to me, Afanasy Ivanovich. You're undoubtedly an excellent man in all
respects

[BOLSHINTSOV *bows slightly*.]

—a man of outstanding qualities . . .

BOLSHINTSOV. Oh please . . . !

SHPIGELSKI. And furthermore, I believe you've got about
three hundred serfs?

BOLSHINTSOV. Yes, three hundred and twenty.

SHPIGELSKI. You're not mortgaged?

BOLSHINTSOV. I don't owe anyone a penny.

SHPIGELSKI. Well then, listen. I told you that you're a splendid
fellow and a good catch as a husband for any girl. But you
yourself say that you've had nothing to do with women. . . .

BOLSHINTSOV [*sighing*]. That's quite right. You might say,
Ignaty Ilyich, that I've avoided the fair sex since the day
I was born.

SHPIGELSKI [*sighing*]. Now look here, that isn't a sin in a man
—quite the contrary in fact—but all the same, on some
occasions—for example, on first declaring one's love—it's
essential to be able to say at least something, isn't it?

BOLSHINTSOV. I quite agree with you.

SHPIGELSKI. Of course, Vera Alexandrovna may just think that
you're not feeling well, and nothing else. But then your
appearance, although quite presentable in every way, doesn't
really have anything striking about it—you know, nothing
that really catches the eye. And that sort of thing is rather
necessary in a case like this.

BOLSHINTSOV [*sighing*]. Rather necessary in a case like this.

SHPIGELSKI. Or at least, young ladies like that sort of thing.
And your age, after all . . . in short, we can't hope to conquer her by charm. And naturally you mustn't start thinking
about sweet nothings—they won't help you much. But you
have got one great advantage, a much more reliable one,

and that's your character, Afanasy Ivanovich, and your three hundred and twenty serfs. If I were you I would just say to Vera . . .

BOLSHINTSOV. In private?

SHPIGELSKI. Oh but definitely in private! I would just say to her: "Vera Alexandrovna . . ."

[*From the movements of his lips, it can be seen that* BOL-SHINTSOV *is repeating every word after him.*]

". . . I love you and wish to marry you. I'm a kind man, simple and inoffensive and not poor. You would be completely free with me, and I would make every effort for your happiness. If you would like to make inquiries about me and pay me a little more attention than before, and give me an answer as and when you like, I'm prepared to wait and would even regard it an honor to do so."

BOLSHINTSOV [*loudly*]. "Regard it as an honor to do so." Yes, that's right, yes—I quite agree with you. But there's just one thing, Ignaty Ilyich. If I remember right, you used the word "inoffensive"—you said "I'm inoffensive. . . ."

SHPIGELSKI. But what do you mean—aren't you inoffensive, then?

BOLSHINTSOV. Yes, of course. But all the same I think . . . would it be right, Ignaty Ilyich? Wouldn't it be better to say, for example . . .

SHPIGELSKI. For example?

BOLSHINTSOV. For example . . . [*Pauses.*] No, on the other hand one might say inoffensive, I suppose.

SHPIGELSKI. Oh, Afanasy Ivanovich, just follow my advice. The simpler you express yourself, the fewer ornaments of speech you use, the better the whole business will go, believe me. The main thing is, don't insist, don't force the pace, Afanasy Ivanovich. Vera is still very young and you might frighten her. . . . Give her time to think over your proposal. Oh, and there's one more thing, I almost forgot. You said that I could give you advice, after all, so I feel that I must point out that sometimes it happens that you get confused and come out with phases like "bed and brutter" or something of the kind. Maybe it's because . . . possible . . . But listen: the words "bread and butter" seem to be rather more effective—one might say that they've come to be more generally accepted. And there's something else I recall now: once I heard you call a friend of ours

who's fond of good living a *bon voleur*—you said "What a
bon voleur he is!" Of course, that's a nice expression, but
unfortunately it means absolutely nothing. I'm no great
shakes as far as French dialect is concerned, you know,
but I'm sure of myself on that point. Don't try to be elo-
quent, and I'm confident you'll win. [*Turns.*] Ah, here
they are—they're all coming this way.

[BOLSHINTSOV *tries to escape.*]

Where are you going—after mushrooms again?

[BOLSHINTSOV *smiles, blushes and stays.*]

The most important thing is: don't be shy!

BOLSHINTSOV [*hastily*]. Tell me—Vera Alexandrovna knows
nothing of this?

SHPIGELSKI. Of course not!

BOLSHINTSOV. I'm depending on you completely. . . . [*Blows
his nose.*]

[*Enter left* NATALYA, VERA, BELIAYEV *with the kite,* KOLYA *followed by* RAKITIN *and* LIZA. NATALYA *is in high spirits.*]

NATALYA [*to* BOLSHINTSOV *and* SHPIGELSKI]. Ah, hello, gentlemen, good afternoon. Doctor, I wasn't expecting you here,
but I'm always glad to see you, How are you Afanasy
Ivanovich?

[BOLSHINTSOV *bows awkwardly.*]

SHPIGELSKI [*to* NATALYA, *pointing to* BOLSHINTSOV]. This
gentleman here insisted on my accompanying him.

NATALYA [*laughing*]. I'm very grateful to him, but do you
really have to be forced into visiting us?

SHPIGELSKI. Of course not . . . it's just that . . . well, I was
here only this morning . . . don't misunderstand me . . .

NATALYA. Ah, you've got yourself tangled up . . . the diplo-
mat's got all tangled up!

SHPIGELSKI. I'm very pleased to see you in such good spirits,
Natalya Petrovna.

NATALYA. And you find it necessary to comment on that?
Does it so seldom happen that I'm cheerful?

SHPIGELSKI. Goodness me no, but . . .

NATALYA. *Monsieur le diplomate,* you're getting into more and
more of a muddle.

KOLYA [*impatiently dancing round them all*]. Oh mother, come on—when are we going to fly the kite?

NATALYA. Whenever you want, dear. . . . Alexei Nikolayich and Vera, let's go on down to the meadow. [*Turns.*] I don't imagine you would find this very amusing, gentlemen. Lizaveta Bogdanovna and you, Rakitin, I leave our friend Afanasy Ivanovich in your care.

RAKITIN. But what makes you think it wouldn't amuse us, Natalya Petrovna?

NATALYA. You're clever people . . . it would probably seem stupid to you. . . . Still, as you wish: we won't stop you coming with us . . . [*To* BELIAYEV *and* VERA.] Come along, then.

[NATALYA, VERA, BELIAYEV *and* KOLYA *exit right.*]

SHPIGELSKI [*after looking at* RAKITAN *in surprise, to* BOLSHINTSOV]. My good Afanasy Ivanovich, give your arm to Lizaveta Bogdanovna, will you?

BOLSHINTSOV [*hastily*]. With the greatest pleasure . . . [*Takes her arm.*]

SHPIGELSKI [*to* RAKITIN]. And we'll go together, if you'll permit, Mikhail Alexandrovich. [*Takes his arm.*] My word, look at them running down the path. Let's go and watch them fly the kite, even if we are clever people. . . . Afanasy Ivanovich, would you like to lead the way?

BOLSHINTSOV [*to* LIZA, *as they go*]. One might say that the weather today is exceedingly pleasant, mightn't one?

LIZA [*affectedly*]. Oh yes, to be sure.

SHPIGELSKI [*to* RAKITIN]. Mikhail Alexandrovich, we must have a talk together.

[RAKITIN *suddenly laughs.*]

What's amusing you?

RAKITIN. Oh, nothing much. . . . It's just funny that we two should be in the rear guard like this, behind everyone else.

SHPIGELSKI. Ah, but don't forget that the rear guard can very easily take the lead. . . . It's all just a question of . . . direction.

[*All exit left.*]

ACT THREE

[*The same setting as in Act One. Enter through the hall door* RAKITIN *and* SHPIGELSKI.]

SHPIGELSKI. You must help me, Mikhail Alexandrovich—I beg of you to help me.

RAKITIN. But in what way, Ignaty Ilyich?

SHPIGELSKI. In what way? Oh, come now, imagine you were in my position. Of course, I'm not really involved in this business at all—I'm acting in it simply from a desire to please, you might say. . . . My kind heart will be the death of me yet!

RAKITIN [*laughing*]. Oh, you've got a long way to go before things get as bad as that!

SHPIGELSKI [*also laughing*]. That remains to be seen. But my position is really an awkward one. Because Natalya Petrovna wanted it, I got Bolshintsov here, and with her permission gave him his answer, but now on the one hand I get black looks as though I'd done something stupid, and on the other Bolshintsov won't leave me alone for a moment. They all avoid him, and won't speak to me. . . .

RAKITIN. To think it was your idea to do this in the first place, Ignaty Ilyich! Well, you know, between ourselves Bolshintsov is simply an idiot.

SHPIGELSKI. Between ourselves—that's good! Thank you for the information. And besides, since when it is only sensible people who get married? Perhaps in other undertakings it might be a good thing, but why discourage fools from getting married? You say that I took on this matter: not a bit of it. This is how it happened—a friend asks me to put in a good word for him. What am I to do? I can't refuse to do it, can I? I'm a kind man—unable to say no. So I do what my friend asks of me, and get the answer: "Thanks very much, we're very grateful—please don't put yourself to any more trouble." I take the hint and drop the matter. Then suddenly they start making overtures and encouraging me, so to speak . . . I obey, and then they get annoyed with me. What have I done wrong?

RAKITIN. But who says you've done anything wrong? I'm

only surprised at one thing, and that's all the trouble you've gone to in this business.

SHPIGELSKI. Well, I only do that because . . . because the fellow won't let me alone.

RAKITIN. Oh, come!

SHPIGELSKI. And anyway, he's an old friend of mine.

RAKITIN [*smiling doubtfully*]. Is he? Oh well, that makes it different.

SHPIGELSKI [*also smiling*]. All right then—nobody can deceive *you*. . . . I'll tell you everything. Well you see, he promised me . . . I should explain that one of my horses has a broken leg, and he promised me . . .

RAKITIN. A new horse?

SHPIGELSKI. No, I must admit—a whole team of them.

RAKITIN. Ah ha! You should have said so earlier!

SHPIGELSKI [*in haste*]. Oh, but please don't think . . . I would never have agreed to act as go-between in this affair if I hadn't known Bolshintsov to be an honest man—it's not in my nature.

[RAKITIN *smiles*.]

And now there's only one thing I want, and that's a definite answer: yes or no.

RAKITIN. Have things really got to that stage?

SHPIGELSKI. What do you mean? I'm not talking about marriage—but only whether he can keep on calling on her.

RAKITIN. But who could forbid that?

SHPIGELSKI. What a word to use: forbid! Of course, if it were anyone else, then perhaps it would apply, but our Bolshintsov is a timid chap, a pure soul straight from the Golden Age of Innocence, hardly born yet, in fact. He lacks confidence in himself, and needs encouraging. But his intentions are completely honorable.

RAKITIN. And his horses are good.

SHPIGELSKI. And his horses are good. [*Takes snuff and offers the box to* RAKITIN.] Would you like some?

RAKITIN. No, thank you.

SHPIGELSKI. Well, there you have it, Mikhail Alexandrovich. You see, I don't want to deceive you—there'd be no point in doing that. The matter's quite clear, clear as a bell. A man of excellent character, with means, yet a modest sort of chap. If he's suitable, then all right. If he's not, then they must say so.

RAKITIN. That's all very fine, but where do I come in? What can I do?

SHPIGELSKI. But Mikhail Alexandrovich, surely we're agreed that Natalya Petrovna respects you very much, and even does what you say occasionally. . . . Come now [*Putting an arm round his back*], be a friend and put in a good word now and then.

RAKITIN. And you think he'll make a husband for Vera?

SHPIGELSKI [*assuming a serious expression*]. I'm certain of it. You don't believe me, but wait and see. After all, the main thing in marriage, as you know, is a solid character. And what could be more solid than Bolshintsov? [*Looks around.*] Here's Natalya Petrovna coming. . . . Now come on, my friend—think of it: two roans on the leading traces, and a bay between the shafts! At least give it a try for me!

RAKITIN [*smiling*]. All right, then, all right.

SHPIGELSKI. Mind now, I'm depending on you. . . . [*Escapes to hall.*]

RAKITIN [*watching him go*]. What a schemer that doctor is! Vera—and Bolshintsov! But after all, what of it? There are worse marriages made. I'll do what he asked me, and after that—well, it's none of my affair. [*Turns.*]

[*Enter* NATALYA *from the study.*]

NATALYA [*stops on seeing him, hesitates*]. Oh, it's you . . . I thought you were in the garden.

RAKITIN. It seems you don't want to see me. . . .

NATALYA [*interrupts*]. Oh, come now! [*Moves downstage.*] Are you alone?

RAKITIN. Shpigelski's just left.

NATALYA [*frowning slightly*]. That village Talleyrand! . . . What was he telling you? He's still hanging around, is he?

RAKITIN. That village Talleyrand, as you call him, is evidently in bad favor with you today . . . but yesterday, apparently . . .

NATALYA. He's amusing, he really is funny, but he's incapable of minding his own business . . . that's not very pleasant . . . and besides, for all his servility, he's very rude and importunate . . . he's a great cynic.

RAKITIN [*approaching her*]. Yesterday you didn't say such things about him. . . .

NATALYA. Maybe not. [*Quickly.*] Anyway, what was he telling you?

RAKITIN. He was talking about Bolshintsov.

NATALYA. Oh, about that idiot?

RAKITIN. You thought differently about him yesterday, too.

NATALYA [*with a forced smile*]. Yesterday isn't today.

RAKITIN. For everyone else it isn't, but for me, evidently, it is.

NATALYA [*lowers her eyes*]. How do you mean?

RAKITIN. Today's always the same as yesterday for me.

NATALYA [*stretching out a hand to him*]. I see why you're reproaching me, but you're wrong. Yesterday I wouldn't have admitted that I'd been behaving badly with you.

[RAKITIN *tries to stop her*.]

. . . please don't interrupt—I know and you know what I want to say . . . and today I do admit it. I've been thinking about many things. . . . Believe me, Mikhail, whatever nonsense I might think, whatever I might say or do, there's no one I depend on as much as you. [*Lowers her voice*.] I don't love anyone as much as you. Don't you believe me?

RAKITIN. Of course I do, but something's depressed you today. What's the matter?

NATALYA [*not listening to him*]. It's just that I've made up my mind about one thing, Rakitin, and that's that whatever happens, it's impossible to answer for oneself, to . . . pledge oneself for anything. We're often completely wrong about the past, so how can we ever be certain of the future? It's wrong to put one's life in chains.

RAKITIN. That's very true.

NATALYA [*after a long silence*]. Listen, I want to be absolutely frank with you, and it's possible that you may be a little hurt by my frankness . . . but I know that silence would hurt you even more. I confess, Mikhail, this young student . . . this Beliayev . . . has made quite an impression on me.

RAKITIN [*quietly*]. I knew it.

NATALYA. Ah, so you've noticed it? Recently?

RAKITIN. Since yesterday.

NATALYA. Ah!

RAKITIN. You remember, only the day before yesterday I mentioned that a change had come over you and that I didn't know what to ascribe it to. But yesterday, after our talk . . . and in the meadow . . . if only you could have seen yourself! I wouldn't have recognized you—you were literally transformed. You laughed, you jumped and skipped about like a little girl, your eyes shone, your cheeks glowed, and you gave him such happy, trusting attention, and smiled at him so . . . [*Glancing at her.*] Even now your face is brightening at the very memory of it. . . . [*Turns away.*]

NATALYA. No, Rakitin, for God's sake don't turn away from me like that. . . . Listen: why should we exaggerate? This young man has infected me with his youth, that's all. I've never been young myself, Mikhail, not from my earliest childhood until now. . . . Oh but you know all about that. . . . I wasn't used to it, and it all went to my head like wine, but I'm convinced that it will go away again as suddenly as it came. . . . It's really not worth talking about. [*Pausing.*] Only don't turn away from me, don't take your hand from mine. . . . Help me.

RAKITIN [*quietly*]. Help you . . . that's very nice. [*Loudly.*] You don't even realize yourself what a muddle you're in, Natalya Petrovna. You insist that it's not worth talking about, and then in the next breath you ask for help. It's clear you need it.

NATALYA. Well yes, I suppose I do . . . I'm turning to you as a friend. . . .

RAKITIN [*bitterly*]. And I'm sure I hope to be worthy of your trust, but you must give me a little time to gather together my courage.

NATALYA. Courage? But is it going to be such an ordeal for you to help me? Has anything really changed?

RAKITIN [*bitterly*]. Oh no, of course not—everything's just as it was.

NATALYA. But what are you thinking, Mikhail? Surely you aren't suggesting . . .

RAKITIN. I'm suggesting nothing.

NATALYA. You can't have such a low opinion of me that . . .

RAKITIN. Oh stop, for goodness' sake. Let's talk about Bolshintsov instead. You know the doctor is waiting for an answer about Verochka. . . .

NATALYA [*sorrowfully*]. You're annoyed with me.

RAKITIN. Annoyed? No, no—I'm sorry for you.

NATALYA. Really, this is too much. You ought to be ashamed of yourself, Mikhail . . .

[RAKITIN *is silent. She shrugs her shoulders and continues in annoyance.*]

You say the doctor is waiting for an answer. But who asked him to interfere . . . ?

RAKITIN. He assured me that you yourself . . .

NATALYA [interrupts]. Well, maybe I did. . . . But I didn't tell him anything definite. . . . And I can always change my mind, can't I? Besides, what's all the fuss about? Shpigelski's been playing that game for long enough to know that you can't expect success every time.

RAKITIN. He just wants to know what answer . . .

NATALYA. What answer . . . [Pausing.] Mikhail, stop it—give me your hand . . . Why this indifference, this icy politeness? What have I done wrong? This isn't my fault, you know: I came to you hoping for some advice, never hesitating for a moment, never thinking of hiding anything from you, but you . . . I see I was frank with you for nothing . . . it would never have entered your head. You never suspected anything—you weren't telling the truth just now about Beliayev. And goodness knows what you're imagining . . .

RAKITIN. What I'm imagining? Oh please.

NATALYA. Take my hand. . . .

[RAKITIN does not move. She continues with an injured air.]

You're turning away once and for all from me? Well, so much the worse for you, though I don't blame you. . . . [Bitterly.] You're jealous!

RAKITIN. I haven't the right to be jealous, Natalya Petrovna. How could I possibly be?

NATALYA [after pausing]. Just as you wish. But about Bolshintsov: I still haven't talked it over with Vera.

RAKITIN. I could send her to you right away.

NATALYA. Why at this minute? Well, all right then—if you like.

RAKITIN [moving to study door]. Would you like me to call her?

NATALYA. For the last time, Mikhail . . . You told me just now that you're sorry for me. . . . Is this the form it takes?

RAKITIN [coldly]. Do you want me to get her?

NATALYA [with annoyance]. Yes, get her then.

[RAKITIN enters the study. NATALYA stays still for some time, then sits down, takes a book from the table, opens it and lets it fall onto her knees.]

He as well! But what does this mean? To think I was relying on him! But my husband—good heavens, I never once even thought about him! [Rises.] I can see it's high time to put a stop to all this. . . .

[*Enter* VERA *from the study.*]

Yes, it's time . . .

VERA [*shyly*]. You sent for me, Natalya Petrovna?

NATALYA [*quickly looks round*]. Ah, Vera! Yes, I sent for you.

VERA [*runs up to her*]. But what's the matter—aren't you well?

NATALYA. Of course I am—why do you ask?

VERA. You look . . .

NATALYA. Oh, it's nothing . . . it's a little too warm for me, that's all. Sit down.

[VERA *sits.*]

Listen Vera, you're not particularly busy at the moment, are you?

VERA. No.

NATALYA. I ask because I've got to have a talk with you, a serious talk. You see, my dear, up to now you've been regarded as a child, but now you're seventeen and sensible . . . it's time you were thinking about your future. You know that I love you like a daughter. My home will always be your home . . . but all the same, in the eyes of the world you're an orphan, and not well off. In time you may get tired of living with strangers all your life. . . . Listen: how would you like to be a lady of the house yourself, and have your own home to run?

VERA [*slowly*]. I don't understand, Natalya Petrovna.

NATALYA [*pausing*]. Someone has asked for permission to marry you, Vera.

[VERA *looks at* NATALYA *in amazement.*]

You didn't expect that, and I must say that it seemed a little strange to me, as well. You're still so young . . . I don't have to tell you that I've absolutely no intention of forcing you; I believe it's too early yet for marriage, but I did think it my duty to tell you. . . .

[VERA *suddenly covers her face with her hands.*]

Vera, what's the matter? . . . You're crying? [*Takes her hand.*] You're trembling all over. Surely you're not frightened of me, are you Vera?

VERA [*tonelessly*]. I'm in your power, Natalya Petrovna . . .

NATALYA [*taking* VERA'S *hands from her face*]. Vera, aren't you ashamed of crying like this? Of saying that you're in my power? What sort of monster do you take me for? I talk to you as though you were my own daughter, and you . . .

[VERA *kisses her hands.*]

So you're in my power, are you? Well then: laugh at once —I order you to.

[VERA *smiles through her tears.*]

There you are, you see. [NATALYA *puts an arm round her and presses her close.*] Vera, behave with me as you would with your mother—no, better imagine that I'm your older sister, and then let's talk about all these strange things, shall we?

VERA. All right, then.

NATALYA. Well, now listen . . . come a little closer—that's right. First of all, since we're sisters there's no need for me to say that you're at home here—eyes like yours would be at home anywhere. Then it follows that you must never think for one moment that anyone in the whole world could be tired of you, could want to be rid of you—do you hear? Well, one day your sister comes to you and says, "Just imagine, Vera, you've got a suitor." . . . Well? What do you answer her? That you're still very young, that you've no thoughts of getting married yet?

VERA [*submissively*]. Yes, of course.

NATALYA. Oh, come now! Sisters don't talk like that to each other.

VERA [*smiling*]. Yes, then.

NATALYA. Your sister agrees with you, they send the suitor packing, and the whole business is forgotten. But what if the suitor were a good man, with means—what if he were prepared to wait, and only wanted permission to come and see you occasionally, in the hope of winning your affection in time?

VERA. But who is this suitor?

NATALYA. Ah ha—inquisitive! Vera, can't you guess?

VERA. I've no idea.

NATALYA. You saw him today. . . .

[VERA *blushes violently.*]

It's true, he's not very handsome, and not very young . . . it's Bolshintsov.

VERA. Afanasy Ivanovich?

NATALYA. Yes, Afanasy Ivanovich.

VERA [*looks at* NATALYA *for some time, then bursts out laughing*]. You're not joking?

NATALYA [*smiling*]. No, but I can see that Bolshintsov hasn't a chance. Had you cried when I mentioned his name, then he might have hoped, but instead you burst out laughing. There's only one thing for him to do, and that's to pack up and go home.

VERA. Do forgive me, but . . . really, I never dreamt . . . Do people really get married at his age?

NATALYA. What next? How old do you take him for? He's not yet fifty—still in the prime of life.

VERA. Perhaps so, but he's got such a funny face.

NATALYA. Well, let's not talk about him any more. He's dead and buried. May he rest in peace. Still, one thing is quite clear, and that is that a man like that can't possibly appeal to a girl of your age. . . . You still want to marry for love and not for convenience, don't you?

VERA. Yes. Natalya Petrovna, surely . . . surely you married Arkady Sergeyich for love, didn't you?

NATALYA [*pausing*]. Of course I did. [*Pausing again and pressing* VERA'S *hand.*] Yes, Vera—a moment ago I called you a child. . . .

[VERA *looks away.*]

Well, the matter is closed. Bolshintsov is finished with. I must admit that I would have felt a bit unhappy at seeing his fat old face next to your bright little cheeks, although he's really a very nice man. And now do you see how silly you were to be frightened of me? How quickly it's all over and done with! [*Reproachfully.*] Though really you've been behaving towards me as though I were your benefactress—ugh, how I hate that word, and you know it.

VERA [*kissing her*]. Oh, forgive me, Natalya Petrovna.

NATALYA. There, there. You're really not frightened of me any more?

VERA. I love you—I'm not frightened of you.

NATALYA. Well thank goodness for that. From now on we'll be real friends and not keep anything from each other. And if I were to ask you: "Vera, whisper to me—did you refuse Bolshintsov only because he's so much older than you and not much to look at?" what would you answer?

VERA. Oh, Natalya Petrovna, that's a good enough reason, isn't it?

NATALYA. I don't say it's not, but is there really no other reason?

VERA. Well, I hardly know him.

NATALYA. That's true, but you're not answering my question.

VERA. There's no other reason I can think of.

NATALYA. Isn't there? In that case perhaps it would be as well if you thought again about his proposal . . . I know it would be hard to fall in love with Bolshintsov, but I repeat, he's a nice man. Of course, if you were in love with someone else—well, that would be quite different. But so far you haven't lost your heart to anyone?

VERA [*shyly*]. How do you mean?

NATALYA. You don't love anyone?

VERA. I love you . . . and Kolya and Anna Semyenovna too.

NATALYA. No, I don't mean that kind of love—you misunderstand me. . . . Let's take an example: of the young men you've seen here or in other people's houses at parties, hasn't one of them attracted you?

VERA. No—one or two of them were nice, but . . .

NATALYA. How about at the Krinitsins' party? I noticed you dancing a lot with that tall officer . . . what's his name?

VERA. With an officer?

NATALYA. Yes, the one with the long moustache . . .

VERA. Oh, that one! No, I don't like him.

NATALYA. Well, how about Shalansky?

VERA. Shalansky's a fine man, but he . . . I don't think he takes me seriously.

NATALYA. What?

VERA. He . . . he seems to pay more attention to Liza Vyelski.

NATALYA [*looking at her*]. Ah, so you noticed that? [*Pause.*] Well then—Rakitin?

VERA. Mikhail Alexandrovich? I love him very much.

NATALYA. Yes, as a brother. Oh, and Beliayev?

VERA [*blushing*]. Alexei Nikolayich? Oh, I'm very fond of him.

NATALYA [*watching her*]. Yes, he's a splendid person. Only he's so shy with everyone.

VERA [*innocently*]. Oh no—he's not shy with me.

NATALYA. Ah.

VERA. He talks with me. Perhaps you think that of him because he . . . because he feels scared of you. He doesn't know you yet.

NATALYA. How is it you know that he's scared of me?

VERA. He told me so.

NATALYA. Ah, so he told you, did he? Then he's more ready to talk to you than to anyone else?

VERA. I don't know what he's like with others, but with me . . . perhaps it's because we're both orphans. And then . . . as far as he's concerned I'm a child.

NATALYA. You think so? Still, I like him too. I should imagine he's very kind.

VERA. Oh yes, exceptionally kind. If you only knew . . . everyone in the house likes him, he's so friendly. He talks to everyone; he's always ready to help. The day before yesterday he carried an old beggar woman all the way from the main road to the hospital. And then not long ago he picked a flower for me from such a steep cliff I had to close my eyes, I was so frightened he'd fall and hurt himself. . . . But he's so quick—yesterday in the meadow you could see for yourself how quick he is.

NATALYA. Yes, that's true.

VERA. D'you remember, when he was running after the kite, how he jumped across that huge ditch? That was nothing for him.

NATALYA. And he really picked you a flower from a dangerous place? It's plain that he loves you.

VERA [pauses]. And he's always so cheerful—always in good spirits.

NATALYA. That's strange—then why, when he's with me, is he . . .?

VERA [interrupts]. But I've told you already: he doesn't know you yet. Just wait a little, I'll tell him . . . I'll tell him that there's no need to be scared of you—that's right isn't it?— and that you're very kind. . . .

NATALYA [smiling forcedly]. Thank you.

VERA. Wait, you'll see . . . He does what I tell him, even if I am younger than he is.

NATALYA. I never dreamt you two were such good friends already. But you must watch out, Vera, and be careful. Of course, he's a very nice young man . . . but you know, at your age . . . It's not right. People might think things . . . I told you about it yesterday in the garden, do you remember?

[VERA looks away.]

And on the other hand, I don't want to try and dictate your likes and dislikes. I've too much trust in you and in him. But all the same . . . don't get annoyed with me for being stuffy, darling: it's the job of us grownups to bore young people with rules and regulations. But anyway, I'm probably wasting my breath saying all this: you just like him, and that's all, isn't it?

VERA [*shyly looking up*]. He . . .

NATALYA. There you go, looking at me as you did before. Does a girl really look at her sister like that? Vera, listen to me, come nearer . . . [*Caressing her.*] If your sister, your real sister, were to whisper in your ear: "Vera, are you really not in love with anyone?" what would you say?

[VERA *looks doubtfully at her.*]

Those eyes seem to want to tell me something.

[VERA *suddenly presses her face to* NATALYA'S *breast.* NATALYA *goes pale, and continues after a pause.*]

You're in love—admit it, you're in love.

VERA [*not lifting her head*]. Oh, I don't know myself what the matter is . . .

NATALYA. Poor thing, you are in love . . .

[VERA *presses closer to her.*]

You love him. And he, Vera—how about him?

VERA [*still not lifting her head*]. Why are you questioning me? . . . I don't know . . . maybe he is . . . I don't know, I don't know. . . .

[NATALYA *shudders and remains still.*]

VERA [*lifts her head, and sees* NATALYA'S *altered expression*]. Natalya Petrovna, what's the matter with you?

NATALYA [*recovering*]. With me? Nothing. . . . What do you mean? Nothing.

VERA. But you're so pale—what is it? Wait, I'll ring. . . . [*Gets up.*]

NATALYA. No, no—don't ring . . . it's nothing, it'll soon pass. Look, it's gone already.

VERA. Oh please let me at least ring for someone. . . .

NATALYA. No, I'd rather be left alone. Leave me, do you hear? We'll have a talk again later. . . . Go away.

VERA. Now you're angry with me, Natalya Petrovna.

NATALYA. I'm not the least bit angry with you. In fact, I'm grateful to you for your trust . . . only leave me now, will you?

[VERA *tries to take her hand, but* NATALYA *turns away as though not seeing this attempt.*]

VERA [*with tears in her eyes*]. Natalya . . .

NATALYA. I'm asking you to leave me.

[VERA *slowly exits to study, leaving* NATALYA *motionless and alone.*]

Now it's all quite clear . . . those two children love each other. . . . [*Stops and passes a hand across her face.*] What of it?—so much the better. Good luck to them! [*Laughing.*] And I . . . I actually thought . . . [*Stops.*] She came out with it pretty quickly . . . I must say I never suspected . . . that piece of news came as quite a shock. But wait, everything's not finished yet. . . . Good God, what am I saying? What is the matter with me? I hardly know myself. And how deeply am I involved in this? [*Pause.*] What is this I am doing, trying to marry off a poor girl to an old man! I send that doctor in secret, he guesses and starts dropping hints . . . Arkady and Rakitin . . . Yes, I. . . . [*Pulls herself together and abruptly raises her head.*] But what is this? Am I jealous of Vera—am I . . . am I in love with him, or something? [*Pausing.*] So you still doubt that, do you? You're in love all right, you poor thing! How it happened I don't know—it's as though I'd been poisoned. Suddenly everything is destroyed, shattered, uprooted . . . he's scared of me . . . everyone is. What have I got to offer him— what would he want with a person like me? He's young and she is too, but I! [*Bitterly.*] What is there in me that he could respect? Both of them are stupid, as Rakitin said —oh how I hate that clever man! And Arkady—my reliable, kind Arkady! Oh God, oh God let me die! [*Rises.*] I think I shall go out of my mind. Why is it I exaggerate everything? Of course I'm hurt. . . . This is all so new to me, it's the first time . . . I . . . yes, it's the very first time! I'm in love for the first time in my life. [*Sits down again.*] He must leave us. Yes, and Rakitin as well . . . it's time I pulled myself together—I took one step off the road, and look where it's led me. And what did I see in him, anyway? Oh, here it is, this terrible feeling again . . . Arkady! Yes, I must run to his embrace and beg him to forgive me, to defend me and save me . . . he, and no one else! All others are strangers to me and must stay strangers. . . . But is there really no other way? That girl—she is still a child. She could have been wrong—after all, it's a lot of childish nonsense . . . why did I think? . . . I'll have a talk with him myself and ask him . . . [*With self-reproach.*] But what is this? Are you still hoping—do you still want to hope? And think what it is you are hoping for! Oh God, don't force me to despise myself! [*Lets her head fall into her hands.*]

RAKITIN [*enters pale and alarmed from study*]. Natalya Petrovna . . .

[*NATALYA doesn't move.*]

[*Quietly.*] What can have happened with her and Vera? [*Loudly.*] Natalya Petrovna . . .

NATALYA [*raising her head*]. Who's there? Oh, it's you.

RAKITIN. Vera told me you weren't feeling well, so I . . .

NATALYA [*turning away*]. I'm perfectly well. Whatever made her think . . . ?

RAKITIN. No, Natalya Petrovna, you aren't well—look at yourself.

NATALYA. Well, perhaps I'm not, but what is it to you? What do you want? Why are you here?

RAKITIN [*moved*]. I'll tell you why I'm here. I've come to ask for your forgiveness. Half an hour ago I was unspeakably stupid and harsh to you . . . forgive me. You see, Natalya Petrovna, it's difficult for a man, however modest his hopes may be, not to lose control of himself, if only for a moment, when they are suddenly snatched away from him. But now I've come to myself, I've seen where I stand and how wrong I was, and I only want one thing—your forgiveness. [*Sits down quietly beside her.*] Look at me—don't you too turn away. Here is the former Rakitin, your friend, the man who demands nothing except permission to help you, as you said I do . . . don't deprive me of your trust . . . forget that I ever said anything that could have hurt you.

NATALYA [*staring at the floor*]. Yes, yes. . . . [*Stops.*] Oh, forgive me, Rakitin, but I haven't been listening to you— what did you say?

RAKITIN [*sadly*]. I said . . . I begged your forgiveness, Natalya

Petrovna. I asked you if you would let me remain your friend.

NATALYA. Rakitin, tell me what the matter with me is. [*Turns slowly to him, placing both hands on his shoulders.*]

RAKITIN. You're in love.

NATALYA [*slowly*]. I'm in love . . . but this is absolute folly, Rakitin. It's impossible. Can such things really happen so quickly? . . . You say I'm in love . . . [*Falls silent.*]

RAKITIN. Yes, you're in love, you poor woman. Don't deceive yourself.

NATALYA [*not looking at him*]. What ever am I to do now?

RAKITIN. I'm prepared to tell you, Natalya Petrovna, if you'll promise me . . .

NATALYA [*interrupts, still not looking at him*]. You know that girl Vera is in love with him . . . that they're both in love.

RAKITIN. In that case all the more reason . . .

NATALYA [*interrupts*]. I suspected it for a long time, and then she admitted it all to me herself, just a few moments ago.

RAKITIN [*to himself*]. Poor woman!

NATALYA [*passing a hand across her face*]. Well anyway, it's time I took hold of myself. You wanted to tell me something, didn't you? Advise me what I should do, Rakitin, for God's sake. . . .

RAKITIN. I'm ready to help you, but only on one condition.

NATALYA. Tell me what it is.

RAKITIN. Promise me that you won't suspect my intentions. Tell me that you believe in my unselfish wish to help you. Help me, too, in your turn—your confidence gives me strength. If you can't do this, then I'd rather not say anything at all.

NATALYA. Oh, speak, speak.

RAKITIN. You won't mistrust me?

NATALYA. Speak.

RAKITIN. Well, then, he must leave.

[NATALYA *looks silently at him.*]

Yes, he must leave here. I don't need to tell you about your husband and your duty—such words would be out of place from me, anyway. But these two children love one another —you told me so yourself just now. Well, try and imagine yourself between them—you would never stand it.

NATALYA. He must leave. . . . [*Pausing.*] But you? Are you staying?

RAKITIN [*embarrassed*]. I? I? . . . [*Pausing.*] I must go too. For your peace, for yours and Vera's happiness both of us must go away for ever.

NATALYA. Rakitin, I'd reached such a point that I was almost ready to give that poor girl, an orphan passed into my care by my mother, to give that girl away in marriage to a stupid, ridiculous old man! . . . I didn't have the courage, Rakitin—the words stuck in my throat when she burst out laughing at my suggestion . . . but I'd plotted with that doctor, I'd let him leer meaningfully, I'd tolerated those smiles, those compliments, those hints . . . Oh, I feel as though I'm on the edge of a cliff—help me!

RAKITIN. You see, I was right, Natalya Petrovna. . . .

[NATALYA *is silent.*]

RAKITIN [*continuing hastily*]. He must leave . . . we both must leave. There's no other way.

NATALYA [*exhaustedly*]. But what will there be to live for afterwards?

RAKITIN. Good Lord, has it come to that? Natalya Petrovna, you'll recover, believe me . . . it will all pass. How can you possibly say there's nothing to live for?

NATALYA. But what *is* there to live for, when everyone leaves me?

RAKITIN. But . . . your family . . .

[NATALYA *looks away.*]

RAKITIN. Listen, if you like, after he's gone I could stay on a few days to . . . to . . .

NATALYA [*gloomily*]. Oh yes, I see what you mean: you're counting on our former friendship, on the force of habit. You hope I'll come to myself—that I'll return to you, don't you? I know what you mean.

RAKITIN [*blushing*]. Natalya Petrovna, why do you insult me?

NATALYA [*bitterly*]. I know what you mean, but you're deceiving yourself.

RAKITIN. How can you say such things? After your promise—after I've thought of you alone, of your happiness and position in society . . .

NATALYA. How long have you let that bother you? Why didn't you ever mention it before?

RAKITIN [*rising*]. I shall leave this very day—instantly—and you'll never see me again. . . . [*About to go.*]

NATALYA [*stretching out a hand to him*]. Mikhail, forgive me.
I really don't know what makes me say these things . . .
you can see what a state I'm in. Forgive me.

RAKITIN [*turns at once and takes her hand*]. Natalya Petrovna . . .

NATALYA. Oh Mikhail, I'm so unhappy. . . . [*Leans on his
shoulder and presses a handkerchief to her eyes.*] Forgive
me—I'll never survive this without you. . . .

[*At that moment the hall door opens and* ISLAYEV *and* ANNA
enter.]

ISLAYEV [*loudly*]. Yes, I've always thought so. . . . [*Stops in
astonishment on seeing* RAKITIN *and* NATALYA.]

[NATALYA *looks round and quickly exits.* RAKITIN *stays, extremely embarrassed.*]

ISLAYEV. What's the meaning of this? Why this scene?

RAKITIN. Oh . . . nothing . . . it's . . .

ISLAYEV. Is my wife unwell, or something?

RAKITIN. No, but . . .

ISLAYEV. Then why did she dash off so suddenly? What were
you talking about? It looked as though she was crying . . .
you were consoling her . . . what is it?

RAKITIN. Really, it was nothing.

ANNA. How do you mean, nothing, Mikhail Alexandrovich?
[*Pausing.*] I'll go and see . . . [*About to exit to study.*]

RAKITIN [*stopping her*]. No, it would be better to leave her
alone—I beg you.

ISLAYEV. But what's this all about? Come on now, tell me.

RAKITIN. I swear to you, it was nothing. . . . Listen, I promise
I'll explain to both of you before the day's out—I give you
my word. But for the moment, if you have any trust in
me, please don't ask anything—and don't bother Natalya
Petrovna.

ISLAYEV. Very well . . . but it's most odd. It's the first time
Natasha has behaved like this—quite extraordinary.

ANNA. What puzzles me is what can have made her cry? And
why did she go away? Anyone would think we were
strangers.

RAKITIN. What do you mean? How can you! . . . but listen:
we were in the middle of a conversation . . . I must ask
both of you to leave us alone for a little.

ISLAYEV. So that's how it is: there's some secret you share, eh?

RAKITIN. There is, but you will be told it.

ISLAYEV [*thinking it over*]. Come along, mother—let's go. We'll let them finish their secret conversation.

ANNA. But . . .

ISLAYEV. Come along, come along. You heard him promise to explain everything to us.

RAKITIN. You can set your minds at rest about that . . .

ISLAYEV [*coldly*]. Oh, I'm not worried. [*To* ANNA.] Come along.

[*Both exit.*]

RAKITIN [*quickly to study door*]. Natalya Petrovna . . . Natalya Petrovna, come out, please come out.

NATALYA [*enters from study*]. What did they say? [*She is very pale.*]

RAKITIN. Nothing—don't worry. Naturally they were a little surprised . . . your husband thought you were ill . . . he noticed how upset you were. Sit down, you can hardly keep on your feet.

[NATALYA *sits.*]

I told him . . . I asked him not to bother you and to leave us alone.

NATALYA. And he agreed?

RAKITIN. Yes. Though I admit, only after I had promised to explain it all tomorrow. . . . Why did you run away?

NATALYA [*bitterly*]. Why? . . . But what will you tell him?

RAKITIN. I'll think of something . . . but that's not the point. . . . We must make full use of this reprieve. You see, this can't go on . . . you're not in a state to take such upsets, and they're not worthy of you . . . I myself . . . but that's not the point. Just you be firm, and don't worry about me! Listen, you do agree with me, don't you?

NATALYA. About what?

RAKITIN. That it's essential I leave? Agreed? In that case, there's no point delaying. If you'll permit, I'll talk to Beliayev immediately. . . . He's a decent person, he'll understand. . . .

NATALYA. You want to talk to him? You? But what can you say to him?

RAKITIN [*embarrassed*]. I'll . . .

NATALYA [*pausing*]. Rakitin, listen. Doesn't it seem to you that we're really both acting like lunatics? I got frightened, and frightened you and everyone else perhaps, over absolutely nothing at all.

RAKITIN. How do you mean?

NATALYA. I'm serious. What is really the matter with you and me? A little while ago everything in this house seemed so quiet and peaceful . . . and suddenly . . . goodness knows how . . . It's true—we've all gone mad. Well, anyway, that's enough of it now . . . we've acted like fools for quite long enough . . . let's live as we did before. You'll have nothing to explain to Arkady—I'll tell him myself all about our foolishness, and we'll both have a good laugh at it together. I don't need anyone to act as a go-between with my husband!

RAKITIN. You frighten me, Natalya Petrovna. You smile, and yet are as pale as death. But at least remember what you said to me a quarter of an hour ago . . .

NATALYA. I may have said anything. . . . But I see what you're up to . . . you're deliberately raising this storm so's not to be the only one to drown.

RAKITIN. More suspicion, more reproaches . . . God forgive you for the way you are torturing me. Maybe you're regretting your frankness?

NATALYA. I don't regret anything.

RAKITIN. Then how am I to understand you?

NATALYA [*with emphasis*]. Rakitin, if you say one word from me or about me to Beliayev, I'll never forgive you.

RAKITIN. So that's it! Don't worry, Natalya Petrovna . . . I'll not only say nothing about you to Beliayev, but I won't even say good-bye to him when I leave. I've no intention of forcing my services on people.

NATALYA [*ashamed*]. Perhaps you think I've changed my mind about his going?

RAKITIN. I think nothing.

NATALYA. Well, quite the contrary, I'm so convinced of how *essential* it is for him to go that I shall dismiss him in person. [*Pausing.*] Yes, I shall dismiss him myself.

RAKITIN. *You* will dismiss him?

NATALYA. Yes, I shall. At once. Please will you send him to me?

RAKITIN. Do you mean this minute?

NATALYA. At once. Please, Rakitin. You can see that I'm perfectly calm now. And besides, no one will interrupt. We must turn all this to advantage . . . I'll be very grateful to you . . . I'll hear his side of the story.

RAKITIN. But he won't tell you anything. He admitted to me that when he's with you he feels uncomfortable.

NATALYA [*suspiciously*]. So you've talked to him about me already?

[RAKITIN *shrugs his shoulders.*]

Oh, forgive me for what I'm saying, Mikhail, and send him to me. You'll see, I'll dismiss him and all will be over. Everything will pass by and be forgotten, like a bad dream. Please send him to me—I've simply got to talk it out once and for all. You won't be ashamed of me.

RAKITIN [*looking at her coldly*]. Very well, I'll do as you wish. [*Goes to hall door.*]

NATALYA [*after him*]. Many thanks, Mikhail.

RAKITIN [*turning*]. Oh, please don't thank me—spare me that much. [*Exits quickly to hall.*]

NATALYA. He is a fine man, but did I really ever love him? [*Rises.*] He's right: that boy must go. But how can I dismiss him? I only want to find out if he's really attracted to that girl. Perhaps it's all nonsense—why did I let myself get so upset? Why did I blurt everything out like that? Well anyway, there's nothing to be done now. I wonder what he'll say to me. . . . But he must go . . . it's essential, essential. Perhaps he won't have anything to say to me in reply. After all, he's afraid of me. . . . They're all afraid of me! Well, what of it? All the better—I haven't got much to say to him. [*Presses a hand to her forehead.*] My head aches. Shouldn't I put it off until tomorrow—I really ought to. Today I feel that everyone's watching me. What a state I'm in. . . . No, it would be best to end the whole thing now, at one blow. . . . Just one final effort and I'm free! Oh, how I long to be free—to be at peace.

[BELIAYEV *enters from the hall.*]

Here he is . . .

BELIAYEV [*going up to her*]. Mikhail Alexandrovich said you wanted to see me, Natalya Petrovna.

NATALYA [*with an effort*]. Yes, that's right . . . there's something . . . there's something I must clear up with you.

BELIAYEV. Something . . . ?

NATALYA [*not looking at him*]. Yes, yes . . . [*Pause.*] I have to tell you, Alexei Nikolayich, that . . . that I'm not pleased with you.

BELIAYEV. Might I ask why?

NATALYA. Please hear me out . . . I . . . I really don't know where to begin. And first of all I must assure you that my displeasure doesn't arise from any negligence on your part . . . on the contrary, the way you've looked after Kolya has pleased me very much.

BELIAYEV. Then what can it be?

NATALYA [*looking at him*]. There's no need for you to alarm yourself . . . your fault isn't as great as all that. You're young, and presumably you've never lived in a strange house before, so you couldn't have been expected to foresee . . .

BELIAYEV. But Natalya Petrovna . . .

NATALYA. Of course, you want to know what all this is about, don't you? I understand your impatience. So I must tell you that Vera . . . [*looking at him*] . . . that Vera has told me everything.

BELIAYEV [*astonished*]. Vera Alexandrovna? What can she have told you? And where do I come in?

NATALYA. Do you honestly not know what she can have told me? Can't you guess?

BELIAYEV. I haven't the slightest idea.

NATALYA. In that case, please forgive me. If you really can't guess, then I must ask your pardon. I imagined . . . and I was mistaken. But let me tell you that you haven't convinced me. I realize why you speak like this, and I greatly admire your discretion.

BELIAYEV. I've no idea what you're talking about, Natalya Petrovna.

NATALYA. Haven't you really? Do you mean to assure me that you haven't noticed that child's feelings towards you?

BELIAYEV. Vera's feelings towards me? I simply don't know what to reply to that . . . please excuse me. I thought that to Vera I'd always behaved as . . . as . . .

NATALYA. As you did with everyone, is that it? [*Pausing a little.*] However that may be, don't you honestly know—aren't you honestly pretending not to know—how things are? That the girl's in love with you? She confessed as much to me. I'm asking you, as an honest man, what you intend to do?

BELIAYEV [*confused*]. What I intend to do?

NATALYA [*folding her hands*]. Yes.

BELIAYEV. All this is so unexpected, Natalya Petrovna . . .

NATALYA [*pausing*]. Alexei Nikolayich, I see that it was wrong of me to interfere in this matter. You don't see what I mean: you think I'm annoyed with you, but in fact I'm just . . . just a little upset. And that's only natural. Don't worry—sit down.

[*Both sit.*]

I'll be quite frank with you, Alexei Nikolayich, and please you be a little less secretive with me. You've really been avoiding me for nothing. Vera loves you . . . of course that's not your fault—I'm willing to believe it wasn't . . . but you see, Alexei Nikolayich, she's an orphan, my adopted child. I'm responsible for her, for her future, for her happiness. She's still young, and I'm sure that the feeling you've aroused in her may pass quickly. At her age love doesn't last long. But you do see that it's my duty to warn you, don't you? It's always dangerous to play with fire. . . . But I don't doubt that, now you know how she feels about you, you'll stop paying so much attention to her and avoid meeting her and going for walks in the garden together . . . you will, won't you? I can rely on you. . . . With anyone else I wouldn't have dared be so frank in discussing it.

BELIAYEV. Believe me, Natalya Petrovna, I'm fully aware of the honor . . .

NATALYA. I don't mistrust you for an instant, believe me. Besides, I trust this will be a secret between us.

BELIAYEV. I assure you, Natalya Petrovna, all you've told me seems so incredible . . . of course, I wouldn't be so rude as to doubt you, but . . .

NATALYA. Listen, Alexei Nikolayich, everything I've said to you has been with the assumption that on your side there's nothing [*Interrupting herself.*] . . . because if that's not so . . . Of course, I hardly know you yet, but I do know you enough to see no reason to object. You're not well off, but you're young and you have a future, and when two people love each other . . . I repeat that I thought it my duty to warn you, as an honest man, of the dangers of your friendship with Vera, but if you . . .

BELIAYEV [*bewildered*]. I don't see what you're trying to tell me, Natalya . . .

NATALYA [*hastily*]. Oh, don't think I'm trying to extort a confession from you, because I see already . . . from your manner I see just what the position is . . . [*Looking at him.*] However, I should say that Vera thought you weren't entirely indifferent to her. . . .

BELIAYEV [*pausing, then rising*]. I see that I mustn't stay in your house any longer, Natalya Petrovna. . . .

NATALYA [*flaring up*]. You might at least have waited until I had asked you to leave myself. [*Rises.*]

BELIAYEV. You were frank with me, so let me be frank with you in return. I'm not in love with Vera—or at least, not in the way you suppose.

NATALYA. But did I ever . . . ? [*Stops.*]

BELIAYEV. And if Vera is attracted to me—if it appears to her that I, to use your expression, am not entirely indifferent to her, then I've no wish to deceive her and will tell her the truth myself. But after such an explanation, you understand, it would be difficult for me to stay here any longer —my position would be too awkward. I don't have to tell you how sad I will be at leaving you . . . but there's nothing else for it. I'll always remember you with gratitude. . . . Allow me to leave . . . I shall still have the honor of making my farewells later on . . .

NATALYA [*with assumed indifference*]. As you wish . . . but, I must admit, I didn't expect this. It wasn't with this in mind that I wanted to talk things over with you . . . I only wanted to warn you . . . Vera is still a child. . . . Perhaps I've been making altogether too much of all this. I wouldn't have thought it would be necessary for you to go—still, it's as you wish.

BELIAYEV. But Natalya Petrovna, it's impossible for me to stay.

NATALYA. It's clearly very easy for you to part from us.

BELIAYEV. No, it's not easy, Natalya Petrovna.

NATALYA. I'm not one to keep a person against his wishes, but I must say that this will be most inconvenient for me.

BELIAYEV [*after some indecision*]. I wouldn't want to cause you any annoyance, Natalya Petrovna. If you like, I'll stay.

NATALYA [*suspiciously*]. Oh . . . [*Pausing.*] I didn't think you would change your mind so quickly . . . I'm grateful to you, but . . . Give me time to think it over. Perhaps you're right—perhaps you really must go. I'll think it over and let you know. . . . May I leave you in doubt until this evening?

BELIAYEV. I'm prepared to wait for as long as you want. [*Bows and tries to go.*]

NATALYA. Will you promise me . . .

BELIAYEV [*stopping*]. What?

NATALYA. You were going to explain to Vera, weren't you . . . I'm not sure if that's the right thing to do. Still, I'll let you know my decision. I'm beginning to think you really ought to leave. *Au revoir.*

[BELIAYEV *bows again and exits to the hall.*]

It's over! He doesn't love her. . . . [*Walks up and down.*] And so, instead of dismissing him, I made him stay myself. For he will stay [*Pausing.*] And what right did I have to announce the love of that girl to everyone? I forced a confession, or rather a half-confession, out of her, and then so pitilessly, so brutally. . . . [*Hides her face in her hands.*] Perhaps he was beginning to care for her . . . what right did I have to crush that flower in the bud? . . . but have I in fact crushed it? Perhaps he has been deceiving me . . . and it was I who wanted to do the deceiving! But no—he's too fine for that . . . he's not like me. And what made me hurry so, go blurting out everything at once? [*Sighing.*] It was quite unnecessary . . . if I could have foreseen . . . How cunning I was!—how I lied to him . . . and he! How boldly and easily he spoke! He made me feel ashamed. . . . He is a man—I didn't realize that until now. . . . He must go! If he stays here . . . I feel I would end by losing all my self-respect. He must go, or I'm lost. Before he's had time to talk to Vera I must write to him. . . . He must go! [*Exits quickly to study.*]

ACT FOUR

[*A large, empty passageway. The walls are bare, the white-washed floor is of uneven stone. Six brick columns in poor repair, three on each side, support the ceiling. Right, a door leading to the house; center, an iron door to the storeroom. At the foot of the first column on the right is a green garden seat; in one corner are some spades, watering cans and pots. Evening. The red rays of the sun fall through the windows onto the floor.* KATYA *enters through door right, cautiously goes to the window and looks out for some time into the garden.*]

KATYA. No, there's nothing to be seen. But they told me that he'd gone into the conservatory—that must mean he hasn't come out yet. Oh well, I'll have to wait till he comes by here: he can't go any other way. . . . [*Sighs and leans against the window.*] They say he's going. . . . [*Sighs again.*] How will we ever manage without him? . . . Poor young mistress. How she begged me . . . Well, it's hard not to do her a favor. And why shouldn't he have a last talk with her? Lord, it's hot today! Oh, I think it's starting to rain. [*Looks out of the window and suddenly moves back.*] But surely they're not going to come in here? Yes, they are for sure! Oh goodness . . .

[KATYA *tries to escape, but doesn't get as far as the door into the corridor before* SHPIGELSKI *and* LIZA *enter from the garden.* KATYA *hides behind a column.*]

SHPIGELSKI [*shakes the rain from his hat*]. We can wait in here until the storm stops—it'll be over soon.

LIZA. All right.

SHPIGELSKI [*looking round*]. What's that building—a storeroom, isn't it?

LIZA [*pointing to iron door*]. No, that's the storeroom there. They say that Arkady Sergeyich's father had this room built when he came home from abroad.

SHPIGELSKI. Ah, I see what the idea is: his lordship had Venice in mind. [*Sits down on the seat.*] Come and sit by me.

[LIZA *does so.*]

[119]

You must agree, Lizaveta Bogdanovna, that this storm's come at a very awkward moment. It's interrupted our conversation at the most moving point.

LIZA [*looking away*]. Ignaty Ilyich . . .

SHPIGELSKI. But no one can stop us resuming it if we want . . . You were saying that Anna Semyenovna's in a bad mood today.

LIZA. Yes she is. She even took dinner alone in her room.

SHPIGELSKI. Did she! What a disaster.

LIZA. This morning she found Natalya Petrovna in tears . . . with Mikhail Alexandrovich. He's like one of us here, of course, but all the same . . . Still he did promise to explain everything.

SHPIGELSKI. Oh well, then, she was getting alarmed over nothing. In my opinion, Mikhail Alexandrovich was never a man to be frightened of, least of all at present.

LIZA. How do you mean?

SHPIGELSKI. Oh, nothing. He talks cleverly enough. Some people work things off by coming out in a rash, but people like him don't need to bother—they just talk it out of their systems instead. Liza, in the future don't be afraid of people who talk a lot—they're not dangerous. It's the silent ones who need watching—the ones with a lunatic streak in them, who are moody and stubborn.

LIZA [*pausing*]. Tell me, is Natalya Petrovna really not well?

SHPIGELSKI. She's no more ill than you are.

LIZA. She didn't eat anything at dinner.

SHPIGELSKI. Illness isn't the only thing that takes away one's appetite.

LIZA. Did you dine with Bolshintsov?

SHPIGELSKI. Yes, I rode over to his place. And to tell you the truth, I only returned so I could see you.

LIZA. Oh come now! Let me tell you something, Ignaty Ilyich —Natalya Petrovna is annoyed with you about something. . . . At table she was discussing you in rather unflattering terms.

SHPIGELSKI. Was she indeed? It's clear that our grand young ladies don't like a man to have a pair of eyes in his head. You've got to do what they want and help them into the bargain, while pretending all the time that you don't see what they're up to. Phew, what creatures they are! Still, let's wait and see. And Rakitin got out of bed on the wrong side, too, did he?

LIZA. Yes, he seemed in a bad mood today too.

SHPIGELSKI. And Vera and Beliayev?

LIZA. Yes, all of them are properly in the dumps. I simply can't imagine what's come over them all today.

SHPIGELSKI. Oh well, too much knowledge bringeth gray hairs, you know, Lizaveta Bogdanovna. However, that's enough of them—let's rather talk about our own affairs. The rain hasn't stopped yet . . . would you like to?

LIZA [*affectedly looking away*]. What exactly do you mean, Ignaty Ilyich?

SHPIGELSKI. Look, Lizaveta Bogdanovna, there's one thing about you that I must criticize: why do you put on such airs, why do you look away like that all of a sudden? After all, we're neither of us exactly adolescents, you know. These little games, these courtesies and sighs aren't our style at all. Let's talk calmly and sensibly, as befits people of our age. Well then, to get to the point: we like each other, or at least, I take it that you like me?

LIZA [*can't shake off her affectedness*]. Ignaty Ilyich, I really . . .

SHPIGELSKI. All right, all right—yes, yes, yes. I suppose for you, a woman, it's only right that you should play the coquette a little. . . . [*Gestures with his hand.*] Well now, it seems we like each other. And we've got other things in common, too. About myself, I should say that I'm not high society, but then you weren't born in exactly the highest class, were you? I'm not rich, but then if I was I shouldn't be standing here now. [*Laughs.*] But I've got a respectable practice, and not all of my patients die on me. You, to use your own words, have got fifteen thousand kopecks doing nothing. All this isn't to be scoffed at, I might say. And what's more, I imagine you're tired of always living as a governess, looking after old women, helping them play cards and saying "yes, madam" to them. It can't be much fun. On my side, I'm not exactly bored with bachelor life, but I'm getting old and my cooks always turn out to be thieves. It looks as though it will all fit like a glove. But there's one snag, Lizaveta Bogdanovna: we don't know each other yet—or rather, to put it more accurately, you don't know me yet. Because you see I know you—you're an open book. I don't say that you haven't got a hundred faults. As you've been living with women for so long, you've turned a little sour, but that's of no importance. In the hands of a good

husband, a wife is soft putty, soft putty. But I want you
to know me, too, before we get married, otherwise later
you might blame me. I wouldn't want to deceive you.

LIZA [*with dignity*]. But Ignaty Ilyich, I think I also have had
a chance to observe your character . . .

SHPIGELSKI. *You* have, have you? Oh, stop, it . . . that's not
a woman's business. Look, I'll bet you think I'm a cheerful
person, a clown, don't you?

LIZA. I've always thought of you as a charming person.

SHPIGELSKI. There you are—look how easy it is to be wrong.
Just because I play the fool in front of others, tell them
stories and dance to their tune, you assume that I'm really
a cheerful person by nature. In actual fact, if I didn't need
them, those people, I'd never give them a glance. . . . And
as it is, whenever I can do so without danger, I make them
into the laughingstock. On the other hand, I don't deceive
myself—I'm well aware that certain people who find me
absolutely indispensable because of my entertainment value
think themselves entitled to despise me. But they'll all get
paid back in full for it, never you mind. Take Natalya
Petrovna, for example. Do you think I don't see through
her? [*Mimicking her.*] "Oh, my dear doctor, I'm really so
fond of you—you've got such a malicious tongue . . ."
Ha-ha, coo away, my little dove, coo away. Ugh, these
women! They smile at you, and flutter their eyelashes, and
all the time disgust is written all over their faces. . . . They
act fastidious with you—there's simply nothing you can
do that they'll approve of. I know why she was complaining
about me today. These women really are an extraordinary
breed. Because they soak themselves in *eau de cologne*
every day, and talk sloppily, letting words fall to the ground
as though implying "Pick them up, you," they imagine
they can't be found out. Oh, but they can be! They're
human beings like the rest of us sinners here below.

LIZA. Ignaty Ilyich you surprise me.

SHPIGELSKI. I know I surprise you. You're obviously just
discovering that I'm not by any means so cheerful a person, and perhaps not even particularly kind, either. But
I don't want to pass myself off to you as something that I
never was. However much I pull faces in front of the
gentry, nobody has ever made a fool of me—they've never
had a laugh at my expense. In fact, you might say that
they're a little afraid of me—they know I bite. Still, three

years ago or so it did happen that one so-called gentleman
began showing off at dinner and stuck a radish in my hair.
What do you think I did? That instant, not turning a hair
and in the most cheerful manner imaginable, I called him
out to a duel. The man was almost paralyzed with fear—
the host made him apologize—the effect was quite sensa-
tional! Though I must confess I knew beforehand that the
man would never fight. So you see, Lizaveta Bogdanovna,
I've got plenty of vanity in me. Though life hasn't been
a bed of roses. I'm not very talented, and I just barely
managed to get through medical school. I'm not a good
doctor, there's no point in hiding the fact, and if you ever
fall ill, it won't be me that'll cure you. If I'd had talent
and a good education, I'd've gone to the city. Oh well, of
course, the savages in these parts don't need anything better.
As far as my character is concerned, I ought to warn you,
Lizaveta Bogdanovna, that at home I'm moody, silent and
demanding. I'm all right so long as people please me and
do as I want—I like to be pampered, and to be well fed—
but on the other hand you won't find me jealous and mean.
When I'm not there, you'll be able to do exactly as you
please. You understand, of course, that romantic love and
all that sort of nonsense is entirely out of the question, but
I think all the same that it would be possible to live under
the same roof as me . . . just do what I want, and don't
ever cry in front of me—I can't stand that! But I'm not
always finding fault. . . . Well, you've heard my confession,
and what do you say?

LIZA. What can I say to you, Ignaty Ilyich? If you haven't
been deliberately running yourself down so as to . . .

SHPIGELSKI. But when did I run myself down? Don't you
forget that anyone else in my place might have cheerfully
kept quiet about his faults, since you hadn't noticed them.
And after the wedding—ah-ha, after the wedding it's too
late! But I've too much pride for that.

[LIZA *looks at him.*]

Yes, too much pride, you don't have to look at me like
that. I've no intention of pretending and lying to my future
wife, not for a hundred thousand kopecks, let alone fifteen,
but to anyone else I'd bow and scrape for next to nothing.
That's my nature, you see. . . . I can grin to someone,
and inside be thinking, "What an idiot you are, my friend,

and how you're swallowing my bait." But to you I say what I think. That is, I don't say everything I think even to you, but at least I don't actually lie. I must seem a pretty odd character, I suppose, but wait a bit and one day I'll tell you my life story and you'll be amazed to hear how well I've managed. I imagine that you weren't born with a silver spoon in your mouth, either, but all the same you can have no idea, my dear, what real out-and-out poverty means. . . . However, more of that later. For the present you'd do better to think over everything I've had the honor of proposing. . . . Decide the matter carefully by yourself, and tell me of your intention. You're a sensible sort of woman, as far as I can tell. Incidentally, how old are you?

LIZA. I'm . . . I'm . . . thirty.

SHPIGELSKI [calmly]. That's not true. You're forty at least.

LIZA [flaring up]. Nothing of the kind—I'm thirty-six!

SHPIGELSKI. That's not thirty, all the same. We'll have to get that notion out of your head somehow, Lizaveta Bogdanovna, the more so because a married woman isn't considered the least bit old at thirty-six. And another thing: this snuff-taking is quite wrong. [Rises.] I think the storm's over.

LIZA [also rises]. Yes, it's stopped.

SHPIGELSKI. And so you'll give me your answer in a few days?

LIZA. I'll let you know tomorrow.

SHPIGELSKI. That's what I like to hear! There's common sense for you, real common sense—splendid, Lizaveta Bogdanovna! Well, give me your arm and we'll go indoors.

LIZA. Let us be going, then. [Gives him her arm.]

SHPIGELSKI. Oh, by the way, I suppose I ought to have kissed your hand—that's what one is supposed to do . . . Oh well, just this once, then! [Kisses her hand.]

[LIZA blushes.]

There you are, then. [Goes to garden door.]

LIZA [stopping]. So you think, do you, Ignaty Ilyich, that Mikhail Alexandrovich really isn't a man to get alarmed about?

SHPIGELSKI. Not in the least.

LIZA. You know for some time now it's seemed to me that Natalya Petrovna . . . that Beliayev . . . that she's noticed him a great deal, don't you agree? Perhaps that has something to do with this morning's scene. . . .

SHPIGELSKI [*interrupting*]. I forgot to tell you one thing, Lizaveta Bogdanovna. I may be very inquisitive myself, but I simply can't stand inquisitive women. Or rather, let me explain: in my opinion a woman should be inquisitive and observant only in company, do you understand?—only with other people. Then it may be a help to her husband. Still, if you really want to know my views on Natalya Petrovna, Verochka, Beliayev, and the local inhabitants in general, listen, and I'll sing you a song. I've got a terrible voice, so don't be too hard on me.

LIZA [*surprised*]. A song?

SHPIGELSKI. Listen! First verse:

> Grandmama had a little gray kid,
> Little gray kid, little gray kid.
> It sometimes didn't do as it was bid,
> Little gray kid, little gray kid.

Second verse:

> It used to wander out in the wood,
> Out in the wood, out in the wood.
> I said before that it wasn't very good,
> Wasn't very good, wasn't very good.

LIZA. I don't understand. . . .

SHPIGELSKI. Listen to me! Third verse:

> Some big gray wolves they wanted some lunch,
> Wanted some lunch, wanted some lunch.
> They ate the kid up crunch, crunch, crunch—
> Crunch, crunch, crunch—crunch, crunch, crunch.

But let's be going. I've got to talk with Natalya Petrovna. I hope she doesn't bite my head off. Unless I'm much mistaken, she still finds me indispensable. Come along.

[*They exit to garden.*]

KATYA [*coming out*]. They've gone at last! Ugh, that horrible doctor! He talked and talked, such awful things! And whatever was that singing? Oh, perhaps Alexei Nikolayich has already returned to the house—they would have to come in here! [*Goes to window.*] And so Lizaveta Bogdanovna's going to be the doctor's wife. . . . [*Laughs.*] And what a wife! Well, I must say I don't envy her. . . . [*Looks out of the window.*] How clean and fresh the grass is! What

a nice smell from the cherry tree. . . . Oh, here he comes!
Alexei Nikolayich! Alexei Nikolayich!

BELIAYEV [*offstage*]. Who's calling? Oh, it's you, Katya.
[*Comes to window.*] What do you want?

KATYA. Come in here . . . I've got something to tell you.

BELIAYEV. Very well, then. [*Leaves the window and enters
from the garden after a moment.*] Here I am.

KATYA. Didn't you get drenched in the storm?

BELIAYEV. No . . . I was sitting in the greenhouse with Potap
—he's your uncle, isn't he?

KATYA. That's right.

BELIAYEV. How pretty you're looking today!

[KATYA *smiles and looks away. He produces a peach from his
pocket.*]

Like one?

KATYA. No, thank you very much.

BELIAYEV. But yesterday I didn't say no to your raspberries,
did I? Take it—I picked it specially for you, really.

KATYA. Thank you then. [*Takes peach.*]

BELIAYEV. Don't mention it. Well, and what was it you wanted
to tell me?

KATYA. The young mistress . . . that is Vera Alexandrovna
. . . asked me . . . she said she wanted to see you.

BELIAYEV. Oh well then, I'll go in and see her right away.

KATYA. Oh, no, she's coming out here. She wants to talk to
you.

BELIAYEV. And it's got to be in here.

KATYA. Yes sir. You see . . . no one ever comes here. There'll
be no one to interrupt . . . [*Sighs.*] She loves you very
much, Alexei Nikolayich. . . . She's so kind. I'll go and
get her, if you've no objection. You will wait, won't you?

BELIAYEV. Of course, of course.

KATYA. I won't be a minute. [*Turns to go, but stops.*] Alexei
Nikolayich, is it true what they say—that you're going?

BELIAYEV. That I'm going? No, it's not true—who's been
saying that?

KATYA. You're not going, then? Oh, thank God! [*Embarrassed.*] We'll be back directly. [*Exits to house.*]

BELIAYEV [*not moving for some time*]. How strange! What
extraordinary things seem to be happening to me! I must
say I never expected all this. . . . Vera loves me . . .
Natalya Petrovna knows it . . . Vera told her everything.

. . . Fantastic! [*Pulls out a small piece of paper.*] From Natalya Petrovna, in pencil. "Don't leave, don't decide anything until I've had a talk with you." What does she want to talk to me about? [*Pausing.*] I'm beginning to imagine all sorts of absurd things . . . this is really most embarrassing. If someone had told me a month ago that . . . that I . . . I simply haven't known what I've been doing since that conversation with Natalya Petrovna. Why is my heart beating so fast? And now Vera, it appears, wants to see me. . . . What shall I tell her? But at least here's a chance to find out what the whole thing's about. . . . Perhaps Natalya Petrovna's angry with me. . . . Yes, but why should she be? [*Reads the note again.*] It's all very strange, very very strange.

[*The door quietly opens. He quickly hides the note. On the threshold are* VERA *and* KATYA. *He goes up to them.* VERA *is very pale and does not move or look up.*]

KATYA. Don't be frightened, miss, go to him. I'll keep watch . . . don't be frightened. [*To* BELIAYEV.] Oh, Alexei Nikolayich. [*Shuts the windows, exits to garden, and shuts the door behind her.*]

BELIAYEV. You wanted to see me, Vera Alexandrovna. Come and sit here.

[*He takes her arm and leads her to the seat.* VERA *sits.*]

There you are. [*Looking at her in surprise.*] Have you been crying?

VERA [*not looking up*]. It's nothing . . . I came to beg your pardon, Alexei Nikolayich.

BELIAYEV. My pardon for what?

VERA. I heard that you had a horrid interview with Natalya Petrovna . . . and that you're going, that you've been told to go.

BELIAYEV. Who said that?

VERA. Natalya Petrovna herself . . . I met her after you'd been to see her. . . . She told me that you yourself didn't want to stay any longer with us. But I'm sure that in fact you've been dismissed.

BELIAYEV. Tell me, does anyone else in the house know of it?

VERA. No . . . only Katya, and I had to tell her . . . I wanted to talk with you, and to ask for your forgiveness. Just think how I must feel about it . . . because after all, I'm the cause of the whole thing, Alexei Nikolayich. It was all my fault.

BELIAYEV. Your fault? What do you mean, Vera Alexandrovna?

VERA. I would have never imagined ... Natalya Petrovna ... still, I forgive her ... and please, you forgive me, too— both of us. This morning I was just a stupid child, but now ... [Stops.]

BELIAYEV. Nothing's been settled yet, Vera Alexandrovna. I may still stay.

VERA [sorrowfully]. Nothing's been settled, you say. No, everything's settled, everything's over. Look how you're acting with me now, and yet, only yesterday in the garden, you remember ... [Pausing.] Oh, I can see that Natalya Petrovna's told you everything.

BELIAYEV [embarrassed]. Vera Alexandrovna ...

VERA. She told you all about it, I can see that ... she wanted to make me give myself away, and like an idiot I went straight into her trap. ... But she gave herself away, too. ... After all, I'm not that much of a child. [Lowering her voice.] Oh no!

BELIAYEV. What are you trying to tell me?

VERA [looking at him]. Alexei Nikolayich, did you really say you were going of your own accord?

BELIAYEV. Yes.

VERA. Why was that?

[BELIAYEV is silent.]

Won't you answer?

BELIAYEV [weakly]. You were quite right, Vera Alexandrovna. ... She told me everything.

VERA. What, for example?

BELIAYEV. Vera ... it's quite impossible for me ... you know what I mean.

VERA. Presumably she told you that I'm in love with you?

BELIAYEV [without conviction]. Yes.

VERA [quickly]. Well it's not true.

BELIAYEV [embarrassed]. How do you mean?

VERA [covers her face with her hands and whispers tonelessly through her fingers]. At least, as far as I can remember I never told her that. ... [Raising her voice.] Oh, how cruelly she treated me! And you ... you want to go away because of that?

BELIAYEV. Vera Alexandrovna, judge for yourself . . .

VERA [*glancing at him*]. He doesn't love me! [*Covers her face again.*]

BELIAYEV [*sits by her and takes her hand*]. Vera, give me you hand. . . . Listen, there mustn't be any misunderstanding between us. I love you like a sister . . . I love you because it's impossible not to. Forgive me, if I . . . I've never been in such a position before . . . I would never knowingly hurt you . . . I shan't start pretending to you—I knew that you liked me, that you started to love me. . . . But judge for yourself, what ever can come of this? I'm only twenty, and haven't a penny to my name. Please don't be cross with me. I simply don't know what to say to you.

VERA [*taking her hands from her face*]. But good Lord, have I ever expected anything from you? All the same, why so cruelly, so heartlessly . . . ? [*Stops.*]

BELIAYEV. Vera Alexandrovna, I didn't mean to distress you.

VERA. I'm not accusing you, Alexei Nikolayich. After all, what have you done? It's all my fault . . . and I've been punished for it! Nor am I saying she's to blame, either. She's really a kind woman, but she couldn't hope to win against herself—it was too much for her.

BELIAYEV [*not understanding*]. Too much for her?

VERA [*turns to him*]. She loves you Beliayev.

BELIAYEV. What?

VERA. She loves you.

BELIAYEV. What are you saying!

VERA. I know what I'm saying. Today has made me grow up. You must realize that I'm no longer a child. She was actually jealous—of me! [*Smiles bitterly.*] What do you say to that?

BELIAYEV. But it's quite impossible!

VERA. Impossible? . . . But why did she suddenly decide to marry me to that man . . . what's his name, Bolshintsov? Why did she send the doctor to me, why did she herself try to persuade me? Oh, I know what I'm saying! Alexei Nikolayich, if you could have seen how her whole face changed when I told her . . . Oh, you can't have any idea how cunningly, how subtly she wormed that confession out of me. . . . Yes, she loves you—it's only too clear.

BELIAYEV. Vera Alexandrovna, you're mistaken, I assure you.

VERA. No, I'm not mistaken—believe me, I'm not. If she doesn't love you then why did she torture me like that?

What have I done to her? [*Bitterly.*] A good deal is excused by jealousy. But what's the use of talking? . . . And now, why is she dismissing you? She thinks that you . . . that you and I . . . Oh, she can set her heart at rest! You can stay. [*Covers her face with her hands.*]

BELIAYEV. She hasn't dismissed me yet, Vera Alexandrovna . . . I've told you already, nothing's been settled. . . .

VERA [*suddenly lifting her head and looking at him*]. Is that so?

BELIAYEV. Yes, but what are you looking at me like that for?

VERA [*as if to herself*]. Oh, I see it now. . . . Yes, yes . . . she's still hoping . . .

[*The house door opens quietly and* NATALYA *appears. She stops on seeing* BELIAYEV *and* VERA.]

BELIAYEV. What do you mean?

VERA. Yes, it's all quite clear to me now. . . . She recovered and saw that there's nothing to worry about as far as I'm concerned. After all, what do I amount to?—a stupid little girl. But she . . . !

BELIAYEV. Vera Alexandrovna, how can you think . . .

VERA. And after all, who knows? Perhaps she's right—perhaps you love her. . . .

BELIAYEV. I?

VERA [*rising*]. Yes, you. What are you blushing for?

BELIAYEV. Blushing? Why . . .

VERA. Do you love her—could you come to love her? [*Pause.*] You don't answer me.

BELIAYEV. But for goodness' sake, what do you want me to answer Vera Alexandrovna? You're so upset . . . Calm down, please. . . .

VERA [*turning from him*]. Oh, you treat me as though I were a child. . . . You don't even think it's worth giving me a serious answer. . . . You just want to end the conversation— you're trying to comfort me! [*Tries to go, but stops short on seeing* NATALYA.] Natalya Petrovna. . . .

[BELIAYEV *looks quickly round.*]

NATALYA [*walking forward*]. Yes, it is I. [*She speaks with some difficulty.*] I've come to get you, Vera.

VERA [*slowly and coldly*]. And what made you think of coming here of all places? Perhaps you were searching for me?

NATALYA. Yes—I was searching for you. You're behaving very foolishly, Vera—I've told you more than once . . . And Alexei Nikolayich, you've forgotten your promise. I'm disappointed in you.

VERA. I won't listen to any more of this—stop it, Natalya Petrovna!

[NATALYA *looks at her in astonishment.*]

You've talked to me like a child for long enough . . . [*Lowers her voice.*] From today I'm a woman . . . as much a woman as you are.

NATALYA [*embarrassed*]. Vera . . .

VERA [*almost whispers*]. You needn't be disappointed in him—it wasn't he who arranged for us to meet here. You see, he doesn't love me—you know that—so there's no need for you to be jealous.

NATALYA [*with growing astonishment*]. Vera!

VERA. It's all true . . . you don't have to be cunning any more. Cunning won't help you now, besides . . . I can see right through you. Oh yes I can. Natalya Petrovna, I'm no longer your adopted daughter whom you watch over like an elder sister. . . . [*Moves up to her.*] I'm your rival. . . .

NATALYA. Vera, you forget yourself . . .

VERA. Perhaps, but who brought me to it? I don't know myself how I dare speak to you like this . . . perhaps it's because I don't hope for anything further—because you tried to trample me underfoot—and succeeded completely too. But listen: I don't intend to be cunning with you like you were with me . . . and so [*Pointing to* BELIAYEV.] I've told him everything.

NATALYA. But what can you have told him?

VERA. What can I have told him? [*Ironically.*] Well, all that I've noticed. You hoped to get everything out of me without giving yourself away. But you made mistakes, Natalya Petrovna. You became too sure of yourself. . . .

NATALYA. Vera, Vera, pull yourself together. . . .

VERA [*in a whisper, moving still closer to her*]. Then tell me that I'm wrong . . . go on, tell me that you don't love him. . . . He's told me that he's not in love with me!

[NATALYA *is silent from embarrassment.* VERA *stays motionless for some time and suddenly presses a hand to her forehead.*]

Natalya Petrovna, forgive me, please have pity on me for
this . . . I don't know what's come over me. . . . [*Bursts
into tears and hurries into the corridor. Silence.*]

BELIAYEV [*going up to* NATALYA]. I promise you, Natalya
Petrovna . . .

NATALYA [*looks at him without moving, then stretches out a
hand towards him*]. Stop, Alexei Nikolayich—Vera's perfectly right . . . it's true . . . it's time for me to stop hiding
the truth. I'm guilty before her and before you—you have
a right to despise me.

[BELIAYEV *makes an involuntary gesture.*]

I've made myself despicable in my own eyes, too. There's
just one way left for me to win your respect again: frankness, complete and utter frankness, whatever the consequences may be. Anyway, I'm talking to you for the last
time. I love you. [*All the time not looking at him.*]

BELIAYEV. You, Natalya Petrovna . . . !

NATALYA. Yes, I love you. Vera wasn't mistaken—I fell in
love with you the first day you arrived here, but only
realized it myself yesterday. I've no intention of justifying
my conduct . . . it was unworthy of me . . . but at least
now you can understand, perhaps even forgive it. Yes, I
was jealous of Vera—I had married her off in my mind
to Bolshintsov, so as to get her away from the two of us.
I took advantage of my age and position to force her secret
out and of course quite without knowing it I gave myself
away at the same time. I love you, Beliayev, but I must
tell you that only pride compels me to say so . . . the farce
which I have been playing till now has at last sickened me.
You can't stay here . . . but in any case, after what I've
just told you, it would probably be too embarrassing for
you to stay in my company—you obviously want to leave
here as soon as you can, don't you? I feel sure of that, and
the certainty has given me courage. Naturally I don't want
you to take away unpleasant thoughts about me. But now
you know it all. . . . Perhaps I ruined everything for you
both . . . perhaps if this hadn't happened, you would have
fallen in love with Vera . . . I have only one excuse, Alexei
Nikolayich: this has all been beyond my control. [*She
stops, after having spoken in a perfectly even, calm voice,
without looking at him. He is silent. She continues with
some emotion, still not looking at him.*] You don't answer

me? . . . But still, that is understandable. You haven't any-thing to tell me. The position of someone who doesn't love but who has to listen to a declaration of love is a very painful one—thank you for your silence. Believe me, when I told you . . . that I love you, I wasn't trying to be cunning in the old way . . . I wasn't planning anything. On the con-trary, I wanted to throw off a mask which I can assure you wasn't proving a very good fit. . . . And anyway, why pose and deceive when everything's known—why go on pretend-ing when there's no one left to be taken in? It's all over now between us. I won't keep you any longer; you may go away without saying a word to me, not even good-bye. I'll not only not regard this as rudeness—I'll even be grateful. There are times when good manners are out of place—worse than rudeness. Obviously we weren't intended to get to know one another properly. Good-bye. No, we weren't intended to get to know each other . . . but at least I hope that I'm no longer persecuting and deceitful in your eyes. . . . Good-bye for-ever. . . .

[BELIAYEV *struggles with his emotions, but can't speak.*]

Aren't you going?
BELIAYEV [*bows, tries to go, but after an inner struggle, stays*]. No, I can't go. . . .

[NATALYA *looks at him for the first time.*]

I can't go like this! Listen, Natalya Petrovna, you've just told me . . . that you don't want me to take away un-pleasant thoughts about you. Well, I too don't want you to remember me as a man who. . . . Oh heavens, how can I put it? . . . Natalya, forgive me . . . I can't talk with ladies like you. . . . Up to now I've only met . . . completely different women. You say that we weren't intended to get to know each other, but forgive me—could I ever . . . I, a simple, uneducated boy—could I ever have even dreamt of getting to know you? Think what you are compared with me. I wouldn't have presumed . . . with your upbring-ing . . . But why am I talking about that? Look at me: at this old suit and at your fine dress . . . my God! Of course, I was frightened of you, and still am . . . without exaggerat-ing, I regarded you as someone from another . . . from a higher world, and now you . . . you tell me that you love me . . . you, Natalya Petrovna! I feel my heart beating as all my life it has never beat—not just from bewilderment, not just because my vanity is flattered—how could this be a time for vanity?—but I can't . . . I can't go away like this, whatever you say!

NATALYA [*pausing, to herself*]. What have I done?

BELIAYEV. For God's sake believe me, Natalya Petrovna . . .

NATALYA [*with altered voice*]. If I didn't know you to be an honest man, a man who wouldn't stoop to lie, God knows what I might be thinking, Alexei Nikolayich. I might even regret my frankness. But I do believe you. I don't want to hide my feelings from you, and I'm grateful to you for saying what you did. I know now exactly why we didn't become friends: it was nothing actually in me that kept you away, it was just my position. . . . [*Stops.*] Everything's for the best, of course . . . now I'll feel easier at parting from you. . . . Good-bye. [*About to go.*]

BELIAYEV [*pausing*]. Natalya Petrovna, I see that I can't stay here, but you've no idea what's going on in me. You love me . . . it's terrible for me to speak those words out loud. . . . All this is so completely new to me—it's as though I were seeing and hearing you for the first time, but I am conscious of one thing, and that is that I must go . . . otherwise I wouldn't be able to answer for myself.

NATALYA [*weakly*]. Yes, Beliayev, you must go . . . after we've had this talk you must go immediately. . . . But in spite of all I've done, do you really . . . Oh believe me, if I could ever have suspected, even remotely, what you've told me, my confession would have gone with me to the grave, Beliayev. I only wanted to end all the misunderstandings, to repent, to punish myself. I wanted to cut right through the last thread at a single stroke. If I could have imagined . . . [*Covers her face.*]

BELIAYEV. I believe you, Natalya Petrovna, I believe you. And I myself, a quarter of an hour ago . . . could I ever have dreamt? . . . Only today, during our talk before dinner, did I feel something unusual, something quite extraordinary, as though a hand had pressed my heart, and a terrible burning in me. . . . It's true that earlier I appeared to be avoiding you, even to dislike you, but when you told me today that Vera thought . . . [*Stops.*]

NATALYA [*involuntarily smiling from happiness*]. That's enough, Beliayev—we mustn't think about it. We mustn't

forget that we're talking together for what will be the last
time—that tomorrow you're going . . .

BELIAYEV. Yes, tomorrow I'm going! Now it's all right for me
to go. . . . All this will pass . . . I don't want to exaggerate,
you see. I shall go wherever God wishes, and I'll take with
me one memory: that you loved me. . . . But how is it
that I didn't know you until now? You're looking at me:
can I ever really have wanted to avoid catching your eye?
—did I ever feel shy with you?

NATALYA [*smiling*]. You just told me that you were afraid of
me.

BELIAYEV. Did I? [*Pausing.*] Oh yes, you're right . . . I'm
amazed at myself. Is this really me who's talking with you
so boldly? I hardly recognize myself.

NATALYA. And you're sure you're not mistaken?

BELIAYEV. What about?

NATALYA. About the fact that you . . . [*Shuddering.*] Oh God,
what am I doing? . . . Listen, Beliayev . . . you must help
me. No woman can ever have been in such a position as
this. I simply haven't the strength to bear it any more. . . .
Perhaps it's all for the best like this, with everything over
at once—at least we've got to know each other. . . . Give me
your hand, and good-bye forever.

BELIAYEV [*taking her hand*]. Natalya Petrovna . . . I don't
know what to say to you in parting . . . my heart is so full
. . . God grant you . . . [*Stops and presses her hand to his
lips.*] Good-bye. [*About to exit to garden.*]

NATALYA [*watching him go*]. Beliayev . . .

BELIAYEV. What is it?

NATALYA. Stay here—may God forgive us! [*Buries her head in
her hands.*]

BELIAYEV [*goes up to her and stretches out a hand to her*].
Natalya Petrovna . . .

[*At that moment the garden door opens, and* RAKITIN *appears.
For some time he watches them both, then approaches
them.*]

RAKITIN [*loudly*]. They're looking everywhere for you, Natalya Petrovna.

[NATALYA *and* BELIAYEV *turn around.*]

NATALYA [*removing her hands from her face as though coming
to herself*]. Oh, it's you. . . . Who's looking for me?

[BELIAYEV, *embarrassed, bows to* NATALYA *and turns to go.*]

You're going, Alexei Nikolayich? Don't forget you know . . .

[*He bows again and exits to garden.*]

RAKITIN. Arkady Sergeyich is looking for you . . . I must admit, I never expected to find you in here, but I was just passing by, and . . .

NATALYA [*smiling*]. You happened to hear our voices. . . . I met Alexei Nikolayich here, and had a long talk with him . . . today's obviously a day of talks. But now we can go indoors. [*About to go to corridor.*]

RAKITIN [*with emotion*]. Might I ask . . . what decision. . . .

NATALYA [*assuming surprise*]. What decision? . . . I don't understand.

RAKITIN [*pausing for a long time, sadly*]. In that case I see it all.

NATALYA. Well, so be it then. . . . More mysterious hints! Listen, I explained things to him, and now everything's settled . . . it was all nonsense, just exaggerations. . . . All that you and I were discussing is sheer childishness and must now be forgotten.

RAKITIN. Natalya Petrovna, I'm not interrogating you.

NATALYA [*with assumed ease*]. Whatever was it I wanted to tell you? I don't remember. It doesn't matter. Come, let's go indoors. All that is over and done with.

RAKITIN [*looking at her intently*]. Yes, everything is over. How annoyed you must feel at yourself now for your . . . frankness earlier today. [*He turns.*]

NATALYA. Rakitin . . .

[*He looks at her again. She is clearly at a loss for words.*]

You've still said nothing to Arkady?

RAKITIN. No, I haven't . . . I haven't had time to think of anything. . . . You realize it's necessary to concoct some sort of story. . . .

NATALYA. How intolerable! What do they want from me— they follow me about everywhere I go! Rakitin, I feel ashamed to see you . . .

RAKITIN. Oh, please don't worry, Natalya Petrovna. . . . What's the point? All this is in the natural order of things. But how easy it is to see that Beliayev is a complete child in such matters! Why did he get so embarrassed and dash away like that? . . . However, in time . . .

[NATALYA *wants to go up to him, but stops. At that moment* ISLAYEV *is heard behind the garden door:* "You say he came in here?" *After which* ISLAYEV *and* SHPIGELSKI *enter.*]

ISLAYEV. Quite right—here he is. Hm, and Natasha also! [*Going up to her.*] What is this? Part two of this morning's conversation? Obviously it's something pretty urgent.

RAKITIN. I happened to meet Natalya Petrovna in here. . . .

ISLAYEV [*looking round*]. You happened to meet her? What kind of public thoroughfare is this, then?

NATALYA. Well, you came along this way too, didn't you?

ISLAYEV. I came here because . . . [*Stops.*]

NATALYA. Because you were searching for me?

ISLAYEV [*pausing*]. Yes, as a matter of fact I was. Wouldn't you like to come back indoors? There's some tea ready. It will be dark soon.

NATALYA [*takes his hand*]. Come along then.

ISLAYEV [*looking around*]. You know, it would be quite possible to turn this place into a couple of nice rooms—for the gardeners or some of the servants, don't you think, Shpigelski?

SHPIGELSKI. It certainly would.

ISLAYEV. Let's go through the garden, Natasha. [*Exits through garden door. Throughout this scene he has not once looked at* RAKITIN. *On the threshold he half turns.*] Gentlemen, what are you waiting for? Come along and have some tea. [*Exits with* NATALYA.]

SHPIGELSKI [*to* RAKITIN]. Well, Mikhail Alexandrovich, let's go . . . give me your arm. . . . It's clear that you and I are fated to remain the rear guard. . . .

RAKITIN [*with feeling*]. Forgive me, doctor, but I'm sick and tired of you.

SHPIGELSKI [*with feigned benevolence*]. Oh, but I'm sick and and tired of myself, too, Mikhail Alexandrovich, if you only knew it!

[RAKITIN *can't help smiling.*]

Come along, come along.

[*Both exit to garden.*]

ACT FIVE

[*Scene as in Acts One and Three. Morning.* ISLAYEV *sits at the table going through papers. He rises suddenly.*]

ISLAYEV. No, I'm definitely not in the mood for work today. It feels exactly as though someone's hammering nails into my head. [*Walks up and down.*] I must say, I never expected it . . . I never thought that I'd alarm myself like this. But what ever shall I do—that's the point. [*Ponders and suddenly shouts.*] Matvey!

MATVEY [*enters*]. You called, sir?

ISLAYEV. Send the foreman to me . . . and tell the men at the dam to wait. . . . Go along.

MATVEY. Very good. [*Exits.*]

ISLAYEV [*returning to table*]. Yes, what a business this is!

ANNA [*enters*]. Arkady, dear . . .

ISLAYEV. Oh, it's you, mother. How do you feel now?

ANNA [*sitting on the couch*]. Thanks be to God, quite well. [*Sighs.*] Quite well. [*Sighs louder.*] Thanks be to God. [*Seeing that he isn't listening, she sighs very loudly, with a groan.*]

ISLAYEV. You're sighing . . . what's the matter?

ANNA [*sighs again, but quieter already*]. Oh Arkady, as though you didn't know what I'm sighing for!

ISLAYEV. What do you mean?

ANNA [*pausing*]. I'm your mother, Arkady. Of course, you're a grown man, and intelligent too, but all the same I'm your mother. It's a big word: mother. . . .

ISLAYEV. Please explain yourself.

ANNA. You're well aware what I'm getting at, my good friend. Your wife Natasha . . . of course, she's a wonderful woman and up to now her behavior has been beyond reproach . . . but she's still so young, Arkady. And youth . . .

ISLAYEV. I understand what you're trying to tell me. . . . You think that her relationship with Rakitin . . .

ANNA. God forbid—I didn't mean . . .

ISLAYEV. You didn't let me finish. . . . You think that her relationship with Rakitin isn't exactly . . . well, clear. These secret conversations, these tears—all this seems strange to you, am I not right?

ANNA. And did he eventually tell you what these conversations
of theirs were about, Arkady? . . . He's told *me* nothing.

ISLAYEV. I didn't inquire, mother, and it would seem that he's
in no great hurry to satisfy my curiosity.

ANNA. So what do you intend to do now?

ISLAYEV. To do, mother? Why, nothing.

ANNA. How do you mean—nothing?

ISLAYEV. Just what I say—nothing.

ANNA [*rising*]. Well, I must say I'm surprised. You're master in
your own house, of course, and you know better than I
what's good and what's bad. But give a thought to the
consequences . . .

ISLAYEV [*animatedly*]. No, I must beg you not to alarm yourself on that account, mother. . . . Please don't.

ANNA. As you wish, Arkady, as you wish. In the future I
won't utter another word. I've warned you, I've done my
duty, and now I'll keep quiet. [*Short pause.*]

ISLAYEV. Aren't you going out at all today?

ANNA. But I must warn you: you're too trusting, son. You
judge everyone else by yourself! Believe me, real friends
aren't so easy to come by these days!

ISLAYEV [*impatiently*]. Mother . . .

ANNA. Oh well, I'll be quiet. . . . What have I got to do with
it, I, an old woman? Perhaps I've become senile, but I was
brought up to think differently about such questions . . .
and I did my best to instill in you something of my . . . Oh
well, get on with your work, I won't interfere . . . I'll go.
[*Goes to door and then stops.*] And so? . . . Oh well, you
know best, I suppose! [*Exits.*]

ISLAYEV. How odd that those who love you always want to
finger your wounds, one after the other! And the absurd
part of it is that they're convinced you'll feel better because
of it. . . . Still, I'm not blaming mother; she's doing what
she thinks right, and never could resist giving advice. But
that's not the point. . . . [*Sits down.*] What am I to do?
[*Thinks it over, then rises.*] Oh, the simpler the better!
Diplomatic subleties aren't for me . . . I'm always the first
to get muddled in them. [*Rings.*]

[*Enter* MATVEY.]

Do you know if Mikhail Alexandrovich is in?

MATVEY. Yes sir—he is. I saw him just now in the billiard
room.

ISLAYEV. Ah! Well, ask him to come here.

MATVEY. Very good, sir. [*Exits.*]

ISLAYEV [*walking up and down*]. I'm not used to such scenes. I hope they won't occur too often. I may be a strong man, but I wouldn't be able to stand this sort of thing for long. [*Presses his chest.*] Ugh!

[*From the hall* RAKITIN *enters, embarrassed.*]

RAKITIN. You wanted to see me?

ISLAYEV. Yes. [*Pausing.*] Mikhail, you owe me something.

RAKITIN. Do I?

ISLAYEV. But what do you mean? Have you really forgotten your promise, your promise about . . . Natasha crying . . . and all that . . . ? When my mother and I found you, you remember, you told me that you had a secret which you wanted to explain.

RAKITIN. I said a secret?

ISLAYEV. You did.

RAKITIN. But what secret could we have had? We were just talking together.

ISLAYEV. What about? And what was she crying about?

RAKITIN. You know, Arkady Sergeyich, there are moments in the life of every woman, even the happiest . . .

ISLAYEV. Rakitin, stop. It's hopeless like this. I can't bear to see you in such a position . . . your embarrassment hurts me more than it does you. . . . [*Takes him by the hand.*] After all, we're old friends—you've known me since we were boys. I'm no good at pretending, and for your part you've always been frank with me too. Let me ask you one question . . . I give you my word beforehand that I won't doubt the honesty of your reply. You love my wife, don't you?

[RAKITIN *looks at him.*]

Don't misunderstand me: you love her like . . . well, not to beat about the bush, you love her with the kind of love that . . . er . . . that it would be difficult to confess to a husband.

RAKITIN [*pausing*]. Yes, I love your wife [*tonelessly*] . . . with that kind of love.

ISLAYEV [*also pausing*]. Thank you for your frankness, Mikhail. You're a fine person. And what are we to do now? Sit down and we'll discuss the matter together.

[RAKITIN *sits.* ISLAYEV *paces about the room.*]

I know Natasha, I know how much I value her . . . but
I know how much I value myself, too. I can't come near
you, Mikhail—don't interrupt me please—I can't come
near you. You're more intelligent, finer, more pleasant than
me. I'm a simple man . . . Natasha loves me, or I think so,
but she has eyes . . . In short, you were bound to appeal to
her. As a matter of fact I should tell you that I noticed
your fondness for one another a long time ago. But I always trusted you both, and as nothing came to the surface
. . . Oh, I'm no good at making speeches! [*Stops.*] But
after that scene yesterday, and after your second meeting
last night, something had to be done. If only I'd come on
you by myself, but there were other witnesses: my mother,
that rogue Shpigelski . . . Well what do you say, Mikhail?

RAKITIN. You're perfectly right, Arkady.

ISLAYEV. Anyway that's beside the point. The question is what
to do now? I ought to tell you, Mikhail—I know I'm a
simple sort of chap, but I do also know one thing, and that is
that it's wrong to wreck another person's life—that there
are times when it's a sin to insist on your rights. And I
didn't read that in a book, old friend—it's my conscience
telling me. Be tolerant . . . that's it, be tolerant. But this
needs thinking over—it's too important.

RAKITIN [*rising*]. Well, I've thought it over already.

ISLAYEV. How do you mean?

RAKITIN. I must go . . . in fact, I'm already going.

ISLAYEV [*pausing*]. Do you think that's necessary? Away from
here altogether?

RAKITIN. Yes.

ISLAYEV [*pacing up and down again*]. That's a terrible thing
to say . . . ! But perhaps you're right. It will be hard for us
here without you . . . And God knows, it might not even
help much, either. . . . But you're better able to see things
straight, better able to know. I suppose you're right to have
decided that . . . You're dangerous to me, old friend . . .
[*Smiling sadly.*] yes, you're dangerous! Of course, there's
always . . . I was talking just now about being tolerant to
people . . . but I probably wouldn't survive it—without
Natasha I'd . . . [*Waves his hand.*] And there is something
else, old friend: for some time, particularly these last few
days. I've noticed a great change in her. I'm worried, be-

cause she always seems to be upset about something. Isn't that so? I'm not mistaken, am I?

RAKITIN [*bitterly*]. Oh no, you're not mistaken.

ISLAYEV. Well, you see, I was right. And so you're going?

RAKITIN. Yes.

ISLAYEV. Hm. How quickly all this has happened! Why did you have to go and get so embarrassed when mother and I came on you together? . . .

MATVEY [*enters*]. The foreman is here, sir.

ISLAYEV. Well, tell him to wait.

[*Exit* MATVEY.]

Mikhail, you're not going away for long, surely? Because really all this has been so much nonsense!

RAKITIN. I just don't know . . . I think perhaps I'd better make it for a long time. . . .

ISLAYEV. But who do you take me for—Othello, or somebody? You know, I doubt if there's ever been a conversation like this between two friends before! I can't part from you like this . . .

RAKITIN [*pressing his hand*]. You'll tell me when you think it would be all right for me to come back?

ISLAYEV. But there's none here who can take your place . . . At least, not Bolshintsov, that's certain . . . !

RAKITIN There are others who can . . .

ISLAYEV. Who? Krinitsin? That dilettante? Of course, Beliayev's a pleasant young fellow, but he's as far below you as I am from the moon.

RAKITIN [*bitterly*]. Do you think so? You don't know him, Arkady. . . . You'd do well to take note of him, do you hear? He's a very . . . a very remarkable man!

ISLAYEV. Bah! Then why did you and Natasha want to take him in hand and finish his education? [*Looking at the door.*] Why, here he comes, I think . . . [*Hurriedly.*] And so it's settled, my friend . . . you'll go away for a bit, just for a few days. . . . There's no need to hurry—Natasha will need to make arrangements . . . I'll calm mother down. . . . And God be with you! You've taken a great weight off my mind . . . embrace me, my dear friend. [*Quickly embraces him, and turns to* BELIAYEV, *who has just entered.*] Oh, it's you . . . well, how goes it?

BELIAYEV. Very well, thank you, Arkady Sergeyich.

ISLAYEV. And where's Kolya?

BELIAYEV. He's with Herr Schaaf.

ISLAYEV. Splendid! [*Takes his hat.*] Well, gentlemen, I must bid you farewell. I still haven't been to either the dam or the building site today. . . . And I've still got all those papers to go through, as well! [*Stuffs them under his arm.*] *Au revoir*! Matvey! Matvey, come with me. [*Exits.*]

[RAKITIN *remains, standing downstage in thought.*]

BELIAYEV [*approaching him*]. How do you feel today, Mikhail Alexandrovich?

RAKITIN. Just as usual, thank you. And you?

BELIAYEV. Quite well.

RAKITIN. That's evident!

BELIAYEV. How do you mean?

RAKITIN. It's in your face . . . Oh, and you've put on a new coat today . . . And what's this?—a flower in your buttonhole!

[BELIAYEV *blushes and pulls it out.*]

But why do that? Why . . . ? It's charming . . . [*Pausing.*] Incidentally, Alexei Nikolayich, if you should want anything, I'm . . . I'm going into town tomorrow.

BELIAYEV. Tomorrow?

RAKITIN. Yes . . . and from there very likely to Moscow.

BELIAYEV [*surprised*]. To Moscow? But you told me only yesterday, didn't you, that you intended to spend a month here?

RAKITIN. Yes, but business . . . Things haven't turned out that way . . .

BELIAYEV. And are you going away for long?

RAKITIN. I don't know . . . perhaps for a long time.

BELIAYEV. Please tell me—does Natalya Petrovna know of this?

RAKITIN. No. What makes you think particularly of her?

BELIAYEV [*embarrassed*]. Oh, I was just asking.

RAKITIN [*pausing and looking about him*]. There's no one in the room but ourselves, Alexei Nikolayich, so why don't we stop acting this farce with each other? What do you say?

BELIAYEV. I don't understand you, Mikhail Alexandrovich.

RAKITIN. Don't you? Do you really not understand why I'm going?

BELIAYEV. No.

RAKITIN. That's odd . . . still, I'm prepared to believe you.

Perhaps you really don't know the reason . . . if you like I'll tell you.

BELIAYEV. Please do.

RAKITIN. Well you see, Alexei Nikolayich—incidentally, I'm relying on your discretion—you saw me just now with Arkady Sergeyich . . . we were having a rather important conversation. It was as a result of just this conversation that I decided to leave. And do you know why? I'm telling you all this because I take you for an honest man—he'd got it into his head that I . . . well, that I'm in love with Natalya Petrovna. What do you make of that, eh? A pretty odd idea, isn't it? But I'm grateful to him for not playing tricks or having us watched, but for asking me about it straight out, to my face. Now tell me, what would you do in my place? Of course, his suspicions are utterly unfounded, but they alarm him nevertheless. . . . A decent man should be able to sacrifice his own pleasure for his friend's peace of mind occasionally. And so it's because of that I'm going . . . I'm sure that you approve of my decision, don't you? Aren't I right—you would act in the same way yourself if you were in my shoes—you'd leave, too?

BELIAYEV [pausing]. Perhaps.

RAKITIN. I'm very glad to hear it. . . . Of course, I don't deny that there's a funny side to my decision: that I should think myself a ladykiller, or something, but you see, Alexei Nikolayich, a woman's honor is such an important thing . . . Of course I'm not now talking of Natalya Petrovna, but I've known the most virtuous and innocent women, absolute children even if they were intelligent, who, because of this virtue and innocence, were all the more likely to surrender themselves to a sudden attraction . . . and why? Who knows? Too much caution in such cases is impossible, the more so, because . . . Incidentally, Alexei Nikolayich, do you still believe that love is the greatest blessing on earth?

BELIAYEV [coldly]. I've yet to experience it, but I should think that to be loved by the woman that you love is a wonderful thing.

RAKITIN. And God grant you keep such pleasant beliefs! In my opinion, Alexei Nikolayich, all love—whether it be happy or unhappy—is sheer misery if you surrender completely to it. . . . Just wait a little, and perhaps you will learn how those tender little hands can torture, and with what loving care they tear your heart to pieces. . . . Wait a little, and you will find out what pangs of hatred lurk beneath the most passionate love! You will remember me when you are longing for peace, the dullest and most ordinary peace, as a sick man longs for good health—when you are envying every carefree, happy man. . . . Wait a bit, and you will learn what it is to belong to a woman, what it means to be enslaved and infected—and how degrading, how wearying that slavery is! And in the end you will learn what trivialities are bought for so dear a price. . . . But why am I telling you all this? You won't believe me now. The point is that I value your approval of my action very highly . . . yes, yes—in such cases one must be careful.

BELIAYEV [*all the time watching him*]. Thank you for the lesson, Mikhail Alexandrovich, although I didn't need it.

RAKITIN [*takes him by the hand*]. I'm sorry—I had no intention . . . It's not for me to give lessons to anyone . . . I was just saying the first thing that came into my head. . . .

BELIAYEV [*slightly ironical*]. Without reference to anyone? . . .

RAKITIN [*confused*]. Exactly, without any reference to anyone. I only wanted . . . Up to now, Alexei Nikolayich, you haven't had much occasion to get to know women, have you? Women are very self-willed.

BELIAYEV. But who are you talking about?

RAKITIN. Oh, no one in particular.

BELIAYEV. About all women in general, then?

RAKITIN. Yes, perhaps . . . I honestly don't know why I've taken on this lecturing tone, but do let me give you one piece of advice in parting. [*Stops and gestures with his hand.*] Oh, but who am I to advise people . . . ? Please excuse my chatter.

BELIAYEV. On the contrary . . . on the contrary . . .

RAKITIN. And so you don't want anything from town?

BELIAYEV. Nothing, thank you. But I'm sorry you're going away.

RAKITIN. That's very nice of you. Believe me, I am, too. . . .

[*Enter* NATALYA *and* VERA *from the study.* VERA *is very sad and pale.*]

It's been most pleasant to make your acquaintance . . . [*Shakes his hand.*]

NATALYA [*looks at both for a while, then approaches them*]. Good morning, gentlemen. . . .

RAKITIN [*quickly turns*]. Good morning, Natalya Petrovna. . . . Good morning, Vera.

[BELIAYEV *bows silently to both. He is embarrassed.*]

NATALYA [*to* RAKITIN]. Are you doing anything in particular?

RAKITIN. Nothing at all.

NATALYA. Vera and I have been for a walk in the garden. . . . It's so lovely in the fresh air today . . . the limes smell so sweet, we were walking under them all the time . . . it's nice to hear the bees buzzing above you. . . . [*Shyly to* BELIAYEV.] We hoped to meet you there, too.

[BELIAYEV *is silent.*]

RAKITIN [*to* NATALYA]. I see you too are noticing the beauties of nature today. [*Pausing.*] Alexei Nikolayich couldn't very well go out into the garden . . . you see, he's got a new coat on today. . . .

BELIAYEV [*irritated*]. Of course, it's the only one I have and in the garden it might get torn—is that what you were trying to say?

RAKITIN. Oh no . . . I didn't mean to imply . . .

[VERA *goes to the sofa right in silence, sits down and picks up her work.* NATALYA *smiles forcedly to* BELIAYEV. *There is a short constrained silence.*]

RAKITIN [*continues with bitterness*]. Oh, I forgot to tell you, Natalya Petrovna—I'm leaving today.

NATALYA [*rather alarmed*]. You're leaving? Where to?

RAKITIN. To town . . . on business.

NATALYA. Not for long, I hope?

RAKITIN. It depends how things go.

NATALYA. Well, mind you come back to us soon. [*To* BELIAYEV, *not looking at him.*] Alexei Nikolayich, were those your sketches that Kolya showed me? Did you paint them?

BELIAYEV. Yes . . . I . . . they're nothing much, really.

NATALYA. On the contrary, they're extremely good. You're very talented.

RAKITIN. It appears you discover something new to admire in Beliayev every day.

NATALYA [*coldly*]. Perhaps . . . so much the better for him. [*To* BELIAYEV.] Have you any other paintings you'd like to show me?

[BELIAYEV *bows.*]

RAKITIN [*who has been like a cat on hot bricks all this time*].
Well, I've just realized that it's time I was getting ready
. . . *Au revoir.* [*Goes to hall door.*]

NATALYA [*after him*]. But you'll come and say good-bye again
properly . . . ?

RAKITIN. Of course.

BELIAYEV [*after some hesitation*]. Mikhail Alexandrovich,
wait and I'll come with you—there's something I must
tell you . . .

RAKITIN. Ah!

[*Both exit to hall.* NATALYA *stays center, then sits down left.*]

NATALYA [*after a short pause*]. Vera . . .

VERA [*not looking up*]. What is it?

NATALYA. Vera, for goodness' sake don't be like this with
me . . . for goodness sake, Vera . . . Verochka . . .

[VERA *says nothing.* NATALYA *rises, crosses stage and kneels
down quietly in front of her.* VERA, *after trying to make
her get up, turns away and covers her face.*]

NATALYA. Vera, forgive me. Don't cry, Vera. I've done wrong
to you, I know, but can't you really forgive me?

VERA [*through her tears*]. Oh get up, get up . . .

NATALYA. I shan't get up till you've forgiven me, Vera . . .
it's hard for you, but think—is it any easier for me? . . .
Think Vera . . . after all, you know everything now. . . .
There's only one difference between us, and that is that
you've done absolutely nothing to me, whereas I . . .

VERA [*bitterly*]. And you think that's the only difference? Oh
no, Natalya Petrovna, there's another . . . today you're so
loving and kind, so friendly . . .

NATALYA [*interrupts*]. That's because I feel so guilty towards
you. . . .

VERA. Indeed? Is that the only reason? . . .

NATALYA [*rises and sits by her*]. But what other reason could
there be?

VERA. Natalya Petrovna, don't torment me any more, stop
interrogating me. . . .

NATALYA [*sighing*]. Vera, I see you can't forgive me . . .

VERA. You're so warm and affectionate today because you're
aware of being loved. . . .

NATALYA [*embarrassed*]. Vera . . . !

VERA [*turns to her*]. Well, it's true, isn't it?

NATALYA [*sadly*]. Believe me, we're both equally unhappy.

VERA. He loves you!

NATALYA. Vera, what point is there in torturing each other? It's time we pulled ourselves together. Think of the position I'm in—the position we're both in. Think that through my fault (of course) two people already know of our secret here. . . . [*Stops.*] Vera, instead of torturing each other with suspicions and reproaches, wouldn't it be better for us both to concentrate on getting out of this terrible position— on saving ourselves? Or perhaps you think that I can stand these upsets and excitements? Perhaps you've forgotten who I am? But you're not listening to me.

VERA [*thoughtfully, looking at the floor*]. He loves you. . . .

NATALYA. Vera, he's going . . .

VERA [*turns*]. Oh, leave me alone!

[NATALYA *looks at her in amazement. At that moment* IS-LAYEV'S *voice is heard from the study:* "Natasha, Natasha where are you?"]

NATALYA [*quickly rising and going to study door*]. I'm here . . . what is it?

ISLAYEV [*still offstage*]. Come in here, I've got something to tell you. . . .

NATALYA. Just a moment. [*Turns to* VERA, *stretching out a hand.* VERA *doesn't move.* NATALYA *sighs and exits to study.*]

VERA [*alone, after a pause*]. He loves her! And I've got to stay under the same roof as her . . . it's too much. . . . [*Covers her face with her hands and stays motionless.*]

[SHPIGELSKI'S *head appears round the hall door. He looks about him cautiously and approaches* VERA *on tiptoe.* VERA *doesn't notice him.* SHPIGELSKI *stops in front of her and folds his arms with a sarcastic smile.*]

VERA [*looking up*]. Who's there? Oh, it's you, doctor. . . .

SHPIGELSKI. What's the matter with my young lady—aren't you well?

VERA. Oh, it's nothing.

SHPIGELSKI. Let me take your pulse. . . . [*Does so.*] Hm! why so fast, eh? You don't pay any attention to me, young lady—I, who have your best interests at heart . . .

VERA [*looks at him with determination*]. Ignaty Ilyich . . .

SHPIGELSKI [quickly]. I'm listening, Vera Alexandrovna . . . but what an expression, for goodness' sake! . . . I'm all ears.

VERA. That gentleman . . . Bolshintsov . . . your friend . . . is he really a good man?

SHPIGELSKI. My friend Bolshintsov? Why, he's an excellent man, a really excellent man . . . he's the absolute model of kindness.

VERA. He's not got a bad temper?

SHPIGELSKI. No, no—he's the soul of amiability, I assure you. He's less of a man than a lump of clay. You've only got to take hold of him to make what you want out of him. You won't find another in the whole world like that, if you were to search for a month of Sundays. . . . He's a little cooing dove, not a man.

VERA. You'd really answer for him?

SHPIGELSKI [laying one hand on his heart, and raising the other in the air]. As I would for myself!

VERA. In that case, you may tell him . . . that I am willing to marry him.

SHPIGELSKI [with joyful astonishment]. You're . . . what?

VERA. Only, as soon as possible, do you hear? As soon as possible . . .

SHPIGELSKI. Oh, tomorrow, if you wish. My goodness, yes! . . . Splendid, Vera Alexandrovna—that's my girl! I'll go right away to tell him the good news. How delighted he will be . . . how unexpectedly things have turned out. . . . You see, he dotes on you, Vera Alexandrovna. . . .

VERA [impatiently]. I didn't ask you that, Ignaty Ilyich. . . .

SHPIGELSKI. Just as you wish, Vera Alexandrovna, just as you wish. It's just that you'll be so happy with him you'll be grateful to me, you'll see. . . .

[VERA makes another impatient movement.]

All right, not another word, not another word, not another word. . . . Then I can tell him?

VERA. You may.

SHPIGELSKI. Excellent—I'll go at once. Au revoir. [Listening.] Someone's coming. . . . [Goes into study, and on the threshold makes a grimace of amazement to himself.] Au revoir. [Exits.]

VERA [watching him go]. Rather anything in the whole world than to stay here. . . . [Rises.] Yes, my mind's made up. I shan't stay in this house . . . not for anything. I can't stand her friendly glances, her smiles—I can't bear to watch how she relaxes all over, melting in happiness. . . . Because she is happy, however much she pretends to be sad and miserable. . . . It's horrible when she kisses me. . . .

[BELIAYEV *enters the hall, looks about himself, and goes up to* VERA.]

BELIAYEV [*quietly*]. Vera Alexandrovna, are you alone?

VERA [*looks round, starts, and speaks after a pause*]. Yes.

BELIAYEV. I'm glad you are . . . otherwise I wouldn't have come in here . . . Vera Alexandrovna, I've come to say good-bye to you.

VERA. Good-bye?

BELIAYEV. Yes—I'm leaving.

VERA. You're leaving? You, as well?

BELIAYEV. I, as well. [*With suppressed feeling.*] Because you see, Vera Alexandrovna, I simply can't stay here. I've done enough harm already. It's not only that I've upset you and Natalya Petrovna—goodness knows how—but now I've started breaking up old friendships. Because of me Rakitin is leaving, and you've quarreled with your benefactress . . . it's time to put a stop to all this. When I've gone I hope everything will calm down and return to normal. I was never cut out to turn rich ladies' heads and break girls' hearts. You'll both forget me and in time perhaps even wonder how all this could ever have happened . . . I've started wondering that already. I don't want to deceive you, Vera Alexandrovna; the thought of staying here terrifies me. There's no explanation I can give for all this. . . . You see, its a completely new situation for me. I'm awkward, I always imagine that everyone's looking at me. . . . And anyway, it would be quite impossible . . . now . . . with both of you . . .

VERA. Oh, please don't worry on my account! I shan't be staying here much longer.

BELIAYEV. How do you mean?

VERA. That's my secret. But there's no question of my being in your way, I assure you.

BELIAYEV. Well, you see, I must go, mustn't I? Judge for yourself. It's as though I'd brought a plague into this house —everyone's running away . . . Wouldn't it be better, while there's still time, if just I went? I've just had a long talk with Rakitin. . . . You've no idea how bitter he was . . .

it serves me right that he made fun of my new coat . . .
he's right. Yes, I must leave. Believe me, Vera Alexandrovna, I can't wait for the moment when I shall be rushing
along the highway in the coach . . . I can't breathe here,
I want to get out into the fresh air. I feel happy and sad
together—you know, like someone feels who is going on
a long journey abroad: he is depressed at parting from his
friends, but all the time the sea is foaming so cheerfully
and the wind is blowing so freshly in his face that he can't
help feeling a tingle in his blood. Yes, I am definitely going.
I shall go back to Moscow, to my friends and my work. . . .

VERA. You love her, don't you, Alexei Nikolayich? And
you're going, just the same?

BELIAYEV. Don't, Vera Alexandrovna—why do you say such
things? Surely you must realize that it's all over? It all
flared up and then went out, like a spark. Let's part friends.
It's time I went—I've pulled myself together. Look after
yourself and be happy—we shall meet again one day . . .
I shall never forget you, Vera Alexandrovna . . . I am very
fond of you, believe me. [*Presses her hand and adds hurriedly.*] Would you give this note to Natalya Petrovna from
me?

VERA [*looking at him embarrassedly*]. A note?

BELIAYEV. Yes . . . I can't say good-bye to her.

VERA. But are you really going at once?

BELIAYEV. Yes, at once . . . I've told no one about it, except
for Mikhail Alexandrovich, and he approves. I'm walking
as far as the next village, where I'll wait for him, and then
we'll drive from there to town together. I can write for my
things to be sent on. So you see, it's all settled. . . . If you
like you can read the note: it's very short.

VERA [*taking the note*]. And you're really going?

BELIAYEV. Yes, yes . . . give her the note and say . . . no,
don't say anything—what's the use? [*Listening.*] Someone's
coming here. Farewell. . . . [*Runs to door, stops for a moment on the threshold and runs out.*]

[VERA *stays holding the note.* NATALYA *enters from the hall.*]

NATALYA [*approaching* VERA]. Verochka . . . [*Looks at her
and stops.*] What's the matter?

[VERA *silently gives her the note.*]

A note? From whom?

VERA [*tonelessly*]. Read it.

NATALYA. You alarm me. [*Reads the note, presses both hands to her face and drops into the armchair.*]

VERA [*approaching her*]. Natalya Petrovna . . .

NATALYA [*not taking her hands from her face*]. He's leaving . . . and he didn't even want to say good-bye to me . . . Oh! At least he did to you!

VERA [*sadly*]. He didn't love me. . . .

NATALYA [*rising*]. But he has no right to go like that . . . I want . . . he can't go like that . . . who said he could go? It's little short of an insult. He knew I'd never make up my mind. . . . [*Drops into the chair again.*] Oh!

VERA. You told me yourself just now that he'd have to go . . .

NATALYA. It's all right for you now . . . he's going . . . now we're even . . . [*Her voice fails her.*]

VERA. Natalya Petrovna, you said just a moment ago—these were your very words—"Instead of torturing ourselves with suspicions and reproaches, wouldn't it be better for us to concentrate on getting out of this terrible position, on saving ourselves" . . . We *are* saved now.

NATALYA [*turning on her almost with hatred*]. Oh . . .

VERA. I know what you mean, Natalya Petrovna . . . don't worry, I shan't burden you with my presence for much longer. We can't go on living together. . . .

NATALYA [*tries to stretch out a hand to her, but instead lets it fall on her knees*]. Verochka, why do you say that? Surely you too don't want to leave me? You're right: we are saved now. Everything's over . . . all's as usual.

VERA [*coldly*]. You needn't worry, Natalya Petrovna. . . . [*Looks at her in silence.*]

[ISLAYEV *enters from the study.*]

ISLAYEV [*after looking at her for some time, quietly to* VERA]. Does she know he's going?

VERA [*bewildered*]. Yes . . . she knows.

ISLAYEV [*to himself*]. But why did he decide to go so suddenly? [*Loudly.*] Natasha . . . [*Takes her hand.*]

[NATALYA *raises her head.*]

ISLAYEV. It's me, Natasha.

[NATALYA *tries to smile.*]

ISLAYEV. Are you ill, my pet? How about lying down for a little?

NATALYA. I'm all right, Arkady . . . it's nothing.

ISLAYEV. Still you're very pale . . . Really, do as I say: go and rest for a while.

NATALYA. Oh well, perhaps. [*Tries to get up, but cannot.*]

ISLAYEV [*helping her*]. There you are, you see.

[NATALYA *on his arm.*]

Do you want me to come with you?

NATALYA. Oh, I'm not as helpless as that! Come along, Vera. [*Goes toward study.*]

[*Enter* RAKITIN *from hall.*]

RAKITIN. Natalya Petrovna, I've come . . .

ISLAYEV [*interrupts*]. Ah, Mikhail! . . . Come here. [*Leads him to one side, speaks quietly and with some annoyance.*] Why did you go and tell her everything at once like that? I'm sure I asked you not to, didn't I? What was to be gained by hurrying? . . . I found her here in such a state . . .

RAKITIN [*in amazement*]. I don't understand you. . . .

ISLAYEV. You told Natasha that you're going, didn't you?

RAKITIN. And you think it's because of that that she's in a state?

ISLAYEV. Sh! she's looking at us. [*Loudly.*] So you're not going to your room, Natasha?

NATALYA. Yes . . . I'm just going.

RAKITIN. Good-bye, Natalya Petrovna!

[NATALYA *holds onto the doorhandle and doesn't answer.*]

ISLAYEV [*putting his hands on* RAKITIN'S *shoulders*]. Natasha, do you know that he's an absolutely splendid man . . . ?

NATALYA [*suddenly bursting out*]. Yes, I know he's a splendid person—all of you are splendid people . . . all of you . . . all of you . . . and yet . . . [*Buries her face in her hands, leans against the door to open it, and quickly exits, followed by* VERA.]

[ISLAYEV *sits in silence at the table, propping himself on his elbows.*]

RAKITIN [*watches him for a moment, and shrugs his shoulders with a bitter smile*]. What a position to be **in**! It's magnificent—there's no way of expressing it! Really, it's quite a relief. Is that how one parts after four years of love? Good, excellent—it serves the fool right. God be praised, it's all for the best. It was time to end this feverish, morbid relationship. [*Loudly to* ISLAYEV.] Well, good-bye, Arkady.

ISLAYEV [*lifts his head. There are tears in his eyes*]. Good-bye, old friend. This is really very difficult . . . I never expected it—just like a storm on a clear day. Still, something good may come of it. Anyway, thank you, thank you—you're a real friend.

RAKITIN [*to himself, through his teeth*]. This is too much! [*Abruptly.*] Farewell. [*He is about to go to the hall, but* SHPIGELSKI *runs in to meet him.*]

SHPIGELSKI. What is it? They told me Natalya Petrovna's not well.

ISLAYEV [*rising.*] Who told you?

SHPIGELSKI. The maid . . .

ISLAYEV. Oh, it's nothing, doctor. I think it would be best not to disturb her just now.

SHPIGELSKI. Very well, then. [*To* RAKITIN.] They say you're off to town.

RAKITIN. Yes, on business.

SHPIGELSKI. Ah, on business.

[*At that moment* ANNA, LIZA, KOLYA *and* SCHAAF *enter from the hall in haste.*]

ANNA. What's the matter? What's wrong with Natasha?

KOLYA. What's wrong with mother? Is she ill?

ISLAYEV. There's nothing wrong with her . . . I've just seen her. . . . Why all this fuss?

ANNA. But please, Arkady—they told us that she's ill . . .

ISLAYEV. Well, you shouldn't have believed them.

ANNA. Why are you cross, Arkady? It's natural we should be worried.

ISLAYEV. Of course, of course.

RAKITIN. Well, it's time I was going.

ANNA. You're going?

RAKITIN. Yes, I'm going.

ANNA [*to herself*]. Ah ha! Now I understand.

KOLYA [*to* ISLAYEV]. Papa . . .

ISLAYEV. What is it?

KOLYA. Why's Alexei Nikolayich gone?

ISLAYEV. Where's he gone to?

KOLYA. I don't know. . . . He kissed me, put on his hat and went. . . . And now it's time for the Russian lesson.

ISLAYEV. He'll probably be back directly. . . . Of course, we could send someone to get him. . . .

[ANNA *tries to hear them;* SHPIGELSKI *whispers to* LIZA.]

RAKITIN [*quietly to* ISLAYEV]. Don't do that, Arkady Sergeyich —he won't be coming back.

ISLAYEV. What do you mean?

RAKITIN. He's leaving, too.

ISLAYEV. Leaving? But where to?

RAKITIN. To Moscow.

ISLAYEV. What do you mean, to Moscow? Have you all gone crazy, or something?

RAKITIN. Between ourselves . . . Verochka fell in love with him . . . and like an honorable man he decided to go.

[ISLAYEV *flings his arms wide apart, and collapses into the armchair.*]

You see now why . . .

ISLAYEV. I see? But I see absolutely nothing. My head's in a whirl. What is there to *see* in all this? Everyone's running off in all directions like partridges rising from the ground, and all because they're honorable people . . . And all this has to happen at once, on one and the same day . . .

ANNA [*coming to his side*]. But what's this? You say that Beliayev . . .

ISLAYEV [*shouting nervously*]. It's nothing, mother, nothing. Herr Schaaf, be good enough to take Kolya now in place of Beliayev. Take him away, please.

SCHAAF. Very good sir. [*Takes* KOLYA *by the hand.*]

KOLYA. But papa . . .

ISLAYEV. Be off with you!

[SCHAAF *takes* KOLYA *out.*]

I'll see you on your way. Rakitin . . . they can saddle me a horse and I'll wait for you down at the dam. . . . But in the meantime, mother, for goodness' sake don't disturb Natasha—nor you, doctor . . . Matvey! Matvey! [*Exits hurriedly.*]

[ANNA *sits down with injured dignity.* LIZA *stands behind her.*
ANNA *turns her eyes upwards, as though trying to detach
herself from all around her.*]

SHPIGELSKI [*furtively and slyly to* RAKITIN]. Well, Mikhail
Alexandrovich, would you like to be driven as far as the
main road?

RAKITIN. Does that mean you've got the horses already?

SHPIGELSKI. Vera Alexandrovna and I had a little talk . . . so
allow me . . .

RAKITIN. With pleasure! Anna Semyenovna, with your leave
. . . [*Bows to her.*]

ANNA [*still with dignity, not moving*]. Good-bye, Mikhail
Alexandrovich. Have a good journey.

RAKITIN. Many thanks. Lizaveta Bogdanovna . . . [*Bows to
her.*]

[LIZA *answers with a curtsey. Exit* RAKITIN.]

SHPIGELSKI [*goes to* ANNA'S *side*]. Good-bye, madam.

ANNA [*less dignified, but still stern*]. Ah, you're going too,
doctor?

SHPIGELSKI. Yes . . . patients, you know . . . And also, as
you can see, my presence here is no longer necessary.
[*Bowing himself out, he winks cunningly at* LIZA *who
smiles in return.*] Au revoir. [*Runs out after* RAKITIN.]

ANNA [*dismissing him, turns to* LIZA *and folds her arms*]. Well,
my dear, and what do you make of all this, eh?

LIZA [*sighing*]. I'm sure I don't know, madam . . . what can
I say?

ANNA. You heard that Beliayev's leaving, too . . . ?

LIZA [*sighing again*]. Oh but Anna Semyenovna, maybe I
shan't be staying here much longer, either . . . I'm leaving
as well.

[ANNA *looks at her with inexpressible astonishment.* LIZA
stands in front of her, not raising her eyes.]

ANTON CHEKHOV

1860–1904

ANTON CHEKHOV, more than any other dramatist of the late nineteenth and early twentieth centuries, was very conscious of the existential loneliness of the human condition. In fact, the central theme of all his plays is estrangement. He was conscious of man's helplessness before the overpowering forces of circumstance; he was aware of man's littleness, his insignificance in a gigantic and impersonal universe; he knew that no matter how closely men huddled together, they could never really communicate. In short, he know the utter impossibility of finding an answer to the question he asks in each of his plays: "What can I do?"

But this is not the whole story. If it were, Chekhov's plays would be little more than unrelieved pictures of gloom, and this we know they are not. This is so because Chekhov, in spite of his realization that man was alone and doomed to failure in all of his attempts to find meaningful relationship and meaningful action, never abdicated his sense of responsibility for human life. Even though Chekhov knew there were no solutions, all his life he sought to find an answer, and his plays are a record of that quest.

In all of his plays we are aware of Chekhov's regard for a certain nobility in the attempts by his characters to alter or overcome their pathetic destinies. Goethe once wrote: "It occurs to me that the hope of persisting, even after fate would seem to have led us back into a state of nonexistence, is the noblest of our sentiments." And this is the quality that informs Chekhov's characters. In all of them we are aware that there is a great disparity between the facts of their animal existence and the aspiring ideals by which they attempt to live. But Chekhov accepted both; he saw the life of a man as the meaningful and at the same time pathetic, ludicrous and tragic attempt to bridge this gap. This conflict is seen in his characters, who embody both a terrible earnestness of purpose and an awkward and ridiculous acting out of that purpose.

Chekhov's career, both as a dramatist and a physician, took its nourishment from a single source: his great capacity to observe and cherish life; not life as an abstraction or as an ideal, but as a doomed phenomenon of which he was a part. His tolerance, sympathy, wisdom and hard-headed vision made it possible for him to achieve, as few writers do, an unflinching but generous perspective on life; a perspective which is a victory over our absurdities, but a victory won at the cost of humility, and won in a spirit of charity and enlightenment.

FROM THE PERSONAL PAPERS

OF ANTON CHEKHOV[1]

Translated by Constance Garnett

TO ALEX P. CHEKHOV,[2] BABKIN: MAY 10, 1886

In my opinion a true description of nature should be very brief and have a character of relevance. Commonplaces such as, "the setting sun bathing in the waves of the darkening sea, poured its purple gold, etc."—"the swallows flying over the surface of the water twittered merrily,"—such commonplaces one ought to abandon. In descriptions of nature one ought to seize upon the little particulars, grouping them in such a way that, in reading, when you shut your eyes, you get a picture.

For instance, you will get the full effect of a moonlight night if you write that on the milldam a little glowing star point flashed from the neck of a broken bottle, and the round, black shadow of a dog, or a wolf, emerged and ran, etc.

In the sphere of psychology, details are also the thing. God preserve us from commonplaces. Best of all is it to avoid depicting the hero's state of mind; you ought to try to make it clear from the hero's actions. It is not necessary to portray many characters. The center of gravity should be in two persons: him and her. . . .

[1] Excerpts from the personal papers of Anton Chekhov are from *Letters to Friends and Family* by Anton Chekhov, translated by Constance Garnett. Reprinted by permission of Mr. David Garnett, A. P. Watt & Son, agents, and Chatto & Windus, executors of Mrs. Garnett's estate.

[2] Chekhov's older brother.

To A. S. Souvorin,[3] Sumi: May 30, 1888

. . . It seems to me that the writer of fiction should not try
to solve such questions as those of God, pessimism, etc. His
business is but to describe those who have been speaking or
thinking about God and pessimism, how, and under what
circumstances. The artist should be, not the judge of his
characters and their conversations, but only an unbiased witness. I once overhead a desultory conversation about pessimism
between two Russians; nothing was solved,—and my business
is to report the conversation exactly as I heard it, and let
the jury,—that is, the readers, estimate its value. My business
is merely to be talented, i.e., to be able to distinguish between
important and unimportant statements, to be able to illuminate
the characters and speak their language. Shcheglov-Leontyev[4]
finds fault with me because I concluded the story with the
phrase: "There's no way of making things out in this world!"
In his opinion an artist-psychologist *must* work things out,
for that is just why he is a psychologist. But I do not agree
with him. The time has come for writers, especially those who
are artists, to admit that in this world one cannot make anything out, just as Socrates once admitted it, just as Voltaire
admitted it. The mob think they know and understand everything; the more stupid they are, the wider, I think, do they
conceive their horizon to be. And if an artist in whom the
crowd has faith decides to declare that he understands nothing
of what he sees—this in itself constitutes a considerable
clarity in the realm of thought, and a great step forward.

To A. S. Souvorin, Moscow: October 27, 1888

In conversation with my literary colleagues I always insist that
it is not the artist's business to solve problems that require
a specialist's knowledge. It is a bad thing if a writer tackles
a subject he does not understand. We have specialists for
dealing with special questions: it is their business to judge
of the commune, of the future, of capitalism, of the evils of

[3] Russian critic and a close friend of Chekhov.
[4] A literary critic for several St. Petersburg newspapers.

drunkenness, of boots, of the diseases of women. An artist must judge only of what he understands, his field is just as limited as that of any other specialist—I repeat this and insist on it always. That in his sphere there are no questions, but only answers, can be maintained only by those who have never written and have had no experience of thinking in images. An artist observes, selects, guesses, combines—and this in itself presupposes a problem: unless he had set himself a problem from the very first there would be nothing to conjecture and nothing to select. To put it briefly, I will end by using the language of psychiatry: if one denies that creative work involves problems and purposes, one must admit that an artist creates without premeditation or intention, in a state of aberration; therefore, if an author boasted to me of having written a novel without a preconceived design, under a sudden inspiration, I should call him mad.

You are right in demanding that an artist should take an intelligent attitude to his work, but you confuse two things: *solving a problem* and *stating a problem correctly*. It is only the second that is obligatory for the artist. In *Anna Karenina* and *Eugen Onegin* not a single problem is solved, but they satisfy you completely because all the problems in these works are correctly stated. It is the business of the judge to put the right questions, but the answers must be given by the jury according to their own lights.

To A. S. Souvorin, Melikhovo: November 21, 1895

Well, I have finished with the play.[5] I began it *forte* and ended it *pianissimo*—contrary to all the rules of dramatic art. It has turned into a novel. I am rather dissatisfied than satisfied with it, and reading over my newborn play I am more convinced than ever that I am not a dramatist. The acts are very short. There are four of them. Though it is so far only the skeleton of a play, a plan which will be altered a million times before the coming season, I have ordered two copies to be typed and will send you one; only don't let anyone else read it. . . .

[5] *The Sea Gull.*

To V. E. Meyerhold[6]

Dear Vsevolod Emilevich, I have not at hand a copy of the text of Johannes' part,[7] and hence I can speak only in general terms. If you will send me the part, I shall read it through, refresh my memory, and give you the details. For the present I shall call your attention to a few things that may be of practical interest to you.

First of all, Johannes is very intelligent; he is a young scientist brought up in a university town. He lacks completely the elements of the bourgeois. He is a well-bred man, accustomed to the society of respectable people (like Anna); in his movements and appearance he is the tender and immature man reared in the bosom of a loving family and still his mother's pet. Johannes is a German scientist; he is, therefore, steady in his relations with men. On the other hand, he is as tender as a woman when in the company of women. As a typical illustration of these traits, there is the scene with his wife, in which he cannot help being tender toward her in spite of the fact that he already loves, or is beginning to love, Anna. Now as to the nervousness. One must not underline this nervous temperament, because the highly strung, neuropathological nature would hide and misrepresent the much more important loneliness—the loneliness experienced only by fine, and at the same time healthy (in the fullest sense of the word) organisms. Depict a lonely man, and represent him as nervous only to the extent indicated by the text. Do not treat this nervousness as a separate phenomenon. Remember that in our day every cultured man, even the most healthy, is most irritable in his own home and among his own family, because the discord between the present and the past is first of all apparent in the family. It is an irritability which is chronic, which has no pathos, and does not end in catastrophic consequences; it is an irritability that guests cannot perceive, and which, in its fullest force, is experienced first by the nearest relatives, the wife, the mother. It is, so to say, an intimate, family irritation and nervousness. Do not spend much time on

[6] Famous Russian director who was an actor at the Moscow Art Theatre when this letter was written.
[7] The letter refers to the performance of Hauptmann's *Lonely Lives* at the Moscow Art Theatre. Meyerhold played the part of Johannes. The letter, not dated, is found in the *Yearbook of the Imperial Theatres*, for 1909, No. 5.

it; present it only as *one* of many typical traits; do not stress it, or you will appear, not a lonely young man, but an irritable one. I know that Konstantin Sergeyevich[8] will insist on this superfluous nervousness; he exaggerates it—but do not yield; do not sacrifice the beauty and power of the voice for the sake of such a detail as the accent. Do not make the sacrifice, because in this case the irritation is only a detail.

To Maxim Gorky, Yalta: September 3, 1899

. . . More advice: when reading the proofs, cross out a host of concrete nouns and other words. You have so many such nouns that the reader's mind finds it a task to concentrate on them, and he soon grows tired. You understand it at once when I say, "The man sat on the grass;" you understand it because it is clear and makes no demands on the attention. On the other hand, it is not easily understood, and it is difficult for the mind, if I write, "A tall, narrow-chested, middle-sized man with a red beard sat on the green grass, already trampled by pedestrians—sat silently, shyly, and timidly looked about him." That is not immediately grasped by the mind, whereas good writing should be grasped at once, in a second. . . .

To Olga Knipper,[9] Yalta: January 2, 1900

I have not congratulated you on the success of *Lonely Lives*. I still dream that you will all come to Yalta, that I shall see *Lonely Lives* on the stage, and congratulate you really from my heart. I wrote to Meyerhold and urged him in my letter not to be too violent in the part of a nervous man. The immense majority of people are nervous, you know: the greater number suffer, and a small proportion feel acute pain; but where—in streets and in houses—do you see people tearing about, leaping up, and clutching at their heads? Suffering ought to be expressed as it is expressed in life—that is, not by the arms and legs, but by the tone and expression; not by gesticulation, but by grace. Subtle emotions of the soul in educated people must be subtly expressed in an external way. You will say—stage conditions. No conditions allow falsity. . . .

---

[8] Stanislavsky—co-founder and co-director of the Moscow Art Theatre.
[9] Famous actress in the Moscow Art Theatre and later Chekhov's wife.

To A. S. Souvorin, Melikhovo: November 25, 1892

You are not hard to understand and you abuse yourself need-lessly for expressing yourself vaguely. You are a hard drinker and I treated you to sweet lemonade; after downing it wryly, you remark with entire justice that it hasn't an alcoholic kick. That is just what our works haven't got—the kick that would make us drunk and hold us in their grasp, and this you set forth clearly. And why not? Leaving me and my "Ward No. 6" out of it, let's talk in general terms, which are more interesting. Let's talk of general causes, if it won't bore you, and let's embrace the whole age. Tell me in all conscience, what writers of my own generation, i.e., people from thirty to forty-five, have given the world even one drop of alcohol? Aren't Korolenko, Nadson, and all today's playwrights lemonade? Have Repin's or Shishkin's paintings really turned your head? All this work is just amiable and talented, and though you are delighted, you still can't forget you'd like a smoke. Science and technical knowledge are now experiencing great days, but for our brotherhood the times are dull, stale and frivolous, we ourselves are stale and dreary. . . . The causes for it are not to be found in our stupidity or lack of gifts and not in our insolence, as Burenin holds, but in a disease which in an artist is worse than syphilis or sexual impotence. Our illness is a lack of *something*, that is the rights of the case, and it means that when you lift the hem of our Muse's gown you will be-hold an empty void. Bear in mind that writers who are con-sidered immortal or just plain good and who intoxicate us have one very important trait in common: they are going somewhere and call you with them; you sense, not with your mind but with all your being, that they have an aim, like the ghost of Hamlet's father, who had a reason for appearing and alarming the imagination. Looking at some of them in terms of their calibre you will see that they have immediate aims—the abolition of serfdom, the liberation of their country, political matters, beauty, or just vodka, like Denis Davidov; others have remote aims—God, life beyond the grave, the happiness of mankind and so on. The best of them are realistic and paint life as it is, but because every line is saturated with juice, with the sense of life, you feel, in addition to life as it is, life as it should be, and you are entranced. Now what about us? Yes, us! We paint life such as it is—that's all, there isn't any more. . . . Beat us up, if you like, but that's as far as we'll go. We have neither immediate nor distant aims, and you can rattle around in our souls. We have no politics, we don't believe in revolution, we don't believe in God, we aren't afraid of ghosts, and personally I don't even fear death or blindness. He who doesn't desire anything, doesn't hope for anything and isn't afraid of anything cannot be an artist. It doesn't matter whether we call it a disease or not, the name doesn't matter, but we do have to admit that our situation is worse than a governor's. I don't know how it will be with us ten or twenty years hence, perhaps circumstances may change by then, but for the time being it would be rash to expect anything really good from us, regardless of whether or not we are gifted. We write mechanically, in submission to the old established order whereby some people are in government service, others in business and still others write. . . . You and Grigorovich hold that I am intelligent. Yes, I am intelligent in that at least I don't conceal my illness from myself, don't lie to myself and don't cover my own emptiness with other people's intellectual rags, like the ideas of the sixties and so on. I won't throw myself down a flight of stairs, like Garshin, but neither will I attempt to flatter myself with hopes of a better future. I am not to blame for my disease, and it is not for me to cure myself, as I have to assume this illness has good aims which are obscure to us and not inflicted without good reason. . . . "It wasn't just the weather that brought them together. . . ."

Well, sir, now as to the intellect. Grigorovich believes the mind can triumph over talent. Byron was as brilliant as a hundred devils, but it was his talent that made him immortal. If you tell me that X spoke nonsense because his intellect triumphed over his talent, or vice versa, I will reply that X had neither intellect nor talent. . . .

. . . The Heavens guard you!

To Olga Knipper, Yalta: September 30, 1899

At your bidding I am dashing off a reply to your letter, in which you ask me about Astrov's last scene with Yelena.[10] You tell me that in this scene Astrov's attitude toward Yelena

---

[10] Chekhov was speaking of *Uncle Vanya.*

is that of the most ardent man in love, that he "snatches at his feelings as a drowning man at a straw." But that is incorrect, absolutely incorrect! Astrov likes Yelena, her beauty takes his breath away, but by the last act he is already aware that the whole business is futile, that Yelena is vanishing forever from his sight—and so in this scene the tone he takes with her is the one he would use in discussing the heat in Africa, and he kisses her simply because that is all he has to do. If Astrov interprets this scene tempestuously, the entire mood of Act IV—a quiet and languid one—will be ruined. . . .

It has suddenly grown cold here, as if a Moscow wind had blown upon us. How I should like to be in Moscow, sweet actress! However, your head is in a whirl, you have become infected and are held in a spell—and you have no time for me. Now you will be able to say, "We are creating a stir, my friend!"

As I write I look out of an enormous window with a very extensive view, so magnificent it cannot be described. I shan't send you my photograph until I get yours, you serpent! I wouldn't think of calling you a "snake," as you say; you are a great big serpent, not a little snake. Now, isn't that flattering?

Well my dear, I press your hand, send my profound compliments and knock my forehead against the floor in worship, my most respected lady.

I am sending you another present soon.

TO JOSEPH TIKHOMIROV,[11] NICE: JANUARY 14, 1901

I have just received your letter—you have given me great pleasure and I thank you enormously. Here are the answers to your questions:

1. Irina does not know that Tusenbach is having a duel, but surmises that something went wrong that may have grave, not to say tragic, consequences. And when a woman guesses, she says, "I knew it, I knew it."

2. Chebutykin only sings the words, "Would it not please you to accept this date . . ." These are words from an operetta which was given some time ago at the Hermitage. I don't remember its title, but you can make inquiries, if you wish, from Shechtel the architect (private house, near the Yer-

---

[11] This letter refers, of course, to the characters in *The Three Sisters*.

molayev Church). Chebutykin must not sing anything else or his exit will be too prolonged.

3. Solyony actually believes he looks like Lermontov; but of course he doesn't—it is silly even to consider a resemblance. He should be made up to look like Lermontov. The likeness to Lermontov is immense, but only in the opinion of Solyony himself.

Forgive me if I haven't answered as I should, or satisfied you. There is nothing new with me, all goes along in the old way. I will probably return earlier than I thought, and it is very possible that in March I will already be at home, i.e., in Yalta.

Nobody writes me anything about the play; Nemirovich-Danchenko[12] never said a word about it when he was here and it seemed to me it bored him and wouldn't be successful. Your letter, for which I thank you, helped to dispel my melancholy. . . . I wish you good health and all the best.

To Konstantin Stanislavsky, Yalta: October 30, 1903

Thank you very much for the letter and for the telegram. Letters are always very precious to me because, one, I am here all alone, and two, I sent the play off three weeks ago and your letter came only yesterday; if it were not for my wife, I would have been entirely in the dark and would have imagined any old thing that might have crept into my head. When I worked on the part of Lopahin, I thought it might be for you. If for some reason it doesn't appeal to you, take Gayev. Lopahin, of course, is only a merchant, but he is a decent person in every sense, should conduct himself with complete decorum, like a cultivated man, without pettiness or trickery, and it did seem to me that you will be brilliant in this part, which is central for the play. (If you do decide to play Gayev, let Vishnevski play Lopahin. He won't make an artistic Lopahin but still he won't be a petty one. Lujski would be a cold-blooded foreigner in this part and Leonidov would play it like a little kulak. You mustn't lose sight of the fact that Varya, an earnest, devout young girl, is in love with Lopahin; she wouldn't love a little kulak.)

[12] Co-founder and co-director, with Stanislavsky, of the Moscow Art Theatre.

I want so much to go to Moscow but I don't know how I can get away from here. It is turning cold and I hardly ever leave the house; I am not used to fresh air and am coughing. I do not fear Moscow, or the trip itself, but I am afraid of having to stay in Sevastopol from two to eight, and in the most tedious company.

Write me what role you are taking for yourself. My wife wrote that Moskvin wants to play Epihodov. Why not, it would be a very good idea, and the play would gain from it.

My deepest compliments and regards to Maria Petrovna, and may I wish her and you all the best. Keep well and gay.

You know, I haven't yet seen *The Lower Depths* or *Julius Caesar*. I would so much like to see them.

To VLADIMIR NEMIROVICH-DANCHENKO, YALTA: NOVEMBER 2, 1903

Two letters from you in one day, thanks a lot! I don't drink beer, the last time I drank any was in July; and I cannot eat honey, as it gives me a stomachache. Now as to the play.

1. Anya can be played by any actress you'd like, even an utter unknown, if only she is young and looks like a young girl, and talks in a young, resonant voice. This role is not one of the important ones.

2. Varya's part is more on the serious side, if only Maria Petrovna would take it. If she doesn't the part will turn out rather flat and coarse, and I would have to do it over and soften it. M.P. won't repeat herself because, firstly, she is a gifted actress, and secondly, because Varya does not resemble Sonya or Natasha; she is a figure in a black dress, a little nunlike creature, somewhat simple-minded, plaintive and so forth and so on.

3. Gayev and Lopahin—have Stanislavsky try these parts and make his choice. If he takes Lopahin and feels at home in the part, the play is bound to be a success. Certainly if Lopahin is a pallid figure, played by a pallid actor, both the part and the play will fail.

4. Pishchik—the part for Gribunin. God have mercy on you if you assign the part to Vishnevski.

5. Charlotta—a big part. It would of course be impossible

to give the part to Pomyalova; Muratova might be good, perhaps, but not funny. This is the part for Mme. Knipper.

6. Epihodov—if Moskin wants the part let him have it. He'll be a superb Epihodov. . . .

7. Firs—the role for Artem.

8. Dunyasha—for Khalutina.

9. Yasha. If it is the Alexandrov you wrote about, the one that is assistant to your producer, let him have it. Moskvin would make a splendid Yasha. And I haven't anything against Leonidov for the part.

10. The passer-by—Gromov.

11. The stationmaster who reads "The Sinner" in Act III should have a bass voice.

Charlotta speaks with a good accent, not broken Russian, except that once in a while she gives a soft sound to a consonant at the end of a word rather than the hard sound that is proper, and she mixes masculine and feminine adjectives. Pishchik is an old Russian fellow broken down with gout, old age and satiety, plump, dressed in a long Russian coat (à la Simov) and boots without heels. Lopahin wears a white vest and tan shoes, flails his arms when he is in motion, takes long strides, is lost in thought when he moves about and walks in a straight line. He doesn't cut his hair short and so he frequently tosses his head back; in reflection he strokes his beard back and forth, i.e., from his neck to his lips. I think Trofimov is clearly sketched. Varya wears a black dress and wide belt.

I have been intending to write *The Cherry Orchard* these past three years and for three years have been telling you to hire an actress who could play a part like Lyubov Andreyevna. This long waiting game never pays.

I have got into the stupidest position: I am here alone and don't know why. But you are unjust in saying that despite your work it is "Stanislavsky's theatre." You are the one that people speak about and write about while they do nothing but criticize Stanislavsky for his performance of Brutus. If you leave the theatre, so will I. Gorky is younger than we and has his own life to lead. As to the Nizhni-Novgorod theatre, this is only an episode in his life; Gorky will try it, sniff at it and cast it aside. I may say in this connection that people's theatres and people's literature are plain foolishness, something to sweeten up the people. Gogol shouldn't be pulled down to the people, but the people raised to Gogol's level.

I would like so much to visit the Hermitage Restaurant, eat some sturgeon and drink a bottle of wine. Once I drank a bottle of champagne solo and didn't get drunk, then I had some cognac and didn't get drunk either.

I'll write you again and in the meantime send my humble greetings and thanks. Was it Lujski's father that died? I read about it in the paper today.

Why does Maria Petrovna insist on playing Anya? And why does Maria Fyodorovna think she is too aristocratic to play Varya? Isn't she playing in *The Lower Depths*, after all? Well, the devil take them. I embrace you, keep well.

UNCLE VANYA

by ANTON CHEKHOV

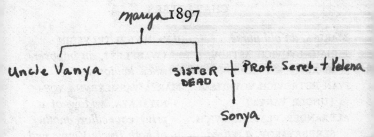

marya 1897

Uncle Vanya — SISTER DEAD + PRof. Sereb. + Yelena

Sonya

DOC. ASTROV

UNCLE VANYA[1]

Translated by Robert W. Corrigan

CHARACTERS

MARINA, *an old nurse*

MIHAIL LVOVICH ASTROV, *a doctor*

IVAN PETROVICH VOYNITSKY (UNCLE VANYA)

ALEXANDER VLADIMIROVICH SEREBRYAKOV, *a retired professor*

YELENA ANDREYEVNA, *his wife*

SOFYA ALEXANDROVNA (SONYA), *his daughter by his first wife*

ILYA ILYICH TELYEGIN (WAFFLES), *an impoverished landowner*

MARYA VASSILYEVNA VOYNITAKAYA, *widow of a privy councillor, mother of both Uncle Vanya and the professor's first wife*

A WORKMAN

SCENE

Serebryakov's estate.

[1] *Uncle Vanya* by Anton Chekhov, from *Six Plays by Chekhov*, edited and translated by Robert W. Corrigan. Copyright © 1962 by Robert W. Corrigan. Reprinted by permission of the translator and the publisher, Holt, Rinehart and Winston, Inc.

ACT ONE

MARINA [*pouring a cup of tea*]. Here, my friend, drink a cup of tea.

ASTROV [*reluctantly taking the cup*]. For some reason I don't seem to care for any.

MARINA. Would you rather have some vodka?

ASTROV. No, I don't drink vodka every day. And besides, the day is too hot and stifling for it. [*A pause.*] Tell me, old nurse, how long have we known each other?

MARINA [*pondering and thoughtfully*]. Let me see, how long is it? God only knows. You first came into these parts, let me see—when was it? Well, Sonya's mother was still alive— she died two years later; that was at least eleven years ago. . . . [*Pondering.*] perhaps even longer.

ASTROV. Have I changed much since then?

MARINA. Oh, yes. You were young and handsome then, and now you seem like an old man. And you drink too.

ASTROV. Yes . . . ten years have made another man of me. And why? Because I am overworked. Do you know, nurse, that I am on my feet from morning till night? I don't know what it is to rest; at night I hide in bed trembling under the blankets in the continual fear that I'll be dragged out to visit someone who is sick. Ever since I have known you, I haven't had a single day all to myself. No wonder I am growing old, how could I help it? And besides, life is tedious; it is senseless, dirty, stupid, and it just drags on and on . . . [*Pause.*] . . . and finally it swallows you up. [*Pause.*] Everyone around here is commonplace, and after you live with them for a couple of years, you, too, become commonplace and queer. It's inevitable. [*Twisting his mustache.*] See what a long mustache I have. A foolish, long mustache. Yes, I am just as silly as all the others, nurse, just as trivial, but not as stupid; no . . . I have not grown stupid. Thank God, my brain is not muddled yet, though my feelings have grown dull. There's nothing I want, there's nothing I need, there's no one I love, except, perhaps, you. [*He kisses her head.*] When I was a little boy, I had a nurse just like you.

MARINA. Don't you want just a little something to eat?

ASTROV. No. During the third week of Lent, a typhoid epidemic broke out in the village, and I had to go. The peasants were all stretched out side by side in their huts, and the calves and the pigs were running about among the sick and the dying. How dirty and filthy it was, and the stench of the smoke, ugh, it was unbearable! I slaved among those people all day, and I didn't have a thing to eat. And then when I returned home there was still no rest for me: a switchman was carried in from the railroad; I laid him on the operating table and he died in my arms under the chloroform. And then, my feelings, which should have been deadened, awoke again; my conscience tortured me as if I had murdered the man. I sat down and closed my eyes—like this—and thought: will those who come after us two hundred years from now, those for whom we are breaking the path . . . will they remember us with grateful hearts? No, nurse, they will forget.

MARINA. Man forgets, but God remembers.

ASTROV. Thank you for that. You spoke the truth.

[*Enter* VANYA *from the house. He has been asleep after dinner and looks somewhat disheveled. He sits down on the bench and straightens his tie.*]

VANYA. H'mm. Yes. [*A pause.*] Yes.

ASTROV. Have a good nap?

VANYA. Yes, very good. [*He yawns.*] Ever since the Professor and his wife came, our daily routine seems to have gone haywire. I sleep at the wrong time, drink too much wine, and I eat the wrong kind of food. It's no good. Sonya and I used to work together and we never had an idle moment. But now she works alone and I . . . I just eat and drink and sleep. Something is wrong.

MARINA [*shaking her head*]. Such confusion in the house! The Professor gets up at twelve, the samovar has to be kept boiling all morning, and everything has to wait for him. Before they came we used to have dinner at one o'clock, like everybody else, but now we eat at seven. The Professor sits up all night writing and reading or something, and suddenly, at two o'clock, the bell rings. Heavens, what's that? The Professor wants tea! Wake up the servants, light the samovar! Lord, what disorder!

ASTROV. Will they be here long?

VANYA [*whistling*]. A hundred years! The Professor has decided to stay here for good.

MARINA. Just look at this, for instance! The samovar has been boiling away on the table for two hours now, and they've gone out for a walk!

VANYA [*calming her brusquely*]. Here they are—here they are —don't get so excited.

[*Voices are heard.* SEREBRYAKOV, YELENA, SONYA, *and* TELYEGIN *enter from the garden, returning from their walk.*]

SEREBRYAKOV. Superb! Superb! What glorious views!

TELYEGIN. They are lovely, your excellency.

SONYA. Tomorrow we shall go to the woods, shall we, father?

VANYA. Ladies and Gentlemen, tea is served.

SEREBRYAKOV. Won't you please send my tea into the library? I have something to do . . . ah, some work to finish.

SONYA. I am sure you will love the woods, father.

[YELENA, SEREBRYAKOV, *and* SONYA *go into the house.* TELYEGIN *takes a seat at the table beside* MARINA.]

VANYA. It is hot and humid, but our eminent scholar walks about in his overcoat and galoshes, wearing gloves and carrying an umbrella.

ASTROV. Which means that he takes good care of himself.

VANYA. But how lovely she is! How lovely! I have never seen a more beautiful woman.

TELYEGIN. Whether I drive through the fields or take a walk under the shady trees in the garden, or look at this table I experience a feeling of indescribable bliss! The weather is enchanting, the birds are singing; we all live in peace and harmony . . . what else do we want? [*Taking a cup of tea.*] Oh, thank you.

VANYA [*dreaming*]. Such eyes—a glorious woman!

ASTROV. Come, Vanya, tell us something.

VANYA [*indolently*]. What shall I tell you?

ASTROV. Haven't you any news for us?

VANYA. No, it is all old. I am the same as ever, no . . . worse, for I've become lazy. I do nothing any more but grumble like an old crow. My mother, the old magpie, is still babbling about the emancipation of women, with one eye on her grave and the other on her learned books, in which she is forever rummaging in the hopes of finding the dawn of a new life.

ASTROV. And the Professor?

VANYA. The Professor as usual sits in his study reading and
writing from morning till night . . .

> "Straining our mind, wrinkling our brow,
> We write, write, write,
> With no respite
> Or hope of praise in the future or now."

Oh, poor unfortunate paper! He ought to write his autobiography; he would make such an excellent subject for a
book! Just think, the life of a retired professor, as stale
as a piece of mildewed bread, racked with gout, headaches,
and rheumatism, his heart bursting with jealousy and envy,
living on the estate of his first wife, although he hates it,
because he can't afford to live in town. He is always whining about his hard fate, although as a matter of fact, he is
extraordinarily lucky. [*Nervously.*] He is the son of a
common, ordinary parson and has achieved a professor's
chair, has become the son-in-law of a senator, is called
"your excellency," but forget it! I'll tell you something; he's
been writing about art for twenty-five years, and he doesn't
know the first thing about it. For twenty-five years he has
been hashing over the thoughts of other men on realism,
naturalism, and all the other nonsensical "isms"; for twenty-
five years he has been pouring water from one empty glass
into another. Yet . . . consider the man's conceit and pre-
tensions! He has been pensioned off . . . Not a living soul
has ever heard of him. He is totally unknown. He is a
nothing. That means that for twenty-five years he has been
treating life as if it were a masquerade ball, and all that it
has accomplished is to have kept a better man out of a
job. But just look at him! He struts across the earth like
a demigod!

ASTROV. You know, I believe you envy him.

VANYA. Yes, I do. Look at the success he's had with women!
Don Juan himself was no luckier. His first wife, my sister,
was beautiful, gentle, as pure as the blue sky, generous, with
more suitors than the number of all his pupils put together
and she loved him as only creatures of angelic purity can
love those who are as pure and beautiful as they are themselves. My mother adores him to this day, and he still in-
spires her with a kind of worshipful awe. And now his
second wife is, as you can plainly see, a great beauty, and
she is intelligent too; and yet she married him in his old

age and surrendered to him all the glory of her beauty and freedom. For what? . . . Why?

ASTROV. Is she faithful to him?

VANYA. Yes, unfortunately she is.

ASTROV. Why "unfortunately"?

VANYA. Because such fidelity is false and unnatural. Oh, it sounds very good, but there is no rhyme nor reason to it. It is immoral for a woman to deceive and endure an old husband whom she hates. But for her to stifle her pathetic youth, those intense longings within her heart—her feelings . . . that is not immoral!

TELYEGIN [*in a tearful voice*]. Vanya, don't talk like that. Really, you know, anyone who is unfaithful to their wife or husband is a disloyal person and will betray his country, too!

VANYA [*crossly*]. Oh, Waffles, dry up!

TELYEGIN. No, allow me, Vanya. My wife ran away with a lover the day after our wedding, because of my . . . ah . . . rather unprepossessing appearance. Since then I have never failed to do my duty. I love her and am true to her to this day. I help her all I can and I've given my fortune to educate the children she had by her lover. I have lost my happiness, but I have kept my pride. And she? Her youth has fled, her beauty has faded according to the laws of nature, and her lover is dead. What does she have left?

[YELENA *and* SONYA *enter, followed by* MARYA *carrying a book. The latter sits down and begins to read. Someone hands her a cup of tea which she drinks without looking up.*]

SONYA [*hurriedly to the nurse*]. Some peasants are waiting inside. Go and see what they want. I'll look after the tea.

[*She pours out several cups.* MARINA *goes out.* YELENA *takes a cup and sits drinking in the swing.*]

ASTROV [*to* YELENA]. I came to see your husband. You wrote me saying he is very ill, that he has rheumatism and what not, but he seems fine, as lively as ever.

YELENA. He had a fit of depression last night and complained of pains in his legs, but he seems all right again today.

ASTROV. And I hurried twenty miles at breakneck speed to get here! But never mind, it isn't the first time. However, now that I am here, I am going to stay until tomorrow; for the first time in ages I am going to sleep as long as I want.

SONYA. Oh, wonderful! You spend the night with us so seldom.
Have you eaten yet?

ASTROV. No.

SONYA. Fine, then you will have dinner with us. We don't
eat until seven now. [*Drinks her tea.*] Oh, the tea is cold!

TELYEGIN. Yes, the samovar has gone out.

YELENA. Never mind, Ivan, we'll just have to drink it cold.

TELYEGIN. I beg your pardon, madam, my name is not Ivan,
it's Ilya, Ilya Telyegin, or Waffles, as some people call me
because of my pock-marked face. I am Sonya's godfather,
and his excellency, your husband, knows me very well. I
now live here on this estate; perhaps, sometime you will be
good enough to notice that I dine with you every day.

SONYA. He is a great help to us—our right-hand man.
[*Tenderly.*] Dear godfather, let me pour you some more tea.

MARYA. Oh! Oh!

SONYA. What is it, grandmother?

MARYA. I forgot to tell Alexander—I must be losing my
memory—I received a letter today from Paul in Kharkov.
He sent me a new pamphlet.

ASTROV. Is it interesting?

MARYA. Yes, but it is so strange. He refutes the very theories
he defended seven years ago. Isn't that queer; in fact, it's
appalling.

VANYA. Oh, there is nothing so appalling about it. Drink your
tea, mother.

MARYA. But I have something to say, I want to talk.

VANYA. But that is all we have been doing for the last fifty
years: talk, read a few pamphlets, and talk some more . . .
talk. Talk. It's time to quit all that nonsense.

MARYA. It seems that you never want to listen to what I have
to say. If you will pardon me, Jean, you have changed so
much this last year that I hardly know you. You used to
be a man of strong convictions and had such an illuminating
personality . . .

VANYA. Oh, yes, to be sure. I had an illuminating personality.
I had elevated ideas, which illuminated or elevated no one.
[*A pause.*] I am forty-seven years old. Until last year I
tried, as you still do, to blind my eyes with meaningless
pedantry to the truths of life. Yes, I did it on purpose, to
avoid seeing life as it really is . . . and I thought I was
doing the right thing. But now . . . Oh, if you only knew!
If you knew how I lie awake at night, heartsick and angry,

to think how stupidly I wasted my time when I might have
been taking from life everything which is now denied me
because I am old.

SONYA. Uncle Vanya, how dreary!

MARYA [to her son]. You talk as if your former convictions
were somehow to blame, but you yourself, not they, were
at fault. You have forgotten that a conviction, in itself, is
nothing but a dead letter. You should have done something.

VANYA. Done something! It isn't every man who is capable of
being a . . . a writing machine like your dear professor.

MARYA. What do you mean by that?

SONYA [imploringly]. Grandmother! Uncle Vanya! Please!

VANYA. I am silent. I apologize and am silent.

[A pause.]

YELENA. What a fine day! Not too hot.

[A pause.]

VANYA. Yes, a fine day to hang oneself.

[TELYEGIN tunes his guitar. MARINA appears near the house,
calling the chickens.]

MARINA. Here chick, chick, here chick!

SONYA. What did the peasants want, nurse?

MARINA. The same old thing, the same old nonsense. Here
chick, chick!

SONYA. Why are you calling the chickens?

MARINA. The speckled hen disappeared with her chicks. I'm
afraid the hawks might get them.

[TELYEGIN plays a polka. Everyone listens in silence. A workman enters.]

WORKMAN. Is the doctor here? [To ASTROV.] Please, Dr.
Astrov, I've been sent for you.

ASTROV. Where do you come from?

WORKMAN. The factory.

ASTROV [annoyed]. Thank you. I suppose I shall have to go
whether I want to or not. [Looking around him for his cap.]
Damn it, this is annoying.

SONYA. Oh, yes, it is too bad. You must come back from the
factory for dinner.

ASTROV. No, I shan't be able to do that. It will be too late. Now where, where—[*To the* WORKMAN.] Look here, good fellow, get me a glass of vodka, will you?

[*The* WORKMAN *goes out.*]

Where—where [*Finds his cap.*] There is a man in one of Ostrovsky's plays, with a long mustache and short wits, like me. However, let me bid you good night, ladies and gentlemen. [*To* YELENA.] I should be most delighted if you came to see me some day with Sonya. My place is small, but if you are interested in such things—things like terraced gardens, sapling beds, and nurseries, the likes of which you'll not find within a thousand miles of here—I'd like to show them to you. My estate is surrounded by government forests. But the old forester is always sick and complains so, that I take care of most of the work myself.

YELENA. I have always heard that you were very fond of the woods. Of course you can do a great deal of good by helping to preserve them, but doesn't that work interfere with your real calling? You're a doctor, aren't you?

ASTROV. God alone can know what a man's real work is.

YELENA. And you find it interesting?

ASTROV. Yes, very.

VANYA [*sarcastically*]. Oh, extremely.

YELENA. You are still young, I should say certainly not over thirty-six or seven, and I have an idea that the woods do not interest you as much as you claim. I should think that you would find them quite monotonous.

SONYA. Dr. Astrov plants new forests every year, and he has been awarded a bronze medal and a diploma. He does his best to prevent the destruction of the forests. If you listen to him you will agree with him entirely. He claims that forests beautify the earth, and so teach man to understand the beautiful and instill in him a feeling of respect and awe. Forests temper the severity of the climate. In countries where the climate is warmer, less energy is wasted on the struggle with nature and that is why man there is more gentle and loving; the people there are beautiful, supple and sensitive, their speech is refined and their movements graceful. Art and learning flourish among them, their philosophy is not so depressing, and they treat women with refinement and nobility.

ecologist

VANYA [*laughing*]. Bravo! bravo! All this is charming, but not convincing, and so, [*To* ASTROV.] I hope you'll permit me, my friend, to go on burning logs in my stove and building my barns with wood.

ASTROV. You can burn peat in your stoves and build your barns of stone. Oh, I don't object, of course, to cutting wood when you have to, but why destroy the forests? The woods of Russia are trembling under the blows of the axe. Millions of trees have perished. The homes of the wild animals and the birds have been laid desolate; the rivers are shrinking, and many beautiful landscapes are gone forever. And why? Because men are too lazy and stupid to bend over and pick up their fuel from the ground. [*To* YELENA.] Am I wrong? Who but a senseless savage could burn so much beauty in his stove and destroy what he cannot create himself? Man has reason and creative powers so that he may increase that which has been given to him. Until now, however, he has not created, he has only destroyed. The forests are disappearing, the rivers are drying up, the game is being exterminated, the climate is spoiled, and the earth becomes poorer and more ugly every day. [*To* VANYA.] Oh, I read irony in your eyes; you do not take seriously what I am saying; and—and—perhaps I am talking nonsense. But when I cross those peasant forests which I have saved from the axe, or hear the rustling of the young trees, which I have set out with my own hands, I feel as if I had had some small share in improving the climate, and that if mankind is happy a thousand years from now I shall have been partly responsible in my small way for their happiness. When I plant a young birch tree and see it budding and swaying in the wind, my heart swells with pride and I . . . [*Sees the* WORK-MAN, *who is bringing him a glass of vodka on a tray.*] However . . . [*He drinks.*] . . . I must be off. Probably it is all nonsense, anyhow. Good-bye.

SONYA. When are you coming to see us again?

ASTROV. I don't know.

SONYA. In a month?

[ASTROV *and* SONYA *go into the house.* YELENA *and* VANYA *walk over to the terrace.*]

YELENA. Vanya, you have been behaving impossibly again. What sense was there in irritating your mother with all

your talk about her pamphlets and the "writing machine."
And this morning you quarreled with Alexander, again.
How petty and small it all is!

VANYA. But suppose I hate him?

YELENA. You hate Alexander without reason; he is like everyone else, and no worse than you.

VANYA. If you could only see your face, your every movement
and gesture! Oh, how tedious your life must be!

YELENA. Yes, it is tedious, and dreary, too! All of you abuse
my husband and look on me with compassion; you think,
"Poor woman, she is married to an old man." How well I
understand your sympathy and compassion! As Astrov said
just now, see how thoughtlessly you destroy the forests,
so that soon there will be nothing left on earth. In just the
same way you recklessly destroy human beings, and soon,
thanks to you, loyalty and purity and self-sacrifice will have
vanished along with the woods. Why can't you look with
calm indifference at a woman unless she belongs to you?
Because . . . the doctor is right. You are all possessed by a
devil of destructiveness; you have no feeling, no, not even
pity, for either the woods or the birds or women, or for
one another.

VANYA. Would you mind stopping all this philosophizing; I
don't like it.

[A pause.]

YELENA. That doctor has a sensitive, weary face . . . an interesting face. Sonya evidently likes him; she is in love with
him, and I can understand her feeling. [Pause.] This is
the third time he has been here since I have come, and I
have not had a real talk with him yet or showed him much
attention. He thinks I am disagreeable. Do you know,
Vanya, why you and I are such friends? I think it is because
we are both lonely and tiresome and unsympathetic.
[Pause.] Yes, unsympathetic. [Pause.] Don't look at me that
way, I don't like it.

VANYA. How can I look at you in any other way since I love
you? You are my joy, my life, my youth. I know that my
chances of your loving me in return are infinitely small
. . . no . . . they are nil, nonexistent; there are no chances,
but I ask nothing of you, I want nothing. Only let me look
at you, listen to you . . .

YELENA. Quiet! Someone may hear you.

VANYA. Let me tell you of my love; don't drive me away. I have no other happiness.

YELENA. Oh, this is agony!

[*Both go into the house.* TELYEGIN *strums the strings of his guitar and plays a polka.* MARYA *writes something on the leaves of her pamphlet.*]

ACT TWO

[*The dining room of* SEREBRYAKOV'S *house. It is night. The click of the watchman's rattle is heard from the garden.* SEREBRYAKOV *sits dozing in an armchair by an open window and* YELENA, *likewise half asleep, is seated beside him.*]

SEREBRYAKOV [*rousing himself*]. Who's there? Is that you, Sonya?

YELENA. It is I.

SRERBRYAKOV. Oh, it's you, Lenotchka. This pain is unbearable.

YELENA. Your blanket has slipped. [*She wraps the blanket around his legs.*] Let me shut the window.

SEREBRYAKOV. No, leave it open; I am suffocating as it is. [*Pause.*] I just dropped off to sleep . . . and . . . I dreamt that my left leg belonged to someone else, and the pain was so agonizing that I awoke. I don't believe this is gout; it is more like rheumatism. [*Pause.*] What time is it?

YELENA. Twenty after twelve.

[*Pause.*]

SEREBRYAKOV. I wish you'd look for Batushkov tomorrow morning; we used to have him, I remember. Oh, why do I find it so hard to breathe?

YELENA. You're exhausted; this is the second night you've been unable to sleep.

SEREBRYAKOV. They say that Turgenev got heart trouble from gout. I'm afraid I'm getting it, too. Oh, damn this terrible, accursed old age! Ever since I've grown old, I have been hateful to myself, and, I'm sure, hateful to all of you, too.

YELENA. You talk as if we were to blame for your old age.

SEREBRYAKOV. I am more hateful to you than to all the others.

[YELENA *gets up, walks away from him and sits down at a distance.*]

You are right, of course. I'm no fool; I can understand. You are young and healthy and beautiful. You want and long for life, and I am an old dotard, almost a corpse. Oh, I know it! Certainly, I see that it's foolish for me to go on

[186]

living for such a long time, but wait! I shall soon set you all free. My life can't drag on too much longer.

YELENA. For God's sake, be quiet! . . . You are exhausting me.

SEREBRYAKOV. It seems that everybody is being exhausted, thanks to me. Everybody is miserable and depressed; everyone's youth is wasting away; only I am enjoying life in blissful triumph. Oh, yes, of course!

YELENA. Be quiet! You're torturing me.

SEREBRYAKOV. Why of course, I torture everybody.

YELENA [on the verge of tears]. This is unbearable! Please, just tell me what you want me to do?

SEREBRYAKOV. Nothing.

YELENA. Then please be quiet.

SEREBRYAKOV. It's funny that everybody listens to Vanya and his old fool of a mother, but the moment I open my mouth, you all begin to feel abused. You can't even bear the sound of my voice. Suppose I am hateful, suppose I am a selfish and egocentric tyrant, haven't I the right to be at my age? Haven't I deserved it? Haven't I, I ask you, the right to be respected, the right to be pampered and cared for . . .

YELENA. No one is disputing your rights.

[The window slams in the wind.]

The wind is rising, I must shut the window. [She shuts it.] We shall have rain in a few minutes. [Pause.] Your rights have never been questioned by anybody.

[The watchman in the garden clicks his rattle.]

SEREBRYAKOV. I have spent my life working for the cause of learning. I am accustomed to my study, the library and the lecture hall and to the regard and admiration of my colleagues. And, now . . . [Pause.] . . . now, I suddenly find myself in this wilderness, in this vault, condemned to see the same stupid people from morning till night and to listen to their inane talk. I want to live; I long for success and fame and the tension of an active world, and here I am in exile! Oh, it's terrible to spend every moment grieving for a past that is lost, to witness the success of others and to sit here with nothing to do but fear death. I can't stand it! It's more than I can endure. And you, you won't even forgive me for being old!

YELENA. Wait; be patient; in four or five years, I shall be old too.

[SONYA *comes in.*]

SONYA. Father, you sent for Dr. Astrov, and now you refuse
    to see him. It is not fair to needlessly trouble a busy man.
SEREBRYAKOV. Oh, what do I care about your Astrov? He
    knows as much about medicine as I do about astronomy.
SONYA. We can't send for famous specialists to come here to
    cure your gout, can we?
SEREBRYAKOV. I refuse to talk to that madman.
SONYA. Do as you wish then. It makes no difference to me.
    [*She sits down.*]
SEREBRYAKOV. What time is it?
YELENA. One o'clock.
SEREBRYAKOV. It's stifling in here . . . Sonya, hand me that
    bottle there on the table.
SONYA [*handing him a bottle of medicine*]. Here you are.
SEREBRYAKOV [*cross and irritated*]. No, not that one! Don't
    you ever understand? Can't I ask you to do a single thing?
SONYA. Please don't be cross with me. Some people may enjoy
    it, but spare me, if you please, because I don't like it.
    Furthermore, I haven't time for it; we are planning to cut
    the hay tomorrow and I have to get up early.

[VANYA *enters dressed in a long gown and carrying a candle.*]

VANYA. A thunderstorm is on its way.

[*The lightning flashes.*]

    There it is! Sonya, you and Yelena had better go and get
    some sleep. I have come to relieve you.
SEREBRYAKOV [*frightened*]. No, no, no! Don't leave me alone
    with him! Oh please don't. He will begin lecturing me
    again.
VANYA. But you must let them have a little rest. They haven't
    slept for two nights now.
SEREBRYAKOV. All right, then let them go to bed, but, please,
    you go away, too! Thank you. I beg of you please to go
    away . . . For the sake of . . . ah . . . our former friendship,
    don't argue. We'll talk some other time . . .
VANYA. Our former friendship! Our former . . .
SONYA. Shh, please be quiet, Uncle Vanya!
SEREBRYAKOV [*to his wife*]. My love, don't leave me alone
    with him. He will begin his infernal lecturing.
VANYA. This is absurd.

[MARINA *comes in carrying a candle.*]

SONYA. You must go to bed, nurse, it's late.

MARINA. I haven't cleaned up the tea things. I can't go to bed yet.

SEREBRYAKOV. No one can. Everyone is completely worn out. I alone enjoy perfect peace and happiness.

MARINA [*going up to* SEREBRYAKOV *and speaking tenderly*]. What's the matter, little man? Does it hurt? My own legs ache, too, oh, such pain. [*She arranges the blanket around his legs.*] You've been sick like this for such a long time. Sonya's mother used to sit up with you night after night, too, and she wore herself out for you. She loved you dearly. [*A pause.*] Old people like to be pitied as much as small children, but somehow nobody cares about them. [*She kisses* SEREBRYAKOV's *shoulder.*] Come to bed, my little man, let me give you some linden tea and warm your poor feet. I shall pray to God for you.

SEREBRYAKOV [*moved*]. Let us go, Marina.

MARINA. My own feet ache so badly, too, oh, so badly! [*She and* SONYA *start leading* SEREBRYAKOV *out.*] Sonya's mother used to wear herself out with sorrow and weeping over you. You were still a small and senseless child then, Sonya. Come along now, come along . . .

[SEREBRYAKOV, MARINA, *and* SONYA *go out.*]

YELENA. He so completely exhausts me, that I can hardly stand up.

VANYA. He has exhausted you and I have exhausted myself. I haven't had a bit of sleep for three nights now.

YELENA. There's something wrong in this house. Your mother hates everything but her pamphlets and the Professor; the Professor is vexed and irritated, he won't trust me and he fears you; Sonya is angry with her father and also with me, and she hasn't spoken to me for two weeks; you hate my husband and openly sneer at your mother. I have reached the limit of my endurance . . . there is no strength left, why I've nearly burst into tears at least twenty times today. There is something wrong in this house.

VANYA. Oh, why don't you stop all your speculating.

YELENA. You are a cultured and intelligent man, Vanya. Certainly you must understand that the world is not destroyed by criminals and fires, but by hate and malice and all this spiteful gossiping and petty wrangling. Your duty is to make peace; your work should be to reconcile everyone and not to growl at everything.

VANYA [*seizing her hand*]. My darling! First, help me to make peace with myself.

YELENA. Let go! [*She drags her hand away.*] Go away!

VANYA. The rain will soon be over, and all nature will awake refreshed. Only I am not refreshed by the storm. Night and day I am haunted by the thought that my life has been hopelessly wasted and is lost forever. My past doesn't count, because I frittered it away on trifles, and the present is so grotesque in its senselessness. What shall I do with my life and my love? What is going to become of them? This glorious passion in my heart will be lost as a ray of sunlight is lost in a dark chasm, and my life will be lost with it.

YELENA. It's just as if I were benumbed when you speak to me of your love, and I don't know how to answer you. Forgive me, I have nothing to say to you. [*She tries to leave.*] Good night!

VANYA [*barring her way*]. If you only knew how it tortures me to think that beside me in this house is another life that is being wasted and is lost forever—yours! What are you waiting for? What accursed philosophy, what damn theory, stands in your way? Oh, understand, understand . . .

YELENA [*looking at him intently*]. Ivan Petrovich, you are drunk.

VANYA. Perhaps . . . perhaps.

YELENA. Where is the doctor?

VANYA. In there. He is going to stay with me tonight. [*Pause.*] Perhaps I am drunk . . . yes, perhaps I am; nothing is impossible.

YELENA. Have you been drinking together? What for?

VANYA. Because in that way at least I experience a semblance of life. Let me do that, Yelena!

YELENA. You never used to drink and you never used to talk so much. Go to bed! You bore me!

VANYA [*falling on his knees before her*]. My darling . . . my precious, beautiful one . . .

YELENA [*angrily*]. Leave me alone! Really, this has become too disgusting. [*She leaves.*]

VANYA [*alone*]. She is gone! [*A pause.*] It was ten years ago that I first met her at her sister's house. She was seventeen and I thirty-seven. Why didn't I fall in love with her then

and propose to her? It would have been so easy . . . then!
And if I had, she would now be my wife. Yes, tonight's
thunderstorm would have awakened us both. But I would
have held her in my arms and whispered: "Don't be afraid!
I am here." Oh, bewitching dream, so sweet that I smile
when I think of it. [*He laughs.*] But, my God! Why are
my thoughts so entangled? Why am I so old? Why won't
she understand me? I despise all that rhetoric of hers, that
indolent morality, that absurd talk about the destruction
of the world . . . [*A pause.*] Oh, how I have been deceived!
For years I have worshiped and slaved for that miserable
gout-ridden professor. Sonya and I have milked this estate
dry for his sake. We have sold our butter and cheese and
wheat like misers, and never kept a bit for ourselves, so
that we could scrape together enough pennies to send to
him. I was proud of him and his learning; I thought all his
words and writings were inspired; he was my life . . . the
very breath of my being. And now? My God . . . Now he
has retired, and what is the grand total of his life? A blank!
Nothing! He is absolutely unknown, and his fame has burst
like a soapbubble. I have been deceived; I see that now,
basely deceived.

[ASTROV *enters. He is wearing his coat but is without waistcoat
or collar and is slightly drunk.* TELYEGIN *follows him, carrying a guitar.*]

ASTROV. Play something!
TELYEGIN. But everyone is asleep.
ASTROV. Play!

[TELYEGIN *begins to play softly.*]

ASTROV. Are you alone? No women around? [*Sings with his
arms akimbo.*]

"The room is cold, the fire is out.
How shall the master cure his gout?"

The thunderstorm woke me. It was a torrential downpour.
What time is it?
VANYA. The devil only knows.
ASTROV. I thought I heard Yelena's voice.
VANYA. She was here a moment ago.
ASTROV. What a beautiful woman! [*Looking at the bottles of
medicine.*] Medicine, is it? What an assortment of pre-

scriptions we have! From Moscow, from Kharkov, from Tula! Why, he has been bothering every city in Russia with his pains! Is he really sick, or simply pretending?

VANYA. He is very ill.

[*Pause.*]

ASTROV. What's the matter with you tonight? You seem gloomy —so melancholic. Is it because you feel sorry for the Professor?

VANYA. Leave me alone.

ASTROV. Or are you in love with the Professor's wife?

VANYA. She is my friend.

ASTROV. Already?

VANYA. What do you mean by "already"?

[TELYEGIN *stops playing to listen.*]

ASTROV. A woman can be a man's friend only after having been his acquaintance and then his mistress . . . then she becomes his friend.

VANYA. What coarse philosophy!

ASTROV. What do you mean? [*Pause.*] Yes, I'll admit I'm growing vulgar, but then, you see, I'm drunk. Usually I drink like this only once a month. At such times my courage and boldness know no bounds. I feel capable of anything. I attempt the most difficult operations and succeed magnificently. The most brilliant plans and ideas evolve in my brain. I'm no longer a poor simpleton of a doctor, but mankind's greatest benefactor. I work out my own system of philosophy and all of the rest of you seem to crawl insignificantly at my feet like so many worms . . . [*Pause.*] . . . or microbes. [*To* TELYEGIN.] Play, Waffles!

TELYEGIN. My dear fellow, I would be delighted to, especially for you, but listen to reason; everyone in the house is asleep.

ASTROV. Play!

[TELYEGIN *plays softly.*]

ASTROV. I want a drink. Come, we still have some brandy left. Then, as soon as morning comes, you'll go home with me. All right?

[SONYA *enters and he catches sight of her.*]

I beg your pardon, I haven't got a tie on. [*He departs hurriedly, followed by* TELYEGIN.]

SONYA. Uncle Vanya, you and the doctor have been drinking again! What a pair you two make! It's all very well for him, he's always been like that. But why must you follow his example? It's wrong at your age.

VANYA. Age hasn't anything to do with it. When the realities of life are gone, or if you've never had them, then you must create illusions. That is better than nothing.

SONYA. All our hay is cut and rotting in these daily rains and here you waste your time living in illusions! You are neglecting the farm completely. I've done all the work myself, until now I'm at the end of my strength . . . [*Frightened.*] Uncle! Your eyes are full of tears!

VANYA. Tears? No . . . ah . . . Nonsense, there are no tears in my eyes. [*Pause.*] You looked at me then just as your dead mother used to, oh my darling child . . . [*He eagerly kisses her face and hands.*] My sister, my dear sister . . . [*Pause.*] . . . where are you now? [*Pause.*] Oh, if you only knew, if you only knew!

SONYA. If she only knew what, Uncle?

VANYA. My heart is bursting. Oh it is dreadful . . . so useless. Never mind, though . . . maybe later on. Now, I must go. [*He goes out.*]

SONYA [*knocking at the door.*] Mihail! Are you asleep? Please come here for a minute.

ASTROV [*behind the door*]. In a moment. [*He appears presently, with his collar and waistcoat on.*] What do you want?

SONYA. Drink as much as you please, if you don't find it disgusting, but I beg of you, don't let my uncle do it. It's bad for him.

ASTROV. All right; we won't drink any more. [*Pause.*] I'm going home at once. That's settled. By the time the horses are harnessed, it will be dawn.

SONYA. It's still raining; wait until morning.

ASTROV. The storm is over. This is only the final blow. I must go. And please don't ask me to visit your father any more. I tell him he has gout, and he insists it is rheumatism. I tell him to lie down and stay in bed, and he sits up and goes about. Today he actually refused to see me.

SONYA. He has been spoiled. [*Looking at the sideboard.*] Won't you have something to eat?

ASTROV. Yes, I think I will.

SONYA. I like to eat at night. I'm sure we shall find something here. [*Pause.*] They say he has been a great favorite with the ladies all his life and women have spoiled him. Here, have some cheese.

[*They stand eating by the sideboard.*]

ASTROV. I haven't eaten a thing all day. I must drink. [*Pause.*] Your father has a very trying temper. [*Taking a bottle out of the sideboard.*] May I? [*Pouring himself a glass of vodka.*] We are alone here and I can speak frankly. Do you know, I couldn't bear to live in this house—not even for a month! This atmosphere would choke me. There is your father, wholly absorbed in his book and his sickness; there is your Uncle Vanya with his melancholy, your grandmother, and finally your stepmother——

SONYA. What about her?

ASTROV. In a human being, everything ought to be beautiful: face and dress, soul and thoughts. She is very beautiful, there's no denying it, but after all, all she does is eat, sleep, go for walks, fascinate us by her beauty and—nothing more. She has no duties, other people work for her . . . isn't that so? And an idle life cannot be a pure one. [*Pause.*] And yet, perhaps I'm judging her too harshly. I'm discontented, like your Uncle Vanya, and so both of us are complainers.

SONYA. Aren't you satisfied with life?

ASTROV. I like life as life, but I hate and despise it when it means frittering it away in a little Russian village. As far as my personal existence is concerned . . . God! . . . it is absolutely beyond redemption! Haven't you noticed when you cross a dense forest in the middle of night and see a small light shining ahead in the distance, how you forget your weariness and the darkness and the sharp branches that lash your face? I work—as you know—perhaps harder than anyone else around here. Fate pursues me relentlessly; at times I suffer unbearably and I see no light ahead of me in the distance. I have no hope; I do not care for people. And . . . it has been a long time since I have loved any one.

SONYA. You love no one?

ASTROV. No one . . . At times I feel a kind of tenderness for your old nurse, but that's only for old time's sake. The peasants are all alike; they are stupid, lazy, and dull. And the educated people are difficult to get along with. I am

tired of them. All our friends are small in their ideas and
small in their feelings. They see no farther than their own
noses; or perhaps, more bluntly, they are dull and stupid.
The ones who have brains and intelligence are hysterical,
morbidly absorbed and consumed in introspection and analysis. They whine, they hate, they find fault everywhere. They
crawl up to me secretively, leer at me and say: "That man
is crazy, he's neurotic or he is fraudulent." Or, if they don't
know what else to call me, if no other label fits, they say I
am peculiar. I like the forests; that is peculiar. I don't eat
meat; that is peculiar, too. Simple, natural and genuine
relations between man and man or between man and nature
have no existence in their eyes. No, none! . . . None! [*He
tries to take a drink;* SONYA *prevents him.*]

SONYA. Please, I beg you, don't drink any more!

ASTROV. Why not?

SONYA. It is so debasing. You are so noble, your voice is
tender, you are, more than any one I know, beautiful. Why
do you wish to be like the common people who drink and
play cards? Oh, don't, I beg you! You are always saying
people never create anything, but only destroy what God
has given them. Why then do you insist on destroying
yourself? Oh, you must not; don't, I implore you! I entreat
you!

ASTROV [*giving her his hand*]. I won't drink any more.

SONYA. Give me your word.

ASTROV. I give you my word of honor.

SONYA [*squeezing his hand*]. Thank you!

ASTROV. I'm through with it. You see, I'm perfectly sober
again; I've come to my senses, and I shall remain so until
the end of my life. [*He looks at his watch.*] But as I was
saying, my time is over; there is nothing for me in life;
the clock has run its race and has stopped. I am old, tired,
unimportant; my feelings are dead. I could never care for
anyone again. I don't love anyone, and I don't think I
shall ever love anyone. The only thing that appeals to me
is beauty. I just can't remain indifferent to it. If, for example,
Yelena wanted to, she could turn my head in a day. Yet,
I know that that isn't love, nor even affection . . . [*He
shudders and covers his face with his hands.*]

SONYA. What is the matter?

ASTROV. Nothing . . . During Lent one of my patients died
on the operating table.

SONYA. It is time to forget that. [*Pause.*] Tell me, Mihail,
if I had a friend or a younger sister, and if you knew that
she, well—that she loved you, what would you do?

ASTROV. I don't know. I don't suppose I'd do anything. I'd
make her understand that I could not return her love . . .
and anyway, my mind cannot be bothered with such affairs
now. I must start at once if I am ever to go. Good-bye, my
dear girl. At this rate, we shall stand here talking till
daylight. [*Shaking hands with her.*] If it's all right, I'll go
out through the drawing room, because I'm afraid your
uncle might detain me. [*He goes out.*]

SONYA [*alone*]. And he really said nothing! His heart and
soul are still hidden from me, and yet for some reason I'm
strangely happy. Why? [*Laughing with pleasure.*] I told him
that he was noble and beautiful and that his voice was
tender. Was that wrong? I can still feel his voice throbbing
in the air as it caresses me. [*Wringing her hands.*] Oh, how
awful it is that I am not beautiful! How awful! And I
know that I'm not beautiful. I know it, I know. Last Sunday,
as people were coming out of church, I heard them talking
about me, and one woman said: "She is so good and generous, what a pity she is not beautiful." Not beautiful . . .

[YELENA *enters and throws open the window.*]

YELENA. The storm has passed. What a refreshing breeze!
[*Pause.*] Where is the doctor?

SONYA. He's gone.

[*Pause.*]

YELENA. Sonya!

SONYA. Yes?

YELENA. How much longer are you going to go on brooding.
We have done nothing to hurt each other. Why should we
be enemies? Certainly we should be friends.

SONYA. I feel this too . . . [*Embracing* YELENA.] Oh, let's be
friends again!

YELENA. With all my heart.

[*Both are strongly moved. Pause.*]

SONYA. Has father gone to bed?

YELENA. No, he is sitting up in the drawing room. [*Pause.*]
You know, it's strange . . . I guess only the Lord knows

what has kept us apart all these weeks. [*Seeing the open sideboard.*] Who left the sideboard open?

SONYA. Mihail has just had supper.

YELENA. Here is some wine. Let's drink to our friendship.

SONYA. Yes, let's.

YELENA. Out of one glass. [*Filling a wine glass.*] Now, we are friends, aren't we?

SONYA. Friends.

[*They drink and kiss each other.*]

I have wished for us to be friends for so long, but somehow I was ashamed. [*She weeps.*]

YELENA. Why do you weep?

SONYA. I don't know. [*Pause.*] Let's forget it.

YELENA. There, there, don't cry. [*She weeps.*] Silly! Now I am crying, too. [*Pause.*] You're angry with me because you think I married your father for his money, but you must not believe all the gossip you hear. I swear to you I married him for love. I was fascinated by his fame and his learning. I know now that it wasn't real love, although it seemed real enough at the time. I am innocent, and yet ever since my marriage your searching, suspicious eyes have been accusing me of an imaginary crime.

SONYA. Peace! Come, let's forget the past.

YELENA. You mustn't look at people that way. It isn't right. You must trust and believe in people [*Pause.*]—or life becomes impossible.

[*Pause.*]

SONYA. Tell me, truthfully, as a friend, are you happy?

YELENA. Truthfully, no.

SONYA. I knew that. One more question: would you like your husband to be young?

YELENA. What a child you are! Of course I would. Go on, ask me something else.

SONYA. Do you like the doctor?

YELENA. Yes, very much indeed.

SONYA [*laughing*]. I have a plain face, haven't I? . . . Yes, I know. He has just left, and his voice still rings in my ears; I can hear the sound of his footsteps; I can see his face in the dark window. Oh, I want so to tell you all that I have in my heart! But I cannot, I am ashamed. Words can never express our feelings. They mean and . . . Oh, what a silly person you must think I am. [*Pause.*] Please talk to me about him.

YELENA. What do you want me to say?

SONYA. He is so wise. He understands everything and he can do anything. He can heal the sick, and plant forests, too.

YELENA. It isn't a question of medicine and trees, my dear. He is a man of genius. Do you realize what that means? It means he is a man of great courage, one with deep insights and clear and far-reaching vision. He plants a tree and his mind swings a thousand years into the future and he envisions the happiness of all mankind. Such people are rare and should be loved. What if he does drink and use coarse language at times. In Russia, a man of genius cannot be a saint. Think of his life. There he lives, cut off from the world by frost and storm and trackless muddy roads, surrounded by coarse and savage people who are crushed by poverty and disease. His life is a continuing and endless struggle, from which he shall never rest. How can a man live like that for forty years and remain sober and free from all sin? [*Kissing* SONYA.] With all my heart, I wish you happiness; you deserve it. [*Getting up.*] As for me, I am worthless—an empty and quite pathetic woman. I have always been futile; in music, in love, in my husband's house—in fact, in everything. If I dared even for a moment to consider . . . Oh, Sonya, I am really very, very unhappy. [*Walking excitedly back and forth.*] I can never achieve happiness in this world. Never. Why do you laugh?

SONYA [*laughing and putting her hands over her face.*] I am so happy [*Pause.*] . . . so happy!

YELENA. How I should like some music at this moment. I believe I could play once more.

SONYA. Oh, do, do! [*Embracing her.*] I couldn't possibly go to sleep now. Do play!

YELENA. Yes, I will. Your father is still awake. Music annoys him when he is ill, but if he says I may, then I shall play a little. Go . . . go and ask him, Sonya.

SONYA. All right. [*She goes out.*]

[*The sound of the watchman's rattle comes from the backyard.*]

YELENA. It's been a long time since I've had the feeling for music. And now, I shall sit and play and cry like a small child. [*Calling out of the window.*] Yefim, is that you out there with your rattle?

VOICE OF WATCHMAN. Yes.

YELENA. Don't make so much noise. Your master is ill.

VOICE OF WATCHMAN. I'm on my way. [*He whistles a tune as* YELENA *closes the window.*]

SONYA [*returning*]. He says "No."

ACT THREE

[*The drawing room of* SEREBRYAKOV'S *house. There are doors right, left and center. It is early afternoon.* VANYA *and* SONYA *are seated.* YELENA *walks back and forth, deep in thought.*]

VANYA. His lordship, the Professor, has deigned to express the wish that we all gather in the drawing room at one o'clock. [*Looking at his watch.*] It is now a quarter to one. He has a message of the greatest importance to convey to the world.

YELENA. It's probably a question of business.

VANYA. He never has any business. He writes nonsense, grumbles and eats his heart out with jealousy; that's all he does.

SONYA [*reproachfully*]. Uncle!

VANYA. Very well. I beg your pardon. [*Pointing to* YELENA.] Look at her. Roaming up and down out of sheer idleness and boredom. A beautiful picture, I must say!

YELENA. I'm surprised that it doesn't bore you to play on the same note from morning to night. [*With despair.*] This tedium is killing me. Oh, what am I going to do?

SONYA [*shrugging her shoulders*]. There is plenty to do if you wish to.

YELENA. For instance?

SONYA. You could help us run the estate, teach the children, look after the sick . . . isn't that enough? Before you and father came, Uncle Vanya and I used to take the grain to market ourselves.

YELENA. I know nothing about such matters, and, besides, I'm not interested in them. It's only in sentimental novels that women go out and teach and look after the sick peasants; furthermore, how could I start in doing it all of a sudden?

SONYA. I don't know how you can live here and not do it. Be patient and you'll get used to it. [*Embracing her.*] Don't be depressed, my dear friend. [*Laughing.*] You feel out of sorts and restless, bored and idle, and unable, somehow, to fit into this life, and your restlessness and idleness is infectious. Look at Uncle Vanya, he does nothing now but follow you about like a shadow, and I have given up my

work today to come here and talk with you. I'm getting
lazy and losing interest in my work and I can't help it.
Dr. Astrov hardly ever came here; it was all we could do
to persuade him to visit us once each month, and now he
has given up his forestry and forgets his patients, and comes
every day. You must be a witch.

VANYA. Why should you pine away here in misery and despair?
[*Eagerly.*] Come, my darling, my sweet one, be sensible!
A mermaid's blood runs in your veins. Why don't you act
like one? Let yourself go for once in your life; fall head
over heels in love with some other water sprite, and plunge
headlong into a bottomless quarry, so that the almighty
Professor and all the rest of us might be so amazed that
we could escape your charms.

YELENA [*in anger*]. Leave me alone! How cruel can you be!
[*She tries to leave.*]

VANYA [*preventing her*]. There, there, my darling, I apologize.
Forgive me. [*He kisses her hand.*] Peace!

YELENA. Admit that you would try the patience of a saint.

VANYA. As a peace offering and as a symbol of true harmony,
I am going to bring you some flowers I picked for you
this morning; some autumn roses, exquisite, glorious, melancholy roses. [*He leaves.*]

SONYA. Autumn roses, exquisite, glorious, melancholy roses
. . . [*She and* YELENA *stand at the window looking out.*]

YELENA. It's September already! How are we ever going to
live through the long winter here? [*Pause.*] Where is the
doctor?

SONYA. He's writing in Uncle Vanya's room. I'm glad Uncle
Vanya left. I must talk to you about something.

YELENA. About what?

SONYA. About what? [*She puts her head on* YELENA'S *breast.*]

YELENA [*carressing her hair*]. There, there! Don't, Sonya.

SONYA. I am not beautiful!

YELENA. You have beautiful hair.

SONYA. No! [*Looks round so as to glance at herself in the
mirror.*] No! When a woman is not beautiful, she is always
told: "You've got beautiful eyes, you've got beautiful hair."
For six years now I have loved him; I have loved him
more than one can love anyone. Every moment, I seem
to hear him by my side. I feel his hand press against mine.
I watch the door constantly, imagining that I can hear his
footsteps. And—don't you see?—I run to you just to talk

about him. He comes here every day now, but he never looks at me, he doesn't even notice that I am here. Yelena, my dear, it is breaking my heart and I have absolutely no hope . . . no hope. [*In despair.*] Oh, God! Give me strength to endure. All last night I prayed. It has gotten so that I go up to him and speak to him and look into his eyes. My pride is gone. I no longer have the strength to control myself. Yesterday I told Uncle Vanya about my love for him. I couldn't help it. And all the servants know it, too. Everyone knows that I love him.

YELENA. Does he?

SONYA. No, he never pays any attention to me; it is as if I didn't exist.

YELENA [*musing*]. He's a strange man. Do you know what? Let me talk to him. I'll do it carefully. I'll just give him a hint. [*Pause.*] Now, really, how much longer do you propose to remain in uncertainty? Please! Let me do it!

[SONYA *nods affirmatively.*]

Wonderful! It will be easy to find out whether he loves you or not. Don't be ashamed, dear one, and don't worry. I shall be careful; he won't have the least suspicion. We only wish to find out whether it is yes or no, don't we? [*A pause.*] And if it is no, then he must stay away from here, isn't that right?

[SONYA *nods.*]

It would be easier not to see him any more. We won't delay this another minute. He said he had some maps he wanted to show me. Go and tell him at once that I wish to see him.

SONYA [*greatly excited*]. Will you tell me the whole truth?

YELENA. Why certainly I will. I'm sure that whatever it is, it will be easier to endure than this uncertainty. Trust me, my dear.

SONYA. Yes, yes. I shall say that you wish to see his charts. [*She starts to go, but stops near the door and looks back.*] No, it is better not to know with certainty . . . one has hope, at least.

YELENA. What did you say?

SONYA. Nothing. [*She leaves.*]

YELENA [*alone*]. There is nothing worse than to know the

secret of another human being, and to realize there's nothing you can do to help them. [*In deep thought.*] Obviously, he is not in love with her. But why shouldn't he marry her? To be sure, she is not beautiful, yet she is good and kind, pure of heart, and so sensible that she would make an excellent wife for a country doctor of his age. [*Pause.*] I can understand the poor child's feelings. Here she lives in the midst of this desperate loneliness with no one about her except these gray shadows who pass for human beings, who do nothing but eat, drink, sleep and talk trivial commonplaces. And then, who from time to time should appear upon the scene among them but this Dr. Astrov, so unlike the rest—so handsome, interesting, fascinating . . . It is like seeing the moon rising, rich and full, in the darkness. Oh, to be able to surrender yourself—to forget oneself—body and soul to such a man! Yes, I too, am a little in love with him! Yes, without him I am lonely; when I think of him, I smile. Uncle Vanya says I have a mermaid's blood in my veins: "For once in your life, let yourself go!" Perhaps I should. Oh, to be free as a bird, to fly away from all those drowsy faces and their monotonous mumblings and forget that they have existed at all! Oh, to forget oneself and what one is . . . But I am a coward; I am afraid, and tortured by my conscience. He comes here every day now. I can guess why, and already my guilt condemns me. I should like to fall on my knees at Sonya's feet and beg her to forgive me and weep . . . But . . .

[ASTROV *enters carrying a portfolio.*]

ASTROV. Hello, how are you this afternoon? [*Shaking hands with her.*] Sonya tells me that you wish to see my maps.

YELENA. Yes, you promised me yesterday that you'd show me what you had been doing. Have you time now?

ASTROV. Of course! [*He lays the portfolio on the table, takes out a sketch and attaches it to the table with thumbtacks.*] Where were you born?

YELENA [*helping him out*]. In Petersburg.

ASTROV. Did you go to school there, too?

YELENA. Yes, at the conservatory of music.

ASTROV. I don't imagine you find our way of life very interesting.

YELENA. And why not? It's true I don't know the country very well, but I've read a great deal about it.

ASTROV. I have my own desk there in Vanya's room. When I become so completely exhausted that I can no longer go on with my work, I abandon everything and rush over here to forget myself with my maps for an hour or two. Vanya and Sonya rattle away at their counting boards, I feel warm and peaceful, the cricket sings, and I sit near them at my table and paint. However, I usually don't indulge in such a luxury very often, certainly not more than once a month. [*Pointing to the picture.*] Look! This is a survey map of our part of the country as it was fifty years ago. Those areas shaded in green, both light and dark, are forest lands. Half the map, you see, is covered with them. Where the green is striped with red, the forests were stocked with elk and wild goats. Here on this lake were large flocks of swans, wild geese and ducks; as the old men used to tell us, there was a "power" of birds of every kind—no end of them. [*Pause.*] Now, they have vanished like thin air. Here, you see, beside the towns and villages, I have jotted down here and there the various settlements, little farms, mon- asteries, and watermills. This country was rich in cattle and horses, as you can see by this expanse of blue. For instance, see how it deepens in this part; there were great herds here, an average of three horses to every house. [*Pause.*] Now, look below to the second map. This is the country as it was twenty-five years ago. Only a third of the map now is green with forests. The goats have disappeared and only a few elk remain. The green and blue are lighter, and so on and so forth. Now, we come to the third drawing, our district as it is today. Still we see spots of green, but very little. The elk, the swans, the black cock have also disap- peared. In fact, everything is gone. On the whole, it is the picture of a continuous and slow decline which will evidently come to completion in about ten or fifteen years. Perhaps you may object that it is the march of progress, that the old order must give way to the new, and you would be right if roads had been built through these ruined forests, or if factories and schools had taken the place of the mon- asteries and the watermills. Then the people would have become better educated and healthier and richer, but as it is, and as you can see, we have nothing of the kind. We have the same swamps and mosquitoes; the same disease, poverty and misery, typhoid, diptheria, fires. The degrada- tion of our country confronts us, brought on by the human race's fierce struggle for existence. This degeneration is due to inertia and ignorance—to a complete lack of understanding. When a man, cold, hungry and sick, simply to save what little there is left in life that has meaning and importance—to help his children survive—why God only knows, he acts in desperation; he instinctively and unconsciously clutches at anything that will fill his belly and keep him warm. Forced to forget what all this will mean tomorrow, the devil of destruction consumes all the land. And so almost everything has been destroyed and nothing has been created to take its place. [*Coldly.*] But I see by your expression that all this does not interest you.

YELENA. I know so little about such things!

ASTROV. There's nothing to know. It simply doesn't interest you, that's all.

YELENA. Frankly, my thoughts were elsewhere. Forgive me! I must ask you something, but I am embarrassed and I don't know how to begin.

ASTROV. Ask me something?

YELENA. Yes, a very innocent and probably not too important question. Sit down. [*They both sit.*] It's about a young girl I know. Let's discuss it like honest and mature people, like friends; and then, when we have finished we will forget all about it, shall we?

ASTROV. All right. Whatever you say!

YELENA. What I want to talk to you about is my stepdaughter, Sonya. Do you like her?

ASTROV. Yes, I respect her.

YELENA. But do you like her as a woman?

ASTROV. [*not at once*]. No.

YELENA. Just one thing more and I am finished. Haven't you noticed anything?

ASTROV. Nothing.

YELENA [*takes him by the hand*]. You don't love her, I can see it from your eyes. She is unhappy. Please, understand that and . . . stop coming here.

ASTROV [*gets up*]. I'm afraid I'm too old for this sort of thing. And, besides, I haven't the time for it. [*Shrugging his shoulders.*] When indeed could I? [*He is embarrassed.*]

YELENA. Oh, God! What a disgusting conversation. I am as breathless as if I had been running three miles uphill. Thank heaven, that's over with. Now let us forget everything that has been said. But you must leave at once. You are in-

telligent and sensible. You do understand, don't you?
[*Pause.*] I am actually blushing.

ASTROV. If you had spoken a month or two ago, perhaps I
might have been able to consider it, but now . . . [*Shrugging
his shoulders.*] Of course, if she is suffering . . . but wait,
there is one thing I can't understand . . . what are your
reasons for bringing all this up? [*Searching her face with his
eyes and shaking an admonishing finger at her.*] Oh, you're
a sly one!

YELENA. What do you mean?

ASTROV [*laughing*]. A sly one! Suppose Sonya is unhappy. I'm
ready to admit it, but what is the real meaning of your
interrogation? [*Preventing her from speaking, quickly.*]
Please, don't look so surprised, you know perfectly well
why I'm here every day. My sweet beast of prey, don't
look at me like that, I'm an old hand at this sort of game
. . . you can't deceive me.

YELENA [*perplexed*]. A beast of prey? I don't understand anything.

ASTROV. A beautiful, fluffy weasel. You must have your victims.
Here I've been doing nothing for a whole month, I've
dropped everything, I seek you greedily, and you're awfully
pleased about it, awfully. Well? I'm conquered, and you
knew all about it without your interrogation. [*Folding his
arms and bowing his head.*] I submit. Here I am . . . eat
me up!

YELENA. You've gone crazy!

ASTROV [*laughing ironically*]. Oh, you're so shy, aren't you?

YELENA. I'm more honorable than you think! I swear it! [*She
tries to leave the room.*]

ASTROV. Wait . . . [*Barring her way.*] I'll go away today. I
shan't come here any more. But [*Taking her hand and
glancing about.*] . . . for the future . . . where are we going
to meet? Tell me quickly, where? Someone may come in.
Tell me quickly! . . . [*Passionately.*] You are so gloriously
and wonderfully beautiful! . . . Let me kiss you but once
. . . Oh, if I could kiss your fragrant hair!

YELENA. I assure you!

ASTROV. Why assure me? You must not! Let's not waste words!
Ah, how lovely you are . . . what hands! [*Kissing her
hands.*]

YELENA. Stop it! Go away! [*Freeing her hands.*] You're forgetting yourself!

ASTROV. Tell me! Tell me! Where will we meet tomorrow? [*Putting his arms around her.*] Don't you see! We must meet! It is inevitable.

[*He kisses her.* VANYA *comes in carrying a bunch of roses, and halts in the doorway.*]

YELENA [*without seeing* VANYA]. Have pity! Leave me! [*She lays her head on* ASTROV'S *shoulder.*] Don't! [*She tries to break away from him.*]

ASTROV [*holding her around the waist*]. Meet me in the forest arbor tomorrow at two. Yes! Oh, yes! Will you come?

YELENA [*seeing* VANYA]. Let me go! [*Breaking free and going to the window deeply embarrassed.*] This is horrible!

VANYA. [*throwing his flowers on a chair, speaking in great excitement and wiping his face with his handkerchief*]. Nothing . . . yes, yes, nothing.

ASTROV [*with bravado*]. It's a fine day, my dear Vanya. This morning, the sky was overcast and it looked like rain, but now the sun is shining again. After all, we've had a very fine autumn, and the wheat crop looks unusually promising. [*Putting his map back into the portfolio.*] But the days are growing short. [*Goes out.*]

YELENA [*quickly approaching* VANYA]. You must do your best; you must use all the power you have to get us away from here today! Do you hear? I say, today!

VANYA [*wiping his face*]. Oh! Ah! Oh! Very well! Yes, I . . . Yelena, I saw everything!

YELENA [*greatly upset*]. Do you hear me? I must leave here today!

[SEREBRYAKOV, SONYA, MARINA, *and* TELYEGIN *enter.*]

TELYEGIN. I'm not feeling very well myself, your excellency. I've been lame for two days, and my head . . .

SEREBRYAKOV. Where are the rest? I hate this house. It winds and sprawls like a labyrinth. Everyone is always scattered through its twenty-six rooms. You can never find a soul. [*To* MARINA.] Ask Marya and Yelena to come here!

YELENA. I am here.

SEREBRYAKOV. Please sit down, all of you.

SONYA [*going to* YELENA *and asking anxiously*]. What did he say?

YELENA. I'll tell you later.

SONYA. You are upset. [*Looking swiftly and with inquiry into her face.*] I understand; he said he would not come here anymore. [*Pause.*] Tell me, did he? . . . Tell me!

[YELENA *nods.*]

SEREBRYAKOV [*to* TELYEGIN]. After all, one can become reconciled to being an invalid, but not to this absurd way of life you have here in the country. I feel as if I had been cast off from this earth and dumped onto a strange planet. Please be seated, ladies and gentlemen. Sonya!

[*She does not hear. She stands with her head sadly bent forward.*]

Sonya! [*A pause.*] I guess she does not hear me. [*To* MARINA.] You sit down, too, nurse.

[MARINA *takes a seat and resumes knitting her stocking.*]

I ask your indulgence, ladies and gentlemen; uh . . . check your ears, as it were, on the hat rack of attention. [*He laughs.*]

VANYA [*in agitation*]. Perhaps I'm not needed . . . May I be excused?

SEREBRYAKOV. No, you are needed now more than anyone else.

VANYA. What do you wish?

SEREBRYAKOV. You—but what makes you so angry and out of sorts? If it is anything I have done, I beg your forgiveness.

VANYA. Oh, forget that and your high and mighty tone, too, and come to the point; what do you want?

[MARYA *enters.*]

SEREBRYAKOV. Here is mother. Ladies and gentlemen, let us begin. I have asked you to gather here, my friends, to inform you that the inspector general is coming. [*Laughs.*] All joking aside, however, I wish to discuss a very important matter. I must ask you for your aid and advice, and realizing your unbounded kindness, I believe I can count on both. I am a scholar and bound to my library, and I am not familiar with practical affairs. I am unable, I find, to dispense with the help of well informed people such as you, Ivan, and you, Ilya, and you, mother. The truth is, *manet omnes una nox*, that is to say, our lives rest in the hands of God, and as I am old and ill, I realize that the time has come for me to dispose of my property in the interests of my family. My life is nearly finished, and I am not thinking of myself, but I must consider by young wife and daughter. [*A pause.*] I cannot go on living in the country; we were just not meant for country life. And yet, we cannot afford to live in town on the income from this estate. We might sell the forests, but that would be an expedient to which we could not resort every year. We must work out some method of guaranteeing ourselves a permanent, and . . . ah, more or less fixed annual income. With this object in view, a plan has occurred to me which I now have the honor of proposing to you for your consideration. I shall give you only a rough outline of it, omitting all the bothersome and trivial details. Our estate does not yield, on an average, more than two percent on the investment. I propose to sell it. If then we invest our capital in bonds and other suitable securities, it will bring us four to five percent and we should probably have a surplus of several thousand roubles, with which we could buy a small house in Finland . . .

VANYA. Wait a minute! Repeat what you said just now; I don't believe I heard you quite right.

SEREBRYAKOV. I said we would invest the money in bonds and with the surplus buy a house in Finland.

VANYA. No, not Finland . . . You said something else.

SEREBRYAKOV. I propose to sell this estate.

VANYA. Aha! That was it! So you are going to sell the estate? Splended! That's a fine idea! And what do you propose to do with my old mother and myself and with Sonya, here?

SEREBRYAKOV. That will be taken care of in due course. After all . . . uh . . . we can't do everything at once, can we?

VANYA. Wait! It is clear that up to now I've never had an ounce of sense in my head. I have always been stupid enough to think that the estate belonged to Sonya. My late father bought it as a wedding gift for my sister, and as our laws were made for Russians and not for Turks, I foolishly imagined that my sister's estate would pass on to her child.

SEREBRYAKOV. Why, of course, it belongs to Sonya. Has anyone denied it? I don't wish to sell it without Sonya's consent; on the contrary, what I am doing is for Sonya's welfare.

VANYA. This is absolutely crazy. Either I have gone insane or . . . or . . .

MARYA. Ivan, don't contradict Alexander. Trust him; he knows better than we do what is right and what is wrong.

VANYA. No! Give me some water. [*He drinks.*] Go on! Say anything you like . . . anything!

SEREBRYAKOV. I can't understand why you are so upset. I don't pretend that my plan is ideal, and if you all object to it, I shall not insist.

[*A pause.*]

TELYEGIN [*looking embarrassed*]. I've always had a great reverence for learning, sir, and, if I may say so, my feelings for it have a certain family connection, I mean, sir, that my brother Gregory's wife's brother, Konstantin Lacedaemonov, as you perhaps know, was an M.A. . . .

VANYA. Wait a minute, Waffles, we're discussing business. Wait a little . . . later . . . [*To* SEREBRYAKOV.] Here, ask him what he thinks; this estate was purchased from his uncle.

SEREBRYAKOV. Ah! Why should I ask questions? What good would it do?

VANYA. The price was ninety-five thousand roubles. My father paid seventy and left a mortgage of twenty-five. Now listen! This estate could never have been bought if I had not renounced by inheritance in favor of my sister, whom I dearly loved . . . and what is more, I worked like a slave for ten years and paid off the mortgage.

SEREBRYAKOV. I regret that I ever brought the matter up.

VANYA. Thanks entirely to my personal efforts, the estate is now free from debt and in good condition, and now . . . as I am getting old, you propose to kick me out!

SEREBRYAKOV. I don't understand what you're talking about.

VANYA. For twenty-five years I have managed this estate. I have sent you the proceeds from it like an honest servant, and you, you have never given me one single word of thanks for my efforts . . . no, not one . . . neither in my youth nor now. You gave me a meager salary of five hundred roubles a year . . . a beggar's pittance, and you have never once thought of adding a rouble to it.

SEREBRYAKOV. How should I know about such things, Ivan? I am not a practical man and I don't understand them. You might have helped yourself to all you desired.

VANYA. Yes, why didn't I steal? Don't you all despise me for not stealing? It would have been only fair, and I wouldn't be a poor man now.

MARYA [*sternly*]. Ivan!

TELYEGIN [*in agitation*]. Vanya, my friend, don't talk like that. Why spoil such a pleasant relationship? Please stop!

VANYA. For twenty-five years I have been sitting here with my mother buried like a mole. Every thought and hope we had was yours and yours alone. All day long we talked with pride of you and your work; and we spoke your name with respect . . . yes, almost with reverence. We wasted our evenings reading your books and articles, which I now detest to the bottom of my heart.

TELYEGIN. Don't, Vanya, don't. I can't stand this sort of thing.

SEREBRYAKOV [*angrily*]. What in God's name do you want, anyhow?

VANYA. We used to consider you a superman, a kind of demi-god, but now the scales have fallen from my eyes and I see you as you are! You write about art without knowing a thing about it. Why, those books of yours which I used to think were so wonderful aren't worth a copper kopeck. You are a fake, a fraud, a . . .

SEREBRYAKOV. Can't anyone stop him? I'm leaving here immediately!

YELENA. Ivan Petrovich, I command you to stop this instant! Do you hear me?

SONYA. Please! Uncle Vanya!

VANYA. I refuse!

[SEREBRYAKOV *tries to escape from the room, but* VANYA *bars the door.*]

Wait! I haven't finished yet! You have destroyed my life. I have never really lived. Thanks to you, my best years have gone for nothing. They have been ruined. I hate you!

TELYEGIN. I can't stand it; I can't stand it. I'm going. [*He leaves in great excitement.*]

SEREBRYAKOV. What do you want from me? What right do you have to speak to me like that? If the estate is yours, take it! I don't want it.

YELENA. I'm leaving this hell right now! [*Shouts.*] I can't stand it any longer!

VANYA. My life's ruined! I'm gifted, I'm intelligent, I'm courageous. If I'd had a normal life, I might have become a Schopenhauer, a Dostoevsky. I'm talking nonsense. I'm going insane! I'm in despair! Oh, Mother!

MARYA. Do as the Professor tells you!

VANYA. Mother, what am I to do? Never mind, don't tell me!
I know myself what I must do! [*To* SEREBRYAKOV.] You
will remember me! [*He goes out through middle door.*
MARYA *goes out after him.*]

SONYA. Oh, nurse, nurse!

SEREBRYAKOV. This is too much! Take that madman away! I
can't live under the same roof with him! He is always
there. [*Points to the middle door.*] Let him move into town
or to another house on the grounds, or I will move myself,
but I cannot stay in the same house with him.

YELENA [*to her husband*]. We are leaving here today; we must
get ready at once.

SEREBRYAKOV. What an utterly insignificant little man.

SONYA [*on her knees beside the nurse, turning to her father
and speaking with emotion*]. You must be merciful, Father.
Uncle Vanya and I are both very unhappy! [*Controlling her
despair.*] Have mercy on us! Remember how Uncle Vanya
and grandmother used to sit up late copying and translating
your books for you every night . . . every night. Uncle
Vanya has worked without rest; we would never spend a
penny on ourselves, but sent it all to you! We earned every
mouthful of bread that we ever ate! I am not speaking as
I should like to, but you must understand, Father, you
must have mercy on us.

YELENA [*to her husband, much excited*]. For heaven's sake,
Alexander, go and talk to him . . . explain!

SEREBRYAKOV. Very well, I shall talk to him. I do not accuse
him of anything, and I am not angry, but you must admit
that his behavior has been strange, to say the least. Very
well, I shall go to him. [*He leaves through the center door.*]

YELENA. Be gentle with him. Try to quiet him. [*She follows
him out.*]

SONYA [*snuggling nearer to* MARINA]. Nurse, oh, nurse!

MARINA. It's all right, child. When the geese have cackled
they will be silent again. First they cackle and then they
stop.

SONYA. Nurse!

MARINA [*carressing her hair*]. You are trembling all over, as
if you had a chill. There, there, my little child, God is
merciful. A little linden tea, and it will pass. Don't cry, my
sweet. [*Looking angrily at the center door.*] See, the geese
have all gone now. The devil take them!

[*A shot is heard.* YELENA *screams behind the scenes.* SONYA shudders.]

MARINA. What's that?

SEREBRYAKOV [*runs staggering in looking terrified*]. Stop him! Stop him! He's gone mad!

[YELENA *and* VANYA *struggle in the doorway.*]

YELENA [*trying to snatch the revolver away from him*]. Give it to me! Give it to me, I tell you!

VANYA. Let go of me. Let go of me, Yelena! [*Freeing himself, he runs in and looks for* SEREBRYAKOV.] Where is he? Ah, there he is! [*Pointing the revolver at* SEREBRYAKOV. *Bang! Pause.*] Missed him! Missed him again! [*Furiously.*] Damn it! Damn! [*Bangs the revolver a few times against the floor and sinks exhausted in a chair.*]

YELENA. Take me away from here! Take me away . . . kill me . . . I can't stay here, I can't.

VANYA [*in despair*]. What have I done! What have I done!

SONYA [*softly*]. Oh, nurse! Nurse!

ACT FOUR

[VANYA'S *bedroom and office. Large table near window; scattered on it are ledgers, scales and papers. Nearby,* ASTROV'S *table with paints and drawing materials. A map of Africa, of no use to anyone, on the wall. A large sofa covered with canvas. A door to an inner room; door right leads to front hall. It is evening in autumn.* TELYEGIN *and* MARINA *sit facing each other, winding wool.*]

TELYEGIN. Hurry, Marina, or we shall have to go out to say good-bye before we've finished. They have ordered the carriage already.

MARINA [*trying to wind more rapidly*]. There isn't much left to wind.

TELYEGIN. They are going to live in Kharkov.

MARINA. It is wise for them to go.

TELYEGIN. They have been frightened. The Professor's wife refuses to stay here an hour longer. She keeps saying: "If we're going at all, let's hurry. We shall go to Kharkov and look around, and then we can send for our things." They're taking practically nothing with them. It seems, Marina, that fate has decreed that they should not live here.

MARINA. And quite rightly. What a storm they raised! It was disgusting!

TELYEGIN. Yes, to be sure! The scene this morning would make a fine story.

MARINA. I wish I'd never laid eyes on them. [*Pause.*] Once more things will be as they used to be; we shall live like normal human beings again: tea at eight, dinner at one, and supper in the evening; everything in order as decent people and Christians like it. [*Sighing.*] It is a long time since I, poor sinner, have eaten noodles.

TELYEGIN. Yes, we haven't had noodles for a great while. [*Pause.*] Not for ages. As I was passing through the village this morning, Marina, one of the storekeepers called after me: "Hi! you hanger-on!" I felt it bitterly.

MARINA. Don't pay any attention to them, my friend; we are all dependent upon God. You, Sonya, Uncle Vanya and

[214]

myself . . . none of us sits idle; we all must work hard.
All! . . . Where is Sonya?

TELYEGIN. In the garden with the doctor, looking for Vanya.
They are afraid he may become violent and attempt to
kill himself.

MARINA. Where is his gun?

TELYEGIN [*whispering*]. I hid it in the cellar.

MARINA [*amused*]. What goings-on!

[VANYA *and* ASTROV *enter.*]

VANYA. Let me alone! [*To* MARINA *and* TELYEGIN.] Go away!
Get out and leave me to myself. Only for an hour! I won't
have you watching me this way!

TELYEGIN [*going out on tiptoe*]. Why certainly, Vanya.

MARINA [*gathering up her wool and leaving*]. The gander is
cackling again; ho! ho! ho!

VANYA. Let me alone!

ASTROV. I would, with the greatest pleasure. I should have
gone long ago, but I shan't leave you until you have returned what you took from me.

VANYA. I took nothing from you.

ASTROV. I'm not joking, don't delay me, I really have to go.

VANYA. I took nothing of yours.

ASTROV [*both sitting down*]. Oh, you didn't? All right, I shall
have to stay a while longer, and if you still don't give it up,
I will have to resort to force. We shall tie your hands and
search you. I warn you, I mean what I say.

VANYA. Do as you please. [*Pause.*] Oh, to think I made such
a fool of myself! To shoot twice and miss him both times!
I can never forgive myself.

ASTROV. When you first felt the impulse to shoot someone, you
would have done better to put a bullet through your own
head.

VANYA [*shrugging his shoulders*]. It's strange! I tried to murder
a man, and they are not going to arrest me or bring me to
trial. That means they think I'm insane. [*Laughing bitterly.*]
I! I am insane, and the ones who hide their futility, their
stupidity, their harsh cruelty behind a professor's mask,
they . . . they are sane! Those who marry old men and then
betray them before the eyes of everyone, they are sane!
Yes, I saw you kiss her; I saw you in each other's arms!

ASTROV. Yes, I did kiss her; which is more than you can say.

VANYA [*watching the door*]. No, it is the earth that is insane,
because it allows us to exist.

ASTROV. That's nonsense.

VANYA. Well? I am a lunatic, aren't I, and therefore irresponsible? Haven't I the right to talk nonsense?

ASTROV. This is a farce! You are not insane; you are simply a ridiculous fool. I used to think every fool was out of his senses—abnormal; but now I see that lack of sense is the normal human condition, and you are perfectly normal.

VANYA [covering his face with his hands]. Oh! If you knew how ashamed I am! There is no pain on earth greater than the bitter sense of shame. [Agonized.] I can't endure it! [Leaning against the table.] What can I do? What can I do?

ASTROV. Nothing.

VANYA. Tell me something! Oh, my God! I am forty-seven. I may live to be sixty; I still have thirteen years ahead of me . . . an eternity! How can I endure life for thirteen years? What shall I do? How can I fill them? Oh, don't you see? [Pressing ASTROV's hand convulsively.] Don't you see, if I could only live the rest of my life in some new manner! If I could only wake up some still sunny morning and feel that my life had begun all over; that the past was forgotten and had vanished like smoke. [Weeping.] Oh, to begin life anew! To start over! Tell me, tell me, how to begin!

ASTROV [crossly]. Nonsense! What kind of a new life can we, yes both of us, you and I—look forward to? We have no hope.

VANYA. None?

ASTROV. None. I am convinced of that.

VANYA. Please give me something to live for. [Putting his hand to his heart.] I feel such a burning pain here.

ASTROV [shouting angrily]. Stop! [More moderately.] It may be that our posterity, despising us for our blind and stupid lives, will find some road to happiness; but we—you and I—have but one hope, the hope that, perhaps, pleasant dreams will haunt us as we rest in our graves. [Sighing.] Yes, my friend, in this entire community there were only two decent and intelligent men, you and I. Ten years or so of this life of ours, this wretched life of the commonplace and the trivial, have sucked us under and poisoned us with their destructive vapors, and we have become as contemptible, as petty, and as despicable as the others. [Resolutely.] But don't try to put me off! Will you give me what you took from me?

VANYA. I took nothing from you.

ASTROV. You took a bottle of morphine out of my medicine

case. [*Pause.*] Listen! If you are positively determined to kill yourself, go into the woods and shoot yourself there. But give me back the morphine, or there will be a great deal of talk and suspicion; people will think I gave it to you. It will be bad enough having to perform your post-mortem. Do you think I shall find it interesting?

[SONYA *enters.*]

VANYA. Leave me alone.

ASTROV [*to* SONYA]. Sonya, your uncle has stolen a bottle of morphine from my medicine case and won't return it to me. Tell him his behavior is—well, unwise. I can't waste any more time, I must be going.

SONYA. Uncle Vanya, did you take the morphine?

[*Pause.*]

ASTROV. Yes, he took it. [*Pause.*] I'm absolutely sure.

SONYA. Give it back! Why do you wish to frighten us? [*Tenderly.*] Give it up, Uncle Vanya! My sorrow is perhaps even greater than yours, but I am not in despair. I endure my grief and shall go on doing so until my life comes to its natural end. You must endure yours, too. [*Pause.*] Give it up! [*Kissing his hands.*] Dear, dear, Uncle Vanya. Give it up! [*Weeping.*] You are so good, I am sure you'll have pity on us and give it back. You must endure your grief with patience, Uncle Vanya; you must endure it.

[VANYA *takes the bottle from the table drawer and gives it to* ASTROV.]

VANYA. There it is! [*To* SONYA.] And now we must get busy at once; we must do something, or else I'll not be able to stand it.

SONYA. Yes, yes, let's work! As soon as we've seen them off, we'll go to work. [*Nervously she straightens out the papers on the table.*] We have neglected everything!

ASTROV [*putting the bottle in the case and closing it*]. Now I can go.

YELENA [*entering*]. Oh, here you are, Vanya. We are leaving soon. Go to Alexander, he wishes to speak to you.

SONYA. Go, Uncle Vanya. [*Taking* VANYA'S *arm.*] Come, you and father must make peace; that is absolutely necessary for us. [SONYA *and* VANYA *leave.*]

YELENA. I'm leaving. [*Giving* ASTROV *her hand.*] Good-bye.

ASTROV. So soon?

YELENA. The carriage is waiting.

ASTROV. Good-bye.

YELENA. You promised me that today you, too, would go away.

ASTROV. I had forgotten. I'll go immediately. [*Pause.*] Were
you afraid? [*Taking her by the hand.*] Was it so terrifying?

YELENA. Yes.

ASTROV. Couldn't you stay? Couldn't you? Tomorrow—in the
forest arbor——

YELENA. No. Everything is settled, and that is why I can
look you so squarely in the eyes. Our departure is definite.
One thing I must ask of you, however; don't think too
harshly of me; I should like you to respect me.

ASTROV. Ah! [*With an impatient gesture.*] Stay, I beg you!
Admit there's nothing for you to do in this world. You have
no object in life; nothing to occupy your attention. Sooner
or later you will give in to your feelings. It is inevitable.
But please not in Kharkov or in Kursk, but here, here in
the lap of nature. Here, at least, it would be poetic, even
beautiful. Here you have forests, Turgenev's half-ruined
houses, the autumn roses . . .

YELENA. How absurd you are! I am angry with you and yet
I shall always remember you with pleasure. You are an
interesting and different kind of man. You and I will never
meet again, and so I shall tell you—why conceal it?—that
I am in love with you. Come, let's shake hands and part as
good friends. Please don't think badly of me.

ASTROV [*pressing her hand*]. Yes, you had better go. [*Thoughtfully.*] You seem sincere and good, and yet there is something strangely restless about your whole personality. The
moment you and your husband arrived here, everyone
whom you found busy and engaged in active, creative work
felt compelled to drop it and give himself up to you and
your husband's gout for the entire summer. You and your
husband have infected all of us with your idleness. I became infatuated with you and I have done nothing for a
whole month, and in the meantime people have been ill
and the peasants have been grazing their herds in my newly
planted woods . . . so that wherever you and your husband
go, you bring destruction everywhere. I am joking, of
course, and yet I am strangely convinced that if you had
remained here, we should have been overtaken by the most

terrible desolation and destruction. I would have perished, and you . . . no good would have come to you either. So go! Our little comedy is over; with a happy ending—Go!

YELENA [*snatching pencil quickly from* ASTROV'S *table*]. I shall keep this pencil as a remembrance!

ASTROV. How strange it is! We meet, and then all of a sudden it seems that we must part forever. So it is with everything in this world. While we are still alone, before Uncle Vanya comes in with a bouquet—allow me—to kiss you good-bye —May I? [*Kissing her on the cheek.*] There! Wonderful!

YELENA. I wish you every happiness. [*Glancing about her.*] For once in my life . . . [*She kisses him impulsively, and they part quickly.*] I must go.

ASTROV. Yes go. Since the carriage is ready, you'd better start at once. [*They stand listening.*] It is finished.

[VANYA, SEREBRYAKOV, MARYA *with her book,* TELYEGIN, *and* SONYA *enter.*]

SEREBRYAKOV [*to* VANYA]. Woe be unto him who cannot forgive past offenses. I have passed through so much—ah, such experience—in the last few hours that I believe I could write a whole treatise for the benefit of all mankind on the art of living. I accept your apology gladly, and I myself ask your forgiveness. [*He kisses* VANYA *three times.*] Good-bye.

VANYA. You will go on receiving your allowance regularly as before. Everything will remain as it was.

[YELENA *embraces* SONYA.]

SEREBRYAKOV [*kissing* MARYA'S *hands*]. Mother!

MARYA [*kissing him*]. Alexander! Have your picture taken again, and send it to me; you know how dearly I love you.

TELYEGIN. Good-bye, your excellency. Don't forget us.

SEREBRYAKOV [*kissing* SONYA]. Good-bye, good-bye, everyone. [*Shaking hands with* ASTROV.] Many thanks for your pleasant company. I have a deep regard for your opinions, your enthusiasm, and your impulses, but permit an old man to add one last observation—let me give you one piece of advice: do something, my friend! Work! You must work! [*They all bow.*] Good luck to you all. [*He goes out followed by* MARYA *and* SONYA.]

VANYA [*fervently kissing* YELENA'S *hand*]. Good-bye . . . forgive me. We shall never meet again!

YELENA [*touched*]. Good-bye, my dear Vanya. [*She kisses his head lightly as he bends over her hand, and then goes out.*]

ASTROV. Tell them to bring my carriage around, too, Waffles.

TELYEGIN. Certainly, my friend. [*He goes out.*]

[ASTROV *and* VANYA *alone are left behind.* ASTROV *gathers together his paints and drawing materials on the table and packs them away in his bag.*]

ASTROV. Why don't you see them off?

VANYA. Let them go! I—I can't go out there. My heart is so saddened. I must busy myself with something at once. To work! To work! [*He rummages through his papers on the table.*]

[*Pause. As the horses trot away, the tinkle of bells is heard.*]

ASTROV. They have gone! Somehow I'm sure the Professor is glad to go. Nothing will tempt him to return.

MARINA [*entering*]. They have gone. [*She sits down in her arm chair and resumes her knitting.*]

[SONYA *comes in drying her eyes.*]

SONYA. They have gone. [*Wipes her eyes.*] God be with them. [*To* VANYA.] And now, Uncle Vanya, let us do something!

VANYA. To work! To work!

SONYA. It has been a long, long time since you and I have sat together at this table. [*Lighting a lamp on the table.*] No ink! [*Taking the inkstand to the cupboard and filling it from an ink bottle.*] How sad it is to see them go!

MARYA [*coming in slowly*]. They have gone. [*She sits down and immediately becomes absorbed in her book.*]

[SONYA *sits at the table and looks through an account book.*]

SONYA. First, Uncle Vanya, let us add up the bills. We have neglected them dreadfully. We received another bill today. Come. We'll both do them.

VANYA. In account with [*Writing.*] . . . in account with . . .

MARINA [*yawning*]. The sandman is on his way.

ASTROV. How silent it is. The pens scratch and the cricket sings; it is so warm and comfortable. You know, I hate to go.

[*The tinkling of bells is heard.*]

ASTROV. Ah, but my carriage has come. All that remains is to say good-bye to you, my friends, and to my table here, and then . . . away! [*He puts the map in the portfolio.*]

MARINA. Why be in such a hurry . . . you can stay a little while longer.

ASTROV. Impossible.

VANYA [*writing*]. And carry forward from the old debt two seventy-five . . .

[*The* WORKMAN *enters.*]

WORKMAN. Your carriage is waiting, sir.

ASTROV. All right. [*He hands the* WORKMAN *his medicine case, portfolio and box.*] Be careful, don't crush the portfolio!

WORKMAN. Yes, sir.

SONYA. When shall we see you again?

ASTROV. Probably not before next summer. Certainly not again till winter's over, at any rate. Of course, if anything happens, let me know, and I'll come at once. [*Shaking hands.*] Thank you for your hospitality, your kindness . . . for all you've done. [*He goes to the nurse and kisses her head.*] Good-bye, old nurse.

MARINA. Are you going without your tea?

ASTROV. I don't care for any, nurse.

MARINA. Won't you have just a little vodka?

ASTROV [*hesitatingly*]. Yes, I guess I might as well.

[MARINA *goes out. After a pause.*]

One of my horses has gone lame for some reason. I noticed it yesterday when Peter was watering him.

VANYA. You should have him reshod.

ASTROV. I shall have to stop at the blacksmith's on my way home. It can't be helped. [*He stands looking up at the map of Africa on the wall.*] I suppose it is terribly hot in Africa now.

VANYA. Yes, I suppose it is.

[MARINA *comes back carrying a tray with a glass of vodka and a slice of bread.*]

MARINA. There you are.

[ASTROV *drinks.*]

Your health! [*Bowing deeply.*] Eat your bread with it.

ASTROV. No, I like it this way. And now, good-bye. [*To*

MARINA.] You needn't come out to see me off, nurse. [*He leaves.*]

[SONYA *follows him with a candle to light him to the carriage.* MARINA *sits in her chair.*]

VANYA [*writing*]. On the second of February, twenty pounds of butter; on the sixteenth, twenty pounds of butter again. Buckwheat flour . . .

[*Pause. The tinkling of bells is heard.*]

MARINA. He has gone.

[*A pause.* SONYA *enters and sets the candlestick on the table.*]

SONYA. He has gone.
VANYA [*adding and writing*]. Total, fifteen . . . twenty-five . . .

[SONYA *sits down and begins to write.*]

MARINA [*yawning*]. Oh, ho! The Lord have mercy on us.

[TELYEGIN *enters on tiptoe, seats himself near the door, and begins to tune his guitar.*]

VANYA [*to* SONYA, *caressing her hair*]. My child, I feel so wretched!
SONYA. What can we do? We must go on living. [*Pause.*] Yes, we shall live, Uncle Vanya. Shall live through the endless procession of days before us, and through all the long evenings. We shall bear patiently the burdens that fate brings to us. We shall work, without rest, for others, both now and when we are old. And, then, when our final hour comes, we shall meet it humbly, and there beyond the grave, we shall know that we have known suffering and tears . . . that our life was bitter. And God will pity us. Oh, then, dear Uncle, we shall enter into a bright and beautiful life. We shall rejoice and look back upon our grief here . . . with tenderness . . . and a smile; [*Pause.*] and we shall have rest. I have faith, Uncle, fervent, passionate faith. [SONYA *kneels down in front of her uncle and lays her head in his hands. She speaks with a weary voice.*] We shall have rest.

[TELYEGIN *plays softly on his guitar.*]

We shall have rest. We shall hear the angels sing. We shall see heaven shining in all its radiant glory. We shall see all the world's evils . . . our every pain, our suffering . . . be engulfed by God's all-pervading mercy that shall enfold the earth. Our life will be peaceful, gentle and sweet—like a child's caress. Oh, I have faith; I have faith—[*Wiping away his tears.*] My poor Uncle Vanya, you are crying! [*Through her tears.*] You have never known joy in your life, but wait, Uncle Vanya, wait! You, too, will have rest. [*Embracing him.*] You, too, will rest.

[*The Watchman's rattle is heard from the garden;* TELYEGIN *plays softly;* MARYA *writes on the margin of her pamphlet;* MARINA *is knitting her stocking.*]

We shall rest. . . .

THE CHERRY ORCHARD

by ANTON CHEKHOV

1904

THE CHERRY ORCHARD[1]

Translated by Robert W. Corrigan

CHARACTERS

MADAME RANEVSKY (LYU-BOV ANDREYEVNA),
owner of the cherry orchard

ANYA, *her daughter, age 17*

VARYA, *her adopted daughter, age 24*

GAEV (LEONID ANDREYE-VICH), LYUBOV's *brother*

LOPAHIN (YERMOLAY ALEXEYEVICH), *a business man*

TROFIMOV (PYOTR SERGE-YEVICH), *a student*

SEMYONOV-PISHCHIK (BORIS BORISOVICH), *a land-owner*

CHARLOTTA IVANOVNA, *a governess*

EPIHODOV (SEMYON PANTA-LEYEVICH), *a clerk on the Ranevsky estate*

DUNYASHA, *a maid*

FEERS, *an old servant, age 87*

YASHA, *a young servant*

A TRAMP

THE STATIONMASTER

A POST-OFFICE CLERK

GUESTS *and* SERVANTS

SCENE

The estate of Madame Ranevsky.

[1] *The Cherry Orchard* by Anton Chekhov, from *Six Plays by Chekhov*, edited and translated by Robert W. Corrigan. Copyright © 1962 by Robert W. Corrigan. Reprinted by permission of the translator and the publisher, Holt, Rinehart and Winston, Inc.

ACT ONE

[*A room which used to be the children's room and is still called the nursery. Several doors, one leading into* ANYA'S *room. It is early in the morning and the sun is rising. It is early in May, but there is a morning frost. The windows are closed but through them can be seen the blossoming cherry trees. Enter* DUNYASHA, *carrying a candle, and* LOPAHIN *with a book in his hand.*]

LOPAHIN. The train's arrived, thank God. What time is it?

DUNYASHA. It's nearly two. [*Blows out the candle.*] It's daylight already.

LOPAHIN. The train must have been at least two hours late. [*Yawns and stretches.*] And what a fool I am! I make a special trip out here to meet them at the station, and then I fall asleep. . . . Just sat down in the chair and dropped off. What a nuisance. Why didn't you wake me up?

DUNYASHA. I thought you'd gone. [*Listens.*] I think they're coming.

LOPAHIN [*also listens*]. No . . . I should've been there to help them with their luggage and other things. . . . [*Pause.*] Lyubov Andreyevna has been abroad for five years. I wonder what she's like now. She used to be such a kind and good person. So easy to get along with and always considerate. Why, I remember when I was fifteen, my father—he had a store in town then—hit me in the face and it made my nose bleed. . . . We'd come out here for something or other, and he was drunk. Oh, I remember it as if it happened yesterday. . . . She was so young and beautiful . . . Lyubov Andreyevna brought me into this very room—the nursery, and she fixed my nose and she said to me, "Don't cry, little peasant, it'll be better by the time you get married." [*Pause.*] "Little peasant" . . . She was right, my father was a peasant. And look at me now—going about in a white waistcoat and brown shoes, like a crow in peacock's feathers. Oh, I am rich all right, I've got lots of money, but when you think about it, I'm still just a peasant. [*Turning over pages of the book.*] Here, I've been reading this book, and couldn't understand a word of it. Fell asleep reading it.

[*Pause.*]

DUNYASHA. The dogs have been awake all night: they know
their mistress is coming.

LOPAHIN. Why, what's the matter with you, Dunyasha?

DUNYASHA. My hands are shaking. I think I'm going to faint.

LOPAHIN. You've become too delicate and refined, Dunyasha.
You get yourself all dressed up like a lady, and you fix
your hair like one, too. You shouldn't do that, you know.
You must remember your place.

[*Enter* EPIHODOV *with a bouquet of flowers; he wears a jacket
and brightly polished high boots which squeak loudly. As
he enters, he drops the flowers.*]

EPIHODOV [*picks up the flowers*]. The gardener sent these. He
says they're to go in the dining room. [*Hands the flowers to*
DUNYASHA.]

LOPAHIN. And bring me some kvass.

DUNYASHA. All right.

EPIHODOV. It's chilly outside this morning, three degrees of
frost, and here the cherry trees are all in bloom. I can't
say much for this climate of ours, you know. [*Sighs.*] No,
I really can't. It doesn't contribute to—well, you know,
things . . . And what do you think, Yermolay Alexeyevich,
the day before yesterday I bought myself a pair of boots
and they squeak so much . . . well, I mean to say, they're
impossible. . . . What can I use to fix them?

LOPAHIN. Oh, be quiet! And don't bother me!

EPIHODOV. Every day something unpleasant happens to me.
But I don't complain; I'm used to it, why I even laugh.

[*Enter* DUNYASHA. *She serves* LOPAHIN *with kvass.*]

Well, I have to be going. [*Bumps into a chair which falls
over.*] There, you see! [*Triumphantly.*] You can see for
yourself what I mean, you see . . . so to speak . . . It's
absolutely amazing! [*Goes out.*]

DUNYASHA. I must tell you a secret, Yermolay Alexeyevich.
Epihodov proposed to me.

LOPAHIN. Really!

DUNYASHA. I don't know what to do. . . . He's a quiet man,
but then sometimes he starts talking, and then you can't
understand a word he says. It sounds nice, and he says it
with so much feeling, but it doesn't make any sense. I

think I like him a little, and he's madly in love with me.
But the poor man, he's sort of unlucky! Do you know,
something unpleasant seems to happen to him every day.
That's why they tease him and call him "two-and-twenty
misfortunes."

LOPAHIN [*listens*]. I think I hear them coming. . . .

DUNYASHA. Coming! . . . Oh, what's the matter with me. . . .
I feel cold all over.

LOPAHIN. Yes, they're really coming! Let's go and meet them
at the door. I wonder if she'll recognize me? We haven't
seen each other for five years.

DUNYASHA [*agitated*]. I'm going to faint . . . Oh, I'm going to
faint! . . .

[*The sound of two carriages driving up to the house can be
heard.* LOPAHIN *and* DUNYASHA *hurry out. The stage is
empty. Then there are sounds of people arriving in the next
room.* FEERS, *who has gone to meet the train, enters the
room leaning on a cane. He crosses the stage as rapidly as
he can. He is dressed in an old-fashioned livery coat and
a top hat and is muttering to himself, though it is impossible to make out what he is saying. The noises offstage
become louder.*]

VOICE [*offstage*]. Let's go through here.

[*Enter* LYUBOV ANDREYEVNA, ANYA, *and* CHARLOTTA IVANOVA,
leading a small dog, all in traveling clothes, VARYA, *wearing
an overcoat and a kerchief over her head,* GAEV, SEMYONOV-
PISHCHIK, LOPAHIN, DUNYASHA, *carrying a bundle and
parasol, and other servants with luggage.*]

ANYA. Let's go through here. Do you remember what room
this is, Mamma?

LYUBOV [*joyfully through her tears*]. The nursery!

VARYA. How cold it is! My hands are numb. [*To* LYUBOV.]
Your rooms are the same as always, Mamma dear, the
white one, and the lavender one.

LYUBOV. The nursery, my dear, beautiful room! . . . I used to
sleep here when I was little. [*Cries.*] And here I am again,
like a little child. . . . [*She kisses her brother, then* VARYA,
then her brother again.] And Varya hasn't changed a bit,
looking like a nun. And I recognized Dunyasha, too. [*Kisses*
DUNYASHA.]

GAEV. The train was two hours late. Just think of it! Such efficiency!

CHARLOTTA [*to* PISHCHIK]. And my dog eats nuts, too.

PISHCHIK [*astonished*]. Think of that!

[*They all go out except* ANYA *and* DUNYASHA.]

DUNYASHA. We've waited and waited for you. . . . [*Helps* ANYA *to take off her hat and coat.*]

ANYA. I haven't slept for four nights . . . I'm freezing.

DUNYASHA. It was Lent when you left, and it was snowing and freezing; but it's spring now. Darling! [*She laughs and kisses her.*] Oh, how I've missed you! I could hardly stand it. My pet, my precious . . . But I must tell you . . . I can't wait another minute. . . .

ANYA [*without enthusiasm*]. What time is it?

DUNYASHA. Epihodov, the clerk, proposed to me right after Easter.

ANYA. You never talk about anything else. . . . [*Tidies her hair.*] I've lost all my hairpins. . . . [*She is so tired she can hardly keep on her feet.*]

DUNYASHA. I really don't know what to think. He loves me . . . he loves me very much!

ANYA [*looking through the door into her room, tenderly*]. My own room, my own windows, just as if I'd never left them! I'm home again! Tomorrow I'm going to get up and run right to the garden! Oh, if only I could fall asleep! I couldn't sleep all the way back, I've been so worried.

DUNYASHA. Pyotr Sergeyevich came the day before yesterday.

ANYA [*joyfully*]. Petya!

DUNYASHA. We put him in the bathhouse, he's probably asleep now. He said he didn't want to inconvenience you. [*Looks at her watch.*] I should have gotten him up, but Varya told me not to. "Don't you dare get him up," she said.

[*Enter* VARYA *with a bunch of keys at her waist.*]

VARYA. Dunyasha, get some coffee, and hurry! Mamma wants some.

DUNYASHA. I'll get it right away. [*Goes out.*]

VARYA. Thank God, you're back! You're home again. [*Embracing her.*] My little darling's come home! How are you, my precious?

ANYA. If you only knew what I've had to put up with!

VARYA. I can just imagine . . .

ANYA. You remember, I left just before Easter and it was cold then. And Charlotta never stopped talking the whole time, talking and those silly tricks of hers. Why did you make me take Charlotta?

VARYA. But you couldn't go all alone, darling. At seventeen!

ANYA. When we got to Paris it was cold and snowing. My French was terrible. Mamma was living on the fifth floor, and the place was filled with people—some French ladies, and an old priest with a little book, and the room was full of cigarette smoke. It was so unpleasant. All of a sudden I felt so sorry for Mamma that I put my arms around her neck and hugged her and wouldn't let go I was so upset. Later Mamma cried and was very kind.

VARYA [*tearfully*]. I can't stand to hear it!

ANYA. She had already sold her villa at Mentone, and she had nothing left, not a thing. And I didn't have any money left either, not a penny. In fact, I barely had enough to get to Paris. And Mamma didn't understand it at all. On the way, we'd eat at the best restaurants and she'd order the most expensive dishes and tip the waiters a rouble each. Charlotta's the same way. And Yasha expected a full-course dinner for himself; it was horrible. You know, Yasha is Mamma's valet now, we brought him with us.

VARYA. Yes, I've seen the scoundrel.

ANYA. Well, how's everything here? Have you paid the interest on the mortgage?

VARYA. With what?

ANYA. Oh dear! Oh dear!

VARYA. The time runs out in August, and then it will be up for sale.

ANYA. Oh dear!

LOPAHIN [*puts his head through the door and moos like a cow*]. Moo-o. . . . [*Disappears.*]

VARYA [*tearfully*]. I'd like to hit him . . . [*Clenches her fist.*]

ANYA [*her arms round* VARYA, *dropping her voice*]. Varya, has he proposed to you?

[VARYA *shakes her head.*]

But he loves you. . . . Why don't you talk to him, what are you waiting for?

VARYA. Nothing will come of it. He's too busy to have time to think of me . . . He doesn't notice me at all. It's easier when he isn't around, it makes me miserable just to see him. Everybody talks of our wedding and congratulates me, but in fact there's nothing to it, it's all a dream. [*In a different tone.*] You've got a new pin, it looks like a bee.

ANYA [*sadly*]. Mamma bought it for me. [*She goes into her room and then with childlike gaiety.*] Did you know that in Paris I went up in a balloon?

VARYA. My darling's home again! My precious one's home.

[DUNYASHA *returns with a coffeepot and prepares coffee.*]

[*Standing by* ANYA'S *door.*] You know, all day long, as I go about the house doing my work, I'm always dreaming. If only we could marry you to some rich man, I'd be more at peace. Then they could go away; first I'd go to the cloisters, and then I'd go on a pilgrimage to Kiev, and then Moscow . . . I'd spend my life just walking from one holy place to another. On and on. Oh, what a wonderful life that would be!

ANYA. The birds are singing in the garden. What time is it?

VARYA. It must be nearly three. Time you went to bed, darling. [*Goes into* ANYA'S *room.*] Oh, what a wonderful life!

[*Enter* YASHA, *with a blanket and a small bag.*]

YASHA [*crossing the stage, in an affectedly genteel voice*]. May I go through here?

DUNYASHA. My, how you've changed since you've been abroad, Yasha. I hardly recognized you.

YASHA. Hm! And who are you?

DUNYASHA. When you went away, I was no bigger than this. . . . [*Shows her height from the floor.*] I'm Dunyasha, Fyodor's daughter. You don't remember me!

YASHA. Hm! You're quite a little peach! [*He looks around and embraces her; she screams and drops a saucer.* YASHA *goes out quickly.*]

VARYA [*in the doorway, crossly*]. What's happening in here?

DUNYASHA [*tearfully*]. I've broken a saucer.

VARYA. That's good luck.

ANYA [*coming out of her room*]. We ought to warn Mamma that Petya's here.

VARYA. I gave strict orders not to wake him up.

ANYA [*pensively*]. Six years ago father died, and then a month later Grisha was drowned in the river. He was such a beautiful little boy—and only seven! Mamma couldn't stand it so she went away . . . and never looked back. [*Shivers.*]

How well I understand her! If she only knew! [*Pause.*]
And Petya was Grisha's tutor, he might remind her . . .

[*Enter* FEERS, *wearing a jacket and a white waistcoat.*]

FEERS [*goes over and is busy with the samovar*]. The mistress
will have her coffee in here. [*Puts on white gloves.*] Is it
ready? [*To* DUNYASHA, *severely.*] Where's the cream?

DUNYASHA. Oh, I forgot! [*Goes out quickly.*]

FEERS [*fussing around the coffeepot*]. That girl's hopeless.
. . . [*Mutters.*] They've come from Paris . . . Years ago
the master used to go to Paris . . . Used to go by carriage.
. . . [*Laughs.*]

VARYA. Feers, what are you laughing at?

FEERS. What would you like? [*Happily.*] The mistress has
come home! Home at last! I don't mind if I die now. . . .
[*Weeps with joy.*]

[*Enter* LYUBOV, LOPAHIN, GAEV *and* SEMYONOV-PISHCHIK, *the
latter in a long peasant coat of fine cloth and full trousers
tucked inside high boots.* GAEV, *as he comes in, moves his
arms and body as if he were playing billiards.*]

LYUBOV. How does it go now? Let me think . . . The red off
the side and into the middle pocket!

GAEV. That's right! Then I put the white into the corner
pocket! . . . Years ago we used to sleep in this room, and
now I'm fifty-one, strange as it may seem.

LOPAHIN. Yes, time flies.

GAEV. What?

LOPAHIN. Time flies, I say.

GAEV. This place smells of patchouli . . .

ANYA. I'm going to bed. Good night, Mamma. [*Kisses her.*]

LYUBOV. My precious child! [*Kisses her hands.*] Are you glad
you're home? I still can't get used to it.

ANYA. Good night, Uncle.

GAEV [*kisses her face and hands*]. God bless you. You're so
much like your mother! [*To his sister.*] You looked exactly
like her at her age, Lyuba.

[ANYA *shakes hands with* LOPAHIN *and* PISHCHICK, *goes out
and shuts the door after her.*]

LYUBOV. She's very tired.

PISHCHIK. It's been a long trip for her.

VARYA [*to* LOPAHIN *and* PISHCHIK]. Well, gentlemen? It's nearly
three o'clock, time to say good-bye.

LYUBOV [*laughs*]. You haven't changed a bit, Varya. [*Draws*
VARYA *to her and kisses her.*] Let me have some coffee,
then we'll all turn in.

[FEERS *places a cushion under her feet.*]

Thank you, my dear. I've got into the habit of drinking
coffee. I drink it day and night. Thank you, my dear old
friend. [*Kisses* FEERS.]

VARYA. I'd better see if they brought all the luggage in. [*Goes
out.*]

LYUBOV. Is it really me sitting here? [*Laughing.*] I'd like to
dance and wave my arms about. [*Covering her face with her
hands.*] But am I just dreaming? God, how I love it here—
my own country! Oh, I love it so much, I could hardly see
anything from the train, I was crying so hard. [*Through
tears.*] Here, but I must drink my coffee. Thank you, Feers,
thank you, my dear old friend. I'm so glad you're still alive.

FEERS. The day before yesterday.

GAEV. He doesn't hear very well.

LOPAHIN. I've got to leave for Kharkov a little after four. What
a nuisance! It's so good just to see you, and I want to talk
with you . . . You look as lovely as ever.

PISHCHIK [*breathing heavily*]. Prettier. In her fancy Parisian
clothes . . . She's simply ravishing!

LOPAHIN. Your brother here—Leonid Andreyevich—says that
I'm nothing but a hick from the country, a tight-fisted
peasant, but it doesn't bother me. Let him say what he likes.
All I want is that you trust me as you always have. Merciful
God! My father was your father's serf, and your grandfather's too, but you've done so much for me that I've
forgotten all that. I love you as if you were my own sister
. . . more than that even.

LYUBOV. I just can't sit still, I can't for the life of me! [*She
jumps up and walks about in great excitement.*] I'm so
happy, it's too much for me. It's all right, you can laugh at
me. I know I'm being silly . . . My wonderful old bookcase!
[*Kisses bookcase.*] And my little table!

GAEV. You know, the old nurse died while you were away.

LYUBOV [*sits down and drinks coffee*]. Yes, you wrote to me
about it. May she rest in peace.

GAEV. Anastasy died, too. And Petrushka quit and is working in town for the chief of police. [*Takes a box of gumdrops out of his pocket and puts one in his mouth.*]

PISHCHIK. My daughter, Dashenka, sends you her greetings.

LOPAHIN. I feel like telling you some good news, something to cheer you up. [*Looks at his watch.*] I'll have to leave in a minute, so there's not much time to talk. But briefly it's this. As you know, the cherry orchard is going to be sold to pay your debts. They've set August 22nd as the date for the auction, but you can sleep in peace and not worry about it; there's a way out. Here's my plan, so please pay close attention. Your estate is only twenty miles from town, and the railroad is close by. Now, if the cherry orchard and the land along the river were subdivided and leased for the building of summer cottages, you'd have a yearly income of at least twenty-five thousand roubles.

GAEV. Such nonsense!

LYUBOV. I'm afraid I don't quite understand, Yermolay Alexeyevich.

LOPAHIN. You'd divide the land into one-acre lots and rent them for at least twenty-five roubles a year. I'll bet you, that if you advertise it now there won't be a lot left by the fall; they'll be snapped up almost at once. You see, you're saved! And really, I must congratulate you; it's a perfect setup. The location is marvelous and the river's deep enough for swimming. Of course, the land will have to be cleared and cleaned up a bit. For instance, all those old buildings will have to be torn down . . . And this house, too . . . but then it's not really good for anything anymore. . . . And then, the old cherry orchard will have to be cut down . . .

LYUBOV. Cut down? My good man, forgive me, but you don't seem to understand. If there's one thing that's interesting and really valuable in this whole part of the country, it's our cherry orchard.

LOPAHIN. The only valuable thing about it is that it's very large. It only produces a crop every other year and then who wants to buy it?

GAEV. Why, this orchard is even mentioned in the encyclopedia.

LOPAHIN [*looking at his watch*]. If you don't decide now, and do something about it before August, the cherry orchard as well as the estate will be auctioned off. So make up your minds! There's no other way out, I promise you. There's no other way.

FEERS. In the old days, forty or fifty years ago, the cherries were dried, preserved, pickled, made into jam, and sometimes . . .

GAEV. Be quiet, Feers.

FEERS. And sometimes, whole wagonloads of dried cherries were shipped to Moscow and Kharkov. We used to make a lot of money on them then! And the dried cherries used to be soft, juicy, sweet, and very good . . . They knew how to do it then . . . they had a way of cooking them . . .

LYUBOV. And where is that recipe now?

FEERS. They've forgotten it. Nobody can remember it.

PISHCHIK [to LYUBOV]. What's it like in Paris? Did you eat frogs?

LYUBOV. I ate crocodiles.

PISHCHIK. Well, will you imagine that!

LOPAHIN. Until recently only rich people and peasants lived in the country, but now lots of people come out for the summer. Almost every town, even the small ones, is surrounded with summer places. And probably within the next twenty years there'll be more and more of these people. Right now, all they do is sit on the porch and drink tea, but later on they might begin to grow a few things, and then your cherry orchard would be full of life again . . . rich and prosperous.

GAEV [indignantly]. Such a lot of nonsense!

[Enter VARYA and YASHA.]

VARYA. There were two telegrams for you, Mamma dear. [Takes out the keys and opens the old bookcase, making a great deal of noise.]. Here they are.

LYUBOV. They're from Paris. [Tears them up without reading them.] I'm through with Paris.

GAEV. Do you know, Lyuba, how old this bookcase is? Last week I pulled out the bottom drawer, and I found the date it was made burned in the wood. Just think, it's exactly a hundred years old. What do you think of that, eh? We ought to celebrate its anniversary. I know it's an inanimate object, but still—it's a bookcase!

PISHCHIK [astonished]. A hundred years! Can you imagine that!

GAEV. Yes . . . That's quite something. [Feeling round the

bookcase with his hands.] Dear, most honored bookcase!
I salute you! For one hundred years you have served the
highest ideals of goodness and justice. For one hundred
years you have made us aware of the need for creative
work; several generations of our family have had their
courage sustained and their faith in a brighter future
fortified by your silent call; you have fostered in us the
ideals of public service and social consciousness.

[*Pause.*]

LOPAHIN. Yes . . .

LYUBOV. You haven't changed a bit, Leonia.

GAEV [*slightly embarrassed*]. I shoot it off the corner into the
middle pocket! . . .

LOPAHIN [*looks at his watch*]. Well, I've got to go.

YASHA [*brings medicine to* LYUBOV]. Would you like to take
your pills now? It's time.

PISHCHIK. You shouldn't take medicine, my dear . . . they
don't do you any good . . . or harm either. Let me have
them. [*Takes the box from her, pours the pills into the palm
of his hand, blows on them, and puts them all into his
mouth and drinks them down with kvass.*] There!

LYUBOV [*alarmed*]. You're out of your mind!

PISHCHIK. I took all the pills.

LOPAHIN. What a stomach!

[*All laugh.*]

FEERS. His honor was here during Holy Week, and he ate
half a bucket of pickles. [*Mutters.*]

LYUBOV. What's he saying?

VARYA. He's been muttering like that for three years now.
We're used to it.

YASHA. It's his age. . . .

[CHARLOTTA IVANOVA, *very thin, and tightly laced in a white
dress, with a lorgnette at her waist, passes across the stage.*]

LOPAHIN. Excuse me, Charlotta Ivanovna, for not greeting
you. I didn't have a chance. [*Tries to kiss her hand.*]

CHARLOTTA [*withdrawing her hand*]. If I let you kiss my hand,
you'd want to kiss my elbow next, and then my shoulder.

LOPAHIN. This just isn't my lucky day.

[*All laugh.*]

Charlotta Ivanovna, do a trick for us.

CHARLOTTA. Not now. I want to go to bed. [*Goes out.*]

LOPAHIN. I'll be back in three weeks. [*Kisses* LYUBOV'S *hand.*] It's time I'm going so I'll say good-bye. [*To* GAEV.] Au revoir. [*Embraces* PISHCHIK.] Au revoir. [*Shakes hands with* VARYA, *then with* FEERS *and* YASHA.] I don't want to go, really. [*To* LYUBOV.] Think over the idea of the summer cottages and if you decide anything, let me know, and I'll get you a loan of at least fifty thousand. So think it over seriously.

VARYA [*crossly*]. Won't you ever go?

LOPAHIN. I'm going, I'm going. [*Goes out.*]

GAEV. What a boor! I beg your pardon . . . Varya's going to marry him, he's Varya's fiancé.

VARYA. Please don't talk like that, Uncle.

LYUBOV. Well, Varya, I'd be delighted. He's a good man.

PISHCHIK. He's a man . . . you have to say that . . . a most worthy fellow . . . My Dashenka says so too . . . she says all sorts of things. . . . [*He drops asleep and snores, but wakes up again at once.*] By the way, my dear, will you lend me two hundred and forty roubles? I've got to pay the interest on the mortgage tomorrow . . .

VARYA [*in alarm*]. We haven't got it, really we haven't!

LYUBOV. It's true, I haven't got a thing.

PISHCHIK. It'll turn up. [*Laughs.*] I never lose hope. There are times when I think everything's lost, I'm ruined, and then—suddenly!—a railroad is built across my land, and they pay me for it! Something's bound to happen, if not today, then tomorrow, or the next day. Perhaps Dashenka will win two hundred thousand—she's got a lottery ticket.

LYUBOV. Well, we've finished our coffee; now we can go to bed.

FEERS [*brushing* GAEV, *admonishing him*]. You've got on the trousers again! What am I going to do with you?

VARYA [*in a low voice*]. Anya's asleep. [*Quietly opens a window.*] The sun's rising and see how wonderful the trees are! And the air smells so fragrant! The birds are beginning to sing.

GAEV [*coming to the window*]. The orchard is all white. You haven't forgotten, Lyuba? How straight that lane is . . . just like a ribbon. And how it shines on moonlit nights. Do you remember? You haven't forgotten, have you?

LYUBOV [*looks through the window at the orchard*]. Oh, my childhood, my innocent childhood! I used to sleep here, and

I'd look out at the orchard and every morning when I woke up I was so happy. The orchard was exactly the same, nothing's changed. [*Laughs happily.*] All, all white! Oh, my orchard! After the dark gloomy autumn and the cold winter, you are young again and full of joy; the angels have not deserted you! If only this burden could be taken from me, if only I could forget my past!

GAEV. Yes, and now the orchard's going to be sold to pay our debts, how strange it all is.

LYUBOV. Look, there's Mother walking through the orchard . . . dressed all in white! [*Laughs happily.*] It is Mother!

GAEV. Where?

VARYA. Oh, please, Mamma dear!

LYUBOV. You're right, it's no one, I only imagined it. Over there, you see, on the right, by the path that goes to the arbor, there's a small white tree that's bending so it looks just like a woman.

[*Enter* TROFIMOV. *He is dressed in a shabby student's uniform, and wears glasses.*]

What a wonderful orchard! Masses of white blossoms, the blue sky . . .

TROFIMOV. Lyubov Andreyevna!

[*She turns to him.*]

I'll just say hello and leave at once. [*Kisses her hand warmly.*] They told me to wait until morning, but I couldn't wait any longer.

[LYUBOV *looks at him, puzzled.*]

VARYA [*through tears*]. This is Petya Trofimov.

TROFIMOV. Petya Trofimov, I was Grisha's tutor. Have I changed that much?

[LYUBOV *puts her arms round him and weeps quietly.*]

GAEV [*embarrassed*]. Now, now, Lyuba . . .

VARYA [*weeps*]. Didn't I tell you to wait until tomorrow, Petya?

LYUBOV. My Grisha . . . my little boy . . . Oh, Grisha . . . my son . . .

VARYA. Don't cry, Mamma darling. There's nothing we can do, it was God's will.

TROFIMOV [*gently, with emotion*]. Don't, don't . . . please.

LUYBOV [*weeping quietly*]. My little boy was lost . . . drowned
. . . Why? Why, my friend? [*More quietly.*] Anya's asleep
in there, and here I'm crying and making a scene. But
tell me, Petya, what's happened to your good looks? You've
aged so.

TROFIMOV. A peasant woman on the train called me "that
moth-eaten man."

LYUBOV. You used to be such an attractive boy, a typical
young student. But now your hair is thin and you wear
glasses. Are you still a student? [*She walks to the door.*]

TROFIMOV. I expect I'll be a student as long as I live.

LYUBOV [*kisses her brother, then* VARYA]. Well, go to bed now.
You have aged, too, Leonid.

PISHCHIK [*following her*]. Yes, I suppose it's time to get to
bed. Oh, my gout! I'd better spend the night here, and in
the morning, Lyubov Andreyevna, my dear, I'd like to
borrow the two hundred and forty roubles.

GAEV. Don't you ever stop?

PISHCHIK. Just two hundred and forty roubles . . . To pay the
interest on my mortgage.

LYUBOV. I haven't any money, my friend.

PISHCHIK. Oh, I'll pay you back, my dear. It's not much,
after all.

LYUBOV. Oh, all right. Leonid will give it to you. You give
him the money, Leonid.

GAEV. Why, of course; glad to. As much as he wants!

LYUBOV. What else can we do? He needs it. He'll pay it back.

[LYUBOV, TROFIMOV, PISHCHIK *and* FEERS *go out.* GAEV, VARYA
and YASHA *remain.*]

GAEV. My sister hasn't lost her habit of throwing money away.
[*To* YASHA.] Get out of the way, you smell like a barnyard.

YASHA [*with a sneer*]. And you haven't changed either, have
you Leonid Andreyevich?

GAEV. What's that? [*To* VARYA.] What did he say?

VARYA [*to* YASHA]. Your mother came out from town yesterday to see you, and she's been waiting out in the servant's
quarters ever since.

YASHA. I wish she wouldn't bother me.

VARYA. Oh, you ought to be ashamed of yourself.

YASHA. What's she in such a hurry for? She could have come
tomorrow. [YASHA *goes out.*]

VARYA. Mamma hasn't changed a bit. She'd give away everything we had, if she could.

GAEV. Yes . . . You know, when many things are prescribed to cure a disease, that means it's incurable. I've been wracking my brains to find an answer, and I've come up with several solutions, plenty of them—which means there aren't any. It would be wonderful if we could inherit some money, or if our Anya were to marry some very rich man, or if one of us went to Yaroslavl and tried our luck with our old aunt, the Countess. You know she's very rich.

VARYA [weeping]. If only God would help us.

GAEV. Oh, stop blubbering! The Countess is very rich, but she doesn't like us . . . To begin with, my sister married a lawyer, and not a nobleman . . .

[ANYA appears in the doorway.]

She married a commoner . . . and since then no one can say she's behaved in the most virtuous way possible. She's good, kind, and lovable, and I love her very much, but no matter how much you may allow for extenuating circumstances, you've got to admit that her morals have not been beyond reproach. You can sense it in everything she does . . .

VARYA [in a whisper]. Anya's standing in the doorway.

GAEV. What? [A pause.] Isn't that strange, something's gotten into my right eye . . . I'm having a terrible time seeing. And last Thursday, when I was in the District Court . . .

[ANYA comes in.]

VARYA. Anya, why aren't you asleep?

ANYA. I don't feel like sleeping. I just can't.

GAEV. My dear little girl! [Kisses ANYA'S face and hands.] My child! [Tearfully.] You're not just my niece, you're an angel, my whole world. Please believe me, believe . . .

ANYA. I believe you, Uncle. Everyone loves you, respects you . . . but, dear Uncle, you shouldn't talk so much, just try to keep quiet. What were you saying just now about mother, about your own sister? What made you say that?

GAEV. Yes, yes! [He takes her hand and puts it over his face.] You're quite right, it was a horrible thing to say! My God! My God! And that speech I made to the bookcase . . . so stupid! As soon as I finished it, I realized how stupid it was.

VARYA. It's true, Uncle dear, you oughtn't to talk so much. Just keep quiet, that's all.

ANYA. If you keep quiet, you'll find life is more peaceful.

GAEV. I'll be quiet. [Kisses ANYA's and VARYA's hands.] I'll be quiet. But I must tell you something about all this business, it's important. Last Thursday I went to the District Court, and I got talking with some friends, and from what they said it looks as if it might be possible to get a second mortgage so we can pay the interest to the bank.

VARYA. If only God would help us!

GAEV. I'm going again on Tuesday to talk with them some more. [To VARYA.] Oh, stop crying. [To ANYA.] Your mother's going to talk with Lopahin, and he certainly won't refuse her. And after you've had a little rest, you can go to Yaroslavl to see your grandmother, the Countess. You see, we'll attack the problem from three sides, and—it's as good as solved! We'll pay the interest, I'm sure of it. [He eats a gumdrop.] On my honor, on anything you like, I swear the estate'll not be sold! [Excited.] I'll bet my happiness on it! Here's my hand, you can call me a worthless liar if I allow the auction to take place. I swear it with all my soul!

ANYA [calmer, with an air of happiness]. How good you are, Uncle, and how sensible! [Embracing him.] I'm not afraid anymore. I feel so happy and at peace.

[Enter FEERS.]

FEERS [reproachfully]. Leonid Andreyevich, aren't you ashamed of yourself? When are you going to bed?

GAEV. In a minute. Now you go away, Feers. I can get ready for bed myself. Come along, children, time for bed. We'll talk about it some more tomorrow, you must go to bed now. [Kisses ANYA and VARYA.] You know, I'm a man of the 'eighties. People don't think much of that period these days, but still I can say that I've suffered a great deal in my lifetime because of my convictions. There's a reason why the peasants love me. You have to know the peasants! You have to know . . .

ANYA. You're beginning again, Uncle!

VARYA. Yes, you'd better keep quiet, Uncle dear.

FEERS [sternly]. Leonid Andreyevich!

GAEV. I'm coming, I'm coming! Go to bed now! Bank the

white into the side pocket. There's a shot for you . . . [*Goes out;* FEERS *hobbles after him.*]

ANYA. I feel better now, although I don't want to go to Yaroslavl, I don't like the Countess at all, but then, thanks to Uncle, we really don't have to worry at all. [*She sits down.*]

VARYA. I've got to get some sleep. I'm going. Oh, by the way, we had a terrible scene while you were gone. You know, there are only a few old servants left out in the servants' quarters: just Yefmushka, Polya, Yevstignay, and Karp. Well, they let some tramps sleep out there, and at first I didn't say anything about it. But then later, I heard people saying that I had given orders to feed them nothing but beans. Because I was stingy, you see . . . Yevstignay was the cause of it all. "Well," I think to myself, "if that's how things are, just you wait!" So I called Yevstignay in. [*Yawns.*] So he came. "What's all this, Yevstignay," I said to him, "you're such a fool." [*She walks up to* ANYA.] Anichka! [*A pause.*] She's asleep! . . . [*Takes her arm.*] Let's go to bed! Come! [*Leads her away.*] My darling's fallen asleep! Come . . .

[*They go towards the door. The sound of a shepherd's pipe is heard from far away, beyond the orchard.* TROFIMOV *crosses the stage, but, seeing* VARYA *and* ANYA, *stops.*]

Sh-sh! She's asleep . . . asleep . . . Come along, come along.

ANYA [*softly, half-asleep*]. I'm so tired. . . . I can hear the bells ringing all the time . . . Uncle . . . dear . . . Mamma and Uncle. . . .

VARYA. Come, darling, come. . . . [*They go into* ANYA'S *room.*]

TROFIMOV [*deeply moved*]. Oh, Anya . . . my sunshine! My spring!

ACT TWO

[*An old abandoned chapel in a field. Beside it are a well, an old bench and some tombstones. A road leads to the Ranevsky estate. On one side a row of poplars casts a shadow; at that point the cherry orchard begins. In the distance, a line of telegraph poles can be seen, and beyond them, on the horizon is the outline of a large town, visible only in very clear weather. It's nearly sunset.* CHARLOTTA, YASHA *and* DUNYASHA *are sitting on the bench;* EPIHODOV *is standing near by, playing a guitar; everyone is lost in thought.* CHARLOTTA *is wearing an old hunting cap; she has taken a shotgun off her shoulder and is adjusting the buckle on the strap.*]

CHARLOTTA [*thoughtfully*]. I don't know how old I am. For you see, I haven't got a passport . . . but I keep pretending that I'm still very young. When I was a little girl, my father and mother traveled from fair to fair giving performances —oh, very good ones. And I used to do the *salto-mortale* and all sorts of other tricks, too. When Papa and Mamma died, a German lady took me to live with her and sent me to school. So when I grew up I became a governess. But where I come from and who I am, I don't know. Who my parents were—perhaps they weren't even married—I don't know. [*Taking a cucumber from her pocket and beginning to eat it.*] I don't know anything. [*Pause.*] I'm longing to talk to someone, but there isn't anybody. I haven't anybody . . .

EPIHODOV [*plays the guitar and sings*]. "What care I for the noisy world? . . . What care I for friends and foes?" How pleasant it is to play the mandolin!

DUNYASHA. That's a guitar, not a mandolin. [*She looks at herself in a little mirror and powders her face.*]

EPIDHODOV. To a man who's madly in love this is a mandolin. [*Sings quietly.*] "If only my heart were warmed by the fire of love requited. . . ."

[YASHA *joins in.*]

CHARLOTTA. How dreadfully these people sing! . . . Ach! Like a bunch of jackals.

DUNYASHA [*to* YASHA]. You're so lucky to have been abroad!

YASHA. Of course I am. Naturally. [*Yawns, then lights a cigar.*]

EPIHODOV. Stands to reason. Abroad everything's reached its maturity . . . I mean to say, everything's been going on for such a long time.

YASHA. Obviously.

EPIHODOV. Now, I'm a cultured man, I read all kinds of extraordinary books, you know, but somehow I can't seem to figure out where I'm going, what it is I really want, I mean to say—whether to live or to shoot myself. Nevertheless, I always carry a revolver on me. Here it is. [*Shows the revolver.*]

CHARLOTTA. That's finished, so now I'm going. [*Slips the strap of the gun over her shoulder.*] Yes, Epihodov, you are a very clever man, and frightening, too; the women must be wild about you! Brrr! [*Walks off.*] All these clever people are so stupid, I haven't anyone to talk to. I'm so lonely, always alone, I have nobody and . . . and who I am and what I'm here for, nobody knows . . . [*Wanders out.*]

EPIHODOV. Frankly, and I want to keep to the point, I have to admit that fate, so to speak, treats me absolutely without mercy, like a small ship is buffeted by the storm, as it were. I mean to say, suppose I'm mistaken, then why for instance should I wake up this morning and suddenly see a gigantic spider sitting on my chest? Like this . . . [*Showing the size with both hands.*] Or if I pick up a jug to have a drink of kvass, there's sure to be something horrible, like a cockroach, inside it. [*Pause.*] Have you read Buckle? [*Pause.*] May I trouble you for a moment, Dunyasha? I'd like to speak with you.

DUNYASHA. Well, go ahead.

EPIHODOV. I'd very much like to speak with you alone. [*Sighs.*]

DUNYASHA [*embarrassed*]. Oh, all right . . . But first bring me my little cape . . . It's hanging by the cupboard. It's getting terribly chilly . . .

EPIHODOV. Very well, I'll get it. . . . Now I know what to do with my revolver. [*Takes his guitar and goes off playing it.*]

YASHA. "Two-and-twenty misfortunes!" Just between you and me, he's a stupid fool. [*Yawns.*]

DUNYASHA. I hope to God he doesn't shoot himself. [*Pause.*] He makes me so nervous and I'm always worrying about him. I came to live here when I was still a little girl. Now I no longer know how to live a simple life, and my hands are as white . . . as white as a lady's. I've become such a delicate and sensitive creature. I'm afraid of everything . . . so frightened. If you deceive me, Yasha, I don't know what will happen to my nerves.

YASHA [*kisses her*]. You sweet little peach! Just remember, a girl must always control herself. Personally I think nothing is worse than a girl who doesn't behave herself.

DUNYASHA. I love you so much, so passionately! You're so intelligent, you can talk about anything.

[*Pause.*]

YASHA [*yawns*]. Yes, I suppose so . . . In my opinion, it's like this: if a girl loves someone it means she's immoral. [*Pause.*] I enjoy smoking a cigar in the fresh air . . . [*Listens.*] Someone's coming. It's the ladies and gentlemen. . . .

[DUNYASHA *impulsively embraces him.*]

Go to the house now, as though you'd been swimming down at the river. No, this way or they'll see you. I wouldn't want them to think I was interested in you.

DUNYASHA [*coughing softly*]. That cigar has given me such a headache . . . [*Goes out.*]

[YASHA *remains sitting by the shrine. Enter* LYUBOV, GAEV *and* LOPAHIN.]

LOPAHIN. You've got to make up your minds once and for all; there's no time to lose. After all, it's a simple matter. Will you lease your land for the cottages, or won't you? You can answer in one word: yes or no? Just one word!

LYUBOV. Who's been smoking such wretched cigars? [*Sits down.*]

GAEV. How very convenient everything is with the railroad nearby. [*Sits down.*] Well, here we are—we've been to town, had lunch and we're home already. I put the red into the middle pocket! I'd like to go in . . . just for one game. . . .

LYUBOV. You've got lots of time.

LOPAHIN. Just one word! [*Beseechingly.*] Please give me an answer!

GAEV [*yawns*]. What did you say?

LYUBOV [*looking into her purse*]. Yesterday I had lots of

money, but today there's practically none left. My poor
Varya feeds us all milk soups to economize; the old servants
in the kitchen have nothing but dried peas, and here I am
wasting money senselessly, I just don't understand it. . . .
She drops her purse, scattering gold coins. Now I've
dropped it again. . . . [*Annoyed.*]

YASHA. Allow me, Madam, I'll pick them right up. [*Picks up
the money.*]

LYUBOV. Thank you, Yasha . . . And why did we go out for
lunch today? And that restaurant of yours . . . the food
was vile, the music ghastly, and the table cloths smelled of
soap. And Leonia, why do you drink so much? And eat
so much? And talk so much? Today at the restaurant you
were at it again, and it was all so pointless. About the
'seventies, and the decadents. And to whom? Really, talking
to the waitress about the decadents!

LOPAHIN. Yes, that's too much.

GAEV [*waving his hand*]. I know I'm hopeless. [*To* YASHA,
irritably.] Why are you always bustling about in front of
me?

YASHA [*laughs*]. The minute you open your mouth I start
laughing.

GAEV [*to his sister*]. Either he goes, or I do. . . .

LYUBOV. Get along, Yasha, you'd better leave us now.

YASHA [*hands the purse to* LYUBOV]. I'm going. [*He can
hardly restrain his laughter.*] Right this minute. . . . [*Goes
out.*]

LOPAHIN. You know, that rich merchant Deriganov is thinking of buying your estate. They say he's coming to the
auction himself.

LYUBOV. Where did you hear that?

LOPAHIN. That's what they say in town.

GAEV. Our aunt in Yaroslavl has promised to send us some
money, but when and how much we don't know.

LOPAHIN. How much will she send? A hundred thousand? Two
hundred?

LYUBOV. Well, hardly . . . Ten or fifteen thousand, perhaps.
And we should be thankful for that.

LOPAHIN. Forgive me for saying it, but really, in my whole
life I've never met such unrealistic, unbusinesslike, queer
people as you. You're told in plain language that your
estate's going to be sold, and you don't seem to understand
it at all.

LYUBOV. But what are we to do? Please, tell us.

LOPAHIN. I keep on telling you. Every day I tell you the same thing. You must lease the cherry orchard and the rest of the land for summer cottages, and you must do it now, as quickly as possible. It's almost time for the auction. Please, try to understand! Once you definitely decide to lease it for the cottages, you'll be able to borrow as much money as you like, and you'll be saved.

LYUBOV. Summer cottages and vacationers! Forgive me, but it's so vulgar.

GAEV. I agree with you entirely.

LOPAHIN. Honestly, I'm going to burst into tears, or scream, or faint. I can't stand it anymore! It's more than I can take! [*To* GAEV.] And you're an old woman!

GAEV. What did you say?

LOPAHIN. I said, you're an old woman!

LYUBOV [*alarmed*]. No, don't go, please stay. I beg you! Perhaps we can think of something.

LOPAHIN. What's there to think of?

LYUBOV. Please don't go! I feel so much more cheerful when you're here. [*Pause.*] I keep expecting something horrible to happen . . . as though the house were going to collapse on top of us.

GAEV [*in deep thought*]. I bank it off the cushions, and then into the middle pocket. . . .

LYUBOV. We've sinned too much. . . .

LOPAHIN. Sinned! What sins have you . . .

GAEV [*putting a gumdrop into his mouth.*] They say I've eaten up my fortune in gumdrops. [*Laughs.*]

LYUBOV. Oh, my sins! Look at the way I've wasted money. It's madness. And then I married a man who had nothing but debts. And he was a terrible drinker . . . Champagne killed him! And then, as if I hadn't enough misery, I fell in love with someone else. We went off together, and just at that time—it was my first punishment, a blow that broke my heart—my little boy was drowned right here in this river . . . so I went abroad. I went away for good, never to return, never to see this river again . . . I just shut my eyes and ran away in a frenzy of grief, but *he* . . . he followed me. It was so cruel and brutal of him! I bought a villa near Mentone because he fell ill there, and for three years, day and night, I never had any rest. He was very sick, and he completely exhausted me; my soul dried up

completely. Then, last year when the villa had to be sold
to pay the debts, I went to Paris, and there he robbed me
of everything I had and left me for another woman. . . . I
tried to poison myself. . . . It was all so stupid, so shameful! And then suddenly I felt an urge to come back to
Russia, to my own country, to my little girl . . . [*Dries her
tears.*] Oh, Lord, Lord, be merciful, forgive my sins! Don't
punish me any more! [*Takes a telegram out of her pocket.*]
This came from Paris today. He's asking my forgiveness,
he's begging me to return. [*Tears up the telegram.*] Sounds
like music somewhere. [*Listens.*]

GAEV. That's our famous Jewish orchestra. Don't you remember, four violins, a flute and a bass?

LYUBOV. Are they still playing? Sometime we should have a
dance and they could play for us.

LOPAHIN [*listens*]. I can't hear anything . . . [*Sings quietly.*]
"And the Germans, if you pay, will turn Russians into
Frenchmen, so they say. . . ." [*Laughs.*] I saw a wonderful
play last night. It was so funny.

LYUBOV. It probably wasn't funny at all. Instead of going to
plays, you should take a good look at yourself. Just think
how dull your life is, and how much nonsense you talk!

LOPAHIN. That's true, I admit it! Our lives are stupid . . .
[*Pause.*] My father was a peasant, an idiot. He knew nothing
and he taught me nothing. He only beat me when he was
drunk, and always with a stick. And as a matter of fact,
I'm just as much an idiot myself. I don't know anything
and my handwriting's awful. I'm ashamed for people to
see it—it's like a pig's.

LYUBOV. You should be married, my friend.

LOPAHIN. Yes . . . That's true.

LYUBOV. You ought to marry our Varya. She's a fine girl.

LOPAHIN. Yes.

LYUBOV. She comes from simple people, and she works hard
all day long without stopping. But the main thing is she
loves you, and you've liked her for a long time yourself.

LOPAHIN. Well. . . . I think it's a fine idea . . . She's a nice
girl. [*Pause.*]

GAEV. I've been offered a job at the bank. Six thousand a year.
Did I tell you?

LYUBOV. Yes, you did. You'd better stay where you are.

[FEERS *enters, bringing an overcoat.*]

FEERS [*to* GAEV]. Please put it on, sir, you might catch cold.

GAEV [*puts on the overcoat*]. Oh, you *are* a nuisance.

FEERS. You must stop this! You went off this morning without letting me know. [*Looks him over.*]

LYUBOV. How you've aged, Feers!

FEERS. What can I do for you, Madam?

LOPAHIN. She says you've aged a lot.

FEERS. I've lived a long time. They were planning to marry me before your father was born. [*Laughs.*] Why, I was already head butler at the time of the emancipation, but I wouldn't take my freedom, I stayed on with the master and mistress. . . . [*Pause.*] I remember everyone was happy at the time, but what they were happy about, they didn't know themselves.

LOPAHIN. That was the good life all right! All the peasants were flogged!

FEERS [*not having heard him*]. That's right! The peasants belonged to their masters, and the masters belonged to the peasants; but now everything's all confused, and people don't know what to make of it.

GAEV. Be quiet, Feers. Tomorrow I've got to go to town. I've been promised an introduction to some general or other who might lend us some money for the mortgage.

LOPAHIN. Nothing will come of it. And how would you pay the interest, anyway?

LYUBOV. He's talking nonsense again. There aren't any generals.

[*Enter* TROFIMOV, ANYA *and* VARYA.]

GAEV. Here come the children.

ANYA. There's Mamma.

LYUBOV. Come here, my dears. Oh, my darling children. . . . [*Embraces* ANYA *and* VARYA.] If only you knew how much I love you! Here now, sit down beside me.

[*All sit down.*]

LOPAHIN. Our perennial student is always with the girls.

TROFIMOV. It's none of your business.

LOPAHIN. He'll soon be fifty, and he's still a student.

TROFIMOV. Oh, stop your stupid jokes.

LOPAHIN. What's bothering you? My, you *are* a strange fellow!

TROFIMOV. Why do you keep pestering me?

LOPAHIN [*laughs*]. Just let me ask you one question: what's your opinion of me?

TROFIMOV. My opinion of you, Yermolay Alexeyevich, is this: you're a rich man, and soon you'll be a millionaire. For the same reason that wild beasts are necessary to maintain nature's economic laws, you are necessary, too—each of you devours everything that gets in his way.

[*Everybody laughs.*]

VARYA. You'd better talk about the planets, Petya.

LYUBOV. No, let's go on with the conversation we had yesterday.

TROFIMOV. What was that?

GAEV. About pride.

TROFIMOV. We talked for a long time yesterday, but we didn't agree on anything. The proud man, the way you use the word, has some mysterious quality about him. Perhaps you're right in a way, but if we look at it simply, without trying to be too subtle, you have to ask yourself why should we be proud at all? Why be proud when you realize that man, as a species, is poorly constructed physiologically, and is usually coarse, stupid and profoundly unhappy, too? We ought to put an end to such vanity and just go to work. That's right, we ought to work.

GAEV. You'll die just the same, no matter what you do.

TROFIMOV. Who knows? And anyway, what does it mean—to die? It could be that man has a hundred senses, and when he dies only the five that are known perish, while the other ninety-five go on living.

LYUBOV. How clever you are Petya!

LOPAHIN [*ironically*]. Oh, very clever!

TROFIMOV. Humanity is continually advancing, is continually seeking to perfect its powers. Someday all the things which we can't understand now, will be made clear. But if this is to happen, we've got to work, work with all our might to help those who are searching for truth. Up until now, here in Russia only a few have begun to work. Nearly all of the intelligentsia that I know have no commitment, they don't do anything, and are as yet incapable of work. They call themselves "the intelligentsia," but they still run rough-shod over their servants, and they treat the peasants like animals, they study without achieving anything, they read only childish drivel, and they don't do a thing. As for their knowledge of science, it's only jargon, and they have no appreciation of art either. They are all so serious, and they go about with solemn looks on their faces; they philosophize and talk about important matters; and yet before our very eyes our workers are poorly fed, they live in the worst kind of squalor, sleeping not on beds, but on the floor thirty to forty in a room—with roaches, odors, dampness, and depravity everywhere. It's perfectly clear that all our moralizing is intended to deceive not only ourselves, but others as well. Tell me, where are the nursery schools we're always talking about, where are the libraries? We only write about them in novels, but in actuality there aren't any. There's nothing but dirt, vulgarity, and decadent Orientalism. . . . I'm afraid of those serious faces, I don't like them; I'm afraid of serious talk. It would be better if we'd just keep quiet.

LOPAHIN. Well, let me tell you that *I'm* up before five every morning, and I work from morning till night. I always have money, my own and other people's, and I have lots of opportunities to see what the people around me are like. You only have to start doing something to realize how few honest, decent people there are. Sometimes, when I can't sleep, I start thinking about it. God's given us immense forests, and wide open fields, and unlimited horizons—living in such a world we ought to be giants!

LYUBOV. But why do you want giants? They're all right in fairy tales, anywhere else they're terrifying.

[EPIHODOV *crosses the stage in the background, playing his guitar.*]

LYUBOV [*pensively*]. There goes Epihodov. . . .

ANYA [*pensively*]. There goes Epihodov. . . .

GAEV. The sun's gone down, my friends.

TROFIMOV. Yes.

GAEV [*in a subdued voice, as if reciting a poem*]. Oh, glorious nature, shining with eternal light, so beautiful, yet so indifferent to our fate . . . you, whom we call Mother, the wellspring of life and death, you live and you destroy. . . .

VARYA [*imploringly*]. Uncle, please!

ANYA. You're doing it again, Uncle!

TROFIMOV. You'd better bank the red into middle pocket.

GAEV. All right, I'll keep quiet.

[*They all sit deep in thought; the only thing that can be heard is the muttering of* FEERS. *Suddenly there is a sound in the distance, as if out of the sky, like the sound of a harp string breaking, gradually and sadly dying away.*]

LYUBOV. What was that?

LOPAHIN. I don't know. Sounded like a cable broke in one of the mines. But it must've been a long way off.

GAEV. Perhaps it was a bird . . . a heron, maybe.

TROFIMOV. Or an owl. . . .

LYUBOV [*shudders*]. Whatever it was, it sounded unpleasant . . .

[*A pause.*]

FEERS. It was the same way before the disaster: the owl hooted and the samovar was humming.

GAEV. What disaster?

FEERS. Before they freed us.

[*A pause.*]

LYUBOV. We'd better get started, my friends. It's getting dark and we should get home. [*To* ANYA.] You're crying, my darling! What's wrong? [*She embraces her.*]

ANYA. Nothing, Mamma. It's nothing.

TROFIMOV. Someone's coming.

[*Enter a* TRAMP *in a battered white hunting cap and an overcoat; he's slightly drunk.*]

TRAMP. Excuse me, but can I get to the station through here?

GAEV. Yes, just follow the road.

TRAMP. Much obliged to you, sir. [*Coughs.*] It's a beautiful day today. [*Declaiming.*] "Oh, my brother, my suffering brother! . . . Come to the Volga, whose groans . . ." [*To* VARYA.] Mademoiselle, could a poor starving Russian trouble you for just enough to . . .

[VARYA *cries out, frightened.*]

LOPAHIN [*angrily*]. Really, this is too much!

LYUBOV [*at a loss what to do*]. Here, take this . . . here you are. [*Looks in her purse.*] I haven't any silver . . . but that's all right, here's a gold one. . . .

TRAMP. Thank you very much! [*Goes off. Laughter.*]

VARYA [*frightened*]. I'm going . . . I'm going . . . Oh, Mamma, you know there's not even enough to eat in the house, and you gave him all that!

LYUBOV. Well, what can you do with a silly woman like me? I'll give you everything I've got as soon as we get home. Yermolay Alexeyevich, you'll lend me some more, won't you?

LOPAHIN. Why of course I will.

LYUBOV. Come, it's time to go now. By the way, Varya, we've just about arranged your marriage. Congratulations!

VARYA [*through her tears*]. Don't joke about things like that, Mother!

LOPAHIN. Go to a nunnery, Okhmelia! . . .

GAEV. Look at how my hands are trembling: I haven't had a game for so long.

LOPAHIN. Okhmelia, nymph, remember me in your prayers!

LYUBOV. Come along, everybody. It's almost supper time.

VARYA. That man frightened me so. My heart's still pounding.

LOPAHIN. My friends, just one thing, please just a word: the cherry orchard's to be sold on the 22nd of August. Remember that! Think of what . . .

[*All go out except* TROFIMOV *and* ANYA.]

ANYA [*laughs*]. We can thank the tramp for a chance to be alone! He frightened Varya so.

TROFIMOV. Varya's afraid—she's afraid we might fall in love —so she follows us about all day long. She's so narrow-minded, she can't understand that we're above falling in love. To free ourselves of all that's petty and ephemeral, all that prevents us from being free and happy, that's the whole aim and meaning of our life. Forward! We march forward irresistibly towards that bright star shining there in the distance! Forward! Don't fall behind, friends!

ANYA [*raising her hands*]. How beautifully you talk! [*A pause.*] It's wonderful here today.

TROFIMOV. Yes, the weather's marvelous.

ANYA. What have you done to me, Petya? Why don't I love the cherry orchard like I used to? I used to love it so very much I used to think that there wasn't a better place in all the world than our orchard.

TROFIMOV. The whole of Russia is our orchard. The earth is

great and beautiful and there are many wonderful places in it. [*A pause.*] Just think, Anya: your grandfather, and your great-grandfather, and all your ancestors were serf owners—they owned living souls. Don't you see human beings staring at you from every tree in the orchard, from every leaf and every trunk? Don't you hear their voices? . . . They owned living souls—and it has made you all different persons, those who came before you, and you who are living now, so that your mother, your uncle and you yourself don't even notice that you're living on credit, at the expense of other people, people you don't admit any further than your kitchen. We're at least two hundred years behind the times; we have no real values, no sense of our past, we just philosophize and complain of how depressed we feel, and drink vodka. Yet it's obvious that if we're ever to live in the present, we must first atone for our past and make a clean break with it, and we can only atone for it by suffering, by extraordinary, unceasing work. You've got to understand that, Anya.

ANYA. The house we live in hasn't really been ours for a long time. I'll leave it, I promise you.

TROFIMOV. Yes, leave it, and throw away the keys. Be free as the wind.

ANYA [*in rapture*]. How beautifully you say things.

TROFIMOV. You must believe me, Anya, you must. I'm not thirty yet, I'm young, and I'm still a student, but I've suffered so much already. As soon as winter comes, I'll be hungry and sick and nervous, poor as a beggar. Fate has driven me everywhere! And yet, my soul is always— every moment of every day and every night—it's always full of such marvelous hopes and visions. I have a premonition of happiness, Anya, I can sense it's coming. . . .

ANYA [*pensively*]. The moon's coming up.

[EPIHODOV *is heard playing the same melancholy tune on his guitar. The moon comes up. Somewhere near the poplars* VARYA *is looking for* ANYA *and calling.*]

VARYA [*offstage*]. Anya! Where are you?

TROFIMOV. Yes, the moon is rising. [*A pause.*] There it is— happiness—it's coming nearer and nearer. Already, I can hear its footsteps. And if we never see it, if we never know it, what does it matter? Others will see it!

VARYA'S VOICE. Anya! Where are you?

TROFIMOV. It's Varya again! [*Angrily.*] It's disgusting!

ANYA. Well? Let's go to the river. It's lovely there.

TROFIMOV. Yes, let's.

[TROFIMOV *and* ANYA *go out.*]

VARYA'S VOICE. Anya! Anya!

ACT THREE

[*The drawing room separated by an arch from the ballroom. The same Jewish orchestra that was mentioned in Act II is playing offstage. The chandelier is lighted. It is evening. In the ballroom they are dancing the Grand-rond.* SEMYONOV-PISHCHIK *is heard calling:* "Promenade à une paire!" *Then they all enter the drawing room.* PISHCHIK *and* CHARLOTTA IVANOVNA *are the first couple, followed by* TROFIMOV *and* LYUBOV, ANYA *and a* POST-OFFICE CLERK, VARYA *and the* STATIONMASTER, *etc.* VARYA *is crying softly and wipes away her tears as she dances.* DUNYASHA *is in the last couple.* PISHCHIK *shouts:* "Grand-rond balancez!" *and* "Les cavaliers à genoux et remerciez vos dames!" FEERS, *wearing a dress coat, crosses the room with soda water on a tray.* PISHCHIK *and* TROFIMOV *come back into the drawing room.*]

PISHCHIK. I've got this high blood pressure—I've had two strokes already, you know—and it makes dancing hard work for me; but, as they say, if you're one of a pack, you wag your tail, whether you bark or not. Actually I'm as strong as a horse. My dear father—may he rest in peace—had a little joke. He used to say that the ancient line of Semyonov-Pishchik was descended from the very same horse that Caligula made a member of the Senate. [*Sitting down.*] But my trouble is, I haven't any money. A starving dog can think of nothing but food . . . [*Starts to snore, but wakes up almost at once.*] That's just like me—I can't think of anything but money . . .

TROFIMOV. You know, you're right, there *is* something horsy about you.

PISHCHIK. Well, a horse is a fine animal, you can sell a horse. . . .

[*The sound of someone playing billiards is heard in the next room.* VARYA *appears under the arch to the ballroom.*]

TROFIMOV [*teasing her*]. Madame Lopahin! Madame Lopahin!
VARYA [*angrily*]. The "moth-eaten man"!
TROFIMOV. Yes, I am a moth-eaten man, and I'm proud of it.

VARYA [*thinking bitterly*]. Now we've hired an orchestra—but how are we going to pay for it? [*Goes out.*]

TROFIMOV [*to* PISHCHIK]. If all the energy you've spent during your life looking for money to pay the interest on your debts had been used for something useful, you'd have probably turned the world upside down by now.

PISHCHIK. The philosopher Nietzsche, the greatest, the most famous—a man of the greatest intelligence, in fact—says it's quite all right to counterfeit.

TROFIMOV. Oh, you've read Nietzsche?

PISHCHIK. Of course not, Dashenka told me. But right now I'm in such an impossible position that I could forge a few notes. The day after tomorrow I've got to pay 310 roubles. I've borrowed 130 already. . . . [*Feels in his pockets, in alarm.*] The money's gone! I've lost the money. [*Tearfully.*] Where's the money? [*Joyfully.*] Oh, here it is, inside the lining! I'm so upset, I'm sweating all over! . . .

[*Enter* LYUBOV *and* CHARLOTTA.]

LYUBOV [*humming the "Lezginka"*]. What's taking Leonid so long? What's he doing in town? [*To* DUNYASHA.] Dunyasha, offer the musicians some tea.

TROFIMOV. The auction was probably postponed.

LYUBOV. The orchestra came at the wrong time, and the party started at the wrong time . . . Oh, well . . . never mind . . . [*She sits down and hums quietly.*]

CHARLOTTA [*hands a deck of cards to* PISHCHIK]. Here's a deck of cards—think of any card.

PISHCHIK. I've thought of one.

CHARLOTTA. Now shuffle the deck. That's right. Now give it to me, my dear Monsieur Pishchik. *Ein, zwei, drei!* Why look! There it is, in your coat pocket.

PISHCHIK [*takes the card out of his coat pocket*]. The eight of spades, that's right! [*In astonishment.*] Isn't that amazing!

CHARLOTTA [*holding the deck of cards on the palm of her hand, to* TROFIMOV]. Quickly, which card's on the top?

TROFIMOV. Well . . . ahh . . . the queen of spades.

CHARLOTTA. You're right, here it is! Now, which card?

PISHCHIK. The ace of hearts.

CHARLOTTA. Right again! [*She claps her hand over the pack of cards, which disappears.*] What beautiful weather we're having today!

[*A woman's voice, as if coming from underneath the floor, answers her.*]

VOICE. Oh yes, indeed, the weather's perfectly marvelous!

CHARLOTTA [*addressing the voice*]. How charming you are! I'm very fond of you!

VOICE. And I like you very much, too.

STATIONMASTER [*applauding*]. Bravo, Madame ventriloquist! Bravo!

PISHCHIK [*astonished*]. Isn't that amazing! Charlotta Ivanovna, you're absolutely wonderful! I'm completely in love with you!

CHARLOTTA [*shrugging her shoulders*]. In love? What do you know about love? *Guter Mensch, aber schlechter Musikant.*

TROFIMOV [*slaps* PISHCHIK *on the shoulder*]. He's just an old horse, he is!

CHARLOTTA. Your attention please! Here's one more trick. [*She takes a shawl from a chair.*] Now there's this very nice shawl . . . [*Shakes it out.*] Who'd like to buy it?

PISHCHIK [*amazed*]. Imagine that!

CHARLOTTA. *Ein, zwei, drei!*

[*She lifts up the shawl and* ANYA *is standing behind it;* ANYA *curtsies, runs to her mother, gives her a hug, and runs back to the ballroom. Everybody's delighted.*]

LYUBOV [*clapping*]. Bravo, bravo!

CHARLOTTA. Once more. *Ein, zwei, drei!*

[*Lifts the shawl again; behind it is* VARYA, *who bows.*]

PISHCHIK [*amazed*]. Isn't that amazing!

CHARLOTTA. It's all over! [*She throws the shawl over* PISHCHIK, *curtsies, and runs into the ballroom.*]

PISHCHIK [*going after her*]. You little rascal! . . . Have you ever seen anything like her? What a girl . . . [*Goes out.*]

LYUBOV. Leonid's still not here. I can't understand what's keeping him all this time in town. Anyway, by now everything's been settled; either the estate's been sold or the auction didn't take place. Why does he wait so long to let us know?

VARYA [*trying to comfort her*]. Uncle's bought it, I'm sure he did.

TROFIMOV [*sarcastically*]. Why of course he did.

VARYA. Our great-aunt sent him power of attorney to buy it in her name, and transfer the mortgage to her. She's done it for Anya's sake . . . God will look after us, I'm sure of it—Uncle will buy the estate.

LYUBOV. Your great-aunt sent us fifteen thousand to buy the estate in her name—she doesn't trust us—but that's not enough to even pay the interest. [*She covers her face with her hands.*] My fate is being decided today, my fate. . . .

TROFIMOV [*to* VARYA, *teasingly*]. Madame Lopahin!

VARYA [*crossly*]. The perpetual student! Why, you've been thrown out of the University twice already!

LYUBOV. But why get so cross, Varya? He's only teasing you about Lopahin, there's no harm in that, is there? If you want to, why don't you marry him; he's a fine man, and he's interesting, too. Of course, if you don't want to, don't. No one's trying to force you, darling.

VARYA. I'm very serious about this, Mother . . . and I want to be frank with you . . . he's a good man and I like him.

LYUBOV. Then marry him. What are you waiting for? I don't understand you at all.

VARYA. But, Mother, I can't propose to him myself, can I? It's been two years now since everybody began talking to me about him, and everybody's talking, but he doesn't say a word, or when he does, he just jokes with me. I understand, of course. He's getting rich and his mind's busy with other things, and he hasn't any time for me. If only I had some money, even a little, just a hundred roubles, I'd leave everything and go away, the farther the better. I'd go into a convent.

TROFIMOV. How beautiful!

VARYA [*to* TROFIMOV]. Of course, a student like you has to be so intelligent! [*Quietly and tearfully.*] How ugly you've become, Petya, how much older you look! [*To* LYUBOV, *her tearfulness gone.*] The only thing I can't stand, Mother, is not having any work to do. I've got to stay busy.

[*Enter* YASHA.]

YASHA [*with difficulty restraining his laughter*]. Epihodov's broken a cue! . . . [*Goes out.*]

VARYA. But what's Epihodov doing here? Who let him play billiards? I don't understand these people. . . . [*Goes out.*]

LYUBOV. Please don't tease her, Petya. Don't you see she's upset already?

TROFIMOV. Oh, she's such a busybody—always sticking her nose into other people's business. She hasn't left Anya and

me alone all summer. She's afraid we might fall in love.
What difference should it make to her? Besides, I didn't
give her any reason to think so. I don't believe in such
trivialties. We're above love!

LYUBOV. And I suppose I'm below love. [*Uneasily.*] Why isn't
Leonid back? If only I knew whether the estate's been sold
or not. It's such an incredible calamity that for some reason
I don't know what to think, I feel so helpless. I think I'm
going to scream this very minute . . . I'll do something silly.
Help me, Petya. Talk to me, say something!

TROFIMOV. What difference does it make whether the estate's
sold today or not? It was gone a long time ago. You can't
turn back, the path's lost. You mustn't worry, and above
all you mustn't deceive yourself. For once in your life you
must look the truth straight in the face.

LYUBOV. What truth? *You* know what truth is and what it
isn't, but I've lost such visionary powers. I don't see anything. You're able to solve all your problems so decisively
—but, tell me, my dear boy, isn't that because you're young,
because life is still hidden from your young eyes, because
you can't believe anything horrible will ever happen to you
and you don't expect it to? Oh, yes, you're more courageous
and honest and serious than we are, but put yourself in our
position, try to be generous—if only a little bit—and have
pity on me. I was born here, you know, and my father and
mother lived here, and my grandfather, too, and I love this
house—I can't conceive of life without the cherry orchard,
and if it really has to be sold, then sell me with it . . .
[*Embraces* TROFIMOV, *kisses him on the forehead.*] You
know, my little boy was drowned here. . . . [*Weeps.*] Have
pity on me, my dear, kind friend.

TROFIMOV. You know that I sympathize with you from the
bottom of my heart.

LYUBOV. But you should say it differently . . . differently.
[*Takes out her handkerchief and a telegram falls on the
floor.*] There's so much on my mind today, you can't
imagine. It's so noisy around here that my soul trembles
with every sound, and I'm shaking all over—yet I can't go
to my room because the silence of being alone frightens me.
. . . Don't blame me, Petya. . . . I love you as if you were
my own son. I'd gladly let Anya marry you, honestly I
would, but, my dear boy, you must study, you've got to
graduate. You don't do anything, fate tosses you from one

place to another—it's so strange—Well, it is, isn't it? Isn't it? And you should do something about your beard, make it grow somehow. . . . [*Laughs.*] You look so funny!

TROFIMOV [*picks up the telegram*]. I don't care how I look. That's so superficial.

LYUBOV. This telegram's from Paris. I get one every day . . . Yesterday, today. That beast is sick again, and everything's going wrong for him. . . . He wants me to forgive him, he begs me to return, and, really, I suppose I should go to Paris and stay with him for awhile. You're looking very stern, Petya, but what am I to do, my dear boy, what am I to do? He's sick, and lonely, and unhappy, and who'll take care of him, who'll stop him from making a fool of himself, and give him his medicine at the right time? And anyway, why should I hide it, or keep quiet about it? I love him; yes, I love him. I do, I do. . . . He's a stone around my neck, and I'm sinking to the bottom with him— but I love him and I can't live without him. [*She presses* TROFIMOV's *hand.*] Don't think I'm evil, Petya, don't say anything, please don't. . . .

TROFIMOV [*with strong emotion*]. Please—forgive my frankness, but that man's swindling you!

LYUBOV. No, no, no, you mustn't talk like that. . . . [*Puts her hands over her ears.*]

TROFIMOV. But he's a scoundrel, and you're the only one who doesn't know it! He's a despicable, worthless scoundrel. . . .

LYUBOV [*angry, but in control of herself*]. You're twenty-six or twenty-seven years old, but you're talking like a schoolboy!

TROFIMOV. Say whatever you want!

LYUBOV. You should be a man at your age, you ought to understand what it means to be in love. And you should be in love. . . . Tell me, why haven't you fallen in love! [*Angrily.*] Yes, yes! Oh, you're not so "pure," your purity is a perversion, you're nothing but a ridiculous prude, a freak. . . .

TROFIMOV [*horrified*]. What is she saying?

LYUBOV. "I'm above love!" You're not above love, you're useless, as Feers would say. Imagine not having a mistress at your age! . . .

TROFIMOV [*horrified*]. This is terrible! What's she saying? [*Goes quickly towards the ballroom, clutching his head between his hands.*] This is dreadful. . . . I can't stand it, I'm going. . . . [*Goes out, but returns at once.*] Everything's over between us! [*Goes out through the door into the hall.*]

LYUBOV [*calls after him*]. Petya, wait! You funny boy, I was only joking! Petya!

[*Someone can be heard running quickly downstairs and suddenly falling down with a crash.* ANYA *and* VARYA *scream, and then begin laughing.*]

What's happened?

[ANYA *runs in.*]

ANYA [*laughing*]. Petya fell down the stairs. [*Runs out.*]

LYUBOV. What a strange boy he is!

[*The* STATIONMASTER *stands in the middle of the ballroom and begins to recite "The Sinner" by Alexey Tolstoy. The others listen to hom, but he's hardly had time to recite more than a little bit when a waltz is played, and he stops. Everyone dances.* TROFIMOV, ANYA, VARYA *come in from the hall.*]

LYUBOV. Poor Petya . . . Poor Petya . . . there, my dear boy . . . Please forgive me . . . Come, let's dance . . .

[LYUBOV *dances with* PETYA, ANYA *and* VARYA *dance. Enter* FEERS, *then* YASHA. FEERS *leans on his cane by the side door.* YASHA *looks at the dancers from the drawing room.*]

YASHA. How are you, old boy?

FEERS. Not too well . . . We used to have generals, barons and admirals at our parties . . . long ago, but now we send for the post-office clerk and the stationmaster, and even they don't want to come, it seems. I seem to be getting weaker somehow . . . My old master, the mistress' grandfather, used to make everyone take sealing wax no matter what was wrong with them. I've been taking it every day for the last twenty years, maybe even longer. Perhaps that's why I'm still alive.

YASHA. How you bore me, old man! [*Yawns.*] Why don't you just go away and die . . . It's about time.

FEERS. Eh, you! . . . You're useless . . . [*Mutters.*]

[TROFIMOV *and* LYUBOV, *dancing, come into the drawing room.*]

LYUBOV. Thank you. I think I'll sit down for a bit. [*Sits down.*] I'm tired.

[*Enter* ANYA.]

ANYA [*agitated*]. There's a man in the kitchen who's been saying that the cherry orchard was sold today.

LYUBOV. Sold? To whom?

ANYA. He didn't say. He's gone. [*She and* TROFIMOV *dance into the ballroom.*]

YASHA. There was some old man gossiping there. A stranger.

FEERS. Leonid Andreyevich isn't back yet, he hasn't come yet. And he's only got his light overcoat on; he'll probably catch a cold. Oh, these youngsters!

LYUBOV. I've got to know, or I think I'll die. Yasha, go and find out who bought it.

YASHA. But the old guy went away a long time ago. [*Laughs.*]

LYUBOV [*with a touch of annoyance*]. What are you laughing at? What's so humorous?

YASHA. Epihodov's so funny—he's so stupid. "Two-and-twenty misfortunes!"

LYUBOV. Feers, if the estate's sold, where will you go?

FEERS. I'll go wherever you tell me to go.

LYUBOV. Why are you looking like that? Aren't you well? You ought to be in bed.

FEERS. Yes . . . [*With a faint smile.*] But if I went to bed, who'd take care of the guests and keep things going? There's no one in the house but me.

YASHA [*to* LYUBOV]. Lyubov Andreyevna! I want to ask you something! If you go back to Paris, will you please take me with you? I couldn't stand staying here. [*Looking round and speaking in a low voice.*] I don't have to say it, you can see for yourself how uncivilized everything is here. The people are immoral, it's frightfully dull, and the food is terrible. And then there's that Feers walking about the place and muttering all sorts of stupid things. Take me with you, please!

[*Enter* PISHCHIK.]

PISHCHIK. May I have this dance, beautiful lady . . .

[LYUBOV *gets up to dance.*]

I'll have that 180 roubles from you yet, you enchantress . . . Yes, I will . . . [*Dances.*] Just 180 roubles, that's all . . . [*They go into the ballroom.*]

YASHA [*sings quietly*]. "Don't you understand the passion in my soul . . . ?"

[*In the ballroom a woman in a grey top hat and check trousers starts jumping and throwing her arms about; shouts of: "Bravo, Charlotta Ivanovna!"*]

DUNYASHA [*stops to powder her face*]. Anya told me to dance: there are so many men and not enough ladies; but I get so dizzy from dancing and it makes my heart beat so fast. Feers Nikolayevich, the post-office clerk said something to me just now that completely took my breath away.

[*The music stops.*]

FEERS. What did he say?
DUNYASHA. You're like a flower, he said.
YASHA [*yawns*]. What ignorance! [*Goes out.*]
DUNYASHA. Like a flower . . . I'm so sensitive, I love it when people say beautiful things to me.
FEERS. You'll be having your head turned if you're not careful.

[*Enter EPIHODOV.*]

EPIHODOV. Avdotya Fyodorovna, you act as if you don't want to see me . . . as if I were some kind of insect. [*Sighs.*] Such is life!
DUNYASHA. What do you want?
EPIHODOV. But then, you may be right. [*Sighs.*] Of course, if one looks at it from a certain point of view—if I may so express myself, and please excuse my frankness, you've driven me into such a state . . . Oh, I know what my fate is; every day some misfortune's sure to happen to me, but I've long since been accustomed to that, so I look at life with a smile. You gave me your word, and though I . . .
DUNYASHA. Please, let's talk later, just let me alone now. I'm lost in a dream. [*Plays with her fan.*]
EPIHODOV. Some misfortune happens to me every day, but I —how should I put it—I just smile, I even laugh.

[*VARYA enters from the ballroom.*]

VARYA. Are you still here, Semyon? Your manners are abominable, really! [*To DUNYASHA.*] You'd better go now, Dunyasha. [*To EPIHODOV.*] First you play billiards and break a cue, and now you're going about the drawing room, like one of the guests.

EPIHODOV. Permit me to inform you, but you have no right to attack me like this.

VARYA. I'm not attacking, I'm telling you. You just wander from one place to another, instead of doing your work. We've hired a clerk, but why no one knows.

EPIHODOV [*offended*]. Whether I work, wander, eat, or play billiards, the only people who are entitled to judge my actions are those who are older than me and have some idea of what they're talking about.

VARYA. How dare you say that to me? [*Beside herself in anger.*] You dare to say that? Are you suggesting that I don't know what I'm talking about? Get out of here! Right now!

EPIHODOV [*cowed*]. I wish you'd express yourself more delicately.

VARYA [*beside herself*]. Get out this minute! Get out!

[*He goes to the door, she follows him.*]

Two-and-twenty misfortunes! Get out of here! I don't want ever to see you again!

EPIHODOV [*goes out; his voice is heard from outside the door*]. I'm going to complain.

VARYA. Oh, you're coming back, are you? [*She seizes the stick which* FEERS *left by the door.*] Well, come along, come in . . . I'll show you! So, you're coming back . . . are you? There, take that . . . [*Swings the stick, and at that moment* LOPAHIN *comes in.*]

LOPAHIN [*whom the stick did not, in fact, touch*]. Thank you very much!

VARYA [*angry and ironically*]. I'm sorry!

LOPAHIN. Don't mention it. I'm much obliged to you for the kind reception.

VARYA. That's quite all right. [*Walks away and then looks round and asks gently.*] I haven't hurt you, have I?

LOPAHIN. No, not at all . . . But there's going to be a huge bump, though.

VOICES [*in the ballroom*]. Lopahin's here! Yermolay Alexeyevich!

PISHCHIK. There he is! You can see him, do you hear him? [*Embraces* LOPAHIN.] You smell of cognac, my good fellow! . . . Well, we're having a party here, too.

[*Enter* LYUBOV.]

LYUBOV. It's you, Yermolay Alexeyevich? What's taken you so long? Where's Leonid?

LOPAHIN. Leonid Andreyevich's here, he'll be along in a minute.

LYUBOV [*agitated*]. Well, what happened? Was there an auction? Tell me!

LOPAHIN [*embarrassed, afraid of betraying his joy*]. The auction was over by four o'clock . . . We missed our train and had to wait until nine-thirty. [*Sighs heavily.*] Ugh! I feel a little dizzy . . .

[*Enter* GAEV; *he carries packages in his right hand and wipes away his tears with his left.*]

LYUBOV. Leonia, what happened, Leonia? [*Impatiently, with tears.*] Tell me quickly, for God's sake! . . .

GAEV [*doesn't answer, but waves his hand. To* FEERS, *crying*]. Here, take these . . . it's some anchovies and Kerch herrings . . . I haven't eaten all day . . . What I've been through!

[*Through the open door leading to the ballroom a game of billiards can be heard and* YASHA'S *voice is heard.*]

YASHA. Seven and eighteen.

GAEV [*his expression changes and he stops crying*]. I'm very tired. Come, Feers, I want to change my things. [*Goes out through the ballroom, followed by* FEERS.]

PISHCHIK. Well, what happened at the auction? Come on, tell us!

LYUBOV. Has the cherry orchard been sold?

LOPAHIN. It has.

LYUBOV. Who bought it?

LOPAHIN. I did.

[*A pause.* LYUBOV *is overcome; only the fact that she is standing beside a table and a chair keeps her from falling.* VARYA *takes the keys from her belt, throws them on the floor in the middle of the room and goes out.*]

I bought it. Wait a moment, ladies and gentlemen, please. I'm so mixed up, I don't quite know what to say . . . [*Laughs.*] When we got to the auction, Deriganov was already there. Leonid had only fifteen thousand roubles, and immediately Deriganov bid thirty thousand over and above the mortgage. I saw how things were, so I stepped in and raised it to forty. He bid forty-five, I went to fifty-five; he kept on raising five thousand and I raised it ten thousand. Well, finally it ended—I bid ninety thousand over and above the mortgage, and it went to me. The cherry orchard's mine now! All right, tell me I'm drunk, tell me I'm crazy and that I'm just imagining all this. . . . [*Stamps his feet.*] Don't laugh at me! If only my father and grandfather could rise from their graves and see all that's happened . . . how their Yermolay, their ignorant, beaten Yermolay, the little boy that ran around in his bare feet in the winter . . . if only they could see that he's bought this estate, the most beautiful place in the world! Yes, he's bought the very estate where his father and grandfather were slaves and where they weren't even admitted to the kitchen! I must be asleep, I'm dreaming, it only seems to be true . . . it's all just my imagination, my imagination must be confused . . . [*Picks up the keys, smiling gently.*] She threw these down because she wanted to show that she's not the mistress here anymore. [*Jingles the keys.*] Well, never mind.

[*The orchestra is heard tuning up.*]

Hey there! you musicians, play something for us! I want some music! My friends, come along and soon you'll see Yermolay Lopahin take an axe to the cherry orchard, you'll see the trees come crashing to the ground! We're going to build hundreds of summer cottages, and our children and our grandchildren will see a whole new world growing up here . . . So play, let's have some music!

[*The band plays.* LYUBOV *has sunk into a chair and is crying bitterly. Reproachfully.*]

Why, why didn't you listen to me? My poor, dear lady, you'll never get it back now. [*With tears.*] Oh, if only all this could be over soon, if only we could change this unhappy and disjointed life of ours somehow!

PISHCHIK [*taking his arm, in a low voice*]. She's crying. Come into the ballroom, let her be by herself . . . Come on . . . [*Takes his arm and leads him away to the ballroom.*]

LOPAHIN. What's the matter! Where's the music? Come on, play! Play! Everything will be as *I* want it now. [*Ironically.*]

Here comes the new owner, here comes the owner of the cherry orchard! [*He tips over a little table accidentally and nearly upsets the candelabra.*] Don't worry about it, I can pay for everything!

[LOPAHIN *goes out with* PISHCHIK. *There is no one left in the ballroom or drawing room but* LYUBOV, *who sits huddled up in a chair, crying bitterly. The orchestra continues to play quietly.* ANYA *and* TROFIMOV *enter quickly;* ANYA *goes up to her mother and kneels beside her.* TROFIMOV *remains at the entrance to the ballroom.*]

ANYA. Mamma! . . . Mamma, you're crying. Dear, kind, good Mamma, my precious one, I love you! God bless you, Mamma! The cherry orchard's sold, that's true, it's gone, but don't cry, Mamma, you still have your life ahead of you, you still have your good, innocent heart. You must come with me, Mamma, away from here! We'll plant a new orchard, even more wonderful than this one—and when you see it, you'll understand everything, and your heart will be filled with joy, like the sun in the evening; and then you'll smile again, Mamma! Come, dearest one, come with me! . . .

ACT FOUR

[*The same setting as for Act I. There are no pictures on the walls or curtains at the windows; most of the furniture is gone and the few remaining pieces are stacked in a corner, as if for sale. There is a sense of desolation. Beside the door, suitcases and other luggage have been piled together. The voices of* VARYA *and* ANYA *can be heard through the door on the left, which is open.* LOPAHIN *stands waiting;* YASHA *is holding a tray with glasses of champagne. In the hall* EPIHODOV *is tying up a large box. Offstage there is a low hum of voices; the peasants have called to say good-bye.* GAEV'S *voice is heard from offstage.*]

GAEV. Thank you, friends, thank you.

YASHA. The peasants have come to say good-bye. In my opinion, Yermolay Alexeyevich, they're good people, but they don't know much.

[*The hum subsides.* LYUBOV *and* GAEV *enter from the hall;* LYUBOV *is not crying but her face is pale and it quivers. She is unable to speak.*]

GAEV. You gave them everything you had, Lyuba. You shouldn't have done that. You really shouldn't.

LYUBOV. I couldn't help it! I couldn't help it! [*Both go out.*]

LOPAHIN [*calls after them through the door*]. Please, have some champagne, please do! Just a little glass before you go. I didn't think to bring some from town, and at the station I could find only this one bottle. Please have some. [*A pause.*] You don't want any, my friends? [*Walks away from the door.*] If I'd known that, I wouldn't have brought it. . . . Well, then I won't have any either.

[YASHA *carefully puts the tray on a chair.*]

Have a drink, Yasha, nobody else wants any.

YASHA. To the travelers! And to those staying behind. [*Drinks.*] This champagne isn't the real thing, believe me.

LOPAHIN. What do you mean, eight roubles a bottle. [*A pause.*] God, it's cold in here.

YASHA. The stoves weren't lit today. What difference does it make since we're leaving? [*Laughs.*]

LOPAHIN. Why are you laughing?

YASHA. Because I feel good.

LOPAHIN. It's October already, but it's still sunny and clear, just like summer. Good building weather. [*Looks at his watch, then at the door.*] Ladies and gentlemen, the train leaves in forty-seven minutes. We've got to start in twenty minutes. So hurry up.

[TROFIMOV, *wearing an overcoat, comes in from outdoors.*]

TROFIMOV. It's time we get started. The horses are ready. God knows where my galoshes are, they've disappeared. [*Calls through the door.*] Anya, my galoshes aren't here; I can't find them.

LOPAHIN. I've got to go to Kharkov. I'm taking the same train. I'll be spending the winter in Kharkov: I've stayed around here too long, and it drives me crazy having nothing to do. I can't be without work: I just don't know what to do with my hands; they hang there, as if they didn't belong to me.

TROFIMOV. We'll be gone soon, then you can start making money again.

LOPAHIN. Have a drink.

TROFIMOV. No, thanks.

LOPAHIN. So, you're going to Moscow?

TROFIMOV. Yes, I'll go with them to town, and then, tomorrow I'll leave for Moscow.

LOPAHIN. I suppose the professors are waiting for you to come before they begin classes.

TROFIMOV. That's none of your business.

LOPAHIN. How many years have you been studying at the university?

TROFIMOV. Can't you say something new for a change, that's getting pretty old. [*Looks for his galoshes.*] By the way, since we probably won't see each other again, let me give you a bit of advice, as we say good-bye: stop waving your arms! Try to get rid of that habit of making wide, sweeping gestures. And another thing, all this talk about building estates, these calculations about summer tourists that are going to buy property, all these predictions—they're all sweeping gestures, too. . . . You know, in spite of everything, I like you. You've got beautiful delicate fingers, like an artist's, you've a fine, sensitive soul. . . .

LOPAHIN [*embraces him*]. Good-bye, my friend. Thanks for everything. I can give you some money for your trip, if you need it.

TROFIMOV. What for? I don't need it.

LOPAHIN. But you haven't got any!

TROFIMOV. Yes, I have, thank you. I got some money for a translation. Here it is, in my pocket. [*Anxiously.*] But I can't find my galoshes.

VARYA [*from the other room*]. Here, take the nasty things! [*She throws a pair of rubber galoshes into the room.*]

TROFIMOV. What are you so angry about, Varya? Hm . . . but these aren't my galoshes!

LOPAHIN. I sowed three thousand acres of poppies last spring, and I've made forty thousand on it. And when they were in bloom, what a picture it was! What I mean to say is that I've made the forty thousand, so now I can lend you some money. Why be so stuck up? So I'm a peasant . . . I speak right out.

TROFIMOV. Your father was a peasant, mine was a druggist. What's that got to do with it?

[LOPAHIN *takes out his wallet.*]

Forget it, put it away . . . Even if you offered me two hundred thousand, I wouldn't take it. I'm a free man. And all that you rich men—and poor men too—all that you value so highly doesn't have the slightest power over me— it's all just so much fluff floating about in the air. I'm strong and I'm proud! I can get along without you, I can pass you by. Humanity is advancing towards the highest truth, the greatest happiness that it's possible to achieve on earth, and I'm one of the avant-garde!

LOPAHIN. Will you get there?

TROFIMOV. Yes. [*A pause.*] I'll get there myself, or show others the way to get there.

[*The sound of an axe hitting a tree is heard in the distance.*]

LOPAHIN. Well, my friend, it's time to go. Good-bye. We show off in front of one another, and all the time life is slipping by. When I work all day long, without resting, I'm happier and sometimes I even think I know why I exist. But how many people there are in Russia, my friend, who exist for no reason at all. But, never mind, it doesn't matter. They say Leonid Andreyevich has a job at the bank, at six thousand a year. That won't last long; he's too lazy. . . .

ANYA [*in the doorway*]. Mamma begs you not to let them cut down the orchard until we've left.

TROFIMOV. Really, haven't you got any tact? [*Goes out through the hall.*]

LOPAHIN. All right, I'll take care of it. . . . These people! [*Follows* TROFIMOV.]

ANYA. Has Feers been taken to the hospital?

YASHA. I told them to take him this morning. He's gone, I think.

ANYA [*to* EPIHODOV, *who passes through the ballroom*]. Semyon Pantaleyevich, will you please find out whether Feers has been taken to the hospital?

YASHA [*offended*]. I told Yegor this morning. Why ask a dozen times?

EPIHODOV. That old Feers—frankly speaking, I mean—he's beyond repair, it's time he joined his ancestors. As for me, I can only envy him. [*He places a suitcase on top of a cardboard hat box and squashes it.*] There you are, you see! . . . I might have known it! [*Goes out.*]

YASHA [*sardonically*]. Two-and-twenty misfortunes!

VARYA [*from behind the door*]. Has Feers been taken to the hospital?

ANYA. Yes.

VARYA. Why wasn't the letter to the doctor taken then?

ANYA. I'll send someone after them with it . . . [*Goes out.*]

VARYA [*from the adjoining room*]. Where's Yasha? Tell him his mother is here and wants to say good-bye to him.

YASHA [*waves his hand*]. This is too much! I'll lose my patience.

[*While the foregoing action has been taking place,* DUNYASHA *has been busy with the luggage; now that* YASHA *is alone, she comes up to him.*]

DUNYASHA. If only you'd look at me just once, Yasha! You're going . . . you're leaving me! . . . [*She cries and throws her arms round his neck.*]

YASHA. What are you crying for? [*Drinks champagne.*] In a week I'll be in Paris again. Tomorrow we'll get on the train—and off we'll go—gone! I can't believe it. *Vive la France!* I can't stand it here and could never live here— nothing ever happens. I've seen enough of all this ignorance.

I've had enough of it. [*Drinks.*] What are you crying for? Behave yourself properly, then you won't cry.

DUNYASHA [*looking into a handmirror and powdering her nose*]. Please, write to me from Paris. You know how much I've loved you, Yasha. Oh, I've loved you so much! I'm very sensitive, Yasha!

YASHA. Sshh, someone's coming. [*Pretends to be busy with a suitcase, humming quietly.*]

[*Enter* LYUBOV ANDREYEVNA, GAEV, ANYA *and* CHARLOTTA IVANOVNA.]

GAEV. We've got to leave soon. There isn't much time left. [*Looks at* YASHA.] What a smell! Who's been eating herring?

LYUBOV. We'll have to leave in the carriage in ten minutes. [*Looks about the room.*] Good-bye, dear house, the home of our fathers. Winter will pass and spring will come again, and then you won't be here any more, you'll be torn down. How much these walls have seen! [*Kisses her daughter passionately.*] My little treasure, how radiant you look, your eyes are shining like diamonds. Are you glad? Very glad?

ANYA. Oh, yes, very glad, Mamma! Our new life is just beginning!

GAEV [*gaily*]. Really, everything's all right now. Before the cherry orchard was sold we were all worried and upset, but as soon as things were settled once and for all, we all calmed down and even felt quite cheerful. I'm working in a bank now, a real financier. . . . The red into the side pocket . . . And say what you like, Lyuba, you're looking much better. No doubt about it.

LYUBOV. Yes, that's true, my nerves are better. [*Someone helps her on with her hat and coat.*] I'm sleeping better, too. Take out my things, Yasha, it's time. [*To* ANYA.] My little darling, we'll be seeing each other again soon. I'm going to Paris—I'll live on the money which your Grandmother sent us to buy the estate—God bless Grandmamma! —but that money won't last very long either.

ANYA. You'll come back soon, Mamma . . . won't you? I'll study and pass my exams and then I'll work and help you. We'll read together, Mamma . . . all sorts of things . . . won't we? [*She kisses her mother's hands.*] We'll read during the long autumn evenings. We'll read lots of books, and a new wonderful world will open up before us . . . [*Dreamily.*] Mamma, come back soon . . .

LYUBOV. I'll come back, my precious. [*Embraces her.*]

[*Enter* LOPAHIN. CHARLOTTA *quietly sings to herself.*]

GAEV. Happy Charlotta! She's singing.

CHARLOTTA [*picks up a bundle that looks like a baby in a blanket*]. Bye-bye, little baby. [*A sound like a baby crying is heard.*] Hush, be quiet, my darling, be a good little boy. [*The "crying" continues.*] Oh, my baby, you poor thing! [*Throws the bundle down.*] Are you going to find me another job? If you don't mind, I've got to have one.

LOPAHIN. We'll find you one, Charlotta Ivanovna, don't worry.

GAEV. Everybody's leaving us, Varya's going away . . . all of a sudden nobody wants us.

CHARLOTTA. There's no place for me to live in town. I'll have to go. [*Hums.*] Oh, well, what do I care.

[*Enter* PISHCHIK.]

LOPAHIN. Look what's here!

PISHCHIK [*gasping for breath*]. Oohhh, let me get my breath . . . I'm worn out . . . My good friends. . . . Give me some water . . .

GAEV. I suppose you want to borrow some money? I'm going . . . Excuse me . . . [*Goes out.*]

PISHCHIK. I haven't seen you for a long time . . . my beautiful lady . . . [*To* LOPAHIN.] You're here, too . . . glad to see you . . . you're a man of great intelligence . . . here . . . take this . . . [*Gives money to* LOPAHIN.] Four hundred roubles . . . I still owe you eight hundred and forty. . . .

LOPAHIN [*shrugging his shoulders in amazement*]. It's like a dream . . . Where did you get it?

PISHCHIK. Wait a minute . . . I'm so hot . . . A most extraordinary thing happened. Some Englishmen came along and discovered some kind of white clay on my land . . . [*To* LYUBOV.] Here's four hundred for you also, my dear . . . enchantress . . . [*Gives her the money.*] You'll get the rest later. [*Takes a drink of water.*] A young man on the train was just telling me that some great philosopher advises people to jump off roofs. You just jump off, he says, and that settles the whole problem. [*Amazed at what he has just said.*] Imagine that! More water, please.

LOPAHIN. What Englishmen?

PISHCHIK. I leased the land to them for twenty-four years. . . . And now you must excuse me, I'm in a hurry and have

to get on. I'm going to Znoikov's, then to Kardamonov's.
. . . I owe them all money. [*Drinks.*] Your health. I'll come
again on Thursday . . .

LYUBOV. We're just leaving for town, and tomorrow I'm going
abroad.

PISHCHIK. What's that? [*In agitation.*] Why to town? Oh, I
see . . . this furniture and the suitcases. . . . Well, never
mind . . . [*Tearfully.*] What difference does it make. . . .
These Englishmen, you know, they're very intelligent . . .
Never mind. . . . I wish you all the best, God bless you.
Never mind, everything comes to an end eventually. [*Kisses*
LYUBOV's *hand.*] And when you hear that my end has come,
just think of a horse, and say: "There used to be a man
like that once . . . his name was Semyonov-Pishchik—God
bless him!" Wonderful weather we're having. Yes . . .
[*Goes out embarrassed, but returns at once and stands in
the doorway.*] Dashenka sends her greetings. [*Goes out.*]

LYUBOV. Well, we can get started now. I'm leaving with two
worries on my mind. One is Feers—he's sick. [*Glances at
her watch.*] We've still got five minutes. . . .

ANYA. Mamma, Feers has been taken to the hospital. Yasha
sent him this morning.

LYUBOV. The other is Varya. She's used to getting up early
and working, and now, with nothing to do, she's like a
fish out of water. She's gotten so thin and pale, and she cries
a lot, the poor dear. [*A pause.*] You know very well,
Yermolay Alexeyevich, that I've been hoping you two
would get married . . . and everything pointed to it.
[*Whispers to* ANYA *and motions to* CHARLOTTA, *and they
both go out.*] She loves you, and you're fond of her, too . . .
I just don't know, I don't know why you seem to avoid
each other. I don't understand it.

LOPAHIN. Neither do I, I admit it. The whole thing's so
strange. . . . If there's still time, I'm ready to. . . . Let's
settle it at once—and get it over with! Without you here,
I don't feel I'll ever propose to her.

LYUBOV. That's an excellent idea! You won't need more than
a minute. I'll call her at once.

LOPAHIN. And there's champagne here, too, we'll celebrate.
[*Looks at the glasses.*] They're empty, someone's drunk
it all.

[YASHA *coughs.*]

They must have poured it down.

LYUBOV [*with animation*]. Oh, I'm so glad. I'll call her, and we'll leave you alone. Yasha, *allez!* [*Through the door.*] Varya, come here for a minute, leave what you're doing and come here! Varya! [*Goes out with* YASHA.]

LOPAHIN [*looking at his watch*]. Yes. . . .

[*A pause. Whispering and suppressed laughter are heard behind the door, then* VARYA *comes in and starts fussing with the luggage. At last she says:*]

VARYA. That's strange, I can't find it. . . .

LOPAHIN. What are you looking for?

VARYA. I packed it myself, and I can't remember . . .

[*A pause.*]

LOPAHIN. Where are you going to now, Varvara Mihailovna?

VARYA. I? To the Rogulins. I've taken a job as their housekeeper.

LOPAHIN. That's in Yashnevo, isn't it? Almost seventy miles from here. [*A pause.*] So this is the end of life in this house. . . .

VARYA [*still fussing with the luggage*]. Where could it be? Perhaps I put it in the trunk? Yes, life in this house has come to an end . . . there won't be any more. . . .

LOPAHIN. And I'm going to Kharkov. . . . On the next train. I've got a lot of work to do there. I'm leaving Epihodov here. . . . I've hired him.

VARYA. Really! . . .

LOPAHIN. Remember, last year at this time it was snowing already, but now it's still so bright and sunny. Though it's cold . . . Three degrees of frost.

VARYA. I haven't looked. [*A pause.*] Besides, our thermometer's broken. . . .

[*A pause. A voice is heard from outside the door.*]

VOICE. Yermolay Alexeyevich!

LOPAHIN [*as if he had been waiting for it*]. I'm coming! Right away! [*Goes out quickly.*]

[VARYA *sits on the floor, with her head on a bundle of clothes, crying quietly. The door opens,* LYUBOV *enters hesitantly.*]

LYUBOV. Well? [*A pause.*] We must be going.

VARYA [*stops crying and wipes her eyes*]. Yes, Mamma, it's time we got started. I'll just have time to get to the Rogulins today, if we don't miss the train.

LYUBOV [*calls through the door*]. Anya, put your things on.

[*Enter* ANYA, *followed by* GAEV *and* CHARLOTTA. GAEV *wears a heavy overcoat with a hood. Servants and coachmen come into the room.* EPIHODOV *is picking up the luggage.*]

Now we can begin our journey!

ANYA [*joyfully*]. Our journey!

GAEV. My friends, my dear, beloved friends! As I leave this house forever, how can I be silent, how can I refrain from expressing to you, as I say good-bye for the last time, the feelings which now overwhelm me. . . .

ANYA [*begging*]. Uncle!

VARYA. Uncle, please, don't!

GAEV [*downcast*]. I put the red into the corner and then . . . I'll keep quiet.

[*Enter* TROFIMOV *and* LOPAHIN.]

TROFIMOV. Well, ladies and gentlemen, it's time we get started.

LOPAHIN. Epihodov, my coat!

LYUBOV. I'll just stay for one more minute. It seems as if I'd never seen the walls and ceilings of this house before, and now I look at them with such longing, such love. . . .

GAEV. I remember when I was six—it was Trinity Sunday . . . I was sitting here at this window watching father on his way to church. . . .

LYUBOV. Have they taken everything out?

LOPAHIN. It looks like it. [*To* EPIHODOV, *as he puts on his coat.*] Be sure to take care of everything, Epihodov.

EPIHODOV [*in a husky voice*]. Don't worry, Yermolay Alexeyevich!

LOPAHIN. What is wrong with your voice?

EPIHODOV. I just had some water, and it went down the wrong throat.

YASHA [*with contempt*]. What a fool!

LYUBOV. After we leave, there won't be a soul here. . . .

LOPAHIN. Not until spring.

VARYA [*pulls an umbrella from a bundle of clothes;* LOPAHIN *pretends to be afraid*]. What are you doing that for? . . . I didn't mean to. . . .

TROFIMOV. Ladies and gentlemen, hurry up, it's time. The train will be here soon.

VARYA. Petya, here are your galoshes beside the suitcase. [*Tearfully.*] How dirty and old they are! . . .

TROFIMOV [*puts them on*]. Hurry up, ladies and gentlemen!

GAEV [*greatly embarrassed, afraid of breaking into tears*]. The train, the station . . . The red off the white into the middle pocket. . . .

LYUBOV. Let us go!

LOPAHIN. Are we all here? No one left? [*Locks the door on the left.*] There are some things stored in there, best to keep it locked up. Come along!

ANYA. Good-bye, old house! Good-bye, old life!

TROFIMOV. Welcome to the new life! . . . [*Goes out with ANYA.*]

[*VARYA looks around the room and goes out slowly. YASHA and CHARLOTTA, with her little dog, follow.*]

LOPAHIN. And so, until the spring. Come, my friends. . . . *Au revoir!* [*Goes out.*]

[*LYUBOV and GAEV alone. They seem to have been waiting for this moment, and now they embrace each other and cry quietly, with restraint, so as not to be heard.*]

GAEV [*in despair*]. Sister, my sister. . . .

LYUBOV. Oh, my orchard, my beloved, my beautiful orchard! My life, my youth, my happiness . . . good-bye! . . . Good-bye!

ANYA [*offstage, calling gaily*]. Mamma! . . .

TROFIMOV [*offstage, gaily and excitedly*]. Yoo-hoo! . . .

LYUBOV. Just one last time—to look at these walls, these windows. . . . Mother loved to walk in this room. . . .

GAEV. Sister, my sister . . .

ANYA [*offstage*]. Mamma!

TROFIMOV [*offstage*]. Yoo-hoo!

LYUBOV. We're coming . . . [*They go out.*]

[*The stage is empty. The sound of doors being locked and then of carriages driving off. Silence. In the stillness the dull sounds of an axe striking on a tree can be heard. They sound mournful and sad. Footsteps are heard and from the door on the right FEERS enters. He is dressed, as usual, in*] *a coat and white waistcoat, and is wearing slippers. He is ill.*]

FEERS [*walks up to the middle door and tries the handle*]. Locked. They've gone . . . [*Sits down on a sofa.*] They've forgotten me. Never mind. . . . I'll sit here for a bit. I don't suppose Leonid Andreyevich put on his fur coat, he probably wore his light one. [*Sighs, preoccupied.*] I didn't take care of it . . . These young people! . . . [*Mutters something unintelligible.*] My life's slipped by as if I'd never lived. . . . [*Lies down.*] I'll lie down a bit. You haven't got any strength left, nothing's left, nothing. . . . Oh, you . . . you old good-for-nothing! . . . [*Lies motionless.*]

[*A distant sound that seems to come out of the sky, like a breaking harp, slowly and sadly dying away. Then all is silent, except for the sound of an axe striking a tree in the orchard far away.*]

MAXIM GORKY

1868–1936

MAXIM GORKY was always a writer of revolutionary protest and is a symbol of the fugitive spirit in modern Russian letters. He lived through the whole of the Russian revolution, from the freeing of the serfs to the ascendancy of the Communist Party in the Soviet state, and in all his works, beginning with his first short story, published in 1892, he sought to give meaning and form to the struggle between the individual outcast and the existing social order. In choosing to write of the proletariat, however, Gorky was more than a rebel. He believed that the forlorn dregs of humanity represented in his plays were the mark of society's failure to meet the individual's most fundamental needs. His characters were the distress signals of a crumbling world, and in all his plays Gorki urges us to inquire into the nature of human disaster, and demands that we accept responsibility for it.

The Lower Depths, Gorky's finest play, is a parable of life that strikes deep at the nature of truth and shows the value of illusion to men whose lives seem to have no worth or meaning. But the play is not, as it is usually interpreted on the stage, a lesson in brotherly love. Gorky made it quite clear that Luka's pampering consolations were only "pulp for the toothless," and were either harmful to man or insulting to human dignity. Satin was his hero, and in the play proclaimed Gorky's belief that truth and reality are not merely philosophical concepts. Gorky's message was a program of conduct: "Let a man become conscious of his dignity and capacity; let him adopt an ideal possible to man and he will realize it as an individual and be happy."

Gorky's plays stirred men to action in the early part of the century. They no longer do so, but they still are important landmarks in the modern theatre, for they were the first plays to indicate the kind of social concern that was to characterize much of the serious theatre of the twentieth century.

OBSERVATIONS ON THE THEATRE[1]

by Maxim Gorky

I HAVE WRITTEN altogether, I think, about ten plays. Among these, however, there is not one that really satisfies me.

The reason for this is probably the fact that, before sitting down to write a play, I first construct its ideological framework, and combine beforehand the course and connection of the various comical and tragical events. But, since I am always and chiefly interested in man and not the group, in the personality and not the society, apparently on account of this, and against my will, every play I have written is about a man with reference to whom all the other characters of the play stand in a subordinate relation, playing the part of illustrations, and characterizing and completing the qualities and faults of the chief hero of the play.

In reality, however, a man does not exist in order to subject the qualities and faults of his neighbor to analysis—although many people busy themselves with such a task, probably because they cannot or will not do anything which carries more purpose!

For the reason given above, my plays acquired a didactical spirit, were saturated with a wordy boredom, and lost their value as works of art. By works of art I mean works in which the will of the author is either absent altogether, or else is so cleverly dissimulated as not to be detected by the reader.

In a play all the characters must act independently of the will of the author, according to their natural and social inclinations; they must follow the inspirations of their "fate," and not of the author. They must of themselves create the

[1] "Observations on the Theatre" by Maxim Gorky, translator unknown. Copyright 1923 by Maxim Gorky. Translation originally published in the *English Review*, April 1924, and reprinted by permission of Eyre & Spottiswood, Ltd., London.

different comical and tragical events, by submitting to the power of their contradictory natures, interests, and passions. The author, on his part, is supposed to act like the host at a party to which he has invited these imaginary guests; and, without preventing them from tormenting or mutilating one another in every manner, morally as well as otherwise, he describes with perfect composure the manner in which they do it.

If an author takes such an attitude, he becomes capable of writing a play that is a pure work of art—a totally impartial play which merely pictures the struggle of differently directed wills, but is devoid of any moral tendencies imposed by the author. Incidentally, in all European literature I know of no drama that is composed according to this principle. Personally, I should not be able to write on such a principle.

But I think I know of people who could create plays penetrated with an inner harmony. The artificiality in such plays is not discernible—it is replaced by art. I consider the comedy of J. M. Synge, the Irishman, entitled *The Playboy of the Western World*, to be such a play. In it the comical side passes quite naturally into the terrible, while the terrible becomes comical just as easily. J. M. Synge, like a truly wise artist, does not inject his own point of view; he just exhibits the people: they are half gods and half beasts, and are possessed of the childish desire to find a "hero" among themselves. (This is, to my mind, an absurd desire, for every one of us is a hero, if he happens to remember all the victories and defeats he has met with in the struggle for life.)

The characters of Synge act in exactly the same way as people usually act and as we shall probably all act for a long time to come; they create heroes in order to ridicule them afterwards. In Synge's play I feel a subtle irony on the cult of the hero. That irony is not very remote from sadness over the stupidity of mankind, but there is in it, I repeat, nothing artificial; it is merely a pure and lawful irony of facts.

Just as perfect as this play is the *Cena delle Beffe* written by the wonderfully gifted Italian author, Sem Benelli. In this play, too, efforts of the author to hypnotize his audience are altogether absent; all the events in it unroll themselves with indisputable logic, the roused will of the hero becomes his fate and leads him unrelentingly to his perdition. I must admit that I watch the development of modern drama altogether with the greatest of hopes, and that I do not believe in the people who cry over the decline of dramatic art. Such playwrights as Sem Benelli, the wonderful Jacinto Benavente, the English Heraclites, Bernard Shaw, and two or three more men in Western Europe, will create, it seems to me, a new theatre, up to the present still rather unfamiliar and incomprehensible to the audience.

Knowing subtly how to handle the methods of the old tragical art, the modern dramatists bring out on the stage all that our tragicomical twentieth century breathes and is tormented with, all that it laughs and cries over. The dramatists I have mentioned fully possess the capacity of true artists: they can stand above reality, they know how to confront facts and characters in such a way that the spectator and the reader can clearly see the nature of the hidden secret powers, the collision of which creates the drama outside the will of the author as well as of his heroes.

Let me recall what I have already said: very often people consider their own stupidity as the ancient *moira*, by creating insurmountable and fatal obstacles out of the easily surmounted trifles of life. This very strongly propagated error probably arises among the people of the twentieth century, from a somewhat sickly imagination, roused by the rush of events, the mad *tempo* of life, a splendid subject for all dramatists! The modern man reminds me somewhat of a toymaker who has made a mechanical doll, and who is beaten on the head by that same doll; in a sudden terror, the toymaker forgets that the doll is a product of his own labor, and imagines that a mysterious power is hidden in it. But in our life there is nothing more mysterious than man himself and his creative instinct—I find that this suffices us.

I believe that the dramatists I have mentioned can see perfectly well the comical helplessness of man in the face of the richness and greatness of all that he has created and is creating. They peer more deeply into life and see it from more angles than did the dramatists of the nineteenth century—psychologists, students of modes and customs, registrars of the trifles of life.

I exclude from these, of course, Henrik Ibsen, and some of the plays of Gerhard Hauptmann.

I think that in spite of this very natural and always wholesome scepticism as regards the present, the art of the twentieth century is more optimistic, vigorous and active.

The complexity of life increases the number of peculiar

collisions and dramatic subjects. The most amusing one is—
man, frightened at his own audacity, amazed by the motley
entanglements with relationships and events which he himself
has created. For this last subject the present political workers
are particularly well adapted to play the part of "heroes."

I have recently written a play, entitled *The Judge*, which
seems to me to be more interesting than any of my other works
written in the form of a dialogue. This does not mean, however, that it is entirely free from didacticism. We all strive
to teach one another something! With the result, however,
that we are taught but this one thing: not to respect the freedom of thought of one another. The reason for this, I believe,
is to be sought in the fact that such a multitude of truths has
lately been disseminated in the world. Every one of us pos-
sesses at least two or three such truths. And everybody tries
to fasten his particular truth around the neck of his neighbor,
like a collar around a dog's neck.

In that play, it seems to me, I tried to show how repulsive
a man can be who is in love with his own torment, and who,
therefore, deems it right to avenge himself for all that he has
had personally to suffer. But when a man is convinced that
suffering gives him the right to consider himself an exceptional being, and to avenge himself upon others for his own
miseries, then, to my mind, he does not belong to those who
deserve the respect of others. You will understand me if you
imagine to yourself an individual setting fire to houses and
towns, merely because he himself suffers from the cold!

It may be that British and American theatre managers will
not be sufficiently interested in this play for them to undertake
its production. It seems to me that among Anglo-Saxons the
theory of purifying the soul through suffering is not so popular
as it used to be in Russia. I say "used to be," in the hope that
Russia may have gone through enough torture to have acquired an organic revulsion against suffering. However, I
have no definite idea concerning the tastes and tendencies of
the contemporary theatre. But rarely do I go to see a play, and
when I do it is only after I have made sure that the theatrical
performance will permit me to rest from the tragedy of reality
which is so abundant in our day.

I should like to see the theatre of today as the Pool of
Siloam, from which a man may emerge softened and restored
physically. I think that the most wholesome theatre is that
in which one can gaily and harmlessly laugh over the stupidity

of mankind. It is exactly this stupidity that men consider to be their "fate." It is extremely healthful, for an hour or two, to forget this reality which we ourselves create so heedlessly and inconsiderately, and which, in making us collide with one another, easily breaks our hearts and heads.

A man works so much that he fully deserves a gay and wholesome leisure period. The place for such a rest ought, to my mind, to be the theatre.

In Russia, at the present time, many new theories on the "new" theatre are blossoming forth. The novelty in these theories is always the same: the theatre should be a center where stage managers compete in wittiness, and should serve as a Procrustean bed for gifted actors. This is not very amusing. It seems to me that the imaginative power of the author, together with the talent of the actor, will always be of considerably greater value to the audience than all the witty artifices of a dozen stage managers.

THE LOWER DEPTHS

by MAXIM GORKY

1902

THE LOWER DEPTHS[1]

Translated by Henry Burke

CHARACTERS

KOSTYLEV, *keeper of the lodging house, age 54*

VASSILISA, *his wife, age 26*

NATASHA, *her sister, age 20*

ABRAM MEDVEDEV, *their uncle, a policeman, age 50*

VASKA PEPPEL, *age 28*

KLETCH, *a locksmith, age 40*

ANNA, *his wife, age 30*

NASTYA, *a prostitute, age 24*

KVASHNYA, *a street seller, age nearly 40*

BUBNOV, *a capmaker, age 45*

THE BARON, *age 33*

SATIN
THE ACTOR } *both nearly 40*

LUKA, *a tramp, age 60*

ALESHKA, *a cobbler, age 20*

SCREWY
THE TARTAR } *longshoremen*

---

[1] *The Lower Depths* by Maxim Gorky, translated by Henry Burke. Copyright © Henry Burke, 1962. Reprinted by permission of the translator. All inquiries concerning performance rights should be addressed to Progressive Management, 36 Baker Street, London, W.1, England.

ACT ONE

[*A cavelike basement. The ceiling heavy, vaulted, blackened with smoke, with the plaster peeling. The light comes from the fourth wall, and from a square window high in the wall on the right.* PEPPEL'S *room is behind a thin partition which cuts off the right corner. A big Russian stove stands in the left corner. The stone wall on the left has a door to the kitchen, where* KVASHNYA, *the* BARON *and* NASTYA *live. By the wall between the stove and the door stands a wide bed, screened off by a dirty cotton-print curtain. There are plank-beds all around the walls. Downstage left stands a block of wood with a vise and a small anvil mounted on it.* KLETCH *sits by it, on a smaller block of wood, trying keys in old locks. At his feet, two large wire rings of keys, a battered tin samovar, a hammer, some files. In the center a big table, two benches and a stool, all unpainted and dirty.* KVASHNYA *sits at the table, serving tea from the samovar. The* BARON *is munching black bread.* NASTYA *sits on the stool, and leans on the table, reading a battered book.* ANNA *is in the bed behind the curtain, where she lies coughing.* BUBNOV *sits on his plank-bed, fitting a torn old pair of trousers over the hat block which he is holding between his knees, and considers how to cut the cloth. A torn hatbox and its contents —cap-peaks, scraps of oilcloth, and rags of old clothes— are scattered around him.* SATIN, *just awake, lies on a plank-bed, grunting. On top of the stove, the* ACTOR *can be heard moving around and coughing. It is morning, in early spring.*]

BARON. Go on.

KVASHNYA. Oh no, I said, no more of that. I've been through all that before, and it's no more marriages for me.

BUBNOV [*to* SATIN]. What are you grunting about?

[SATIN *continues to grunt.*]

KVASHNYA. I'm a free woman, I said. My own mistress. Me make myself slave to a man?—not on your life! Why, I wouldn't marry him, not if even he was an American prince.

KLETCH. Lies, all lies.

KVASHNYA. What's that?

KLETCH. Lies. You'll marry Abram all right.

BARON [*snatches* NASTYA'S *book, reads title*]. "Fatal Love" . . . [*Laughs.*]

NASTYA [*holding out hand*]. Give it back! Come on . . . stop playing around!

[BARON *looks at her, waves book in air.*]

KVASHNYA [*to* KLETCH]. You red-haired old goat! I'm lying, am I? How dare you speak to me like that!

BARON [*hits* NASTYA *on head with the book*]. You're a fool, Nastya . . .

NASTYA [*takes the book from him*]. Give me that book! Give it to me . . .

KLETCH. Oh, the fine lady! All the same, you'll marry Abram all right . . . that's all you've been waiting for . . .

KVASHNYA. Oh yes! Very likely . . . You drive *your* wife nearly to her grave.

KLETCH. Shut up, you old bitch! Mind your business.

KVASHNYA. Oho! You don't like to hear the truth!

BARON. There they go! What's the matter, Nastya?

NASTYA [*without lifting her head*]. Mm? . . . Go away!

ANNA [*looks out from behind curtain*]. Another day starting! For God's sake . . . stop shouting . . . stop quarrelling, all of you!

KLETCH. Now she's whining again.

ANNA. Every blessed day . . . Let me die in peace, can't you?

BUBNOV. Noise never stopped anyone dying yet.

KVASHNYA [*goes to* ANNA]. My God! How do you put up with such a brute?

ANNA. Leave me alone . . .

KVASHNYA. Well! . . . You poor thing . . . Does your chest feel any better?

BARON. Kvashnya! Time to go to the market.

KVASHNYA. All right, I'm coming. [*To* ANNA.] Would you like some nice hot dumplings?

ANNA. No . . . thank you. What's the good of eating?

KVASHNYA. You eat. Something hot—do you good. I'll leave some in this cup for you. You can eat them when you want. [*To* BARON.] Come on, your lordship . . . [*To* KLETCH.] you filthy bastard . . . [*Goes off into kitchen.*]

ANNA [*coughing*]. Oh, God . . .

BARON [*taps* NASTYA *on back of neck*]. Leave it alone, you fool!

NASTYA [*snaps*]. Go away . . . Do you mind?

[BARON *goes out after* KVASHNYA, *whistling*.]

SATIN [*lifting himself up on his bunk*]. Who beat me up last night?

BUBNOV. What difference does it make who?

SATIN. S'pose not. But what for?

BUBNOV. You playing cards?

SATIN. Yes.

BUBNOV. That's why you got beat up.

SATIN. The bastards!

ACTOR [*looks down from the stove*]. They'll kill you one day.

SATIN. Don't talk such crap.

ACTOR. What do you mean?

SATIN. I mean a man can't be killed twice.

ACTOR [*after a pause*]. What do you mean? How . . . Why not?

KLETCH. You come down off that stove and sweep the floor. You've been loafing up there long enough.

ACTOR. You mind your own business.

KLETCH. You wait till Vassilisa comes. She'll show you whose business it is.

ACTOR. To hell with Vassilisa! It's the Baron's turn to sweep the floor . . . Baron!

BARON [*coming from the kitchen*]. I haven't got time to sweep the floor . . . I'm going to the market with Kvashnya.

ACTOR. I don't care if you're going to jail. It's your turn to sweep the floor . . . I'm not going to do someone else's work.

BARON. Oh, go to hell! Nastya will sweep up. Hey you, Fatal Love! Wake up! [*Snatches her book away*.]

NASTYA [*rises*]. What do you want? Give it here! You son-of-a-bitch! And you call yourself a baron?

BARON [*returns her book*]. You're going to sweep the floor for me, Nastya, all right?

NASTYA [*going into kitchen*]. Ha! What do you think I am?

KVASHNYA [*at the kitchen door—to* BARON]. Are you coming? They can sweep the floor without you . . . Actor! You were asked to do it—well, do it . . . it won't kill you.

ACTOR. Always me. I don't see why. I don't get it.

BARON [*comes in from the kitchen, carrying large, cloth-covered pots in two baskets on a yoke*]. Heavy today . . .

SATIN. A lot of good it does being born a Baron.

KVASHNYA [*to* ACTOR]. See to it that you sweep the floor.
[*Exit after* BARON.]

ACTOR [*comes down from the stove*]. It's bad for me to breathe
dust. [*Proudly.*] My organism is poisoned with alcohol.
[*Sits down on plank-bed thoughtfully.*]

SATIN. Organism . . . organon . . .

ANNA. Andrey . . .

KLETCH. What is it now?

ANNA. Kvashnya's left me some dumplings there . . . You
eat them.

KLETCH [*goes to her*]. What about you?

ANNA. I don't want any . . . What's the good of me eating?
You work—you need to eat.

KLETCH. You afraid? Don't be afraid. May be all right.

ANNA. Go on. Eat. I feel all in. It won't be long now.

KLETCH [*moves away*]. Don't worry. May be all right yet.
It does happen. [*Goes into kitchen.*]

ACTOR [*loudly, as if suddenly waking up*]. Yesterday at the
hospital the doctor says to me, "Your organism," he says,
"is completely poisoned with alcohol . . ."

SATIN [*smiling*]. Organon . . .

ACTOR [*insistently*]. Not organon. Or-gan-ism.

SATIN. Sycamore . . .

ACTOR [*waves his hand*]. Ach, nonsense. I'm serious. If my
organism is poisoned with alcohol, then it's bad for me to
sweep the floor, to breathe dust.

SATIN. Macrobiotics—ha!

BUBNOV. What are you mumbling about?

SATIN. Words—here's another one: transcendental . . .

BUBNOV. What's that mean?

SATIN. I don't know. Can't remember.

BUBNOV. Why are you saying them, then?

SATIN. Well . . . I'm fed up with all words, chum . . . all
human speech. Sick of it all! I've heard it all a thousand
times . . .

ACTOR. There's a line in *Hamlet:* "Words, words, words!" A
wonderful play . . . I played the gravedigger . . .

KLETCH [*coming from the kitchen*]. When are you going to
start playing with that broom?

ACTOR. Mind your own business. [*Strikes himself on the chest.*]
"The fair Ophelia! O nymph in thy orisons be all my sins
remembered."

[*Somewhere in the distance, a muffled noise, cries, a police-man's whistle.* KLETCH *sits down to work, rasping with a file.*]

SATIN. I like rare words I don't understand . . . I had a job in a telegraph office when I was a boy . . . read a lot of books.

BUBNOV. You worked the telegraph?

SATIN. Once . . . [*Smiling.*] there's some good books . . . lots of wonderful words . . . I was educated, you know.

BUBNOV. So you've told us before. So you were educated—much good it's done you! Well, I was a fur-dresser once. Had my own shop. My hands got all yellow from dye—I dyed furs—all yellow they were, brother. I thought I'd go to my grave with yellow hands, never wash it off. Now look at them. Look—just dirty, that's all.

SATIN. Well?

BUBNOV. Well, nothing.

SATIN. What are you getting at?

BUBNOV. Just . . . food for thought . . . It's just—doesn't matter how you paint yourself up, it all rubs off . . . yes, it all rubs off.

SATIN. Oh, my bones ache!

ACTOR [*sits, with his arms round his knees*]. Education is rubbish. The main thing is talent. I knew an actor, he could hardly read his own parts, but when he was on the stage the whole theatre used to shake with the applause he got.

SATIN. Bubnov, give me five kopecks.

BUBNOV. I've only got two kopecks myself.

ACTOR. I say talent's what you need. And talent's just be-lieving in yourself, in your own ability . . .

SATIN. Give me five kopecks and I'll believe you've got talent. I'll believe you're a genius, a crocodile, a police inspector . . . Kletch, give me five kopecks.

KLETCH. Go to hell! There's too many of your sort here.

SATIN. What are you cursing for? You haven't got a penny in the world.

ANNA. Andrey . . . It's stuffy . . . can't breathe . . .

KLETCH. What do you want me to do?

BUBNOV. Open the hall door.

KLETCH. Oh yes! You sit up there on a bed, and I'm on the

floor. Give me your bed, and you can open the door all
you want. I've got a cold as it is.

BUBNOV [*unconcernedly*]. I don't care if you open the door.
It's your wife who's asking.

KLETCH [*sulkily*]. I don't care who's asking.

SATIN. My head's ringing! Why do people hit each other over
the head?

BUBNOV. Why do they hit each other at all? [*He gets up.*]
Going to buy some thread . . . Mr. and Mrs. Landlord
haven't been around yet today—perhaps they've dropped
dead. [*Exit.*]

[ANNA *coughs.* SATIN *lies motionless, his arms under his head.*]

ACTOR [*looks around sadly, goes to* ANNA]. Feeling bad? Eh?

ANNA. I'm choking.

ACTOR. If you like—I'll take you out in the hall. Get up then.
[*Helps her up, throws an old gown over her shoulders, and
holds her under the arm, leading her out to the hall.*] Come
on, carefully now. I'm sick too . . . poisoned with alcohol.

KOSTYLEV [*at the door*]. Going for a walk? Ha! You make a
fine pair . . .

ACTOR. Well, get out of the way. Can't you see that invalids
are trying to get through.

KOSTYLEV. Come on then, if you want to . . . [*Humming some
hymn, he looks about suspiciously, and leans his head to
the left as if trying to overhear something in* PEPPEL'S
room. KLETCH *watches him while continuing to rattle his
keys and to rasp his file firmly.*] Scraping away?

KLETCH. Uh?

KOSTYLEV. I say, you're scraping away. [*Pause.*] Er . . .
What was I going to ask you? [*Suddenly in a low voice.*]
Has my wife been in here?

KLETCH. Haven't seen her.

KOSTYLEV [*cautiously goes up to* PEPPEL'S *door*]. You get a
lot of space for only two rubles a month. A bed . . . place
to sit . . . hm . . . it's worth five rubles at least. I think
I'll have to raise your rent another half ruble.

KLETCH. Raise me by the neck and hang me while you're
about it. There you stand, with one foot in the grave, and
all you can think about is another half ruble.

KOSTYLEV. Why should I want to hang you? That wouldn't
do anybody any good. God be with you—live as much as
you want to, but I will raise your rent another half ruble.

I can buy more oil for my icon lamp—as atonement for my sins. Then my sins will be forgiven. And yours too. You never think of your sins, do you, Andrey? . . . Ah well . . . Ah, you're a wicked man, Andrey! Your wife is fading away, you're so wicked . . . Nobody likes you, respects you . . . your work grates on everyone's ears, disturbs everybody——

KLETCH [*shouts*]. What did you come here for?—to bait me?

[SATIN *roars loudly.*]

KOSTYLEV [*jumps*]. Oh, God!

ACTOR [*entering*]. I sat her down in the hall, wrapped her up . . .

KOSTYLEV. Ah, you're a good fellow. You'll be rewarded . . .

ACTOR. When?

KOSTYLEV. In the next world, my friend. All your good deeds are written down, there.

ACTOR. Suppose you were to repay my good deeds here.

KOSTYLEV. How can I do that?

ACTOR. Half of what I owe you.

KOSTYLEV. Ha, ha! You will have your little joke, always play-acting . . . You can't measure kind-heartedness in money. Kind-heartedness is the greatest of all gifts. And your debt to me—that's all it is—a debt! So you have to pay me. You mustn't ask an old man like me to pay you for being kind-hearted.

ACTOR. You old bastard. [*Goes into kitchen.*]

[KLETCH *rises and goes into the hall.*]

KOSTYLEV [*to* SATIN]. Ha, ha! Old scraper's gone away. Doesn't like me.

SATIN. Who does—except the devil?

KOSTYLEV [*laughing*]. You've got a sharp tongue! But I like you. I like you all. I do. My unhappy, lost, wretched friends . . . [*Suddenly.*] Is Vaska in?

SATIN. Go and look.

KOSTYLEV [*goes to door and knocks*]. Vaska!

[ACTOR *appears at the kitchen door, munching.*]

PEPPEL [*off*]. Who is it?

KOSTYLEV. It's me, Vaska.

PEPPEL. What do you want?

KOSTYLEV [*moves from the door*]. Open the door . . .

SATIN [*not looking at* KOSTYLEV]. She's in there.

[ACTOR *laughs*.]

KOSTYLEV [*uneasily, in a low voice*]. Uh? Who? Who's there? Eh?

SATIN. You speaking to me?

KOSTYLEV. What did you say just now?

SATIN. I was . . . talking to myself . . .

KOSTYLEV. You watch out. Don't get too funny . . . see! [*Knocks hard on* PEPPEL'S *door*.] Vaska!

PEPPEL [*opens door*]. Well? What's the matter with you?

KOSTYLEV [*looking into the room*]. I . . . you see . . .

PEPPEL. Brought the money?

KOSTYLEV. What money? I . . .

PEPPEL. The money. The seven rubles for the watch. Come on.

KOSTYLEV. What watch? Ach, Vaska, you . . .

PEPPEL. You know damn well what watch. The one I sold you yesterday, in front of witnesses. Ten rubles. You gave me three. Come on, then, where's the other seven? What are you blinking for? You hang around here, waking people up, and now you don't know yourself what you want.

KOSTYLEV. Sh—sh! Dont' lose your temper, Vaska . . . The watch . . . was . . .

SATIN. Stolen.

KOSTYLEV [*sternly*]. What do you mean? I don't buy stolen goods.

PEPPEL [*takes him by the shoulder*]. Well, what did you wake me up for? What do you want?

KOSTYLEV. Me? I . . . nothing. I . . . I'll go away, if that's your attitude.

PEPPEL. Well, get out of here, then. And next time be sure you bring the money.

KOSTYLEV [*going*]. Miserable, unpleasant people! Ay, ay . . .

ACTOR. What a farce!

SATIN. Who'd have believed it?

PEPPEL. What was he after?

SATIN [*laughing*]. Don't you know? He's looking for his wife. Why don't you take care of him for good, Vaska?

PEPPEL. Risk my life for trash like that?

SATIN. There's no risk. You're too smart. You could marry Vassilisa, become our landlord . . .

PEPPEL. Ho, that's a good one! All of you living off me! I'm too soft—you'd drink every penny I had. [*Sits on bunk.*] Old devil—woke me up. Such a good dream I was having. I was fishing. Caught an enormous trout. Huge—never seen one so big. I thought the line would snap. Any minute now I thought . . .

SATIN. That wasn't no trout—that was Vassilisa.

ACTOR. He hooked Vassilisa long ago.

PEPPEL [*angrily*]. Oh, go to hell, all of you—and take her with you when you go!

KLETCH [*comes from hall*]. Cold. Damn cold.

ACTOR. You left Anna out there? She'll freeze.

KLETCH. Natasha's taken her into the kitchen.

ACTOR. The old man will throw her out.

KLETCH [*sits down to work*]. Oh, Natasha will look after her.

SATIN. Vaska, give us five kopecks.

ACTOR [*to* SATIN]. You and your five kopecks! Give us twenty, Vaska.

PEPPEL. Here—take it quick, before you ask for a ruble.

SATIN. Gibraltar! There's no people like thieves.

KLETCH [*grumpily*]. Easy money—they don't work for it.

SATIN. Lots of people make easy money . . . not many give it away easy though . . . Work? You make work pleasant enough, and perhaps I'll work. Might do. When work's pleasant, life's all right. When work's a duty, life's just slavery. [*To* ACTOR.] Come on, then, Sardanapalus!

ACTOR. Come on, Nebuchadnezzar! God, I'm going to get so damn drunk!

[*They go out.*]

PEPPEL [*yawns*]. How's your wife?

KLETCH. Not long now.

PEPPEL. You know, looking at you—I can't see the sense of all that scraping.

KLETCH. What else can I do?

PEPPEL. Nothing.

KLETCH. Nothing! How am I supposed to live?

PEPPEL. Some people manage.

KLETCH. Huh—call them people! Rabble, scum—people! I'm a working man. I'm ashamed to look at them. I've been working ever since I was a kid. You think I won't get out of this hole? I'll get out of here if I have to leave my skin here behind me. You wait . . . when my old woman dies . . . I've been here six months, and it feels more like six years . . .

PEPPEL. There's no one here any worse than you are—say what you like.

KLETCH. No worse than me? They've got no honor, no conscience . . .

PEPPEL [*indifferently*]. What's the good of honor and conscience? You can't wear them on your feet instead of boots. Honor and conscience are all right for rich people, people in authority . . .

BUBNOV [*re-enters*]. Oo-oo-oo-oh! I'm frozen, it's so cold.

PEPPEL. Bubnov, have you got a conscience?

BUBNOV. What? A conscience?

PEPPEL. That's right.

BUBNOV. What do I want with a conscience? I can't afford it.

PEPPEL. Just what I say. Honor and conscience is all right for the rich, yes. But Kletch here is blaming *us*, because we haven't got any conscience.

BUBNOV. Why—does he want to borrow some?

PEPPEL. He's got plenty of his own.

BUBNOV. Oh, he's trying to sell some. You won't find any customers here. I wouldn't mind buying some marked cards, but they'd have to be on credit.

PEPPEL [*sermonizing*]. You're a fool, Andrey! You should try talking to Satin about conscience . . . or the Baron.

KLETCH. I wouldn't talk to them about anything.

PEPPEL. They've got more brains than you've got—for all their drinking.

BUBNOV. If a man is drunk and wise, he's a man that all should prize.

PEPPEL. Satin says everybody wants everyone else to have a conscience, but nobody wants to have one himself. It's true too . . .

[*Enter* NATASHA, *followed by* LUKA, *who carries a stick, a knapsack on his back, and a kettle and teapot hanging from his waist.*]

LUKA. Good morning, honest people!

PEPPEL [*smooths his moustache*]. Ah, Natasha!

BUBNOV [*to* LUKA]. I was honest up to last spring.

NATASHA. Here's a new lodger.

LUKA. It's all the same to me. I have just as much respect for crooks. All fleas are the same. All black, and all good jumpers. Where shall I squeeze myself, child?

NATASHA [*points to the kitchen door*]. In there, grandpa.

LUKA. Thank you, dear. Anywhere you say. Anywhere the old man can be warm. [*Exit.*]

PEPPEL. An interesting old man you've brought us, Natasha.

NATASHA. A lot more interesting than you . . . Andrey! Your wife's in our kitchen. You'd better come and get her.

KLETCH. All right. I'll come.

NATASHA. You ought to try and be kinder to her. She hasn't got long.

KLETCH. I know.

NATASHA. You know . . . It's no good just knowing. You should do something. It's a terrible thing to die.

PEPPEL. I'm not afraid of death.

NATASHA. Oh, you're a marvel, aren't you?

BUBNOV [*whistling*]. This thread's rotten.

PEPPEL. God's truth, I'm not afraid. If I was to die now. Take a knife and stab me in my heart. I'll die without a murmur. In fact, I'd be glad to, because it comes from a pure hand.

NATASHA [*turns to go*]. You keep your soft soap for those who like it.

BUBNOV [*drawls*]. Thread's rotten . . .

NATASHA [*at hall door*]. Don't forget your wife, Andrey . . .

KLETCH. All right.

[*Exit* NATASHA.]

PEPPEL. She's a nice girl.

BUBNOV. Not bad.

PEPPEL. Why does she get like that with me? What for? She'll come to no good here.

BUBNOV. Through you she will.

PEPPEL. What do you mean, through me? I feel sorry for her.

BUBNOV. Like the wolf feels sorry for the sheep.

PEPPEL. That's a lie. I feel very sorry for her. She has a hard life here, I can see she does.

KLETCH. You wait till Vassilisa catches you talking to her.

BUBNOV. Vassilisa? Mm, yes. She won't give up what's hers as easily as that. She's a bitch, she is.

PEPPEL [*lies down on the planks*]. You two prophets can go to hell!

KLETCH. Well, you just wait and see!

LUKA [*in the kitchen, sings*].

> Night is dark, your feet are lead,
> You cannot see the road ahead . . .

KLETCH [*goes into the passage*]. Another one bawling.

PEPPEL. God, I'm bored. Why do I get so bored? Everything's fine, and all of a sudden—bored. Like catching a cold.

BUBNOV. Bored? Hmm . . .

PEPPEL. O-o-o-oh!

LUKA [*sings*].

No sir, you cannot see the road ahead . . .

PEPPEL. Hey, there, old man!

LUKA [*at door*]. Who, me?

PEPPEL. Yes, you. Stop singing!

LUKA [*comes in*]. What's wrong? Don't you like it?

PEPPEL. I like good singing.

LUKA. So mine isn't good, then.

PEPPEL. That's right.

LUKA. Well, well. I thought I sang well. That's always the way. A man thinks he's doing something well, and then—suddenly, bang!—everybody's criticizing.

PEPPEL [*laughs*]. That's the way it is.

BUBNOV. You say you're bored, and there you are laughing.

LUKA. Who's bored?

PEPPEL. Me . . . I am . . .

[*Enter the* BARON.]

LUKA. Well, well! And in the kitchen there's a girl reading a book, and crying! Yes, crying! Tears falling down her cheeks. I say to her, "What's the matter, child? Eh?" "It's so sad," she says. "What's sad?" I say. "The book" she says . . . Some people find funny things to worry about. All from boredom.

BARON. She's a fool, that girl.

PEPPEL. Baron, have you had your tea?

BARON. Yes, what about it?

PEPPEL. Like me to buy you a drink?

BARON. What do you think?

PEPPEL. Get down on all fours and bark like a dog, then.

BARON. Idiot! Are you drunk or something?

PEPPEL. Go on, bark! That'll amuse me. You're a Baron. Used to look down on people like me.

BARON. So what?

PEPPEL. So now I make you bark like a dog. You will, too. You know you will.

BARON. What if I do? Idiot! What good is it to you to know

I've sunk lower than you? You should have tried to make me walk on all fours when I was better than you.

BUBNOV. That's right!

LUKA. Very good, I'd say!

BUBNOV. What's past is past, and what's left isn't worth talking about. There's no aristocracy here. No class distinction. Just man, that's all.

LUKA. So everybody's equal . . . Were you really a baron, mister?

BARON. What's that? Who are you? A ghost?

LUKA [*laughs*]. I've seen counts, and I've seen princes. But this is the first time I've seen a baron—and this one's a damaged one, at that.

PEPPEL [*laughs*]. That's one for you, Baron!

BARON. We live and learn, Vaska.

LUKA. Hey, hey! To look at you, my brothers, your way of life . . .

BUBNOV. Our way of life is nothing but uproar from morning to night

BARON. We knew better times once . . . I used to drink coffee in bed in the mornings . . . coffee!—with cream . . .

LUKA. But we're all human beings. Pretend all you like, give yourself airs, but a man you were born, and a man you must die. I can see everyone getting cleverer and cleverer. They live worse and want more out of life—stubborn lot!

BARON. Who are you, old man? Where do you come from?

LUKA. Who, me?

BARON. Are you a tramp?

LUKA. We're all of us tramps. They even say the world's a tramp in the universe.

BARON [*sternly*]. I daresay—but have you got a passport?

LUKA [*after a slight pause*]. And what are you, a police inspector?

PEPPEL [*delighted*]. That's the way, old man. That had you, Baron—eh?

BUBNOV. Yes, that was one for our fine gentleman.

BARON [*embarrassed*]. What's the matter? I was only joking, old man. I haven't got any papers myself.

BUBNOV. Lies, all lies.

BARON. Well . . . I have got papers . . . but they're no use, any of them.

LUKA. All papers are like that—no use, any of them.

PEPPEL. Baron, let's go and have a drink.

BARON. All right! Well, good-bye, old man. You're an old bastard.

LUKA. Who isn't, brother—eh?

PEPPEL [*at hall door*]. Well, are you coming?

[*Exit* PEPPEL. BARON *quickly follows him.*]

LUKA. Is that man really a Baron?

BUBNOV. God knows. He's been a gentleman all right. Every now and then it breaks out. He can't get rid of it yet.

LUKA. It seems like breeding's like the smallpox. You get cured, but you've still got the marks.

BUBNOV. He's all right . . . Only now and then he goes off, like about your passport today.

ALESHKA [*enters, drunk, whistling, with a concertina*]. Hello everyone!

BUBNOV. What are you yelling about?

ALESHKA. Oh, I beg your pardon . . . 'scuse me! I'm polite . . .

BUBNOV. You on another binge?

ALESHKA. You damned right! Just now Inspector Medyakin throws me out of the police station, and he says, "Never let me smell you on the streets again," he says. And I'm a sensitive sort of fellow. My boss just snarls at me. And what is he, my boss, eh? He's just a goddamned drunkard, my boss is. And I don't ask for nothing. Not a thing. That's flat! Here's twenty rubles, you say. But I don't want nothing.

[*Enter* NASTYA *from the kitchen.*]

Here's a million. I don't want it. But I won't be ordered around by another man—a drunkard too. I won't have it. I won't.

[NASTYA, *standing in the doorway, looks at* ALESHKA *and shakes her head.*]

LUKA [*good-naturedly*]. Well, you have got yourself in a mess, my boy . . .

BUBNOV. What fools people are!

ALESHKA [*lying on floor*]. A-a-ah, eat me up! I don't care, I'm a miserable fool! Show me, why am I worse than other people? What other people? Eh? Medyakin says to me, "You keep off the streets or I'll knock your block off." But I'm going to lie down in the middle of the street— run over me! I don't care . . .

NASTYA. Poor boy! . . . Such a kid, and . . . look at him.

ALESHKA [*sees her, gets on his knees*]. Mam'sel! Parlez français? Prix-fixe? I'm on a binge . . .

NASTYA [*a loud whisper*]. Vassilisa!

VASSILISA [*opens door with a bang; to* ALESHKA]. Are you here again?

ALESHKA. How do you do? Do come in . . .

VASSILISA. You brat, I told you not to show your face in here again, didn't I? And you're here again!

ALESHKA. Vassilisa . . . Shall I play you a funeral march?

VASSILISA [*grabs him by shoulder*]. Clear out!

ALESHKA [*moves to door*]. No, wait . . . you can't do that! A funeral march . . . I just learnt it! New tune . . . Wait . . . you can't . . .

VASSILISA. I'll show you "can't." I'll set the whole street on you, you little dirty-mouthed . . . pig! Who do you think you are talking about me like that. . . .

ALESHKA [*runs out*]. All right, I'm going.

VASSILISA [*to* BUBNOV]. Never let him set foot here again, do you hear?

BUBNOV. I'm not your blasted watchdog.

VASSILISA. I don't care what you are. You're living here on charity, don't you forget that! How much do you owe me?

BUBNOV [*calmly*]. Never worked it out.

VASSILISA. You be careful—I'll work it out!

ALESHKA [*opens door, shouts*]. Vassilisa! I'm not scared of you! I'm not scared! [*Disappears.*]

[LUKA *laughs.*]

VASSILISA. Who are you?

LUKA. Just passing through. Bird of passage.

VASSILISA. For the night, or are you stopping?

LUKA. That all depends.

VASSILISA. Where's your passport?

LUKA. I'll let you have it.

VASSILISA. Let me have it then.

LUKA. I'll bring it to you—right to your door.

VASSILISA. Bird of passage—huh! Jailbird would be more the truth.

LUKA [*with sigh*]. Ayy . . . You're a hard woman, aren't you?

[VASSILISA *goes to* PEPPEL'S *door.*]

ALESHKA [*peers round kitchen door, whispers*]. Hey! She gone?

VASSILISA [*turns on him*]. You still here?

[ALESHKA *disappears, whistling.* NASTYA *and* LUKA *laugh.*]

BUBNOV [*to* VASSILISA]. He isn't there.

VASSILISA. Who isn't?

BUBNOV. Vaska.

VASSILISA. Did I ask you if he was?

BUBNOV. I can see you're looking for him.

VASSILISA. I'm looking to see if the place is tidy. Why isn't the floor swept yet? How many times do I have to tell you to sweep the floor?

BUBNOV. It's the Actor's turn.

VASSILISA. I don't care whose turn. If the Health Inspector comes and fines me, then—out you go, the lot of you!

BUBNOV [*calmly*]. Then what will you live on?

VASSILISA. I won't have all this mess. [*Goes towards kitchen. To* NASTYA.] What's the matter with you? Your face is all swollen. Don't stand there—sweep the floor! Have you seen Natasha? Has she been in?

NASTYA. Don't know. I haven't seen her.

VASSILISA. Bubnov! Has my sister been here?

BUBNOV. Er . . . she brought him in.

VASSILISA. Was he . . . has he been in?

BUBNOV. Vaska? Yes . . . She was here talking to Kletch, your Natasha.

VASSILISA. I wasn't asking who she was talking to! Dirt everywhere—filth! Ach, you pigs! See the place is clean, you hear? [*Exit quickly.*]

BUBNOV. My God, what a bitch!

LUKA. Quite a temper—eh?

NASTYA. You'd be a bitch if you had her life. Tied to a husband like she's got!

BUBNOV. Well, she isn't tied too fast.

LUKA. Does she always have these fits?

BUBNOV. All the time. She came after her lover, you see. And he isn't here.

LUKA. So she has to get angry. Huh! Everybody is trying to be boss. They throw their weight around, and make all sorts of threats, and punish each other. And the world still doesn't make any sense . . . and is dirty.

BUBNOV. Everybody wants order, and their brains are all disorder. Still, the floor's got to be swept. Hey, Nastya— you do it.

NASTYA. Like hell! Do you think I'm your kitchen maid? [*After a pause.*] I'm going to get drunk today—dead drunk!

BUBNOV. There you are!

LUKA. What do you want to get drunk for, girl? Just now you were crying. Now you want to get drunk.

NASTYA [*defiantly*]. And when I'm drunk, I'll cry again—so there!

BUBNOV. So what?

LUKA. Yes, but what for, girl? Even a pimple has a reason.

[NASTYA *shakes her head in silence.*]

So . . . hey, hey . . . What's going to happen to the human race? Well, suppose I sweep the floor. Where's the broom?

BUBNOV. In the hall behind the door.

[LUKA *goes out to the hall.*]

Nastya!

NASTYA. Uh?

BUBNOV. Why did Vassilisa go for Aleshka?

NASTYA. He went round saying Vashka's fed up with her, and wants to drop her for Natasha. I'm getting out of here. Going somewhere else.

BUBNOV. Why? Where to?

NASTYA. I'm fed up. I'm not wanted here.

BUBNOV [*calmly*]. You're not wanted anywhere. Nobody's wanted anywhere the whole world over, for that matter.

[NASTYA *shakes her head, rises, and slowly goes out to the hall. Enter* MEDVEDEV, *followed by* LUKA *with broom.*]

MEDVEDEV. Don't think I know you.

LUKA. Do you know everybody else, then?

MEDVEDEV. I have to know everybody in my area. But I don't know you.

LUKA. That's because the whole world couldn't quite get inside your district, uncle. There's a little bit left outside. [*Goes into kitchen.*]

MEDVEDEV. He's right . . . my district isn't very big. But it's worse than some of the big ones. [*Going up to* BUBNOV.] Just now, coming off duty, I had to run in Aleshka, the cobbler. Lying there right in the middle of the road, playing his concertina, and yelling, "I don't want anything! I don't care! I don't want anything!" Horses and traffic everywhere. Could have been run over, crushed to death. He's a wild one. Well, I had to take him in. He sure loves to cause trouble.

BUBNOV. You coming for a game of checkers tonight?

MEDVEDEV. Tonight? Yes . . . And what's this about Vaska?

BUBNOV. What about him? Same as usual.

MEDVEDEV. Same as usual, eh?

BUBNOV. What's wrong with that? He's allowed to live, isn't he?

MEDVEDEV [doubtfully]. Is he?

[LUKA crosses the room to the hall with a bucket.]

Mm, yes. There's some talk . . . about Vaska . . . haven't you heard it?

BUBNOV. I've heard lots of talk.

MEDVEDEV. About Vassilisa . . . haven't you noticed?

BUBNOV. What?

MEDVEDEV. "What!" I think you know—you're just lying. Everyone knows . . . [Sternly.] Don't lie to me, old man.

BUBNOV. Why should I lie?

MEDVEDEV. I know, I know . . . Oh, come on! They say Vaska and Vassilisa are . . . carrying on . . . Well, so what? I'm her uncle, not her father. It can't make me a laughing stock.

[Enter KVASHNYA.]

That's what people are these days—they'll laugh at anything. Ah, its you!

KVASHNYA. My darling keeper of the peace! Bubnov, he's been pestering me to marry him again.

BUBNOV. Well, why not? He's got money. He's still got his health and strength.

MEDVEDEV. Me? Ho, ho!

KVASHNYA. You old bear! Leave me alone—it's my sore spot. I've been through it all once, honey. It's like falling through a hole in the ice. You never forget it.

MEDVEDEV. Wait a minute. Husbands aren't all the same.

KVASHNYA. No, but I'm the same. When my old man died, it took me a whole day before I could believe my own luck.

MEDVEDEV. If your husband beat you, you should have complained to the police.

KVASHNYA. I complained to God for eight years—it didn't do any good.

MEDVEDEV. It's a punishable offense for a man to beat his wife. That's the law today. Nobody's allowed to beat anyone—except the police.

LUKA [*leads in* ANNA]. Careful now . . . There you are! You're
  too weak to go about on your own. Where do you go?

ANNA [*points it out*]. Thank you, grandpa . . .

KVASHNYA. Look, there's a married woman for you. Look at
  her!

LUKA. The poor thing's very weak. She was in the hall, holding
  onto the wall, groaning. Why do you leave her by herself?

KVASHNYA. Sorry, we didn't notice, grandpa. Her maid must
  have gone out for a walk.

LUKA. You can laugh! How can you neglect a human being?
  Whoever it is, we all have some value.

MEDVEDEV. People have got to be looked after. What if she
  dies suddenly? No end of trouble. Got to watch out for that.

LUKA. That's true, Inspector.

MEDVEDEV. Of course it is . . . but I'm not an inspector yet.

LUKA. Oh, I thought you were. That strong, commanding
  manner of yours.

[*Noise and scuffling in the hall. Loud cries.*]

MEDVEDEV. Not a fight?

BUBNOV. Sounds like it.

KVASHNYA. I'm going to see.

MEDVEDEV. I'd better go too. Duty calls! People ought to be
  left to fight. They'd stop when they got tired. Let them
  knock each other about as much as they like—they won't
  do it again in a hurry. They'd remember what it's like.

BUBNOV [*rises from bunk*]. Tell that to the Chief of Police.

KOSTYLEV [*flings open door, cries*]. Abram! Quickly . . .
  Vassilisa . . . killing Natasha! Come quick . . .

[KVASHNYA, MEDVEDEV, BUBNOV *rush into hall.* LUKA *looks
  after them, shaking his head.*]

ANNA. Oh, God . . . Poor Natasha!

LUKA. Who is fighting?

ANNA. The mistress . . . and her sister.

LUKA [*goes to* ANNA]. What's it about?

ANNA. They've nothing better to do . . . they're both well and
  strong.

LUKA. What's your name?

ANNA. Anna. You look like my father . . . kind like he was
  . . . soft . . .

LUKA. It's all the kicks I've had—they've made me soft . . .
  [*He laughs with a grating laugh.*]

ACT TWO

[*The same scene. Night. On the bunk by the stove,* SATIN, *the* BARON, SCREWY *and the* TARTAR *are playing cards.* KLETCH *and the* ACTOR *are watching. On his bunk,* BUBNOV *is playing checkers with* MEDVEDEV. LUKA *sits on a stool by* ANNA'S *bed. The cellar is lighted by two lamps. One hangs on the wall by the card players, the other stands on* BUB- NOV'S *bunk.*]

TARTAR. One more game, then I stop.
BUBNOV. Screwy! Sing! [*Sings.*]

> The sun comes up, the sun goes down . . .

SCREWY [*harmonizes*].

> In my prison night won't go . . .

TARTAR [*to* SATIN]. Shuffle! Shuffle well! I know what you're like . . .
BUBNOV *and* SCREWY [*sing together*].

> Day and night the warder paces
> Past the bars of my window . . .

ANNA. Beaten black and blue—nothing but curses all my life, all my blessed life . . .
LUKA. There, there, don't upset yourself, my dear.
MEDVEDEV. Where do you think you're moving? You blind?
BUBNOV. Ah! yes, of course . . .
TARTAR [*shakes his fist at* SATIN]. Why you try to hide a card? I see it—you . . . !
SCREWY. Forget it, Hassan! They'll skin us anyway. Come on, Bubnov—sing!
ANNA. I can't remember a time when I wasn't hungry . . . counted every last crumb of bread . . . Never known where the next bite's coming from . . . Been in rags all my miserable life. Why? What's it all for?
LUKA. You poor child. You're tired. Don't worry yourself so.
ACTOR [*to* SCREWY]. Play the Jack . . . the Jack, damn you!
BARON. And we have the king.

KLETCH. They win every time.

SATIN. Can't help it—force of habit.

MEDVEDEV. King!

BUBNOV. And me . . . mm . . .

ANNA. I'm dying.

KLETCH. Look at that! You might as well give up now, Hassan.
Go on, throw in your cards!

ACTOR. He can play without your advice! Leave him alone.

BARON. Shut up, Andrey, or I'll hit you. I'm warning you!

TARTAR. Deal again. You may as well break me all the way.

[KLETCH *shakes head, goes over to* BUBNOV.]

ANNA. Oh, God, will I be punished with suffering in the next
world too? There as well?

LUKA. No, you won't. You won't. Don't upset yourself. Listen:
you won't suffer there—you'll only rest. Have a little
patience—everybody has to suffer a bit in this life . . .
[*Rises, goes quickly into kitchen.*]

BUBNOV [*sings*].

Warder, watch my prison window . . .

SCREWY [*sings*].

Warder, guard my prison cell . . .

BOTH [*sing*].

How I long, I long for freedom!
But my chains they hold me well!

TARTAR [*cries out*]. You hide a card up your sleeve!

BARON [*embarrassed*]. Well, where do you want me to hide it?
Up your ass?

ACTOR [*emphatically*]. You're wrong, Hassan. . . . Nobody
ever . . .

TARTAR. I saw him! Bloody cheat! I won't play no more!

SATIN [*gathers cards*]. For Christ's sake, Hassan! You know
we're cheats—why do you play with us at all, then?

BARON. He loses half a ruble, and he makes three rubles'
worth of noise about it . . . Come on, Hassan! Sit down.

TARTAR [*hotly*]. Well, play straight then.

SATIN. Why should we?

TARTAR. What do you mean, why should you?

SATIN. What I say. Why should we?

TARTAR. Don't you know?

SATIN. No, I don't. Do you?

[TARTAR *spits in disgust. Everybody laughs at him.*]

SCREWY [*good-naturedly*]. You're a funny guy, Hassan. Can't you see, if they turned honest, they'd die of starvation in three days . . .

TARTAR. That's nothing to do with me! Everyone should be honest.

SCREWY. He's off again. Come on and have some tea . . . Bubnov! And [*sings*]

Oh, you heavy chains that bind me . . .

BUBNOV [*sings*].

Oh, you heavy clanking chains . . .

SCREWY. Come on, Hassan! [*Exit singing.*]

I will never break you ever . . .

[TARTAR *shakes his fist at* BARON, *and follows his friend.*]

SATIN [*laughing, to* BARON]. Well, your majesty—you sure messed us up again, didn't you? You've learned a lot, but you still don't know how to cheat at cards.

BARON [*shrugs*]. God knows how it happened.

ACTOR. No talent . . . No faith in yourself . . . and without that . . . you're nothing, nothing at all . . .

MEDVEDEV. I have one king. You've got two . . . mm!

BUBNOV. One's enough, if you use him right. Your move!

KLETCH. You've had it, Abram!

MEDVEDEV. Mind your own business, will you? And shut up . . .

SATIN. Fifty-three kopecks in.

ACTOR. Three of those are mine . . . Though what do I want with three kopecks?

LUKA [*coming in from the kitchen*]. So you've cleaned out the Tartar? Going for a drink now?

BARON. Come and have a drink with us!

SATIN. Let's see what you're like drunk!

LUKA. No better than I am sober . . .

ACTOR. Come on, old man . . . I'll recite to you . . .

LUKA. What's that?

ACTOR. Poetry, you know.

LUKA. Poetry? What do I want with poetry?

ACTOR. It's funny . . . sometimes it's sad . . .

SATIN. Hey, recitationist! Are you coming? [*Exit with* BARON.]

ACTOR. I'm coming . . . I'll catch you up! Here, here's one, old man. It's a speech from a play . . . can't remember how it begins . . . I've completely forgotten it! [*Strikes his forehead.*]

BUBNOV. There! I take your king . . . Your move!

MEDVEDEV. You had me, wherever I moved.

ACTOR. I had a good memory once, old man, before my organism got poisoned with alcohol. Now I'm finished— done for. I used to do that speech well . . . used to bring the house down! You don't know what it's like—applause. It's . . . it's like vodka! I used to come on . . . stand like this . . . [*Strikes a pose.*] stand like this, and [*Silence.*] I can't remember a thing! Not a single word! Can't remember! My best speech . . . In a bad way, eh, old man?

LUKA. Yes, it's bad, all right, forgetting something you used to love. Something you had your heart and soul in . . .

ACTOR. I've drunk up my soul, old man . . . I'm lost, my friend. Why am I lost? Because I've lost faith in myself . . . I'm finished . . .

LUKA. Finished? You go and get yourself cured! Listen. They cure people of drunkenness nowadays. Cure them for nothing. They've built a special hospital to cure drunkards for nothing. They realize a drunkard's a man like any other. They're glad when he wants to be cured! So there it is for you. You go there!

ACTOR [*reflectively*]. Where? Where is it?

LUKA. It's . . . in a town . . . what's its name? Never mind. I'll think of it. But you get ready to go. Pull yourself together, and keep off the vodka. Then go and get cured, and you can start life over again. Sounds good, doesn't it, my brother? All over again—eh? Well, just make up your mind, and you can do it.

ACTOR [*smiles*]. All over again . . . from the beginning . . . that would be marvelous . . . yes . . . all over again. [*He laughs.*] Oh . . . yes! Can I? Can I really do it? Eh?

LUKA. Of course you can do it! A man can do anything, once he makes up his mind to it.

ACTOR [*as if woken up suddenly*]. You're a strange duck! Well, g'bye! [*Whistles.*] G'bye, old man! . . . [*Exit.*]

ANNA. Grandpa!

LUKA. What is it, dear?

ANNA. Come and talk to me.

LUKA [*goes up to her*]. All right. Let's have a chat.

[KLETCH *looks round, silently comes up to his wife, looks at her, and gestures, as though wanting to say something.*]

LUKA. What's the matter, my brother?

KLETCH [*quietly*]. Nothing. [*Goes slowly to hall door, stands there for a moment, and exits.*]

LUKA [*watching him*]. Takes it to heart, your old man.

ANNA. I can't worry about him any more.

LUKA. Did he used to beat you?

ANNA. Did he! I'm dying because of him . . .

BUBNOV. My wife had a lover. Bastard played a good game of checkers.

MEDVEDEV. Hm . . .

ANNA. Grandpa! Talk to me. I can't breathe.

LUKA. It's all right. Like that before you die, my child. It's nothing, dear. Just keep hoping. You're going to die, and then you'll have peace. There's nothing to be afraid of—nothing. Peace and quiet . . . Lie still, now! Death settles everything . . . it's kind to us . . . When you die, they say you go to rest. Well, it's true, dear! After all you can't find rest in this world.

[PEPPEL *enters, slightly drunk, dishevelled and sullen. He sits on a bunk by the door, and stays silent and motionless.*]

ANNA. But what if there's suffering there, too?

LUKA. There won't be! There won't be, believe me! Just rest, that's all there'll be. They'll call you up to God, and they'll say, "Look Lord, this is your servant, Anna . . ."

MEDVEDEV [*sternly*]. How do you know what they'll say? Ach . . .

[*Hearing* MEDVEDEV'S *voice*, PEPPEL *raises his head, and listens.*]

LUKA. I just do, that's all, Inspector.

MEDVEDEV [*conciliatory*]. Yes, yes, yes . . . That's up to you. But I'm not an inspector yet . . .

BUBNOV. I take two.

MEDVEDEV. Damnation!

LUKA. And God will look at you gently and kindly, and He'll say, "I know this Anna. Take her into Heaven," He'll say,

"Give her rest. I know she's had a hard life. She's weary.
Give Anna rest."

ANNA [*gasping*]. Oh, grandpa! If only it would be . . . if only
. . . rest . . . feel nothing more . . .

LUKA. You won't. I tell you. You must believe me. Die happy,
no worry. Death's like a mother to little children for us,
I tell you.

ANNA. Perhaps . . . perhaps I'll . . . get well?

LUKA. What for? To suffer some more?

ANNA. But . . . to live just a bit longer . . . just a bit longer!
If I won't have to suffer there, I can stand it here a bit
longer.

LUKA. But there's nothing there. So easy . . .

PEPPEL [*rises*]. That's true. Or maybe it isn't!

ANNA [*frightened*]. Oh, God!

LUKA. Hello, handsome.

MEDVEDEV. Who's that shouting?

PEPPEL [*goes up to him*]. Me. What of it?

MEDVEDEV. There's no need to go shouting, that's what.
People should be quieter.

PEPPEL. Oh, shit! Call yourself an uncle—huh!

LUKA [*to* PEPPEL, *in a low voice*]. Listen, don't shout. There's
a woman dying here. One foot in the grave. Don't upset her.

PEPPEL. Grandpa, I'd do anything for you. You're all right!
A damn fine liar, that's what you are. Damned good stories
you make up. I don't mind you lying. You carry on! There
aren't many good things in this life!

BUBNOV. Is she really dying?

LUKA. Do you think she's pretending?

BUBNOV. Won't have any more coughing, then. Been disturb-
ing everybody . . . I take two!

MEDVEDEV. Oh, damn your eyes!

PEPPEL. Abram!

MEDVEDEV. Don't call me Abram.

PEPPEL. Abram—is Natasha ill, Abram?

MEDVEDEV. What business is it of yours?

PEPPEL. I want to know. Did Vassilisa beat her up badly?

MEDVEDEV. It's nothing to do with you. Family matter. Who
do you think you are, anyway?

PEPPEL. Never mind about who I am. If I want, you won't
ever see Natasha again. That's who I am.

MEDVEDEV [*leaves the game*]. What's that? What do you say?
My niece . . . You thief, you!

PEPPEL. A thief, perhaps, but you haven't caught me yet!

MEDVEDEV. Just you wait! I'll catch you all right, before long.

PEPPEL. You catch me, it'll be so much the worse for all your precious family. Think I'll keep quiet before the judge? I'm a thief, aren't I? "Who taught you to thieve" they'll say, "and showed you the cribs?" Mishka Kostylev and his wife! "Who was your fence?" Mishka Kostylev and his wife!

MEDVEDEV. You liar! They won't believe you.

PEPPEL. They'll believe me all right, because it's true. I'll drag you in it too—ha! I'll sink the lot of you, you bastard, you see.

MEDVEDEV [*shaken*]. Lies, all lies! What harm have I done you? You scabby cur!

PEPPEL. What good have you done me?

LUKA. Aha!

MEDVEDEV [*to* LUKA]. What are you croaking about? None of your business. This is family matters.

BUBNOV. Keep out of this. Let them hang each other if they want.

LUKA [*meekly*]. I didn't say anything. I only say, if a man doesn't do someone any good, he does him harm.

MEDVEDEV [*misunderstands*]. That's right. Now, we all know one another here . . . who are you? [*Spits angrily and goes out.*]

LUKA. The gentleman's angry. Oho-ho! You've gotten yourselves all twisted up, haven't you?

PEPPEL. He's gone crying to Vassilisa.

BUBNOV. You're a damn fool, Vaska. What's the good of all the tough stuff? All very well being brave, but it doesn't cut much ice here. They'll break your neck before you know it.

PEPPEL. No, they won't. A Yaroslav doesn't give in without a fight. If there's a fight, I'm ready for it.

LUKA. I tell you, my boy, you ought to get out of this place.

PEPPEL. And go where? You tell me.

LUKA. To . . . Siberia.

PEPPEL. Ha! When I go to Siberia, it'll be at the government's expense.

LUKA. Listen to me, you go there. You'll do all right there. You're the kind who do.

PEPPEL. My life's already marked out for me. My father spent all his life in prisons, and that's my life too. When I was only a kid, everybody called me a thief, and son of a thief.

LUKA. But it's a wonderful place, Siberia. Golden land! A strong fellow, with brains, he can make a fortune there!

PEPPEL. Why do you tell lies, old man?

LUKA. What?

PEPPEL. Are you deaf? I said, why do you tell lies?

LUKA. When was I lying?

PEPPEL. All the time. You say it's fine here, and its wonderful somewhere else. All lies! What for?

LUKA. You take my word for it, and go there and see for yourself. You'll thank me all right. What's the good of hanging around here? And what do you want with the truth anyway? It'll do you more harm than good.

PEPPEL. I don't care. I can face it, whatever it is!

LUKA. Oh, you're crazy! Are you trying to get yourself killed?

BUBNOV. What is all this nonsense? I don't get it. What's this truth you're after, Vaska? What for? You know the truth.

PEPPEL. Shut up, Bubnov. I want to ask him something. Listen, old man, is there a God?

[LUKA *smiles, silently.*]

BUBNOV. We're all just somebody's garbage, that's all.

PEPPEL. Well? Is there?

LUKA [*quietly*]. If you believe in him, there is. If you don't, there isn't. Whatever you believe in, exists.

[PEPPEL *stares silently at* LUKA, *puzzled.*]

BUBNOV. I'm going to get a drink. Coming? Hey!

LUKA [*to* PEPPEL]. What are you staring at?

PEPPEL. Wait a minute. You mean . . .

BUBNOV. I'll go on my own then. [*Goes to door, where he meets* VASSILISA.]

PEPPEL. Then . . . you . . .

VASSILISA [*to* BUBNOV]. Is Nastya here?

BUBNOV. No. [*Exit.*]

PEPPEL. Oh . . . look who's here.

VASSILISA [*goes to* ANNA]. Still alive?

LUKA. Leave her alone.

VASSILISA. What are you hanging around here for?

LUKA. I'll go, if you want.

VASSILISA [*goes towards* PEPPEL's *door*]. Vaska! I want to talk to you.

[LUKA *goes to hall door, opens it, and closes it again loudly. Then he clambers up on the stove.*]

VASSILISA [*from* PEPPEL'S *room*]. Vaska! Come here!

PEPPEL. No. I don't want to.

VASSILISA. What's wrong? What's the matter?

PEPPEL. I've had enough. I'm sick of the whole bloody business.

VASSILISA. Sick . . . of me?

PEPPEL. And sick of you.

[VASSILISA *pulls her shawl tight across her shoulders, presses her hands to her breast. Goes to* ANNA'S *bed, looks carefully behind the curtain, and turns to* PEPPEL.]

Well, what did you want to talk about?

VASSILISA. What can I say? I can't force you to love me. It isn't in me to grovel. Thank you for speaking the truth.

PEPPEL. Speaking what truth?

VASSILISA. That you're sick of me. Or isn't it the truth?

[PEPPEL *looks at her in silence*.]

VASSILISA [*goes up to him*]. What are you staring for? Haven't you seen me before?

PEPPEL [*sighs*]. You're beautiful, Vassilisa. [*She puts hand on his shoulder, but he shakes it off*.] But I never loved you. We slept together, all right, but I never loved you.

VASSILISA [*quietly*]. I see . . . Well . . .

PEPPEL. Well, there's nothing for us to say. Not a thing. Go away.

VASSILISA. Is there someone else?

PEPPEL. Forget it. I wouldn't ask your advice if there was.

VASSILISA [*significantly*]. That's too bad. I might be able to help.

PEPPEL [*suspiciously*]. What do you mean?

VASSILISA. You know what I mean. What are you pretending for? Vaska, let's be honest about it. [*Lowering her voice*.] I won't hide it—you've hurt me . . . All of a sudden, as if you hit me with a whip. For no reason at all. You said you loved me . . . and all of a sudden . . .

PEPPEL. Not sudden at all. A long time . . . You've got no heart, Vassilisa. A woman's got to have a heart. We men are just beasts. You've got to tame us and make something of us. How have you tamed me? What have you made me?

VASSILISA. What's done is done. People can't help their own feelings. You don't love me any more. All right then. That's how it is.

PEPPEL. That's how it is. Finish! Let's part friends. No fuss. That's the way.

VASSILISA. No, wait. Listen . . . When I lived with you, I always hoped you were going to get me out of this mess. Free me from my husband, from my uncle . . . all this life . . . Maybe I didn't love you at all, Vaska—just this hope I kept thinking about, that I loved. Don't you see? I thought you were going to pull me out of here.

PEPPEL. You aren't a nail. I'm not a pair of pliers. I'd have thought with your brains . . . After all, you're smart enough, aren't you?

VASSILISA [bends close to him.] Vaska! Let's help one another . . .

PEPPEL. How do you mean?

VASSILISA [quietly but strongly]. I know . . . you like my sister.

PEPPEL. That's why you beat her, you cat! Listen, you dare lay a finger on her . . .

VASSILISA. Wait a minute! Keep calm! We can manage all this peacefully, and properly . . . Do you want to marry her? All right—marry her. I'll even give you money. Three hundred! More if I can.

PEPPEL [moves away]. Wait a minute. What is this? What's the idea?

VASSILISA. Help me—get rid of my husband. Take that noose from around my neck.

PEPPEL [whistles softly]. So that's it! Oho! You've thought it all out, haven't you? Your husband in his grave, your lover in prison, and you . . .

VASSILISA. No, Vaska, why should you go to prison? Get some of the others to do it. Even if you do do it yourself, who's to know? Think of Natasha! And the money. You can go anywhere you like. Set me free for good. It'll be a good thing for Natasha, not to be near me. I can't even look at her without getting furious, on account of you. I can't help it. I torment the girl, I beat her. I beat her so hard, I could cry myself I feel so sorry for her. But I beat her all the same. And I'll go on beating her!

PEPPEL. You bitch! Are you boasting?

VASSILISA. Not boasting—it's the truth. Look, Vaska, you've been to prison twice because of my husband. He's been like a vampire sucking my blood for four years. And what sort of a husband is he? And he pushes Natasha around, shouts at her, calls her a beggar. He's poison to everybody.

PEPPEL. This is some clever scheme of yours . . .

VASSILISA. No. Everything I say is true. It's clear enough—you're not a fool.

[KOSTYLEV *enters cautiously, steals in.*]

PEPPEL [*to* VASSILISA]. Oh, go away!

VASSILISA. Think it over. [*Sees husband.*] What are you doing here? Following me around!

[PEPPEL *jumps up, stares wildly at* KOSTYLEV.]

KOSTYLEV. It's me . . . me! Are you here by yourselves? Aah! You were having a little chat? [*Suddenly stamps his feet and screams out.*] You swine, Vaska! You filthy beggar! [*Startled at his own voice, as the others watch motionless and silent.*] God forgive me—you've led me to sin again, Vassilisa . . . I've been looking for you everywhere. [*Screaming.*] It's time for bed! And you haven't filled the lamps, you devil! . . . you hellcat! [*Points at her with trembling hand.*]

[VASSILISA *goes slowly to the hall, looking round at* PEPPEL.]

PEPPEL [*to* KOSTYLEV]. Clear out of here! Go on, get out!

KOSTYLEV [*screams*]. I'm the landlord! You clear out—you thief!

PEPPEL [*sullenly*]. Get out, Mishka.

KOSTYLEV. How dare you? I—I—I'll . . .

[PEPPEL *grabs him by the collar and shakes him. A noise and a loud yawning are heard from the stove.* PEPPEL *lets go of* KOSTYLEV, *who runs into the hall screaming.*]

PEPPEL [*jumps on the bunk*]. Who's that? Who's that up there?

LUKA [*raises his head*]. Eh?

PEPPEL. You!

LUKA [*calmly*]. Yes, it's me. Oh, Jesus Christ!

PEPPEL [*closes hall door, looks for the bolt, but cannot find it*]. Ach, the devils! Come down, old man.

LUKA. All right. I'm coming.

PEPPEL [*threateningly*]. What were you doing up there?

LUKA. Where else do you want me to go?

PEPPEL. I thought you went out in the hall.

LUKA. I'm an old man, my friend—it's cold out in the hall.

PEPPEL. You heard?

LUKA. How could I help hearing? I'm not deaf, am I? Ah, you're a lucky fellow. You're lucky, all right.

PEPPEL [*suspiciously*]. What do you mean lucky? What do you mean?

LUKA. Lucky I was up there.

PEPPEL. Why did you make that noise just then?

LUKA. I was getting a bit uncomfortable—lucky for you. And then again, I thought maybe you were accidentally going to strangle the old man.

PEPPEL. Maybe I would have. Maybe I hate his guts.

LUKA. It's easy enough. People often make mistakes like that.

PEPPEL [*smiles*]. What about you? Have you ever made a mistake like that?

LUKA. Listen. Steer clear of that woman. Don't let her anywhere near you. She'll drive her husband to his grave well enough without your help. Don't you listen to her—she's a witch! Look at my head. Bald, eh? And why? Because of women. I should say I've known more women than I ever had hairs on my head. And, I say, that Vassilisa's worse than the devil incarnate.

PEPPEL. Should I be thanking you for this? Or maybe you, as well . . .

LUKA. Don't say anything. You won't say anything better than what I've said. Listen. This girl you like, whoever she is, take her away from here, fast as you can. Get out of here right away.

PEPPEL [*darkly*]. Can't make people out. Some are kind, and and some are just out to get you. Can't tell which are which.

LUKA. What's the point? People just live the way they want to. Kind today, and out to get you tomorrow. That's all. If you really love this girl of yours, go away with her, and that's all there is to it. Or go on your own. You're young. There'll be plenty of women around.

PEPPEL [*takes him by the shoulder*]. No, wait a minute. What are you telling me this for?

LUKA. Let me go. I must see to Anna. She was breathing funny. [*Goes to* ANNA'S *bed, opens curtains, looks, touches her.* PEPPEL, *distraught and pensive, follows him.*] Oh Jesus Christ, merciful Lord! Receive in peace the soul of Thy newly departed servant Anna!

PEPPEL [*quietly*] Is she dead? [*Stays where he is, leans forward to look.*]

LUKA [*quietly*]. She's dead. Where's her husband?

PEPPEL. Having a drink, I expect.

LUKA. We'll have to tell him.

PEPPEL [*shudders*]. I don't like dead people.

LUKA [*goes to door*]. What's there to like about them? It's living people we ought to like. Living people.

PEPPEL. I'll come with you.

LUKA. You afraid?

PEPPEL. I don't like . . .

[*They hurry out. The stage is deserted and quiet. An indistinct noise comes from the passage. Then the* ACTOR *enters, stands in the doorway, leaning on the doorposts.*]

ACTOR [*calls*]. Hey, old man! Where are you? Listen! I've remembered it! [*Staggers forward two steps, strikes a pose, and declaims:*]

> There is no truth, my friends! Seek far and near:
> I say there is no truth here in this world.
> So honor the madman, friends, I say!
> The madman's brain will spin us golden lies.

[NATASHA *appears in the door behind him.*]

> Old man!

> Put out the sun, my friends! No more its rays
> Will shine upon this miserable globe.
> But see the golden light that shines instead——
> Born of the fire within the madman's head!

NATASHA [*laughs*]. You idiot! You're drunk . . .

ACTOR [*turns*]. Who's that? Ah, where's the old man? The darling little old man? Nobody here, it seems. Good-bye Natasha. Yes, good-bye.

NATASHA [*comes in*]. Never known you to say good morning before. Now you say good-bye.

ACTOR [*bars her way*]. I'm going away. I'm going right away. Spring will come back again, but I won't.

NATASHA. Rubbish! Where are you going?

ACTOR. To a town . . . to get cured. You should go away too. "Ophelia—get thee to a nunnery!" You know, there's a hospital for organisms, for drunkards. A wonderful hospital. Marble . . . marble floors! Light. Clean floors. Food —all free! Marble floors—yes! I'm going to find it, get

cured, and start life all over again. I'll be reborn! That's
from . . . King—Lear . . . Natasha, my stage name . . . is
Sverchkov-Zavolski. Nobody knows that. Nobody. I haven't
got a name here. Do you know how terrible it is, not to
have a name? Even a dog has a name.

[NATASHA *goes carefully round* ACTOR, *stops at* ANNA'S *bed,
looks.*]

ACTOR. You don't exist without a name.

NATASHA. Look . . . the poor thing . . . she's dead.

ACTOR [*shakes head*]. Can't be.

NATASHA [*backs away*]. Oh, God! She's dead. Look.

BUBNOV [*at door*]. Look at what?

NATASHA. Anna. She's dead.

BUBNOV. That means she won't cough any more. [*Goes to*
ANNA'S *bed, and looks, and goes to his own place.*] You'd
better tell Kletch. It's his business.

ACTOR. I'll go and tell him. She's lost her name. [*Exit.*]

NATASHA [*in the center of the room*]. That's the way I'll end
up one day, dying in a cellar . . . forgotten . . .

BUBNOV [*spreading rugs over his bunk*]. What are you mumbling about?

NATASHA. Nothing. I was talking to myself.

BUBNOV. You waiting for Vaska? You see—your Vaska will
break your neck for you.

NATASHA. I don't care. Rather he broke it than anyone else.

BUBNOV [*lies down*]. Well, it's your lookout.

NATASHA. It's as well she did die, really. But I feel sorry for
her. Oh, God! What do people live for?

BUBNOV. It's the same for everybody. Born, live a while, die.
I'll die—so will you. Nothing to be sorry for.

[*Enter* LUKA, TARTAR, SCREWY *and* KLETCH. KLETCH *comes
slowly after the others, stooping.*]

NATASHA. Sh! Anna——

SCREWY. We know . . . God rest her soul, if she is dead.

TARTAR [*to* KLETCH]. You got to take her out! Take her into
the hall! Can't have dead people in here. Living people got
to sleep in here.

KLETCH [*low voice*]. We'll take her out.

[*They all go to the bed.* KLETCH *looks at his wife over the
others' shoulders.*]

SCREWY [to TARTAR]. You think she'll smell? No, she won't
smell. She all dried up while she was alive.

NATASHA. Oh, God! You might feel sorry for her! You might
say a kind word, some of you! Oh, you . . .

LUKA. Don't take on like that, girl. It's all right. How can we
be sorry for the dead? We can't even be sorry for the living.
Not even sorry for ourselves! What do you expect?

BUBNOV [yawns]. Anyway, death isn't afraid of talk. Illness
may be, but not death.

TARTAR [moves away]. Must call police.

SCREWY. Police—yes, of course! Kletch, have you reported
to the police?

KLETCH. No . . . she's got to be buried . . . I've only got 40
kopecks.

SCREWY. Well, you'll have to borrow. We'll all chip in and
give you what we can. But you'd better report this to the
police quickly. Or they'll think you killed the old woman
. . . [Goes to his bunk and prepares to lie down beside
TARTAR.]

NATASHA [moves away, towards BUBNOV]. Now I'll dream
about her. I always dream about people who die. I'm scared
of going back by myself. It's dark in the hall . . .

LUKA. You be scared of the living, I tell you . . .

NATASHA. Come with me, grandpa . . .

LUKA. All right. Come on, then. [Exeunt.]

[A pause.]

SCREWY. Ho, ho, ho! Hassan! Spring's coming, buddy. It'll
be warm again soon. Farmers are mending their ploughs
. . . getting ready to plough . . . yes! And what about us,
eh, Hassan? . . . Old Mohammed's fast asleep, the bastard!

BUBNOV. Seem to like sleeping, these Tartars.

KLETCH [stands in the middle of the floor, gazing vacantly
ahead]. What am I going to do now?

SCREWY. Lie down and go to sleep. That's all you can do.

KLETCH [quietly]. What about her?

[Nobody answers. Enter SATIN and the ACTOR.]

ACTOR [shouts]. Old man! Hither, my faithful Kent! . . .

SATIN. Here comes Marco Polo! Ho, ho!

ACTOR. I've made up my mind. Where's the town, old man?
Where are you?

SATIN. Fata Morgana! The old man's kidding you . . . There's nothing! No town, no people—nothing!

ACTOR. You're a goddamned liar!

TARTAR [*jumps up*]. Where's the landlord? I'm going to speak to the landlord. Can't get any sleep—then I won't pay him. Dead women, drunken men . . . [*Rushes out.*]

[SATIN *whistles after him.*]

BUBNOV [*sleepily*]. Go to bed, boys. Stop making a row. People want to sleep at night.

ACTOR. Oh, yes. There's a corpse here. "We caught a corpse in our fishing nets . . ." poem, by—Shakespeare!

SATIN [*shouts*]. Corpses can't hear! Corpses can't feel . . . Shout! Yell! Corpses can't hear!

[LUKA *appears in the doorway.*]

ACT THREE

[*The yard, a bit of waste ground, littered with various junk and overgrown with weeds. At the back, a high brick wall, which cuts off the sky. Near it is a cluster of elder. To the right, the dark log wall of some stable building. To the left, a grey wall with patches of plaster, which is part of* KOSTY-LEV'S *lodging house. It stands at an angle, its far corner projecting almost to the middle of the yard. There is a narrow passage between this wall and the brick wall. In the grey wall are two windows, one at ground level, the other five feet higher up, and nearer the brick wall. Along the wall are a large sledge turned upside down, and a log about ten feet long. Old planks are piled up on the right near the wall.*

Evening. The sun is setting, throwing a red glow on the brick wall. Early spring, and the snow has recently thawed. As yet, there are no buds on the black elder bushes.

NATASHA *and* NASTYA *are seated side by side on the log.* LUKA *and the* BARON *are on the sledge.* KLETCH *is lying on the heap of wood, right.* BUBNOV'S *face is at the lower window.*]

NASTYA [*her eyes closed, her head nodding in time to the words, speaks in a sing-song voice.*] So one night he comes into the garden, to talk to me in the arbor as we'd arranged . . . And I've been waiting for him a long time, trembling all over, I was so afraid. And he's trembling all over too, and his face is white as a sheet, and in his hands he's got a revolver . . .

NATASHA [*cracking sunflower seeds*]. Oh, my goodness! So it's true what they say about students—how desperate they get . . .

NASTYA. And in a terrible voice he says to me, "My dearest precious love . . ."

BUBNOV. Ho, ho! Precious!

BARON. Shut up! If you don't like it, don't listen. Don't spoil a good lie . . . Go on.

NASTYA. "My beloved," he says, "My darling! My parents refuse to give their consent for me to marry you . . . and they say they'll curse me forever because of my love for you. So," he says, "I've got to kill myself . . ." And he's got a huge revolver, with ten bullets in it . . . "Goodbye, my dearest heart," he says. "I've decided . . . I can't live without you." And I said to him, "I can never forget you, my darling Raoul . . ."

BUBNOV [*astonished*]. What's that? Growl?

BARON [*laughs*]. Oh, look here, Nastya. Last time it was Gaston!

NASTYA [*jumps*]. Shut up, you . . . miserable bastards! Ach! How can you understand what love is—true love? It was true love! [*To* BARON.] You! you worthless trash, you! Educated man! Used to drink coffee in bed—so you say!

LUKA. Now, stop it, all of you! Don't interrupt her! Show a bit of regard for other people . . . It isn't so much what people say—it's why they say it. Go on, girl. Don't worry about them.

BUBNOV. No, don't worry about us—we're not worrying about you!

BARON. Go on.

NATASHA. Don't pay any attention to them. They're just jealous. Because nothing's ever happened to them.

NASTYA [*sits again*]. I won't tell any more! Why should I? They don't believe me. They laugh at me . . . [*Suddenly breaks off, remains silent for several seconds, and, closing her eyes again, and waving her hands as though in time with some distant music, continues loudly and heatedly.*] So I said to him, "Joy of my life! My bright star! I just couldn't go on living in this world without you. I love you so madly, and I'll go on loving you as long as my heart goes on beating in my breast. But," I said, "you mustn't take your young life, your dear parents' only hope and joy. Forget me! Better to let me suffer for my love for you, my darling heart. For I have nobody . . . People like me are always alone. Let me die—what does it matter? I have nothing. I am nothing. Nothing at all . . . [*Covers her face with her hands, and cries noiselessly.*]

NATASHA [*turns to one side, in a low voice*]. Don't cry . . . you mustn't!

[LUKA, *smiling, strokes* NASTYA'S *head.*]

BUBNOV [*laughs*]. Ha! What a damned fool!

BARON [*also laughing*]. Do you believe that, old man? It's all out of a book—"Fatal Love." A lot of trash! Leave her alone! . . .

NATASHA. What's that to you? Shut up, can't you? Just because you haven't got any heart . . .

NASTYA [*bitterly*]. God damn your soul! You worthless pig! Soul—ugh—you haven't got one!

LUKA [*takes* NASTYA *by the arm*]. Come on, my dear. Don't worry. Don't get angry. I know. I believe you. You're right, not them. If you believe it was a true love you had, then it was. It was! But don't upset yourself. Don't quarrel with your Baron. Maybe he does laugh, but he's only jealous. Because he's never had a true love like that. Never had anything at all! Come on, then . . .

NASTYA [*presses her hands to her breasts*]. Honest, grandpa, it's true. It did happen. He was a student. A French boy, Gaston, his name was. He had a moustache, and he wore big black boots. Cross my heart and hope to die! And he loved me so . . .

LUKA. I know. It's all right. I believe you. Wore big, black boots, you say? Ay-ay-ay! And you—you loved him too?

[*They go round corner.*]

BARON. She's a fool, that girl. A good girl, but—such a damned fool, it's incredible!

BUBNOV. Why is it people are so fond of lying? Just as if they were up before the judge? It's amazing.

NATASHA. Perhaps it's more fun lying than telling the truth. That's why I . . .

BARON. Well, go on.

NATASHA. That's why I like imagining things. I dream and dream, and—wait.

BARON. What for?

NATASHA [*smiles, embarrassed*]. Oh, I don't know. Perhaps someone will come along, tomorrow . . . or something's going to happen . . . something that never happened before . . . I wait, and I look forward—I'm always looking forward to something. But what have I got to look forward to—I don't know.

[*A pause.*]

BARON [*smiles*]. There's nothing to look forward to. I don't look forward to anything. It's all happened already. Over and done with! Finished . . . Go on.

NATASHA. And then sometimes I get the feeling that tomorrow I'm going to die suddenly. It frightens me. It always happens in the summer, when there are thunderstorms, and you can get killed by lightning.

BARON. You have a hard life, don't you? That sister of yours has one hell of a temper.

NATASHA. Who has an easy life? Nobody! Everywhere you look, people are unhappy.

KLETCH [*until this time motionless and indifferent, suddenly jumps up*]. Everybody? It's a lie! Not everybody! If everybody had a hard life, it would be all right. Then it wouldn't hurt so much.

BUBNOV. What the devil's got into *you*—shouting like that?

[KLETCH *lies down on the wood pile as before, mumbling to himself.*]

BARON. Mm . . . I suppose I'd better go and make up with Nastya or I won't get any money for a drink . . .

BUBNOV. Mm . . . people telling lies . . . I can understand it with Nastya. She's used to painting her face; now she wants to paint her soul . . . put rouge on her soul . . . But why do other people do it? That Luka for instance . . . lies all the time . . . and he don't get nothing out of it . . . An old man, too . . . Why does he do it?

BARON [*moves away, with a smile*]. Everybody's got grey souls . . . and they all want to brighten them up . . .

LUKA [*comes from round the corner*]. Why do you upset the girl, Baron? You should leave her alone. Let her cry if it gives her pleasure . . . She enjoys crying, you should know that . . . What harm does it do you?

BARON. The whole thing's stupid, old man! I'm sick of it. Today it's Raoul, tomorrow it's Gaston . . . but it's the same story all the time. Still, I'll go and make up with her . . . [*Exit.*]

LUKA. That's it. Go and be nice to her. Never does any harm being nice to people . . .

NATASHA. You're a kind man, grandpa. Why are you so kind?

LUKA. Kind, you say? Well, yes, if it's true . . .

[*Behind the red wall, the sound of singing to an accordion is softly heard.*]

LUKA. Somebody's got to be kind, girl. Somebody's got to be sorry for other people. Christ felt sorry for other people—

told us to do the same. I can tell you, if you feel sorry for somebody at the right time, it can do a lot of good. For instance, the time I was caretaker at a country house near Tomsk. Well . . . the house was in the middle of a forest. It was winter time, and I was all alone in the house. Well, one day, I heard a noise at the window.

NATASHA. Burglars?

LUKA. That's right. Burglars. Trying to break in. So I took my gun and went out. I looked around and saw two men trying to open the window. They were working at it so hard they didn't even see me until I yelled at them and told them to get out! And what did they do? They came at me with an axe! "Keep away," I said, "or I'll shoot." And I pointed my gun right at them. They both went down on their knees and begged for mercy. Still I was mad about that axe. "You wouldn't go away when I told you, you devils," I said. "Now you go and break some branches off that tree." So they did. "Now," I said to one of them, "you lie down while he flogs you." So they obey me and flog each other. Then they said to me, "Mister, for God's sake, give us some bread. We've been tramping for miles with nothing to eat. We're hungry!" There are your burglars, my dear . . . And with axes, no less! Good honest peasants, both of them . . . I said to them, "Why didn't you come and ask for bread in the first place, you fools?" And they said, "We were tired of asking. You beg and beg, and nobody gives you even a crumb. It's hell!" . . . And those two stayed with me all winter. One of them, Stepan his name was, used to take my gun sometimes and go into the forest for days, shooting. The other one, Yakov, he was ill most of the time, and he coughed a lot. The three of us took care of the house. And when spring came they said, "Good-bye, Grandpa," and went away, back home to Russia.

NATASHA. Were they escaped convicts?

LUKA. That's right. Escaped convicts. Honest peasants! And if I hadn't felt sorry for them, they might have killed me or something. They'd have been tried and sent back to Siberia—what's the sense in that? Prison doesn't teach a man to be good, and Siberia doesn't either. But a man—yes! a man can teach another man kindness, believe me!

[*Pause.*]

BUBNOV. Mm . . . yes . . . but me, I don't know how to tell

lies, I don't. What's the use of lies? What I say is, give us the truth, just as it is. Why try to hide anything?

KLETCH [*leaps up suddenly, shouts*]. What truth? Well, what truth—eh? Where do you find it, this precious truth of yours? [*Runs his hands through his ragged clothes.*] There's your truth! No work . . . no strength . . . nowhere to live even. Not a goddamned place to live! You just die like a dog, that's all. There's the truth for you! Hell! What do I want with truth? Just give me room to breathe, that's all. Room to breathe! What have I done wrong? What do I want with truth? Christ Almighty—they won't let you live, damn it! You can't live—that's the truth for you!

BUBNOV. Don't worry about him, he's a little bit titched!

LUKA. Heavenly Jesus! . . . listen to me, my brother. You . . .

KLETCH [*shaking with emotion*]. You talk about truth, truth! You, old man, you go around comforting everybody. I tell you, I hate you all! The whole goddamned bunch of you! And to hell with your goddamned truth! To hell with it! Do you hear? To hell with it! [*Runs off round the corner, looking back as he goes.*]

LUKA. Ay-ay-ay! How upset he is! Where's he run off to?

NATASHA. Has he gone mad or something?

BUBNOV. God, how fantastic! Just like they do it on the stage. . . . Sometimes it happens like that. . . . He can't get used to life.

PEPPEL [*slowly comes round the corner*]. Hello, you honest people! Hello, Luka, you old bastard! Still telling them stories, eh?

LUKA. You should have been here just now. There was a man here screaming his lungs out.

PEPPEL. Kletch, was it? What's wrong with him? He just ran past me like a madman.

LUKA. You'd do the same thing, if your heart were breaking.

PEPPEL [*sits*]. I don't like him. Who does he think he is? [*Imitates* KLETCH.] "I'm a working man." And so nobody's as good as he is . . . Well, work if you like it—but don't get so goddamned pompous about it! If you start judging people by how much work they do, then a horse is better than any man. He works and he keps quiet about it! Your people at home, Natasha?

NATASHA. They went down to the cemetery—said they were going to the evening service afterwards.

PEPPEL. So that's why you're free. That's a novelty!

LUKA [*to* BUBNOV, *pensively*]. You say "truth" . . . Truth's not always the best thing for people, though. Not when people are in a bad way. I once knew a man, for instance—he believed in a Land of Truth . . .

BUBNOV. In what?

LUKA. The Land of Truth. "Somewhere on earth," he used to say, "there must be a Land of Truth. The people there," he says, "are a special sort of people—good people! They love one another, they help one another, and everything they do is good and kind!" Every day he'd talk about going to find it, this Land of Truth. A poor man, he was; had a hard life. And when he got so bad he was ready to lie down and die, he didn't give in. He'd just laugh and say, "Never mind—I can stand it! Just a bit longer, then I'll quit this life and go to the Land of Truth . . ." That was all he lived for, the Land of Truth.

PEPPEL. Well, did he go?

BUBNOV. Where? Ho, ho!

LUKA. This all happened in Siberia. And one day along comes an exile. He was a scholar with all sorts of books and maps. So the man asks him, "Will you show me where the Land of Truth is? How do you get there?" So the scholar gets out his books and his maps, and he looks and looks, and he can't find the Land of Truth—it doesn't exist!

PEPPEL [*softly*]. Doesn't exist?

[BUBNOV *laughs.*]

NATASHA. Stop it. What happened, grandpa?

LUKA. Well, the man doesn't believe him. "It must exist," he said. "Take another look! If it isn't there, then your books and maps are no good." The scholar got angry at this. "My maps are the best there are, and your Land of Truth isn't on them anywhere." So the man got angry. "What's that?" he said. "I've lived and suffered all these years and I've always thought there was a Land of Truth. Now your maps say there isn't. It's a fraud! You swine! You're a goddamned cheat, not a scholar." And he hit him on the nose—bang! And another and another . . . [*Pause.*] Then he went home and hung himself! . . .

[*They are all silent.* LUKA *smiling, looks at* PEPPEL *and* NATASHA.]

PEPPEL [*softly*]. To hell with your story! I don't call it very funny . . .

NATASHA. He couldn't stand it—the disappointment . . .

BUBNOV [*sullen*]. You made it all up.

PEPPEL. Well . . . There's your Land of Truth for you. Doesn't exist after all . . .

NATASHA. I'm sorry for him, that man . . .

BUBNOV. He made it all up! Ho, ho! Land of Truth! What an idea! Ho, ho!

LUKA [*nods towards window where* BUBNOV *is*]. He's laughing! Well, my children, God be with you! I'll be leaving you soon . . .

PEPPEL. Where are you going?

LUKA. To the Ukraine . . . I hear they've discovered a new religion there. I want to see—yes! People are always seeking—they want something better—God give them patience!

PEPPEL. You think they'll find it?

LUKA. The people? They will find it! He who seeks will find! He who desires strongly, will find!

NATASHA. If only they could find something better—invent something better . . .

LUKA. They're trying to! But we must help them, my child—we must respect them.

NATASHA. How can I help them? I'm helpless myself!

PEPPEL [*resolutely*]. Listen! I'm going to . . . to ask you again, Natasha . . . He knows about it . . . Come away with me!

NATASHA. Where to? From one jail to another?

PEPPEL. I tell you, I'll stop stealing. I swear I will. I will! I can read and write. I'll work . . . Luka says I ought to go to Siberia, before they send me there. Come with me—what do you say? Don't you think my life makes me sick? Oh, Natasha! I know . . . I can see it all . . . I console myself that other people steal more than I do, and get honor heaped on them—but that doesn't help. It's no answer. I'm not repenting—I don't believe in conscience. But I know one thing: I can't go on living like this. Got to find something better. So I can have some self-respect . . .

LUKA. That's right, my son! May God help you! You're right, a man's got to have self-respect.

PEPPEL. I've been a thief all my life. That's all they called me: "Vaska's a thief, and the son of a thief." So I'm a thief! But maybe it's only because nobody ever called me anything else. You won't call me a thief, will you, Natasha? Tell me . . .

NATASHA [*melancholy*]. I can't believe in all this talk somehow

... I feel strange, uneasy today. Funny aching feeling round my heart ... as if something's going to happen. I wish you hadn't started this, Vaska.

PEPPEL. Well, how long do you want me to wait, then? It isn't the first time ...

NATASHA. How can I go away with you, Vaska? I'm not in love with you. Not enough ... Sometimes I like you. Sometimes it makes me sick to look at you. I can't be in love with you. When you're in love with someone, you can't see any faults in them. And I do ...

PEPPEL. Never mind—you'll love me after a while! I'll make you love me ... if you'll just say yes! I've been seeing you here for over a year ... and you're a good, decent girl ... you're kind, and reliable ... and I'm very much in love with you ...

[VASSILISA, *in her Sunday clothes, appears at the window.*]

NATASHA. I know all about that. You say you love me—and what about my sister?

PEPPEL [*embarrassed*]. Well, what about her? She's nothing ... She doesn't mean anything to me ...

LUKA. Never mind that, girl! When you can't get fresh bread, you have to take stale bread ...

PEPPEL [*gloomily*]. You might feel sorry for me! My life's no bed of roses ... It's one hell of a life! I feel like I'm sinking in a swamp—everything I catch hold of is ... rotten ... no hold anywhere ... I thought your sister ... was different ... I'd have done anything for her! If she'd have been mine ... But she's after something else ... after the money ... and her own way ... Her own way, so she can be free. She's no good to me. But you—you're like a young fir tree. You're prickly to touch, but strong to hold on to.

LUKA. You marry him, girl. That's my advice! He's all right. He's a good man! You just keep reminding him he's a good man, so he won't forget it himself! He'll believe you. Just keep on saying, "Don't forget, Vaska, you're a good man!" And where else could you go dear—just think! Your sister, she's a vixen. And her husband—nothing you can say about him is as bad as he is. All this life of yours here—where's it leading you? But this man ... he's good, he's strong ...

NATASHA. I know I've got nowhere else to go. I've thought all about that. But I don't seem to be able to trust anybody

. . . But you're right, there's nowhere else for me to go . . .

PEPPEL. There's only one other way for you here . . . and I won't let you go that way . . . I'd sooner kill you first.

NATASHA [*smiles*]. You see, I'm not his wife yet, and he's talking of killing me already.

PEPPEL [*puts arms round her*]. Come on, Natasha. Say yes!

NATASHA [*presses close to him*]. One thing Vaska—God be my Judge! If you beat me just once, or get angry with me . . . the first time will be the last time. I'll go and hang myself, or . . .

PEPPEL. Let this hand rot off if I ever touch you! . . .

LUKA. Don't you worry about him, my child. He needs you more than you need him.

VASSILISA [*from window*]. So they all lived happily ever after! Congratulations to the happy pair!

NATASHA. They're back! Oh, God, they saw us! Oh, Vaska . . .

PEPPEL. What are you scared of? They can't touch you now.

VASSILISA. Don't be afraid, Natasha. He won't beat you. He can't beat you and he can't love you. I know.

LUKA [*in a low voice*]. Rotten old hag! Snake in the grass . . .

VASSILISA. But he hurts you with his tongue.

KOSTYLEV [*enters*]. Natasha! What are you doing here, you leech? Gossiping? Telling lies about your family behind their back? Why isn't the samovar ready? And the table set?

NATASHA [*going out*]. I thought you said you were going to church . . .

KOSTYLEV. It's none of your business where we go! You just do your work, and do what you're told!

PEPPEL. You leave her alone! She isn't your slave any longer . . . Don't go, Natasha. Don't do it.

NATASHA. Don't you start giving orders. You're starting a little early, aren't you. [*Exit.*]

PEPPEL [*to* KOSTYLEV]. Leave her alone! You've been bullying the girl long enough. She's mine now.

KOSTYLEV. Yours, is she? When did you buy her? For how much?

[VASSILISA *laughs.*]

LUKA. Vaska! Go away . . .

PEPPEL. You think it's funny don't you? Well, you'll be laughing on the other side of your face before long!

VASSILISA. Oh, how terrible! Oh, how you frighten me!

LUKA. Go away, Vaska! Can't you see they're leading you on?

PEPPEL. Oh, no. Not me. You won't get away with it.

VASSILISA. It'll be just the way I want it, Vaska.

PEPPEL [*shakes a fist at her*]. We'll see about that! [*Exit.*]

VASSILISA. I'll arrange a wedding for you that you won't forget!

KOSTYLEV [*goes up to* LUKA]. Well, old man, how's everything with you?

LUKA. All right.

KOSTYLEV. They say you're going away.

LUKA. Soon.

KOSTYLEV. Where?

LUKA. I'll just follow my nose . . .

KOSTYLEV. A wanderer, eh? Don't stay in one place for very long, do you?

LUKA. Even water won't pass under a stone that's sunk too deep in the ground . . .

KOSTYLEV. That's all right about stones, but a man has to settle down in one place. Men can't live like roaches crawling about wherever they feel like it . . . A man's got to stay in one place, and can't go wandering about.

LUKA. But suppose home is wherever he happens to be?

KOSTYLEV. Then, he's nothing but a useless vagabond . . . A human being's got to work—be of some use to somebody.

LUKA. So, that's what you think, eh?

KOSTYLEV. That's right . . . Look. What's a vagabond? He's different, he's not like the rest of us. If he's a real pilgrim, why then he's some good to the world . . . like maybe he's discovered a new truth, or something. Well . . . but not every truth is good. Let him keep it to himself and shut up about it! Or else—let him talk so we can understand him. But he shouldn't interfere with our business and upset us without any good reason. It's none of his business how other people live! If he wants to be righteous, all right, but alone—in the woods, or in a monastery, away from everybody. But he shouldn't bother people, or condemn them—he should just pray—pray for all of us, for the sins of the whole world—for mine, for yours, for everybody's. To pray—that's why he forsakes the turmoil of the world. That's the truth, see! But you . . . What sort of pilgrim are you? You don't even have a passport! An honest person has a passport, all honest people do. Isn't that right?

LUKA. In this world there are people . . . and just ordinary men.

KOSTYLEV. Don't give me any double talk! And don't try to be so smart! I'm as smart as you, and don't you forget it. What's the difference . . . people and men?

LUKA. Where is there any double talk? I say there's sterile and there's fertile ground. You can sow in some ground and it grows and other ground it don't . . . that's all.

KOSTYLEV. What do you mean?

LUKA. Take yourself for instance . . . If the Lord God himself said to you: "Mikhailo, be a man!"—it would be useless— nothing would happen—you're doomed to remain just as you are . . .

KOSTYLEV. Oh, yeah! Listen, my wife's uncle is a policeman, and if I want to . . .

VASSILISA [enters]. Mishka, come and have your tea.

KOSTYLEV [to LUKA]. Listen. Get out of here! Get out of this place!

VASSILISA. Yes, old man, you clear out! Your tongue's too long. And for all we know, you've run away from prison.

KOSTYLEV. Don't let me see a sign of you after today—or else!

LUKA. Or else you'll send for your uncle? Well, go ahead, send for him. Just suppose he caught a wanted man! Uncle might collect a reward. Three kopecks.

BUBNOV [at window]. What's that for sale? What's going for three kopecks?

LUKA. They want to sell me.

VASSILISA [to her husband]. Come on.

BUBNOV. For three kopecks? Listen, old man, they'd sell you for one.

KOSTYLEV [to BUBNOV]. Where did you come from all of a sudden, you busybody? [Goes off with his wife.]

VASSILISA. There's far too many suspicious people around here—too many good-for-nothings!

LUKA. Bon appetit!

VASSILISA [turns back]. You shut your mouth, you viper! [Goes out round corner with her husband.]

LUKA. I'd better go tonight.

BUBNOV. I would if I was you. Don't outstay your welcome.

LUKA. You're right there.

BUBNOV. I know I'm right. If I hadn't gone away in time, I'd probably be in Siberia right now.

LUKA. Oh?

BUBNOV. It's true. It was like this. My wife got mixed up with a furrier. He was a good worker, I'll say that for him. He could dye dogskins to look like raccoon. And cats to look like kangaroo. And muskrats. All sorts of things. He was a real genius! Well, my wife got herself mixed up with him, and they were mad about each other. I could see they'd be poisoning me any minute, or find some other way of getting rid of me. I used to beat my wife, and the furrier beat me. Oh, we had dreadful fights! One time he pulled out half my beard and broke one of my ribs. Another time I hit my wife over the head with a poker. It was a real war going on! Well, I could see I wasn't going to get anything out of all that—they were getting the best of me. So I decided to kill my wife—had it all planned! But I came to my senses . . . and got out of there . . .

LUKA. That was best! Let them go on making dogs into raccoons.

BUBNOV. Only my workshop was in my wife's name. And I was left, just as you see me now. Though, to be honest, I'd have drunk away the shop anyway. I get pretty drunk sometimes, you know.

LUKA. You drink? Ah . . .

BUBNOV. You don't know! Once I get started, I don't stop until I don't have a penny left . . . nothing left but my skin and bones. And another thing—I'm lazy. You've no idea how I hate working! . . .

[*Enter* SATIN *and the* ACTOR, *quarrelling.*]

SATIN. Nonsense! You aren't going anywhere. Just a god-damned pipe dream! Look here, old man. What sort of lies have you been stuffing into this broken-down windbag here?

ACTOR. It's not a lie! I am going! Grandpa, tell him I am going! I had work today. I swept the streets. And I haven't had a drink all day! What do you think of that? Here, look—here's the thirty kopecks and I'm sober!

SATIN. It's absurd! You're mad! Give them to me. I'll drink it up for you, or gamble them away.

ACTOR. Oh, go to hell! I'm saving them—for my journey.

LUKA [*to* SATIN]. Don't tease him. Why are you trying to lead him astray?

SATIN. "Tell me, O wizard, beloved of the gods, what fate do my stars hold in store?" Listen brother, I've lost every kopeck I ever had—blown myself to smithereens!! There's still some people who can cheat at cards better than me!

LUKA. You're a funny guy, Konstantin . . . I like you.

BUBNOV. Actor! Come over here!

[*The* ACTOR *goes to the window, and sits on the sill talking to* BUBNOV.]

SATIN. I was one of the smart ones when I was a kid, old man. It's great to look back on those days. I was a happy-go-lucky . . . I danced like a dream, played on the stage, liked to make people laugh—it was great!

LUKA. What went wrong then?

SATIN. You're pretty damn curious old man. You want to know everything. What for?

LUKA. So I can understand people. I can't make you out. A fellow like you, Konstantin—with your brains, too. Yet, all of a sudden . . .

SATIN. Prison, old man. Four years and seven months in prison. And after you've been in prison, you're finished. Can't go anywhere.

LUKA. I see . . . What were you in for?

SATIN. For a dirty swine. I lost my temper and killed him . . . I learnt to play cards in prison . . .

LUKA. Was it . . . did you kill him because of a woman?

SATIN. My sister . . . Oh, leave me alone! I don't like being cross-examined . . . Anyway, it was a long time ago. My sister's been dead nine years now . . . She was a fine girl, my sister was . . .

LUKA. I must say you take life casually enough. Not like old Kletch here just now. He starts screaming something horrible. Ooooh . . .

SATIN. Kletch?

LUKA. Yes. "No work!" he shouts. "No nothing!"

SATIN. He'll get used to it . . . Now, what can I do with myself, I wonder?

LUKA [*quietly*]. Look! Here he comes . . .

[*Enter* KLETCH *slowly, his head hung down.*]

SATIN. Hey, widower! What are you looking so miserable for? What's the matter?

KLETCH. What will I do? No tools—sold them all for the funeral.

SATIN. I'll give you a bit of advice. Don't do anything. Just be a burden to the world.

KLETCH. You and your advice. I've got some sense of shame before other people . . .

SATIN. Well, forget it! Other people aren't ashamed to let you live worse than a dog! Look here—supposing you don't work, I don't work, hundreds, thousands of others, everybody stops working, see? Nobody does anything—then what will happen?

KLETCH. They'll all starve to death.

[NATASHA *is heard from* KOSTYLEV'S *window, crying out,* "Why? Stop it! What have I done?"]

LUKA [*agitated*]. Natasha? She was crying out—eh? Oh . . .

[*Noise, scuffling, the sound of dishes being broken, from* KOSTYLEV'S *window, and* KOSTYLEV'S *shrill cry,* "Ah, you heathen! You slut!"]

VASSILISA. Wait a minute, I'll show her . . .

NATASHA. They're killing me! Murdering me! Help!

SATIN [*shouts in at the window*]. Hey you in there!

LUKA [*trembling*]. Vaska . . . call Vaska . . . Oh, God! Listen brothers . . .

ACTOR [*runs off*]. I'll get him.

BUBNOV. They're always beating her these days. Nothing unusual.

SATIN. Come on, old man. We'll be witnesses.

LUKA [*follows* SATIN]. I'm no sort of witness. No good. Go and get Vaska. Get him quick!

NATASHA. Vassilisa! I'm your sister! Va-a-ass——

BUBNOV. They've gagged her. I'll go and see . . .

[*The noise dies down, fades away as if they have gone into the hall. The old man shouts* "stop it!" *A door is slammed, cutting off all sound, as though with an axe. Quiet on stage. Twilight.*]

KLETCH [*sits on sledge, rubbing hands hard. Then starts to mumble something, at first indistinguishable, then*]. But how? Got to live . . . [*Aloud.*] Got to have somewhere to live. Got to. Haven't got anywhere. Haven't got anything. I'm alone. Alone. No-one to help me . . . [*Goes out slowly, hunched up.*]

[*Ominous silence. Then a confused chaos of shouting in the hallway. It grows louder and nearer. Individual voices can be distinguished.*]

VASSILISA. I'm her sister. Let me go!

KOSTYLEV. You haven't any right to . . .

VASSILISA. You jailbird!

SATIN. Call Vaska, quick! Go on, Screwy, hit him!

[*A police whistle.*]

TARTAR [*rushes in, his right arm in a sling*]. What a business! Murder in broad daylight!

SCREWY [*followed by* MEDVEDEV]. Ha, I hit him good!

MEDVEDEV. What are *you* fighting about?

TARTAR. What about you? Why don't you do your duty?

MEDVEDEV [*runs after* SCREWY]. Come here! Give me my whistle!

KOSTYLEV [*runs in*]. Abram! Arrest him! Stop him! It's murder!

[KVASHNYA *and* NASTYA *come in round the corner, supporting* NATASHA, *dishevelled. Then* SATIN, *who comes in backwards, fighting off* VASSILISA *who is trying to hit* NATASHA. ALESHKA *skips madly round* VASSILISA, *whistling in her ears, shouting, yelling. Then come a few other tattered figures.*]

SATIN [*to* VASSILISA]. What are you trying to do? Goddamned bitch . . .

VASSILISA. Let me go, you jailbird! I'll tear her apart if it kills me!

KVASHNYA [*pulls* NATASHA *out of the way*]. Now stop it, Vassilisa. You ought to be ashamed! Are you mad?

MEDVEDEV [*grabs* SATIN]. Aha! I've got you!

SATIN. Screwy! Hit him! . . . Vaska! Vaska!

[*They are all struggling together by the hall, near the red wall. They bring* NATASHA *to the right, and sit her down on the woodpile.*]

PEPPEL [*runs out of the hall, elbows his way through the crowd silently, with strong movements*]. Natasha, where are you? Where are you?

KOSTYLEV [*hiding behind corner*]. Abram! Arrest him! Help catch Vaska, all of you! He's a thief! Vaska's a thief!

PEPPEL. You old goat! [*Swinging round violently, strikes* KOSTYLEV *who falls so that only the upper part of his body can be seen round the corner.* PEPPEL *rushes to* NATASHA.]

VASSILISA. Get Vaska! All of you! Beat him up—he's a thief!

MEDVEDEV [*shouts to* SATIN]. It's none of your business—it's a family matter. Relations—what are you?

PEPPEL. What did she do to you? She stab you?

KVASHNYA. Look at that! The brutes! Scalded the poor girl's feet with boiling water!

NASTYA. Knocked over the samovar.

TARTAR. Maybe an accident. Must make sure. Mustn't make wild accusations.

NATASHA [*half fainting*]. Vaska . . . Take me away . . . Help me . . .

VASSILISA. My God! Look! Look here! . . . He's dead. They've killed him.

[*Everybody crowds round* KOSTYLEV, *by the passage.* BUBNOV *comes out of the crowd towards* PEPPEL.]

BUBNOV [*quietly*]. Vaska! The old man. You're in trouble now . . .

PEPPEL [*looks at him uncomprehendingly*]. Send for . . . take her to a hospital . . . I'll take care of them.

BUBNOV. I tell you, someone's killed the old man.

[*The noise on stage dies down like a fire extinguished with water. Murmured exclamations are heard: "Is he really?" "What do you think of that?" "Well, then?" "Let's get out of here." "What the hell!" "Someone's in for it!" "Get out before the police come." The crowd decreases.* BUBNOV *and* TARTAR *exeunt.* NASTYA *and* KVASHNYA *rush over to* KOSTYLEV'S *body.*]

VASSILISA [*gets up off the ground, shouts triumphantly*]. He killed my husband! He killed him! Vaska killed him! I saw it. All of you, I saw it. Well, Vaska—the police!

PEPPEL [*leaves* NATASHA]. Get out! Leave me alone! [*Looks at the old man. To* VASSILISA.] Well, are you happy now? [*Touches the body with his foot.*] The old bastard's dead. Just what you wanted. Well, I'll give you the same! [*Rushes at her.* SATIN *and* SCREWY *catch him quickly.* VASSILISA *rushes into the hall.*]

SATIN. Don't be a fool!

SCREWY. Hey, what are you trying to do?

VASSILISA [*comes back*]. Well, Vaska—darling! You can't escape fate, can you? The police! Abram, blow your whistle.

MEDVEDEV. They stole it, the beggars!

ALESHKA. Here it is! [*Blows it.*]

[MEDVEDEV *runs after him.*]

SATIN [*leads* PEPPEL *to* NATASHA]. Don't worry, Vaska. It's nothing, killing a man in a fight. Won't be much.

VASSILISA. Arrest Vaska! He killed him. I saw it!

SATIN. I hit him a couple of times myself. Sure didn't take much. Call me as a witness, Vaska . . .

PEPPEL. I don't need an alibi. I'm going to get Vassilisa in this. I will. She wanted it. Egged me on to kill her husband. Egged me on.

NATASHA [*suddenly, in a loud voice*]. Ah! Now I see it! So that's it, Vaska! What nice people they are! They'd arranged it all, my sister and him. They'd arranged it all! Hadn't you, Vaska? That's why you talked to me the way you did— so she could overhear it? What nice people they are! She's his mistress. She is—everybody knows it! They're in it together! She got him to kill her husband. He was in the way. Look what they've done to me!

PEPPEL. Natasha! What are you saying? What are you saying?

SATIN. Oh—hell!

VASSILISA. It's a lie! She's lying! I . . . He killed him, Vaska did!

NATASHA. They're both in it together. Damn both of you! Both of you!

SATIN. What the hell's going on here? Vaska, watch it—they'll finish you between them.

SCREWY. I don't understand. What a mess!

PEPPEL. Natasha—you can't believe . . . You don't think she and I were . . .

SATIN. For God's sake, Natasha. Use your brain.

VASSILISA [*in the hallway*]. My husband's been murdered, your Honor. Vaska Peppel did it—the thief. I saw it, your Honor. We all saw it . . .

NATASHA [*her mind wandering*]. What nice people . . . My sister and Vaska killed him! Listen, officer. My sister here got him to do it. Her lover. There he is, the miserable bastard! They killed him. Take them . . . arrest them . . . And take me as well . . . Take me to prison! For Christ's sake, take me to prison!!

ACT FOUR

[*Same as Act One. But* PEPPEL'S *room is no longer there, and the partition has been taken down.* KLETCH'S *anvil is also gone. In the corner where* PEPPEL'S *room was, lies the* TARTAR, *restless and groaning from time to time.* KLETCH *is at the table, tinkering with a concertina and trying it out. At the other end of the table are* SATIN, *the* BARON *and* NASTYA. *They have a bottle of vodka, three bottles of beer and a large chunk of black bread. The* ACTOR *is on the stove, turning about and coughing. Night. The stage is lit by a lamp standing in the middle of the table. Outside, a wind is blowing.*]

KLETCH. Yes . . . In the middle of all the trouble, he just disappears . . .

BARON. Vanished from the police—just like fog when the sun comes out.

SATIN. Thus the sinner vanisheth from the sight of the righteous.

NASTYA. He was good, the old man was! You—you aren't men. You're just mildew!

BARON [*drinks*]. Your very good health, my lady!

SATIN. He was an interesting old guy . . . Nastya here fell madly in love with him.

NASTYA. Yes, I did. I did fall in love with him. He knew everything—understood everything.

SATIN [*laughing*]. In fact, for some people, he was like slops to the toothless.

BARON [*laughs*]. Or plaster to a boil.

KLETCH. He had pity for other people. You haven't got any pity . . .

SATIN. What good's it do you if I pity you?

KLETCH. You can . . . well, it's not so much having pity for people. But you shouldn't hurt them.

TARTAR [*sits on his bunk, and nurses his wounded arm*]. The old man was good. Had the law in his soul. People who has the law—is good. People who lose the law—is lost.

BARON. What kind of law, Hassan?

TARTAR. Different kind. You know what kind.

[344]

BARON. Go on.

TARTAR. Not hurt a man—that is law!

KLETCH [*trying the concertina*]. Oh, hell! Still wheezes . . . Hassan's right. Must live by the law . . . by the gospel . . .

SATIN. Well, go ahead and do it!

BARON. Just try it.

TARTAR. Mohammed gave the Koran. He says, "Here is the law! Do what is written here!" Then comes a time, Koran is not enough. Every age has its own law—a new law. Every age has its own law.

SATIN. That's right. And our age has the law called the Penal Code. A strong law, that is. Won't wear out in a hurry.

NASTYA [*bangs her glass on the table*]. Why do I go on living here with you? What for? I'm going away—anywhere. The end of the world.

BARON. Without your shoes on, my lady?

NASTYA. Stark naked! On all fours if I have to!

BARON. Extremely picturesque, my lady—if you're on all fours.

NASTYA. Yes, I'll crawl—I don't mind. Anything, as long as I don't have to see your stupid face any more! Oh, I'm so sick of it all! Sick of living . . . sick of people . . .

SATIN. Well, then, go away! You can take the Actor with you. He wants to go there too. It's come to his attention that half a mile from the end of the world there's a hospital for organons . . .

ACTOR [*sticks his head out from on top of the stove*]. Organisms, you fool!

SATIN. For organons poisoned with alcohol . . .

ACTOR. Yes, and he'll go! He'll go there—just wait and see!

BARON. He? Who's he, *monsieur*?

ACTOR. Me!

BARON. *Merci*, servant of the goddess . . . what's her name? The goddess of plays, of the theatre—what's her name?

ACTOR. The muse, idiot! Not a goddess—muse!

SATIN. Lachesis . . . Hera . . . Aphrodite . . . Atropos . . . Oh, what the hell! You see what the old man did, Baron? Getting the Actor all excited like this?

BARON. The old man's a fool . . .

ACTOR. And you're a lot of ignorant savages! It's Mel-po-me-ne! You with no soul—he'll go, just wait and see! "Go on and stuff yourselves, you dismal mortals," . . . poem by . . . Shakespeare. Yes, he's going to find the place where there isn't any . . . any . . .

BARON. Anything at all, *monsieur*?

ACTOR. That's right! Where there isn't anything at all! "This hole my grave will be . . . I die of sickness and infirmity." What do you go on living for? Why?

BARON. Listen you! You Edmund Kean! Or God or genius or whatever you are! Don't make such a noise!

ACTOR. You hear! I'll make all the noise I want to.

NASTYA [*lifts her head from table, waves her arms about*]. Go on, yell! Let 'em hear you!

BARON. What's the sense of that, my lady?

SATIN. Leave them alone, Baron. To hell with them! Let them yell if they want to. Let them split their goddamned heads open. Let them! There's sense in that. Don't interfere with people, as the old man used to say. Yes, the old bastard, he got them all like this.

KLETCH. He told them all to get out and go somewhere. But he didn't tell them where.

BARON. He's a charlatan, that old man.

NASTYA. That's a lie! You're a charlatan yourself.

BARON. Shut up! My lady!

KLETCH. The old man didn't like the truth. In fact, he resented the truth. And he was right. Look! Where is there any truth? And yet you can't breath without it! Look at Hassan—gets his hand crushed at work—have to get it cut off, I suppose. There's the truth for you!

SATIN [*bangs his fist on the table*]. Shut up, you sons of bitches! Shut up about the old man, all of you! [*Calmer.*] You, Baron, you're the worst of the lot! You don't understand a thing, and you lie. The old man wasn't a charlatan. What's the truth? Man—there's the truth! He understood that—you don't understand a thing. You're about as sensitive as a block of wood. I understand the old man. Oh, yes, he lied—but out of pity for you, goddamn it, out of pity for you! Some people do—they tell tall tales out of pity for other people. I know—I've read about them. Beautiful, exciting, inspiring lies! . . . The soothing lie, the consoling lie, the lie that justifies the load that crushes the workman's hand, the lie that blames a man for being hungry—I know all about lies! People who are weak in spirit, people who live by the sweat of other people's brows —they need lies! Lies are their support, their shield, their armor! But the man who is strong, who's his own master, who's free and doesn't feed off others . . . he needs no lies!

Lying is the creed of slaves and masters of slaves! Truth is
the religion of the free man!

BARON. Bravo! Well said! I—agree! You speak like an honest
man.

SATIN. And why can't a crook tell the truth sometimes?—
Honest people usually speak like crooks. I've forgotten a lot,
but I still know some things. The old man? Oh, he was wise,
all right! He worked on me like acid on an old, dirty
coin . . . Let's drink to his health! Come on, fill the glasses!

[NASTYA *pours a glass of beer and gives it to* SATIN.]

[*Laughs.*] The old man lives his own way, looks at everything his own way. I asked him once, "Grandpa, what do
people live for?" [*Tries to imitate* LUKA'S *voice and man-
nerisms.*] "So that one day people will be better, my boy.
For example, let's take carpenters. Just ordinary, miserable
carpenters. Then one day there's born a carpenter—a
carpenter like there never was in all the world. Not another
carpenter like him—he shines above them all. He revolu-
tionizes the whole carpenter trade, the whole trade's ad-
vanced twenty years by one person. And the same thing
with locksmiths there, and cobblers—all the trades, peasants
too—even the aristocrats. They're all living in hopes of a
better life. It may take a hundred years. May be more.
But we go on living so there'll be a better life one day."

[NASTYA *stares at* SATIN. KLETCH *stops work on the concertina
to listen. The* BARON, *his head bowed low, softly drums
with his fingers on the table. The* ACTOR *has got off the
stove, carefully lowers himself onto his bunk.*]

"Everybody lives so there'll be something better one day,
my boy. That's why we should show respect to everybody
we meet. How do we know what he is, what he was born
to do, what he can do? Maybe he's going to make us happy.
Maybe he's going to help us. And especially we should be
kind to children. Give them plenty of elbow room. Don't
interfere with their little lives. Be kind to children!" [*He
laughs quietly. A pause.*]

BARON [*reflectively*]. Yes . . . Something better one day? That
reminds me of our family . . . An old family—goes back
to the time of Catherine the Great . . . noblemen . . .
warriors! . . . French in origin . . . We served our country
and rose higher and higher. My grandfather Gustave De-

bille, held a very important position in Nicholas the First's time. We were rich. Hundreds of serfs . . . horses . . . cooks . . .

NASTYA. Liar! There weren't!

BARON [*jumps up*]. What? Well, what? Go on.

NASTYA. There weren't!

BARON [*shouts*]. We had a house in Moscow! And a house in St. Petersburg! And carriages . . . carriages with our coat of arms!

[KLETCH *takes the concertina to the side, where he watches the scene.*]

NASTYA. There weren't!

BARON. Shut up! I tell you, we had dozens of footmen! . . .

NASTYA [*enjoying it*]. There weren't!

BARON. I'll kill you!

NASTYA [*ready to run*]. There weren't any carriages!

SATIN. Stop it, Nastya. Don't ride him.

BARON. Wait till I get you, you little bitch! My grandfather . . .

NASTYA. There weren't any grandfathers! There wasn't anything!

[SATIN *laughs.*]

BARON [*exhausted by his shouting, sits on the bench*]. Satin, tell this—slut . . . You're laughing at me, too! You don't believe me either! [*Shouts in despair, bangs the table.*] It's true, damn you! It's true!

NASTYA. Ah! You see? You see what it's like when people don't believe you?

KLETCH [*comes back to the table*]. I thought there was going to be a fight.

TARTAR. Ach, people are stupid. It's bad!

BARON. I . . . I won't have people laughing at me! I've got proofs. I've got papers to prove it, damn it!

SATIN. Forget it. And forget about all your carriages. You can't go very far in carriages of the past.

BARON. But how can she have the nerve?

SATIN. You see—she has got the nerve! Is she any worse than you? Maybe she didn't have any carriages, or any grandfather—not even a father and mother . . .

BARON [*calmer*]. Oh go to hell! You can argue without getting upset. I don't have the will power. . . .

SATIN. Get some. It's useful. [*Pause.*] Nastya! Are you going to the hospital?

NASTYA. What for?

SATIN. To see Natasha.

NASTYA. You're a bit late, aren't you? She's been out a long time. She came out and—just disappeared! Nowhere to be found . . .

SATIN. So . . . she's vanished . . .

KLETCH. I'd like to know who'll hurt the other the most. Vaska or Vassilisa.

NASTYA. Vassilisa will. She's shrewd. And Vaska will go to Siberia.

SATIN. It's only prison for manslaughter.

NASTYA. That's a pity. He'd be better off in Siberia. So would the whole bunch of you. In Siberia. Swept onto the rubbish heap, like the dirt you are!

SATIN [shaken]. What's that? Have you gone mad?

BARON. I'm going to hit her one so hard, she'll . . . don't be so wise . . .

NASTYA. You just try! Go ahead, just try and hit me!

BARON. I'll try all right!

SATIN. Leave her alone! Leave her. Don't interfere with other people. I can't get him out of my head, that old man. [He laughs.] Don't interfere with other people. And what if someone wrongs me, wounds me for the rest of my life— am I supposed to forgive him? Huh! Not on your life!

BARON [to NASTYA]. You've got to understand, once and for all, we're from different classes. You're just dirt under my feet.

NASTYA. Oh, you good-for-nothing bastard! Why, you live off me like a worm in an apple!

[The men burst into laughter.]

KLETCH. Ha! What a fool! An apple . . .

BARON. You can't be angry with her . . . She's a goddamned fool.

NASTYA. You're laughing are you? You old fraud! It isn't funny and you know it!

ACTOR [gloomily]. Go ahead, beat them up!

NASTYA. If I could, I'd . . . smash you to bits—[Throws cup on floor.] like that!

TARTAR. What are you breaking things for? That's stupid.

BARON [gets up]. Now, stop it! . . . I'll teach you some manners!

NASTYA [runs away]. Go to hell!

SATIN [*after her*]. Hey, that's enough! Who are you trying
to scare! What's all the fuss about anyway?

NASTYA. Dogs! Drop dead! You bastards!

ACTOR [*gloomily*]. Amen!

TARTAR. Ach! She's a bad woman—the Russian woman.
Spiteful, willful . . . Tartar woman not like that. Tartar
woman knows the law.

KLETCH. Give her a good hiding.

BARON. What a bitch!

KLETCH [*tries concertina*]. There—it's finished. But no sign
of the owner. He's on a binge again . . .

SATIN. Have a drink.

KLETCH. Thank you. Soon be time for bed . . .

SATIN. You getting used to us?

KLETCH [*finishes drink, goes to his bunk in the corner*]. It's all
right . . . People are the same everywhere. You don't
see it at first. Then you look around, and you see they're
all human beings. They're all right.

[TARTAR *spreads something on his bunk, kneels down, and
prays.*]

BARON [*to* SATIN, *points to the* TARTAR]. Look at him!

SATIN. Leave him alone. He's a good fellow . . . Leave him
alone! [*Laughs.*] I'm in a good mood today. God knows
why! . . .

BARON. You're always in a good mood, when you're drunk.
That's when you talk the most sense too.

SATIN. I like everybody when I'm drunk. All right, so he's
praying—so what? A man can believe or not believe—
that's his business. He's free—he pays for everything himself, for belief, for disbelief, for love, or intelligence.
That's what makes him free. Man—that's the truth! What
is man? Not you, not me, not them . . . No! it's you, and
me, and them, and the old man, and Napoleon and
Mohammed, all in one. [*Draws the figure of a man in the
air.*] Do you see? It's marvellous! This is the beginning, and
the end. Everything's in man, everything's for man! Man's
the only thing that exists. Everything else is just the work
of his hands and the work of his brain. Man! It's marvellous!
It sounds—great! Man. We should respect him. Not pity
him . . . you degrade him with pity. Respect him! Let's
drink to man, Baron! [*Stands up.*] It's good to be a man!
I'm a convict, a murderer, I cheat at cards—all right.

When I walk down the street, people look at me like a
crook. They step to one side and stare after me. Sometimes
they shout after me, "Why don't you work, you lazy
beggar?" Work? What the hell for? To stuff my belly?
[*Laughs.*] I hate people who worry all the time about
stuffing their bellies. That doesn't matter, Baron. No.
Man's above that. Man's for something much better than
stuffing his belly!

BARON [*shakes his head*]. You've got brains. You're lucky—
must be nice. I haven't. I haven't got brains. [*Looks
around, speaks in a low voice, cautiously.*] You know,
sometimes I get scared. Do you know what I mean? I'm
scared. I don't know what's going to happen to me.

SATIN [*walks up and down*]. Nonsense! What's a man got
to be afraid of?

BARON. You know, for as long as I can remember I've had
a sort of fog in my head. Cant' understand things. I get
an awful feeling I've never done anything in life except
change clothes. What for? I don't know. I went to school
and I had to wear a uniform—College for the Sons of the
Nobility. And what did I learn? I can't remember. I got
married—wore a frock coat, and then I wore a dressing
gown. But I picked the wrong wife. Why? I don't know.
Squandered all my money and had to wear an old grey
jacket and faded trousers. How did I lose it all? I didn't
notice. I got a job in the Civil Service, wore a uniform and
a cap with a badge. Then I embezzled government money,
and they put me in prison clothes. And now I'm wearing
these. And it all happened like a dream. It's funny, isn't it?

SATIN. Not really. I'd say it was stupid.

BARON. Yes, I suppose it is stupid. But I must have been born
for some reason—eh?

SATIN [*laughs*]. Probably . . . People are born so that one day
there'll be better people! [*Nods his head.*] So there you are!

BARON. Wonder where Nastya went off to. I'll go and see.
After all, she . . . [*Exit.*]

[*A pause.*]

ACTOR. Tartar! [*Pause.*] Hassan!!

[TARTAR *looks up.*]

Pray . . . for me . . .

TARTAR. What for?

ACTOR [*softly*]. Pray . . . for me . . .

TARTAR [*after a pause*]. Pray yourself!

ACTOR [*quickly gets down, goes to table, pours himself some vodka with trembling hands, drinks it, and almost runs out into the hall*]. I'm off.

SATIN. Hey, Organism! Where are you going? [*Whistles.*]

[*Enter* MEDVEDEV, *in a woman's quilted jacket, and* BUBNOV. *Both are slightly drunk, but not very.* BUBNOV *carries some pretzels in one hand, and some smoked fish in the other: a bottle of vodka under one arm, and another bottle sticking out of his pocket.*]

MEDVEDEV. Camel—it's a kind of donkey! Only without ears.

BUBNOV. Oh, shut up! You're a kind of donkey yourself.

MEDVEDEV. Camel—hasn't got any ears at all . . . Hears—with his nostrils.

BUBNOV [*to* SATIN]. Ah, there you are! I've been looking for you in every saloon in the street. Here, take a bottle—my hands are full.

SATIN. Put the pretzels on the table—then you'll have one hand free.

BUBNOV. Oh, you . . . Look, policeman! Isn't he clever!

MEDVEDEV. All crooks are clever, I know that! They've got to be clever. An honest man can be stupid. But a crook's got to have brains. But about this camel—you're wrong. It's a sort of animal, and it's got no horns, no teeth . . .

BUBNOV. Where is everybody? Where are they all? Why isn't everybody here? Come on, get up. It's my treat. Who's that in the corner?

SATIN. You drinking up all your money at once? You idiot!

BUBNOV. Yes, all at once! Haven't saved up much money this time . . . Screwy! Where's Screwy?

KLETCH [*comes to table*]. He isn't here.

BUBNOV. Come on, enjoy yourselves! Cheer up! The drinks are on me! If I was rich, I'd run a free saloon. My God, yes, I would! with music, and singing. Come in, and drink, and eat, and sing songs, and enjoy yourselves. You a poor man? Come in, mister, come in—into my free saloon! Satin, I'd make you . . . I'd give you half my capital. There!

SATIN. You'd better give it all to me, right now.

BUBNOV. All of it? Now? Here, take it. Here's a ruble . . . and twenty kopecks . . . five kopecks . . . two kopecks . . . that's all there is!

SATIN. That's fine. It's safer with me. I'll gamble with it.

MEDVEDEV. I'm a witness. He gave you the money to take care of. How much was it?

BUBNOV. You? You're a camel. We don't want any witnesses.

ALESHKA [enters barefoot]. Hello everyone! My feet are soaking wet!

BUBNOV. Come over here and wet your whistle. I like you . . . you're a good guy. Sing and play . . . very well! But you shouldn't drink. That's bad for you, brother. Drinking's bad! . . .

ALESHKA. I can tell by looking at you! It's only when you're drunk that you look like a human being. Kletch. You mended my concertina? [Sings, dances.]

> If I didn't have such a handsome face,
> My girl wouldn't have me round the place.

Boy, I'm frozen. It's cold.

MEDVEDEV. And who is the girl, might I ask?

BUBNOV. Oh, shut up! You're not a policeman now. Forget it! You're not a policeman, and you're not an uncle.

ALESHKA. Just Auntie Kvashnya's husband!

BUBNOV. One of your nieces is in prison, the other one's dying . . .

MEDVEDEV [proudly]. It's a lie! She isn't dying. She's just disappeared without telling anybody.

[SATIN laughs.]

BUBNOV. Just the same, my friend—an uncle without any nieces isn't an uncle.

ALESHKA. Your majesty, the retired drum-major!

> My girl's got money, and I've got none,
> And that is why I treat her nice!

It's so cold!

[Enter SCREWY; from now until the end of the Act, other men and women come in, undress, get onto bunks and start to snore.]

SCREWY. Bubnov! What did you run off for?

BUBNOV. Come over here and sit down . . . Let's sing a song—my favorite one, eh?

TARTAR. Night time you should sleep. Sing songs in daytime.

SATIN. Never mind, Hassan. Come over here.

TARTAR. What do you mean, "never mind"? There'll be noise . . . always noise when you sing songs . . .

BUBNOV [goes up to him]. How's your arm, Hassan? They cut it off yet?

TARTAR. Why should they? May not have to cut it off. I wait a bit. An arm . . . not made of iron. Can easy cut it off.

SCREWY. Means the gutter for you, Hassan! What use are you without an arm? You're only worth what your arm and your back's worth. No arm—no man! Might as well be dead. Come and have some vodka . . . That's all you're good for now.

KVASHNYA [enters]. Hello, inmates! Ooh, it's terrible out there! Cold and wet! Is my policeman here?

MEDVEDEV. Here I am.

KVASHNYA. Wearing my jacket again, are you? And you're a bit tight by the look of you—how come?

MEDVEDEV. It's his birthday—Bubnov's. And besides it's cold . . .

KVASHNYA. Cut the stories! Now get to bed with you, go on!

MEDVEDEV. Yes, it's time I did. Time I went to bed . . . [Exit to kitchen.]

SATIN. What are you so damn strict with him for?

KVASHNYA. You've got to, boy. It's the only way. You got to be strict with a man like him. When I married him I thought I was really getting something. After all, he's a military man, and you're a rough bunch . . . and I'm only a woman. And then he goes and starts taking to drink! And I don't want any of that.

SATIN. You picked the wrong man.

KVASHNYA. No, he's better than you are. You couldn't live with me. You couldn't stand me. A fellow like you! I'd see you one week in twenty. And you'd gamble me away in no time—me and everything else you could lay your hands on.

SATIN [laughs]. You're right there, lady! I'd gamble you away all right!

KVASHNYA. Well, then! . . . Aleshka!

ALESHKA. That's me.

KVASHNYA. What have you been saying about me?

ALESHKA. Me? Only the truth, that's all. That you're a wonderful woman, all flesh, fat and bones—weigh 400 pounds —and have got no brain at all.

KVASHNYA. You're wrong there. I've got plenty of brains. But why do you go telling people I beat my husband?

ALESHKA. I thought you were, when you pulled his hair.

KVASHNYA [*laughs*]. You fool! You aren't blind, are you! What do you go about telling tales for? And you've hurt his feelings, too—he's took to drink because of you.

ALESHKA. Then it's true what they say—even a camel drinks!

[SATIN *and* KLETCH *laugh*.]

KVASHNYA. Oh, Aleshka, you're some kid!

ALESHKA. That's right, some kid! A jack of all trades. And I just follow my nose wherever it takes me!

BUBNOV [*by the* TARTAR'S *bunk*]. Come on! It's no use. You won't get any sleep. We'll be singing—all night long! Eh, Screwy?

SCREWY. A song? All right!

ALESHKA. And I'll play.

SATIN. And we'll listen!

TARTAR [*smiles*]. All right, Bubnov, you bastard . . . give me a drink! We'll drink, and we'll enjoy ourselves—and when death comes, we'll die!

BUBNOV. Fill them up, Satin! Sit down, Screwy! Oh, what does a man need after all? Look at me—give me a drink, and I'm happy! Screwy! Let's have my favorite song. I'm going to sing, and I'm going to cry!

SCREWY [*sings*].

The sun comes up, the sun goes down . . .

BUBNOV [*harmonizing*].

In my prison night won't go . . .

[*The door opens suddenly*.]

BARON [*stands on the threshold, cries*]. Hey . . . you! Come on . . . come out here in the yard . . . out here . . . the Actor . . . he's hanged himself!

[*Silence. They all look at the* BARON. NASTYA *appears behind him, and slowly, with wide eyes, goes to table*.]

SATIN [*quietly*]. The damn fool—he ruined the song!

VLADIMIR MAYAKOVSKY

1893–1930

VLADIMIR MAYAKOVSKY, the poet laureate of the Soviet state, was a wild man of prodigous talents and profligate habits who was more than a little in love with death. In fact, the whole of his short life might be best described as a headlong rush towards death, and when he killed himself playing Russian roulette on the morning of April 14, 1930 it was no surprise to anyone who knew him. They marvelled that he had been lucky for so long.

As one of Russia's greatest poets, Mayakovsky was—like Lorca, only more directly and self-consciously—the lyric voice of the Revolution; and during the years 1917–21 he was the unrivalled leader of the new Soviet literary circles. But he was not satisfied with this (he was never satisfied with anything or anyone, including his countless women); the writing of poetry was too private, too personal, for a leader of the People's Revolution, and he longed to enter the public forum of the theatre which was rapidly emerging as Russia's dominant art form and the tribunal where the rest of the world was judged and found wanting.

Mayakovsky wrote his first play, *Opera Bouffe*, for Meyerhold in 1918, and it was clear from the start that the lyric poet could not make the jump to the theatre. In his first play, he pictured not only the Soviet revolution, but insurrection throughout the whole world, including "the cosmic revolution of the universe." The play was written in the form of a morality play, with scenes on earth, in hell and finally in a new-found Soviet paradise. He continued to write for the theatre with varying success, but it was with his last play, *The Bedbug*, that he hoped to achieve his greatest success.

The Bedbug opened in Moscow on February 15, 1929, under the direction of Meyerhold. Mayakovsky assisted him, and the famous director thought highly of the poet's talents. Of him, he wrote: "Mayakovsky knew what theatre is. . . . he was not only a brilliant playwright but also a brilliant director. I have been staging plays for many years but I have never allowed myself the luxury of letting a dramatist work with me directing a play. But not only did I permit Mayakovsky to work with me, but I found I could not work without him." Meyerhold may have been right, but their production failed in Moscow, as did a subsequent one in Leningrad. *The Bedbug* was successfully revived in 1955, however, and since that time it has been in the repertoire of Russian theatres in most major cities of the Soviet Union.

HOW ONE WRITES A POEM

by Vladimir Mayakovsky

I MUST explain my title. In the course of various literary dis-
cussions and conversations with young workers about
verbal assonances ["soap," "rope," "Pope," and so on] and in
writing criticism it has often fallen to my lot to discredit, if
not to destroy, the ancient art of poetry. It is not that I have
anything against ancient poetry, which is innocent of all evil.
I attacked it only because the zealous defenders of what is
old-fashioned used to shield themselves against new art by
hiding behind the monuments of great men. The point was that
by knocking down these monuments I made readers see a
completely obscured and ignored aspect of these great men.

Children and young literary schools are always curious to
know what is hidden inside cardboard horses. The labors of
the formalists have clearly revealed what the intestines of
paper horses and elephants contain, and we must not feel
aggrieved if the horses are degraded. There is no use doing
injury to the poetry of the past, for it presents us with material
for study.

My chief and abiding hatred goes out against the ro-
mantico-critical, petty bourgeois spirit, against those good
gentlemen for whom the grandeur of ancient poetry consists
of the fact that they, too, have loved as Onegin loved Tatiana
in one of Pushkin's poems. They understand poets because
iambics caress their ears—a trick they learned in school.
This facile hocus-pocus revolts me because it surrounds an
important, serious work of poetry with an atmosphere of sexual thrills and swoons. It is based an the belief that only
eternal poetry is above all dialectic and that the creative
process merely consists in throwing one's hair back with in-

spiration and waiting until celestial poetry descends on one's bared head in the form of a pigeon, a peacock or an ostrich.

It is not difficult to confute these gentlemen. One need only compare Tatiana's love and the "art that Ovid sung" with the projected marriage law, to read to Donets miners the story of the coxcomb who was made a cuckold, or to rush to the aid of May Day parades shouting "My uncle has very honest principles," these words being drawn from the beginning of Pushkin's story of Onegin. After such an experiment it is doubtful whether a young man who is burning with desire to devote his powers to the Revolution will still want to occupy himself seriously with the antiquarian element in poetry. Much has been written and said about this theme and we who have written and talked have always received the enthusiastic approval of our audiences. But after they have given their approval, skeptical phrases rise. "You only destroy; you do not create." "The old manuals are bad, but where are the new ones?" "Give us the rules of your poetic art, give us manuals."

To say that the ancient art of poetry existed for fifteen centuries and that our own has existed for only thirty years is a shabby excuse. You want to write and you want to know how it is done. Why do people refuse to regard as poetry the kind of work that is composed in strict accordance with the rules formulated by Chengeliev, with perfect rhymes, metres, and refrains? You have the right to demand that poets should not take the secret of their calling with them to the tomb.

II

I am going to write about my calling not as a theorist but as a practitioner. My article has no "scientific value." I speak of my work. In the light of my own observations and convictions there are no great distinctions between it and the work of other professional poets. Once more I warn the reader categorically that I am not laying down rules that will enable any man to become a poet and write verse. A poet is a man who creates poetic rules. For the hundredth time I shall resort to a comparison that I am reluctant to employ.

A mathematician is a man who creates, develops and perfects mathematical laws. He is a man who brings something new to mathematical science. The man who first stated that two and two make four was a great mathematician even if he got this result by adding two pebbles to two other pebbles. All other men, even those who add incomparably greater things, locomotives, for instance, are not mathematicians at all. What I am saying does not detract from the value of the work performed by the man who adds locomotives. When transportation gets disorganized this work may be a hundred times more precious than pure mathematics, but it is not necessary to assign the task of comparing figures on locomotives to the Mathematicians' Society and to demand that it put that task on a level with the geometry of Lobachevski. It would enrage the Planning Commission, overtax the mathematicians, and confuse the railway offices.

It will be said that I am drawing a farfetched analogy, that the thing is clear enough without this comparison. But nothing could be more false. Eighty out of a hundred rhymed imbecilities that the editors of our magazines publish are brought out simply because the editors either have not got the least idea of poetry or do not understand its purposes. Magazine editors only know enough to think, "I like that" or "I don't like that." They forget that taste is a faculty that one can and must develop. Almost all magazine editors have complained to me that when manuscripts of poems arrive they do not know why they reject them. A really literary editor should be able to say to the poet, "Your verses are very regular. They are composed in accordance with the third edition of Brodovski's versification manual. All your rhymes are well tested and have long been found in N. Abramov's *Complete Dictionary of Russian Rhymes*. Since I do not have any good verse now I shall accept them and pay for them as I pay for the work of any trained copyist, that is to say, thirty rubles per printed page."

The so-called poet will not know what to reply to this. Either he will stop writing or he will begin to consider verse as something that demands a great deal of work. In any case, the poet will stop putting on airs in front of a reporter who does real work and who is paid so much per line for what he writes even if it is not printed. For a reporter wears out his clothes running to scandals and fires, whereas our poet uses only saliva in turning over the leaves of his manual.

In order to raise the level of poetry, in order to contribute to the future development of art, we must stop considering poetry independently of other forms of human activity. But watch out. The creation of rules is not the ultimate purpose of poetry, for in that case the poet would degenerate into a research investigator who would spend all his energies making up rules to explain nonexistent or useless things and situations. For instance, there would be no use inventing rules to count the stars while one is riding full speed on a bicycle.

Life creates the situations that must be expressed and for which rules must be invented. The form of expression and the purpose of the rules are determined by the social class, by the exigencies of our struggle. For instance, the Revolution has given the rude language of the masses the right to circulate anywhere; the popular language of the working-class districts is moulded by the broad streets on which it is spoken. But the weak, slender language of the intellectuals, with its overworked expressions: "ideal," "the elements of justice," "the divine principle," "the transcendental face of Christ and the Antichrist"—all these phrases that are murmured in chic restaurants have worn thin. Language is being carried away by a new torrent. How can it be made poetic? The old rules with all their dreams, roses and Alexandrines do not fit any more. How can current speech be introduced into poetry, how can poetry be extracted from current conversation? Must we spit on the Revolution in the name of iambic verse? Certainly not.

III

Let us therefore give the keys of the city to this new language. Let us let shouts take the place of refrains. Let drumbeats take the place of lullabies.

> Let us march
> in step
> with the revolution.
>
> —BLOK

> Form yourselves in line of march . . .
> —MAYAKOVSKY

It is not enough to give samples of the new verse, to show how words act on revolutionary crowds. We must adjust this action in such a way as to bring the maximum help to the working class. It is not enough to say, as Blok does, "the old, implacable enemy"; we must indicate precisely the aspect of this enemy or else enable people to visualize it exactly. It is not enough to form in line of march. We must do so in accordance with all the rules of street fighting, taking the telegraph services, the banks and the arsenals and causing them to fall into the hands of the revolutionary workers. Thus I have written:

> Eat your pineapples
> Devour your pullets
> Your last day has come, bourgeois.

Classic poetry could hardly consider such lines worth quoting. In 1820 Gretch did not know the *chastuchki* (Russian popular songs) and even if he had known them he would have spoken of them as he did of popular poetry, disdainfully: "These verses have no rhythm, no assonance." But "these verses" were adopted by the Petersburg streets, and when our gentlemen critics have leisure they will be able to discover what rules were used in composing them. Novelty is obligatory in a work of poetry. The verbal matter that offers itself to the poet must be transformed by his labor. If one uses old verbal scrap iron to make a poem one must take care that a definite proportion of new material is added. It is the quality and quantity of this new material that determine the value of the mixture.

Of course, novelty does not mean that one keeps producing unheard-of truths. Iambic verse, free verse, alliteration and assonance are not created every day. One can try to develop them, to expand them, and make them penetrate the public. "Two and two make four" has no life of its own. One must apply this truth (rules of addition). One must also make this truth easy to remember (more rules). One must clearly reveal the character of this truth through a whole series of visual representations (examples, subjects).

It is clear from what I have said that poetry does not consist in describing and representing bare facts. Of course, there is need for this kind of work, but it is on a par with the minutes that a secretary takes at a great meeting. It consists of nothing but "We have heard," "It has been decided." That is the whole tragedy of the "fellow travelers" [the writers who came over to the Revolution after it had triumphed]. They "agreed" only five years afterward, and "decided" too late, when the others had already achieved.

Poetry begins with tendency. To my mind, Lermantov's poem, "I go alone on the road," is a kind of propaganda to encourage girls to go walking with poets. To walk alone is boring, you know. If one could only write a poem as forceful as Lermontov's but appealing to people to join coöperatives.

The old manuals of poetic art are of no use. They only catalogue different ways of writing, all of which have become conventional. Actually such books should not be called, *How to Write*, but *How People Wrote*. Let me be honest. I know nothing about iambics or trochees. I have never been able to distinguish them and never shall be able to. Not that it is difficult, but I have never had to concern myself with such things in my poetic work. If my poetry contains fragments of rhythm it is simply because I have repeated too frequently those boring motifs that one encounters everywhere. Several times I have attempted to study these matters. I have succeeded in understanding the mechanism of regular verse and have then promptly forgotten it. But these trifles, which occupy ninety percent of our manuals of poetry, do not occupy three percent of my own practical activity.

In poetic work there exist only certain general rules for getting one's work under way, and even those rules are purely conventional. As in chess, the opening moves are almost always the same, but after you have played them once you try to find others. The most brilliant *coup* cannot be repeated in a given situation a second time. For one's adversary can be defeated only by unexpected attacks. The same thing is true of unexpected rhymes in poetry.

IV

What, then, are the necessary conditions for getting one's poetic work started?

1. The existence of a social task that can be accomplished only through poetic work. There must be a social "command." Here, incidentally, is an interesting subject for special research: the lack of connection between the social command and the command actually given.

2. You must have an exact knowledge of or at least a feeling for the aspirations of the class or group you represent toward this social task, in other words, a final attitude, an end.

3. You must have the material, the words. The store house, the reserves of your mind should be equipped with the necessary words—expressive, rare, new, renovated and invented words of every kind.

4. Means of production are necessary. These include a pen,

a pencil, a typewriter, a telephone, clothes to wear when going out for food. A bicycle to ride on to the editorial office, a table, an umbrella to enable one to write in the rain, a room in which one can take a certain number of steps (this is necessary for one's work), connections with a clipping bureau in order to make sure of receiving a continual supply of material on subjects that are of interest to your district, a pipe and a supply of cigarettes.

5. One must have formed the habit of elaborating words. This habit is infinitely individual and comes only after years of daily work. It covers rhymes, measures, alliterations, images, gradations, style, pathos, endings, titles, plans and so on.

For instance, the social task is to find the words for a song to be sung by the Red Guards, who are going to defend Petersburg. The purpose is to defeat Yudenich. The material is words, drawn from the common speech of soldiers. The tool is a pencil point. The form, a rhymed *chastuchka*. Here is the result:

> Milkoï mne v podarok burka
> I noski podareni
> Mchit Yudenich s Peterburga
> Kak naskipidareni.

> (My girl friend made me a present
> Of a jacket and some socks.
> Yudenich is fleeing from Petersburg
> As if he were soaked in turpentine.)

The novelty of the quatrain that justifies the production of this particular *chastuchka* rests in the rhyme, *noski podareni* and *naskipidareni*. This novelty makes the thing necessary, poetic, typical. For the *chastuchka* to attain maximum effectiveness, the rhyme must be unexpected and the first two lines must have no relation to the other two. Moreover, the first two lines can be regarded as purely accessory. To any man who wants to evaluate and qualify poetic work these very general rules will open up more possibilities than the rules that now exist. It is enough to consider as coefficients the elements of material equipment and form. Is there a social command? Yes. Two points. A purpose? Two points. Is it rhymed? One more point. Are there alliterations? Half a point. Then one point for the rhyme because one had to take an autobus to arrive at this unaccustomed measure.

Do not smile, critic. The truth is that I should prefer the

verses written by an inhabitant of Alaska, provided, of course, he had the same talent, to those written by a man who lived on the Côte d'Azur. And quite rightly. An inhabitant of Alaska suffers from cold. He has to buy a fur coat and the ink in his fountain pen freezes. The inhabitant of the Côte d'Azur writes surrounded by palm trees in a setting that makes even his poems pleasant.

To qualify a poem is equally easy. The verses of Demian Biedni correspond to an urgent, well understood social command. Their purpose is clear. They are adapted to the needs of workers and peasants. The words are those of the daily life of the semi-peasant class, mixed with remnants of poetic rhymes.

The verses of Kruchenikh, with their alliterations, dissonances, and purpose, are destined to aid future poets. I shall not occupy myself here with the metaphysical problem of discovering which is the better—a poem by Demian Biedni or a poem by Kruchenikh. They are made up of different elements that belong on different planes and each can exist without embarrassing the other or competing against it. For my part, I believe that the best poetic work will be written in accordance with the social command laid down by the Communist International and that it will tend to assure the victory of the proletariat. It will be written in new, striking words comprehensible to everybody. It will be born in the hour when it is wanted and will be sent to the editor by express airplane. I insist on this last point, for the poetic way of living is also one of the most important factors in our production.

Of course, the process of evaluating poetry is really something much more complex and subtle than I have indicated here. I am simplifying, enlarging, exaggerating my thought intentionally. I simplify to show more clearly that the essence of this study of literature does not reside in individual appreciation of any particular piece of writing but rather in a fair way of approaching the study of the process of literary production. The purpose of the present essay is not to discuss already existing examples and forms but to try to show the actual process of poetic production.

V

How, then, is a poem written? Work begins long before the social command has been received, all unknown to one's consciousness. Preparatory poetic work continues uninterruptedly. One can write a piece of poetry within a given time only if one has previously accumulated considerable poetic reserves. For instance—and I am merely mentioning what comes to my mind at the moment—a good family name, Glitzeron, happens to come into my head. It came by chance during some conversation about glycerine. I also have a reserve of good rhymes and I shall always remember a passage taken from some American song that needs to be Russified and that gives me infinite pleasure:

> The vamp of Sovani
> The vamp of Sovani
> J. A.

I also have in my storehouse of alliterations one that was suggested to me by an advertisement that I happened to see out of the corner of my eye and that bore the name, "Nita Jo":

> Gde jiviot Nita Jo
> Nita nije etajom.
>
> (Where does Nita Jo live?
> One story below.)

I also can choose between various subjects, some clear, some confused. First, rain in New York. Secondly, the prostitute on the Boulevard des Capucines in Paris. It is said to be particularly chic to make love to her because she has only one leg. She lost the other in a streetcar accident, I believe. Thirdly, the old man who is stationed in the wash room of the huge Heissler restaurant in Berlin. Fourthly, the immense subject of the October Revolution, which is something that one cannot imagine if one did not live in a village.

All these reserves exist in my mind, and I have noted down here those that are particularly delicate. All my time is spent accumulating these reserves, and on this work I lose eighteen and twenty hours a day. I am almost always murmuring something. It is this concentrated effort that accounts for the supposed distraction of the poet. I pursue this work of accumulation so intensely that eight times out of ten I can recall the place and particular circumstances in which during fifteen years of work certain rhymes, certain alliterations, certain images came to me and received their definite form.

The notebook is one of the essential factors in any real

piece of work. Ordinarily one does not learn of the existence of the notebook until after the death of the writer. For years it is ignored, and it is only published posthumously after his complete works have appeared, but for the writer the notebook is everything.

Beginners in poetry do not possess such a notebook, for they have no practice, no experience. Rarely does one find in their work really finished verses, and that is why their poems are so long-drawn-out. It is only with the aid of reserves that have been carefully worked over that I have been able to do a thing by a given date, because my normal production is eight or ten verses a day when I am occupied with a real task. To the poet every encounter, every lesson, every event, has value only in so far as it provides verbal material. I used to be so immersed in this work that I even feared to express myself in the words and phrases that my futurist verse seemed to demand, and I therefore became sombre, boring, and taciturn.

About 1913, as I was coming back from Saratov to Moscow in the company of a certain young lady, I told her, in order to prove my complete loyalty to her, that I was "not a man but a cloud in trousers." At once I realized that this expression might serve in a poem and I was afraid that she would repeat it and prevent my turning it to profit. In great anxiety I questioned the girl for half an hour, asking her insidious questions, and I only became calm when I was convinced that my words had gone in one ear and out the other. Two years later I used the "cloud in trousers" as the title of a poem.

Here is another example. For two days I meditated on the best way to express the tenderness a solitary man feels for a woman he loves above all else. How would he care for her, how would he love her? The third night I went to bed with a headache, not having discovered anything. But in the middle of the night it finally came to me:

> I shall guard and I shall love
> your body
> as a soldier
> mutilated by war
> —of no use to anybody—
> guards
> his remaining leg.

I jumped up half awake. In the darkness I wrote down on

a cigarette box with the blackened end of a match the words "one leg" and fell asleep again. The next morning I spent two hours trying to remember what leg it was and how the words happened to be written on the box.

When you are about to seize on a rhyme but have not yet found it, life is poison. You talk without understanding what you say, you do not know what you are eating, and you cannot sleep because you are continually obsessed by the rhyme that is fluttering before your eyes. Yet here is an advertisement from the Kharkov *Proletarian*: "How to be a writer. Detailed reply for fifty kopecks in postage stamps. Slaviansk Station, Donets Line, Post Office Box 11." What do you think of that? Simply a survival of the old régime, and already the magazine *Distraction* is giving away as a supplement a book entitled *How to Be a Poet in Five Lessons*. I think that my little examples are enough to prove that poetry belongs to the category of the most difficult things in the world, the category of reality. A poem must be considered in the same way in which this immortal quatrain of Pasternak's considers a woman:

> From that day, from your head to your feet,
> I carried you with me and knew you by heart
> As a provincial actor knows a play of Shakespeare's.
> I took you about with me in the city and repeated you.

THE BEDBUG

by VLADIMIR MAYAKOVSKY

1929

THE BEDBUG[1]

Translated by Max Hayward

CHARACTERS

IVAN PRISYPKIN (*otherwise known as* PIERRE SKRIP-KIN), *a former Party member, former worker, and now the fiancé of*

ELZEVIR DAVIDOVNA RENAISSANCE, *manicurist and cashier of a beauty parlor*

ROSALIE PAVLOVNA RENAISSANCE, *her mother*

DAVID OSIPOVICH RENAISSANCE, *her father*

ZOYA BERYOZKINA, *a working girl*

OLEG BARD, *an eccentric house owner*

MILITIAMAN
PROFESSOR
DIRECTOR OF ZOO
FIRE CHIEF
FIREMEN
USHER AT WEDDING
REPORTER
WORKERS
CHAIRMAN OF CITY SOVIET
ORATOR
HIGHSCHOOL STUDENTS
MASTER OF CEREMONIES
MEMBERS OF PRESIDIUM OF CITY SOVIET, HUNTERS, CHILDREN, OLD PEOPLE

[1] From *The Bedbug and Selected Poetry* by Vladimir Mayakovsky. Copyright © 1960 by Meridian Books, Inc. Published by arrangement with The World Publishing Company, Cleveland and New York—A Meridian Book.

Scene 1

[*1929. Tambov, U.S.S.R. Center: Huge revolving door of State Department Store. Sides: Display windows full of goods. People entering empty-handed and coming out with bundles. Private peddlers walking through the aisles.*]

MAN SELLING BUTTONS. Why get married on account of a button? Why get divorced on account of a button? Just press your thumb against your index finger and you won't lose your pants, citizens! Dutch grippers! They sew themselves on! Twenty kopecks for half a dozen! Here you are, gentlemen!

MAN SELLING DOLLS.
Dancing dolls!
Straight from the ballet studios!
The best toy for indoors and outdoors!
Dances to the order of the People's Commissar!

WOMAN SELLING APPLES.
We ain't got no pineapples!
We ain't got no bananas!
Top-grade apples at fifteen kopecks for four!
Like some, lady?

MAN SELLING WHETSTONES.
Unbreakable German whetstones!
Any one you choose for thirty kopecks!
Hones where you like and how you like!
Sharpens razors, knives—and tongues for political
    discussions!

MAN SELLING LAMPSHADES.
Lampshades! Lampshades!
All sizes and colors!
Blue for comfort and red for passion!
Get yourselves a lampshade, comrades!

MAN SELLING BALLOONS.
Sausage balloons!
Fly like a bird!
Nobile could have used one at the North Pole!
Step right up, citizens!

MAN SELLING SALTED HERRINGS.
  Best herrings! Best herrings!
  Indispensable with pancakes and vodka!
WOMAN SELLING UNDERWEAR.
  Brassieres! Brassieres!
  Lovely fur-lined brassieres!
MAN SELLING GLUE.
  Why throw out your broken crockery?
  Famous Excelsior glue!
  Fixes anything from Venus de Milo to a chamber pot!
  Like to try it, lady?
WOMAN SELLING PERFUME.
  Coty perfume by the ounce!
  Coty perfume by the ounce!
MAN SELLING BOOKS.
  What the wife does when the husband's away!
  A hundred and five funny stories by the ex-Count
    Leo Nikolaevich Tolstoy!
  Fifteen kopecks instead of a ruble twenty!
WOMAN SELLING UNDERWEAR.
  Lovely brassieres!
  Fur-lined brassieres!

[*Enter* PRISYPKIN, ROSALIE PAVLOVNA, *and* OLEG BARD.]

PRISYPKIN [*excitedly*]. Look at those aristocratic bonnets!
ROSALIE. They're not bonnets, they're . . .
PRISYPKIN. Think I'm blind? Suppose we have twins? There'll
  be one for Dorothy and one for Lillian when they go out
  walking together. . . . That's what I'm going to call them:
  Dorothy and Lillian—aristocratic—like the Gish sisters.
  Now you buy those bonnets, Rosalie . . . my house must
  be like a horn of plenty.
OLEG BARD [*giggling*]. Buy 'em, buy 'em, Rosalie Pavlovna!
  He doesn't mean to be vulgar—that's how the up-and-
  coming working class sees things. Here he is, bringing an
  immaculate proletarian origin and a union card into your
  family and you count your kopecks! His house must be
  like a horn of plenty.

[ROSALIE *buys with a sigh.*]

OLEG BARD. Let me carry them—they're quite light. Don't
  worry—it won't cost you any more. . . .
MAN SELLING TOYS. Dancing dolls from the ballet studios. . . .

PRISYPKIN. My future children must be brought up refined. There, buy one, Rosalie Pavlovna!

ROSALIE PAVLOVNA. Comrade Prisypkin. . . .

PRISYPKIN. Don't call me comrade! You're not a proletarian yet—not till after the marriage!

ROSALIE PAVLOVNA. Well, *Mister* Prisypkin, for this money fifteen men could have a shave—beards, whiskers, and all. What about an extra dozen beers for the wedding instead?

PRISYPKIN [*sternly*]. Rosalie Pavlovna, my house must be filled like a horn. . . .

OLEG BARD. His house must be like a horn of plenty. Beer must flow like a river, and dancing dolls, too—like out of a cornucopia.

[ROSALIE PAVLOVNA *buys.*]

OLEG BARD [*seizing the parcels*]. Don't worry—it won't cost you any more.

MAN SELLING BUTTONS.
    Why get married on account of a button?
    Why get divorced on account of a button?

PRISYPKIN. In our Red family there must be no petty bourgeois squabbles over fly buttons. There we are! Buy them, Rosalie Pavlovna!

OLEG BARD. Rosalie Pavlovna, don't provoke him until you get that union card. He is the victorious class and he sweeps away everything in his path, like lava, and Comrade Prisypkin's pants must be like a horn of plenty. . . .

[ROSALIE PAVLOVNA *buys with a sigh.*]

OLEG BARD. Allow me . . . I'll take them and it won't cost you. . . .

MAN SELLING SALTED HERRINGS. Finest republican herrings! Indispensable with every kind of vodka!

ROSALIE PAVLOVNA [*brightening, pushing everybody aside, loudly*]. Yes! salted herrings! Now that's something for the wedding, I'll sure take some of them. Let me through, sir! How much is this sardine?

MAN SELLING SALTED HERRINGS. This salmon costs two-sixty the kilo.

ROSALIE PAVLOVNA. Two-sixty for that overgrown minnow?

MAN SELLING SALTED HERRINGS. Really, madam! Only two-sixty for this budding sturgeon!

ROSALIE PAVLOVNA. Two-sixty for these marinated corset stays!

Did you hear that, Comrade Skripkin? Oh, how right you were to kill the Tsar and drive out Mr. Ryabushinsky! Oh, the bandits! I shall claim my civic rights and buy my herrings in the Soviet State Co-op!

OLEG BARD. Wait a moment, Comrade Skripkin. Why get mixed up with petty bourgeois elements and haggle over herrings like this? Give me fifteen rubles and a bottle of vodka and I'll fix you up with a wedding in a million.

PRISYPKIN. Comrade Bard, I'm against all this petty bourgeois stuff—lace curtains and canaries . . . I'm a man with higher needs. What I'm interested in is a wardrobe with a mirror. . . .

[ZOYA BERYOZKINA *nearly runs into them as they stand talking. Steps back in astonishment and listens.*]

OLEG BARD. When your cortege . . .

PRISYPKIN. What's that? Some kind of card game?

OLEG BARD. Cortege, I say. That's what they call processions of all kinds, particularly wedding processions, in these lovely foreign languages.

PRISYPKIN. Well, what do you know!

OLEG BARD. As I was saying, when the cortege advances I'll sing you the epithalamium of Hymen.

PRISYPKIN. Huh? What's that about the Himalayas?

OLEG BARD. Not the Himalayas . . . an epithalamium about the god Hymen. That was a god these Greeks had. I mean the ancient republican Greeks, not these mad-dog guttersnipe opportunists like Venizelos.

PRISYPKIN. What I want for my money is a real Red wedding and no gods! Get it?

OLEG BARD. Why, of course, Comrade Skripkin! Not only do I understand, but by virtue of that power of imagination which, according to Plekhanov, is granted to Marxists, I can already see as through a prism, so to speak, the triumph of your class as symbolized by your sublime, ravishing, elegant and class-conscious wedding! The bride steps out of her carriage and she's all red—that is, she's all steamed up. And leading her by the arm is her red escort, Yerikalov, the bookkeeper—he's fat, red and apoplectic . . . and you are brought in by the red ushers, the table is covered with red hams, and the bottles all have red seals.

PRISYPKIN [*approvingly*]. That's it! That's it!

OLEG BARD. The red guests shout "Kiss, kiss!" and your red spouse puts her red lips to yours. . . .

ZOYA BERYOZKINA [*seizes both of them by the arms; they remove her hands and dust off their sleeves*]. Vanya! What's he talking about, this catfish in a cravat? What wedding? Who's getting married?

OLEG BARD. The Red nuptials of Elzevir Davidovna Renaissance and . . .

PRISYPKIN.

I love another, Zoya,
She's smarter and cuter
With a bosom held tighter
By a beautiful sweater.

ZOYA BERYOZKINA. But what about me, Vanya? Who do you think you are? A sailor with a girl in every port?

PRISYPKIN [*wards her off with outstretched hand*]. "We part like ships in the sea . . ."

ROSALIE PAVLOVNA [*rushing from the shop, holding a herring above her head*]. Whales! Dolphins! [*To the herring peddler.*] Now then, show me that snail! [*She compares. The street vendor's herrings are larger. Wrings her hands.*] Longer by a tail's length! What did we fight for, Comrade Skripkin, eh? Why, oh, why did we kill the Tsar? Why did we throw out Mr. Ryabushinsky? This Soviet regime of yours will drive me to my grave. . . . A whole tail's length longer!

OLEG BARD. My dear Rosalie Pavlovna, try comparing them at the other end. They're only bigger by a head and what do you want the heads for? You can't eat them and you'll cut them off and throw them out anyway.

ROSALIE PAVLOVNA. Did you hear that? If I cut off your head, Comrade Bard, it will be no loss to anyone, but if I cut off these herrings' heads I lose ten kopecks to the kilo. Well, let's go home. . . . I sure want a union card in the family, but my daughter's in a good business, and that's nothing to sniff at!

ZOYA BERYOZKINA. We were going to live and work together . . . so it's all over. . . .

PRISYPKIN. Our love is liquidated. I'll call the militia if you interfere with my freedom of love as a citizen.

ROSALIE PAVLOVNA. What does she want, this slut? Why have you got your hooks on my son-in-law?

ZOYA BERYOZKINA. He's mine!

ROSALIE PAVLOVNA. Ah! She's pregnant! I'll pay her off, but I'll smash her face in first!

MILITIAMAN. Citizens! Stop this disgusting behavior!

Scene 2

[*Hostel for young workers.* INVENTOR *huffs and puffs over a blueprint.* YOUTH *lolls around.* GIRL *sits on the edge of the bed.* YOUTH IN SPECTACLES *with nose buried in a book. Whenever the door opens, a long corridor with doors off and lightbulbs is seen.*]

BAREFOOT YOUTH [*howling at the top of his voice*]. Where are my boots? Someone's swiped my boots again! Am I supposed to check them every night in the baggage room at the Kursk Station? Is that what I've got to do? Is that it?

CLEANER. Prisypkin took them to go see his ladylove, his she-camel. He cursed while he put them on. "This is the last time," he said. "In the evening," he said, "I shall present myself in a get-up more appropriate to my new social status."

YOUTH. The bastard!

YOUNG WORKER [*tidying up the room*]. The trash he leaves behind him is kind of more refined nowadays. It used to be empty beer bottles and fishtails and now it's cologne bottles and ties all the colors of the rainbow.

GIRL. Shut your trap! The kid buys a new tie and you curse him like he was Ramsay MacDonald.

YOUTH. That's just what he is—Ramsay MacDonald! The new tie don't matter. Trouble is that he's tied to the tie—not the tie to him. He don't even use his head any more, so his tie shouldn't get twisted.

CLEANER. If there's a hole in his sock and he's in a hurry, he paints it over with indelible ink.

YOUTH. His feet are black anyway.

INVENTOR. But maybe not black in the places where the holes are. He ought to just switch his socks from one foot to the other.

CLEANER. There's the inventor for you! Why don't you take out a patent before somebody steals the idea? [*Whisks a duster over the table, upsets a box from which visiting cards drop out fanwise. Bends down to pick them up, holds them to the light, laughs so hard he can barely manage to motion his comrades toward him.*]

ALL [*reading and repeating after each other*]. Pierre Skripkin! Pierre Skripkin!

INVENTOR. That's the name he's invented for himself. Prisypkin. Who is Prisypkin? What good's Prisypkin? What's the
point of Prisypkin? But Pierre Skripkin—that's not a name,
it's a romance!

GIRL [*dreamily*]. But it's true! Pierre Skripkin is very fine
and elegant. You roar your heads off but how do you know
he's not carrying out a cultural revolution in his own home?

YOUTH. Yeah, Pushkin's got nothing on him with those sideburns of his. They hang down like a pair of dog's tails and
he doesn't even wash them to keep them neat.

GIRL. There's that movie star with sideburns. . . .

INVENTOR. Prisypkin got the idea from him.

YOUTH. And what does his hero's hair grow on, I'd like to
know? He's got no head at all, but a whole halo of fuzz.
Wonder what makes it grow? Must be the dampness.

YOUTH WITH BOOK. Anyway, he's no movie star. . . . He's a
writer. I don't know what he's written, but I know he's
famous! They've written about him three times in *Evening
Moscow*: they say that he sold Apukhtin's poetry as his
own, and Apukhtin got so mad he wrote a denial. And so
what's-his-name came back and said: "You're all crazy, it's
not true, I copied it from Nadson." I don't know which
of them is lying. It's true they don't print him any more,
but he's very famous. He gives lessons to young people—
how to write verse, how to dance, and, well, you know . . .
how to borrow money.

YOUTH WITH BROOM. Painting over holes with ink—that's no
way for a worker to behave!

[MECHANIC, *grease-covered, comes in halfway through this
sentence. Washes his hands and turns around.*]

MECHANIC. He's no worker. He quit his job today. He's
marrying a young lady—a hairdresser's daughter. She's the
cashier and the manicurist too. Mademoiselle Elzevir
Renaissance'll clip his claws for him now. . . .

INVENTOR. Elzevir—that's the name of a type face.

MECHANIC. I don't know about her type face, but she's certainly got a figure! He showed her picture to our payclerk
today . . .

      What a honey, what a peach——
      Both her breasts weigh eighty pounds each!

BAREFOOT YOUTH. He's sure fixed himself up!

GIRL. Jealous, eh?

BAREFOOT YOUTH. So what? When I get to be foreman and earn enough to buy myself a pair of boots, I'll start looking around for a cozy little apartment.

MECHANIC. Here's my advice to you: get yourself some curtains. You can either open them and look out at the street or close them and take your bribes in private. It's better to work with other people, but it's much more fun to eat your sirloin by yourself. Right? We had men who tried to run away from the trenches, too, and we just swatted them down like flies. Well, why don't you just get out?

BAREFOOT YOUTH. Okay. Okay. Who do you think you are? Karl Liebknecht? If a dame gives you the glad eye out of a window, I bet you fall for it, too, hero!

MECHANIC. I'm no deserter. You think I like wearing these lousy rags? Like hell I do! There are lots of us, you know, and there just aren't enough Nepmen's daughters to go around. . . . We'll build houses for everybody! But we won't creep out of this foxhole with a white flag.

BAREFOOT YOUTH. You and your trenches! This isn't 1919. People want to live their own lives now.

MECHANIC. Well, isn't it like the trenches in here?

BAREFOOT YOUTH. Nuts!

MECHANIC. Look at the lice!

BAREFOOT YOUTH. Nuts!

MECHANIC. Our enemies attack silently now—that's the only difference. And people shoot with noiseless powder!

BAREFOOT YOUTH. Nuts!

MECHANIC. Look at Prisypkin—he's been shot by a two-eyed, double-barreled gun!

[*Enter* PRISYPKIN *in patent leather shoes. In one hand he holds a pair of worn-out shoes by the laces and tosses them over to* BAREFOOT YOUTH. OLEG BARD *carries his purchases. He stands between* PRISYPKIN *and the* MECHANIC, *who is dancing a jig.*]

OLEG BARD. Don't pay any attention to this vulgar dance, Comrade Skripkin, it will only spoil the refined taste that is awakening in you.

[*The youths in the hostel turn their backs.*]

MECHANIC. Quit bowing and scraping. You'll crack your skull.

OLEG BARD. I understand, Comrade Skripkin! You are too

sensitive for this vulgar crew. But don't lose your patience
for just one more lesson. The first foxtrot after the nuptial
ceremonies is a crucial step—it should leave a deathless
impression. Well now, take a few steps with an imaginary
lady. . . . Why are you stamping your feet like at a May
Day parade?

PRISYPKIN. Comrade Bard, let me take my shoes off; they
pinch and besides they'll wear out.

OLEG BARD. That's the way! That's right! Tread softly like
you were coming back from a saloon on a moonlit night,
full of sadness and dreams. That's the way! But don't
wriggle your hind parts! You're supposed to be leading
your partner, not driving a pushcart. . . . That's the way!
. . . Where's your hand? Your hand's too low!

PRISYPKIN [*passes his hand over an imaginary shoulder*]. It
won't stay up!

OLEG BARD. And now, Comrade Skripkin, you discreetly
locate the lady's brassiere, hook your thumb into it, and
rest your hand—it's pleasant for the lady and makes it
easier for you. Then you can think about your other hand.
. . . Why are you rolling your shoulders? That's not a
foxtrot. You're giving a demonstration of the shimmy.

PRISYPKIN. No, I was just scratching myself.

OLEG BARD. That's not the way to do it, Comrade Skripkin!
If any such emergency occurs while you're carried away
by the dance, roll your eyes, as if you were jealous of the
lady, step back to the wall in the Spanish manner, and rub
yourself rapidly against some statue or other. In the smart
society where you'll be moving there's always a hell of a lot
of statues and vases. So rub yourself, screw up your face,
flash your eyes, and say: "I understand, tr-r-reacherous one,
you are playing a game with me. . . ." Then you start
dancing again and pretend you're gradually calming down
and cooling off.

PRISYPKIN. Like this?

OLEG BARD. Bravo! Well done! How clever you are, Comrade
Skripkin! A man of such talents just doesn't have elbow
room in Russia, what with capitalist encirclement and the
building of socialism in one country. I ask you—is Lower
Goat Street a worthy scene for your activities? You need
a worldly revolution, you must break through into Europe.
Once you've smashed the Chamberlains, the Poincarés, you
will delight the Moulin Rouge and the Pantheon with the

beauty of your bodily movements. Just remember that!
Now hold it! Hold it! Magnificent! But I must be off. I
have to keep an eye on the ushers. I'll give them one glass
in advance before the wedding and not a drop more. When
they've done their job, they can drink straight out of the
bottle, if they like. *Au revoir!* [*Shouts from the doorway
as he leaves.*] And don't put on two ties at once—particularly if they're different colors. And remember, you can't
wear a starched shirt outside your pants!

[PRISYPKIN *tries on his new clothes.*]

YOUTH. Vanya, why don't you cut it out?

PRISYPKIN. Mind your own goddamn business! Respected
comrade. What did I fight for? I fought for the good life,
and now I've got it right here in my hands—a wife, a
home and real etiquette. I'll do my duty, if need be, but
it's only we who held the bridgehead who have a right to
rest by the river! So there! Mebbe I can raise the standards
of the whole proletariat by looking after my own comforts.
So there!

MECHANIC. There's a warrior for you! A real Suvorov! Bravo!

> For a while I worked my best
> Building a bridge to Socialism
> But before I was through I wanted a rest
> By the bridge to Socialism.
> Now it's grown with grass that's grazed by sheep
> And all I do is lie and sleep
> By the bridge to Socialism.

So that's it, eh?

PRISYPKIN. Leave me alone with your cheap propaganda
ditties . . . [*Sits down on bed and sings to guitar.*]

> On Lunacharsky Street
> There's an old house I know
> With stairs broad and neat
> And a most elegant window.

[*A shot. All rush to the door.*]

YOUTH [*from the doorway*]. Zoya Beryozkina's shot herself!
They'll give her hell for this at the Party meeting!

VOICES. Help! First aid! Help! First aid!

A VOICE [*on the phone*]. First aid! Help! What? She's shot

herself! Right through the breast! This is Lower Goat Street, number sixteen.

[PRISYPKIN *hurriedly collects his belongings.*]

MECHANIC. And a woman like that shoots herself on account of you, you hairy skunk! [*Grabs* PRISYPKIN *by the jacket and throws him out of the room, hurling his belongings after him.*]

CLEANER [*running in with doctor; jerks* PRISYPKIN *to his feet and gives him his hat, which has fallen off*]. You're walking out on your class with a hell of a bang!

PRISYPKIN [*turns away and yells*]. Cab! Seventeen Lunacharsky Street—and my luggage!

Scene 3

[*Huge beauty parlor. Mirrors decorated with paper flowers. Liquor bottles on small shaving tables. On the left a grand piano with gaping maw. On the right a coal stove whose pipes climb all around the walls. In the middle of the room a banquet table at which sit* PIERRE SKRIPKIN, ELZEVIR RENAISSANCE, *the* BEST MAN (*an accountant*) *and the* MATRON OF HONOR (*accountant's wife*). OLEG BARD *is master of ceremonies and sits in the center of the table.*]

ELZEVIR. Shall we begin, Skrippy, my pet?

PRISYPKIN. Just a minute.

ELZEVIR. Skrippy darling, shall we start?

PRISYPKIN. Wait. I said I wished to get wed in an organized fashion—in the presence of the guests of honor, and particularly in the presence of the secretary of our factory committee, respected Comrade Lassalchenko. . . . Here we are!

GUEST [*running in*]. My dear bride and bridegroom, please forgive me for being late and allow me to convey to you the congratulations of our respected leader, Comrade Lassalchenko. "Tomorrow," he says, "I would even go to the church, if need be, but today," he says, "I can't make it. Today," he says, "is a Party meeting, and like it or not, I have to go to the Party cell. . . ." So let us proceed to current business, as the saying goes.

PRISYPKIN. I hereby declare the wedding open.

ROSALIE PAVLOVNA. Comrades and *Messieurs*! Please eat! Where would you find pigs like these nowadays? I bought this ham three years ago in case of a war with Greece or Poland. . . . But there's still no war and the ham is getting moldy. . . . Eat, gentlemen!

ALL [*raising their glasses*]. Kiss! Kiss!

[ELZEVIR *and* PIERRE *kiss.*]

Kiss! Kiiii-ss-ss!

[ELZEVIR *throws herself around* PIERRE's *neck and he kisses her staidly, conscious of his working-class dignity.*]

BEST MAN. Let's have some Beethoven! Shakespeare! Give us a show! What do they think we celebrate their anniversaries for!

[*The piano is dragged to center of stage.*]

VOICES. By the side! Grab it by the side! Look at its teeth— makes you want to smash them in!

PRISYPKIN. Don't trample on the legs of my piano!

OLEG BARD [*stands up, staggers, and spills his glass*]. I am happy, I am happy to see, as we are gathered here today, that the road of Comrade Skripkin's fighting career has come to such a splendid conclusion. It's true that along that road he lost his Party card, but, on the other hand, he did acquire many state lottery tickets. We have succeeded in reconciling, in co-ordinating the couple's class and other contradictions. We who are armed with the Marxist vision cannot fail to see, as in a drop of water, so to speak, the future happiness of humanity—or as it is called in popular parlance: socialism.

ALL. Kiss! Kiss!

[ELZEVIR *and* PRISYPKIN *kiss.*]

OLEG BARD. What gigantic steps we are making on the road to the rebuilding of family life! When we all lay dying at the battle of Perekop, and when many of us, indeed, did die, could we have foreseen that such fragrant roses would blossom forth in this day and age? Could we have imagined, when we groaned under the yoke of autocracy, could even our great teachers Marx and Engels have imagined in their dreams, or dreamed in their imaginations that the bonds of

Hymen would one day join together Labor—obscure but
grandiose—and Capital—dethroned but ever enchanting?

ALL. Kiss! Kiss!

OLEG BARD. Respected comrades! Beauty is the motive force of
progress! What would I have been as a simple worker?
Botchkin—just plain Botchkin! What could Botchkin do
except bray like an ass? But as Oleg the Bard I can do
anything you like! For instance:

> I'm Oleg the bard
> A happy drunkard

And so now I'm Oleg Bard and enjoy all the blessings of
culture as an equal member of society. And I swear—well,
no swearing here—but at least I can talk like an ancient
Greek:

> Prithee, give me, Elzevir
> A herring and a glass of beer!

And the whole country responds, just like they were trouba-
dours:

> Here's to you, Oleg dear,
> A herring's tail and a glass of beer,
> To whet your whistle
> In style and good cheer!

ALL. Bravo! Hurray! Kiss!

OLEG BARD. Beauty is pregnant with . . .

USHER [jumps up, menacingly]. Pregnant? Who said "pregnant"? I'll ask you to watch your language in the presence
of the newlyweds!

[USHER is dragged off.]

ALL. Give us Beethoven! Give us the Kamarinsky!

[OLEG BARD is dragged to the piano.]

OLEG BARD.

> The tramcars drew up to the Registry Office
> Bringing the guests to a Red marriage service. . . .

ALL [singing in chorus].

> Dressed in his working clothes was the spouse
> And a union card stuck out of his blouse!

ACCOUNTANT. I get the idea! I get the whole thing!

> Hail to thee, Oleg Bardkin
> Curly-headed like a lambkin. . . .

HAIRDRESSER [*poking his fork at the* MATRON OF HONOR]. No, madam, no! Nobody has curly hair now, after the Revolution! Do you know how we make a *chignon gaufré*? You take the curling iron [*He twists his fork.*], heat it on a low flame—*à l'étoile*—[*thrusts his fork into the blazing stove.*] and then you whip up a kind of *soufflé* of hair on the crown of the head . . . like this.

MATRON OF HONOR. You insult my honor as a mother and a virgin. . . . Leave me alone, son of a bitch!!!

USHER. Who said "son of a bitch"? I'll ask you to watch your language in the presence of the newlyweds!

[*The* ACCOUNTANT *separates them and continues his song, turning the handle of the cash register as though it were a barrel organ.*]

ELZEVIR [*to* OLEG BARD]. Ah, play us the waltz "Makarov's Lament for Vera Kholodnaya". . . . Ah, it's so *charmant*; it's simply a *petite histoire*. . . .

USHER [*armed with a guitar*]. Who said *"pissoir"*? I'll ask you to watch . . .

[OLEG BARD *separates them and pounces on the piano keys.*]

USHER [*looks over his shoulder, threateningly*]. Why do you play only on the black keys? I suppose you think black is good enough for the proletariat. You play on all the keys only for the bourgeoisie, is that it?

OLEG BARD. Please, citizen, please! I'm concentrating on the white ones!

USHER. So you think white is best? Play on both!

OLEG BARD. I *am* playing on both!

USHER. So you compromise with the Whites, opportunist!

OLEG BARD. But, comrade . . . the keyboard is . . .

USHER. Who said "broad"? And in the presence of the newlyweds! Take that!

[*Hits him on the back of the neck with guitar. The* HAIRDRESSER *sticks his fork into the* MATRON OF HONOR'S *hair.* PRISYPKIN *pushes the* ACCOUNTANT *away from his wife.*]

PRISYPKIN. What do you mean by sticking a fish into my wife's breast? This is a bosom, not a flower bed, and that's a fish, not a chrysanthemum!

ACCOUNTANT. And who gave us salmon to eat? You did, huh? So what are you screaming about, huh?

[*In the tussle the bride is pushed onto the stove. The stove overturns. Her wedding veil catches fire. Flames. Smoke.*]

VOICES. We're on fire! . . . Who said "on fire"? . . . Salmon! . . . "The tramcars drew up to the Registry Office. . . ."

Scene 4

[*A fireman's helmet gleams in the darkness, reflecting the light of a nearby fire. Firemen rush on stage, report to their CHIEF and exit.*]

FIRST FIREMAN. We can't control it, Comrade Chief! We weren't called for two hours . . . the drunken swine! It's burning like a powder magazine. [*Exit.*]

CHIEF. No wonder it burns—cobwebs and liquor.

SECOND FIREMAN. It's dying down . . . the water's turning to icicles. The cellar looks like a skating rink. [*Exit.*]

CHIEF. Found any bodies?

THIRD FIREMAN. One with a smashed skull—must have been hit by a falling beam. Sent it straight to the morgue. [*Exit.*]

FOURTH FIREMAN. One charred corpse of undetermined sex with a fork in its hand.

FIRST FIREMAN. An ex-woman found under the stove with a wire crown on her head.

THIRD FIREMAN. One person unknown of prewar build with a cash register in his hands. Must have been a bandit.

SECOND FIREMAN. No survivors . . . one person unaccounted-for—since the corpse has not been found, I assume it must have burned up entirely.

FIRST FIREMAN. Look at the fireworks! Just like a theater, except that all the actors have been burned up!

THIRD FIREMAN.

> They were driven from the marriage
> In a Red Cross carriage. . . .

[*A bugler summons the FIREMEN. They form ranks and march through the aisles of the theater reciting.*]

FIREMEN.

Comrades and citizens! vodka is toxic!
Drunks can easily burn up the Republic!
A primus stove or an open fire can turn your home into a
    funeral pyre!
You can start a fire if you chance to doze off
So no bedside reading of Nadson and Zharoff!

Scene 5

[*Fifty years later. An immense amphitheater for conferences.
Instead of human voters, radio loudspeakers equipped with
arms like directional signals on an automobile. Above each
loudspeaker, colored electric lights. Just below the ceiling
there are movie screens. In the center of the hall a dais
with a microphone, flanked by control panels and switches
for sound and light. Two technicians—an* OLD MAN *and a*
YOUTH—*are tinkering around in the darkened hall.*]

OLD MAN [*flicking dust from loudspeakers with a bedraggled
feather duster*]. It's an important vote today. Check up on
the voting apparatus of the agricultural zones and give it
a spot of oil. There was a hitch last time. . . .

YOUTH. The agricultural zones? Okay! I'll oil the central zones
and polish up the throat of the Smolensk apparatus—they
were a bit hoarse again last week. I must tighten up the
arms on the metropolitan auxiliary personnel—they're deviating a bit—the right arm tangles with the left one.

OLD MAN. The Ural factories are ready. We'll switch in the
Kursk metal works—they've just installed a new apparatus
of sixty-two thousand votes for the second group of Za-
porozhe power stations. It's pretty good and doesn't give
any trouble.

YOUTH. And you remember how it was in the old days? Must
have been queer, wasn't it?

OLD MAN. My mother once carried me to a meeting in her
arms. There weren't many people—only about a thousand.
They were just sitting there, the parasites, and listening.
It was some important motion and it was passed by a
majority of one. My mother was against it but she couldn't
vote because she was holding me in her arms.

YOUTH. Yes . . . That was amateur stuff, of course!

OLD MAN. Apparatus like this wouldn't even have been any good in the old days. A fellow used to have to raise his hand to draw attention to himself—he'd thrust it right in the chairman's face, put both his hands right under his nose. He could have used twelve hands like the ancient god Isis. And lots of people avoided voting. They tell a story about one fellow who sat out some important discussion in the men's room—he was too frightened to vote. He just sat and thought, trying to save his skin.

YOUTH. And did he?

OLD MAN. I'll say he did! But they appointed him to another job. Seeing how much he liked the men's room they put him there permanently in charge of the soap and towels. . . . Everything ready?

YOUTH. Everything!

[*They run down to the control panels. A man with glasses and beard flings open the door and walks straight to the rostrum. Standing with his back to the auditorium, he raises both hands.*]

ORATOR. Plug in all the zones of the Federation!

OLD MAN *and* YOUTH. Okay!

[*All the red, green and blue bulbs light up simultaneously.*]

ORATOR. Hello, hello! This is the President of the Institute for Human Resurrection. The motion has been circulated by telegram and has been discussed. The question is clear and simple. At the corner of 62nd Street and 17th Avenue in the former town of Tambov, a building brigade, while excavating at a depth of seven meters, has discovered a caved-in, ice-filled cellar. A frozen human figure is visible through the ice. In the opinion of the Institute this individual, who froze to death fifty years ago, could be resurrected. Let us regulate the difference of opinions!

The Institute considers that the life of every worker must be utilized until the very last second.

An X-ray examination has shown that the hands of the individual are callused. Half a century ago calluses were the distinguishing mark of a worker. And let me remind you that after the wars that swept over the world, after the civil wars that led to the creation of our World Federation, human life was declared inviolable by the decree of November 7th, 1965. I have to bring to your attention the objections of the Epidemological Office, which fears a spread of the bacteria known to have infected the former inhabitants of what was once Russia.

In putting the question to the vote, I am fully aware of my responsibility. Comrades, remember, remember, and once again remember:

We are voting for a human life!

[*The lights are dimmed, a high-pitched bell rings. The text of the motion is flashed onto a screen and read out by the* ORATOR.]

"For the sake of research into the labor habits of the proletariat, for the sake of comparative studies in human life and manners, we demand resurrection!"

[VOICES *from half the loudspeakers:* "Quite right! Adopted!" *Some other* VOICES: "Rejected!" *The* VOICES *trail off and the screen darkens. A second bell. A new motion is flashed onto the screen and the* ORATOR *reads it out.*]

"Moved by the sanitary inspection stations of the metallurgical and chemical enterprises of the Don Basin: In view of the danger of the spread of the bacteria of arrogance and sycophancy, which were epidemic in 1929, we demand that the exhibit remain in its refrigerated state."

[VOICES *from the loudspeakers:* "Rejected." *A few shouts of* "Adopted."]

ORATOR. Any further motions or amendments?

[*Another screen lights up and the* ORATOR *reads from it.*]

"The agricultural zones of Siberia request that the resurrection be postponed until the fall—until the termination of work in the fields—in order to make possible the presence of the broad masses of the people."

[*Overwhelming majority of loudspeakers:* "Rejected!" *The bulbs light up.*]

I put it to a vote. All in favor of the first motion please raise their hands!

[*Overwhelming majority of the steel hands are raised.*]

Who is in favor of the amendment from Siberia?

[*Two lone hands are raised.*]

The Assembly of the Federation accepts the motion in favor of RE-SUR-RECTION!

[*Roar from all the loudspeakers: "Hurrah!" The* VOICES *die away.*]

The session is closed!

[REPORTERS *rush in through swinging doors. The* ORATOR *cannot restrain himself and shouts joyfully.*]

Resurrection it is! Resurrection! Resurrection!

[*The* REPORTERS *pull microphones from their pockets.*]

FIRST REPORTER. Hello! 472.5 kilocycles calling. . . . *Eskimo Izvestia.* . . . Resurrection!

SECOND REPORTER. Hello! Hello! 376 kilocycles. . . . *Vitebsk Evening Pravda.* . . . Resurrection!

THIRD REPORTER. Hello! Hello! Hello! 211 kilocycles. . . . *Warsaw Komsomol Pravda.* . . . Resurrection!

FOURTH REPORTER. *Armavir Literary Weekly.* . . . Hello! Hello!

FIFTH REPORTER. Hello! Hello! Hello! . . . 44 kilocycles. . . . *Izvestia of Chicago Soviet.* . . . Resurrection!

SIXTH REPORTER. Hello! Hello! Hello! . . . 115 kilocycles. . . . *Red Gazette of Rome.* . . . Resurrection!

SEVENTH REPORTER. Hello! Hello! Hello! . . . 78 kilocycles. . . . *Shanghai Pauper.* . . . Resurrection!

EIGHTH REPORTER. Hello! Hello! Hello! . . . 220 kilocycles. . . . *Madrid Dairy-Maid.* . . . Resurrection!

NINTH REPORTER. Hello! Hello! Hello! . . . 11 kilocycles. . . . *Kabul Pioneer.* . . . Resurrection!

[*Newsboys burst in with newssheets fresh from the press.*]

FIRST NEWSBOY.

Read how the man froze
Lead stories in verse and prose!

SECOND NEWSBOY.

Worldwide poll on number-one question!
Can obsequiousness spread by infection?

THIRD NEWSBOY.

> Feature on ancient guitars and romances
> And other means of drugging the masses!

FOURTH NEWSBOY.

> Interview! Interview! Read all about it!

FIFTH NEWSBOY.

> Complete list of so-called "dirty words."
> Don't be scared, keep your nerve!

SIXTH NEWSBOY.

> *Science Gazette! Science Gazette!*
> Theoretical discussion of ancient problem—
> Can an elephant die from a cigarette?

SEVENTH NEWSBOY.

> It'll make you cry and give you colic——
> Explanation of the word "alcoholic"!

Scene 6

[*Sliding door of frosted glass behind which gleam metal parts of surgical apparatus. In front of it are an old* PROFESSOR *and his elderly assistant, who is recognizable as* ZOYA BERYOZKINA. *Both are in white hospital gowns.*]

ZOYA BERYOZKINA. Comrade! Comrade professor! Don't do this experiment, I beg you! Comrade professor, that awful business will start all over again. . . .

PROFESSOR. Comrade Beryozkina, you have begun to live in the past and you talk an incomprehensible language. Just like a dictionary of obsolete words. What's "business"? [*Looks it up in the dictionary.*] Business . . . business . . . bootlegger . . . Bulgakov . . . bureaucracy . . . ah, here we are: "business: a kind of activity that prevented every other kind of activity. . . ."

ZOYA BERYOZKINA. Well, this "activity" nearly cost me my life fifty years ago. . . . I even went so far as to attempt suicide. . . .

PROFESSOR. Suicide? What's "suicide"? [*Looks in dictionary.*]

. . . supertax . . . surrealism . . . here we are: "suicide."
[*Surprised.*] You shot yourself? By a court order? A revolutionary tribunal?

ZOYA BERYOZKINA. No . . . by myself. . . .

PROFESSOR. By yourself? Carelessness?

ZOYA BERYOZKINA. No . . . love. . . .

PROFESSOR. Nonsense! Love should make you build bridges
and bear children. . . . But you . . . my-my-my!

ZOYA BERYOZKINA. Let me go; I simply can't face it!

PROFESSOR. That really is . . . what was the word? . . . "a
business." My-my-my! A business! Society needs you. You
must bring all your feelings into play so as to enable this
being, whom we are about to unfreeze, to recover from
his fifty anazooic years with the maximum of ease. Yes,
upon my word! Your presence is very, very important! . . .
He and she—that's you I mean! Tell me, were his eyelashes brittle? They might break during the process of
rapid defrigeration.

ZOYA BERYOZKINA. Comrade professor, how can I remember
eyelashes of fifty years ago!

PROFESSOR. Fifty years ago . . . that was yesterday! And how
do you think I manage to remember the color of the hairs
on the tail of a mastodon that died half a million years ago?
My-my-my! Well, do you remember whether he dilated his
nostrils very much while breathing in a state of excitement?

ZOYA BERYOZKINA. Comrade professor, how can I remember?
It's thirty years since people dilated their nostrils under
such conditions.

PROFESSOR. Well, well, well! And do you have information
about the size of his stomach and liver?—in case there is
any quantity of alcohol that might ignite at the high voltage
we require. . . .

ZOYA BERYOZKINA. How can I remember all that, Comrade
professor? I know he had a stomach. . . .

PROFESSOR. Ah, you don't remember anything, Comrade
Beryozkina! But you can at least tell me, was he impulsive?

ZOYA BERYOZKINA. I don't know . . . perhaps . . . but not with
me.

PROFESSOR. Well, well, well! I fear that while we're unfreezing
him, you are freezing up! My-my-my! Well, let's proceed.

[*Presses a button. The glass door slides back silently. In the
middle a shining, zinc-covered, man-sized box on an operat-*

ing table. Around it are faucets with pails under them. Wires lead into the crate. Oxygen cylinders. Six calm, white-clad DOCTORS *stand around the crate. Six washbasins in the foreground. Six towels hang, as though suspended in mid air, on an invisible wire.*]

PROFESSOR [*to* FIRST DOCTOR]. Switch on the current only at my signal. [*To* SECOND DOCTOR.] Bring temperature up to 98.6 at intervals of fifteen seconds. [*To* THIRD DOCTOR.] Have the oxygen cylinder ready. [*To* FOURTH DOCTOR.] Drain off the water gradually as you replace the ice with air pressure. [*To* FIFTH DOCTOR.] Raise the lid at once. [*To* SIXTH DOCTOR.] Follow the stages of his revival in the mirror.

[*The* DOCTORS *nod their heads to show they have understood. They watch the temperature. Water drips. The* SIXTH DOCTOR *stares at a mirror in the right side of the crate.*]

SIXTH DOCTOR. His natural color is returning! [*Pause.*] He's free from ice! [*Pause.*] His chest is heaving! [*Pause.*] Professor, look at these unnatural spasms!

PROFESSOR [*comes up and looks closely; in a calm voice*]. That's a normal movement—he's scratching himself. Evidently the parasites inseparable from these specimens are reviving.

SIXTH DOCTOR. Professor, what do you make of this? That movement of his left hand from the body. . . .

PROFESSOR [*looking closely*]. He's what used to be called a "sentimental soul," a music lover. In antiquity there was Stradivarius and there was Utkin. Stradivarius made violins and Utkin played on this thing—"guitar" they called it. [*Inspects thermometer and apparatus registering blood pressure.*]

FIRST DOCTOR. 98.6.

SECOND DOCTOR. Pulse 68.

SIXTH DOCTOR. Breathing regular.

PROFESSOR. To your places!

[*The* DOCTORS *walk away from the crate. The lid flies open and out comes* PRISYPKIN. *He is disheveled and surprised. He looks around, clutching his guitar.*]

PRISYPKIN. Well, I've slept it off! Forgive me, comrades, I was boiled, of course! What militia station is this?

PROFESSOR. This isn't the militia. This is the defrigeration station. We have unfrozen you.

PRISYPKIN. What's that? Unfrozen me? We'll soon see who was drunk! I know you doctors—always sniffing at alcohol! I can prove my identity; I've got my documents on me [*Jumps down from crate and turns out his pockets.*] . . . seventeen rubles, sixty kopecks in cash . . . paid up all my dues . . . Revolutionary Defense Fund . . . Anti-illiteracy campaign . . . Here you are, look! . . . What's this? A marriage certificate [*Whistles.*] . . . Where are you, my love? Who is kissing your finger tips? There'll be hell to pay at home! Here's the best man's receipt. Here's my union card. [*Happens to see the calendar; rubs his eyes, looks around in horror.*] May 12th, 1979! All my unpaid union dues! For fifty years! The forms I'll have to fill out! For the District Committee! For the Central Committee! My God! My wife! Let me out of here!

[*Shakes the hands of the* DOCTORS *and makes for the door. Alarmed,* ZOYA BERYOZKINA *goes after him. The* DOCTORS *crowd around the* PROFESSOR *and speak in chorus.*]

DOCTORS. What's that he was doing—squeezing our hands like that?

PROFESSOR. An antihygienic habit they had in the old days.

[*The six* DOCTORS *and the* PROFESSOR *thoughtfully wash their hands.*]

PRISYPKIN [*bumping into* ZOYA BERYOZKINA]. For heaven's sake, who are you? Who am I? Where am I? You wouldn't me Zoya Beryozkina's mother? [*Turns his head at the screech of a siren.*] Where the hell am I? Where've they put me? What is this? Moscow, Paris, New York??? Cab!

[*Blaring of automobile horns.*]

Not a soul in sight! Not a single horse! Just automobiles, automobiles, automobiles! [*Presses against door, scratches his back, gropes with his hand, turns around, and sees a bedbug crawling from his collar onto the white wall.*] A bedbug! My sweet little bedbug, my darling little bedbug, my own little bedbug! [*Plays a chord on guitar and sings.*] "Leave me not, abide with me awhile . . ." [*Tries to catch bedbug with his hand, but it crawls away.*] "We part like ships in the sea . . ." He's gone! . . . I'm all alone! "No

one replies, alone I am again, alone . . ." Cab! Automobiles!
. . . Seventeen Lunacharsky Street, no luggage . . . [*Clutches
his head, swoons into the arms of* ZOYA BERYOZKINA, *who
has run out after him.*]

Scene 7

[*A triangular plaza. Three artificial trees. First tree has green
square leaves on which stand enormous plates with tangerines. Second tree has paper plates with apples. Third tree
has open perfume bottles shaped like pine cones. Sides:
glass-fronted buildings. Long benches running along the
sides of the triangle. Enter* REPORTER *and four other people,
men and women.*]

REPORTER. Over here, comrades! In the shade! I'll tell you
about these grim and astonishing events. In the first place
. . . Pass me some tangerines. How right the municipality
was to make the trees tangerine today. Yesterday it was
pears—so dry, insipid, unnutritious!

[GIRL *takes a plate of tangerines from the tree. The people
sitting on the bench peel them, eat them, and turn ex-
pectantly to the* REPORTER.]

FIRST MAN. Well, come on, comrade, let's have all the details.
REPORTER. Well, the . . . how juicy they are! Want some?
Well, okay, here's the story. . . . How impatient you are!
. . . Naturally, as dean of the correspondents I know every-
thing. . . . Look, look! See that?

[*A* MAN *with a box full of thermometers walks quickly
through.*]

He's a vet. The epidemic's spreading. As soon as it was left
alone this resurrected mammal made contact with the do-
mestic animals in the skyscraper, and now all the dogs
have gone mad. It taught them to stand on their hind legs.
They don't bark or frisk around any more—all they do
is "beg." They pester everybody at mealtimes, whining and
fawning. The doctors say that humans bitten by these
animals will get all the primary symptoms of epidemic
sycophancy.
ALL. O-h!

REPORTER. Look, look!

[*A* MAN *staggers past. He is loaded with hampers containing bottles of beer.*]

PASSER-BY [*singing*].

> Back in the nineteenth cent-ury
> A fella could live in lux-ury
> Drinking beer and drinking gin
> His nose was blue and hung down to his chin!

REPORTER. See? That man's sick—finished! He's one of the one hundred and seventy-five workers of the Second Medical Laboratory. To make its transitional existence easier the doctors ordered the resurrected mammal to be fed with a mixture that is toxic in large doses and repulsive in small ones—"beer" it's called. The poisonous fumes made them dizzy and some of them took a swig of it by mistake, as a refresher. Since then they've had to change the working personnel three times. Five hundred and twenty workers are in the hospital, but the terrible epidemic continues to rage, mowing everybody down in its foaming path.

MAN [*dreamily and longingly*]. I don't mind sacrificing myself in the cause of science. Let them inoculate me with a dose of this mysterious illness!

REPORTER. He's done for, too. . . . Quiet! Don't startle this sleepwalker! . . .

[GIRL *comes by. She stumbles through the steps of a foxtrot and the Charleston and mutters verses from a booklet held between two fingers of one outstretched hand. She holds an imaginary rose between two fingers of the other hand. Presses it to her nose and inhales imaginary fragrance.*]

Poor girl. She lives next door to this crazed mammal and at night, when the town is asleep, she hears the throb of his guitar through the wall—and then there are long heart-rending sighs and sobs. What was it they called this sort of thing? "Crooning," wasn't it? . . . It was too much for the poor girl and she began to go out of her mind. Her parents were heartbroken and called in the doctors. The professors say it's an acute attack of an ancient disease they called "love." This was a state in which a person's sexual energy, instead of being rationally distributed over the whole of his life, was compressed into a single week and concentrated in one hectic process. This made him commit the most absurd and impossible acts.

GIRL [*covers her face with her hands*]. I'd better not look. I can feel these "love" microbes infecting the air!

REPORTER. She's finished, too. The epidemic is taking on oceanic proportions.

[*Thirty* CHORUS GIRLS *dance onto the stage.*]

Look at this thirty-headed centipede! Just think, this raising of the legs is what they [*He turns to the audience.*] called art!

[*A foxtrotting couple comes on.*]

The epidemic has reached it . . . its—what's the word?— [*Looks in dictionary.*] its "apo-gee." . . . Well, this is nothing less than a hermaphrodite quadruped.

[DIRECTOR *of zoo runs in. He is carrying a small glass case. After him comes a crowd of people armed with telescopes, cameras, and fire ladders.*]

DIRECTOR [*to all*]. Seen it? Seen it? Where is it? Oh, you've seen nothing! A search party reported they saw it here about a quarter of an hour ago. It was making its way up to the fourth floor. Its average speed is one and a half meters an hour, so it can't have got very far. Comrades, search the walls immediately!

[*The searchers extend their telescopes. The people sitting on the benches jump up and, shading their eyes with their hands, peer into the distance. The* DIRECTOR *gives instructions.*]

VOICES. This the way to find it? . . . We should put a naked man on a mattress in every window. . . . It goes for humans. . . . Don't shout! You'll frighten it away! . . . I won't give it to anybody if I find it! . . . Don't you dare; it's public property! . . .

EXCITED VOICE. Found it! Here it is, crawling . . . !

[*Binoculars and telescopes are all focused on one spot. The silence is interrupted only by the clicking and whirring of cameras.*]

DIRECTOR. Yes . . . that's it! Put guards around it! Firemen, over here!

[*People with nets surround the place. The firemen put up their ladder and people clamber up in Indian file.*]

DIRECTOR [*lowering telescope. In tearful voice*]. It's got away! . . . Crawled to the next wall. . . . SOS! It'll fall and kill itself! Volunteers! Heroes! This way!

[*The ladder is run up a second wall. People climb up. Others watch with bated breath.*]

EXCITED VOICE [*from above*]. Got it! Hurrah!
DIRECTOR. Quick! Careful! Don't let it go! Don't crush the insect's legs! [*The insect is passed down the ladder and handed to the* DIRECTOR. *He puts it in the glass case and flourishes it over his head.*] My thanks to you, comrades, for your humble efforts on behalf of science! Our zoo has been enriched by a *chef-d'oeuvre*. . . . We have captured a most rare specimen of an extinct insect which was extremely popular at the beginning of the century. Our city may be justly proud of itself. Scientists and tourists will flock to us. . . . Here in my hands I have the only living specimen of *bedbugus normalis*. . . . Move back there, citizens, the insect has fallen asleep, it has crossed its legs and wishes to rest! I invite all of you to the solemn opening of an exhibition in the Zoological Garden. The capture, so supremely important and so fraught with anxiety, has been successfully completed!

Scene 8

[*A room with smooth, opalescent, translucent walls. Hidden, bluish lighting from the ceiling. A large window on the left. A large table in front of the window. On the right, a bed let down from the wall. On the bed, lying under the cleanest of blankets, is* PRISYPKIN. *He is filthy. Electric fans.* PRISYPKIN'S *corner is like a pigsty. The table is littered with cigarette butts and overturned bottles. A piece of pink paper has been stuck on the reading lamp.* PRISYPKIN *is groaning. A* DOCTOR *paces the room nervously.*]

PROFESSOR [*entering*]. How's the patient?
DOCTOR. I don't know, but I feel terrible. If you don't order a change of staff every half-hour he'll infect everybody.

Every time he breathes, my legs give way! I've put in seven
fans to disperse his breath.

PRISYPKIN. A-a-a-a-a-a-a-h! [PROFESSOR *runs over to him.*]
Professor! Oh, profes-s-or!!! [PROFESSOR *takes one sniff
and staggers back, clawing the air from dizziness.*] Give
me a drink. . . . [PROFESSOR *pours a little beer into a glass
and hands it to him.* PRISYPKIN *raises himself on his elbows.
Reproachfully.*] You resurrect me and now you make fun
of me! Like giving lemonade to an elephant!

PROFESSOR. Society hopes to raise you up to a human level. . . .

PRISYPKIN. To hell with society and to hell with you. I didn't
ask you to resurrect me. Freeze me back!

PROFESSOR. I don't know what you're talking about! Our lives
belong to the collective and neither I nor anybody else . . .

PRISYPKIN. What kind of a life is it when you can't even
pin a picture of your best girl on the wall? The tacks break
on this goddamn glass. . . . Comrade professor, give me a
drink. . . .

PROFESSOR [*filling glass*]. All right, only don't breathe in my
direction.

[ZOYA BERYOZKINA *comes in with two piles of books. The*
DOCTORS *talk with her in a whisper and leave.*]

ZOYA BERYOZKINA [*sits next to* PRISYPKIN *and unpacks books*].
I don't know whether this is what you want. Nobody knows
anything about what you asked for. Only textbooks on
horticulture have anything about roses, and daydreams are
dealt with only in medical works—in the section on hyp-
nosis. But here are two very interesting books more or less
of your period—Hoover: *An Ex-President Speaks* . . .
translated from the English.

PRISYPKIN [*takes the book and hurls it aside*]. No . . . I want
something that . . . plucks at my heartstrings. . . .

ZOYA BERYOZKINA. Well, here's a book by someone called
Mussolini: *Letters from Exile.*

PRISYPKIN [*takes it and throws it aside*]. No, that's not for the
soul. . . . I want something that gives me that melting
feeling . . . leave me alone with your crude propaganda.

ZOYA BERYOZKINA. I don't know what you mean . . . heartstrings, melting feeling. . . .

PRISYPKIN. What is all this? What did we fight for? Why did
we shed our blood, if I can't dance to my heart's content—
and I'm supposed to be a leader of the new society!

ZOYA BERYOZKINA. I demonstrated your bodily movement to the director of the Central Institute of Calisthenics. He says he's seen things like that in an old collection of French post cards, but now, he says, there isn't even anybody to ask about it. Except a couple of old women—they remember, but they can't demonstrate it because of their rheumatism.

PRISYPKIN. Why then did I bother to acquire such an elegant education? I could always *work* before the revolution.

ZOYA BERYOZKINA. Tomorrow I'll take you to see a dance performed by twenty thousand male and female workers on the city square. It's a gay rehearsal of a new work system on the farms.

PRISYPKIN. Comrades! I protest! I didn't unfreeze for you to dry me up! [*Tears off the blanket, jumps out of bed, seizes a pile of books and shakes them out of the broadsheet in which they are wrapped. He is about to tear up the paper when he looks at it more closely. He runs from lamp to lamp, studying the text.*] Where . . . where did you get this?

ZOYA BERYOZKINA. It was being distributed to everybody in the streets . . . they must have put copies in all the library books. . . .

PRISYPKIN. Saved!! Hurrah!! [*He rushes to the door, waving the paper like a flag.*]

ZOYA BERYOZKINA [*alone*]. And to think that fifty years ago I might have died on account of this skunk. . . .

Scene 9

[*Zoo. In the center a platform on which stands a cage draped with a cloth and decked with flags. Two trees behind the cage. Behind the trees two more cages with elephants and giraffes. On the left of the cage a rostrum and on the right a grandstand for guests of honor.* MUSICIANS *standing around the cage.* SPECTATORS *approaching it in groups.* STEWARDS *with armbands assign them to their places according to profession and height.*]

STEWARD. Over here, comrades of the foreign press! Closer to the platform! Move over there and leave room for the Brazilians! Their airship is now landing at Central Airport. [*Steps back and admires his arrangement of the guests.*]

Comrade Negroes, mix in with the Britons and form nice multicolored groups with them. . . . Their Anglo-Saxon pallor will set off your complexions to even greater advantage! High-school students, over there to the left. Four old people from the Union of Centenarians have been assigned to you. They will supplement the professor's lecture with eyewitness accounts. . . .

[*Two* OLD MEN *and two* OLD WOMEN *are wheeled in in wheel-chairs.*]

FIRST OLD MAN. *I* remember like it was now . . .

FIRST OLD WOMAN. No, it's me who remembers like it was now!

SECOND OLD WOMAN. You remember like it was now, but I remember like it was before.

SECOND OLD MAN. But I remember like it was before, like it was now.

THIRD OLD WOMAN. I remember how it was even before that, a long, long time before!

THIRD OLD MAN. I remember how it was before *and* like it was now!

STEWARD. Quiet there, eyewitnesses, no squabbling! Clear the way, comrades, make way for the children! Over here, comrades! Hurry, hurry!

CHILDREN [*marching in a column and singing*].

> We study all day
> But we know how to play
> We're through with math
> And now we're off to see the giraffe
> We're going to the zoo
> Like the grown-ups do!

STEWARD. Citizens who wish to please the exhibits and also to examine them for scientific purposes are requested to obtain various exotic products and scientific equipment from the official zoo attendants. Doses prepared without expert knowledge can be fatal. We ask you to use only the products and equipment supplied by the Central Medical Institute and the Municipal Laboratories of Precision Engineering.

[ATTENDANTS *walk around the zoo and the theater.*]

FIRST ATTENDANT.
> Comrade, when looking at germs

Don't be a dope!
Use a magnifying glass or a microscope!

SECOND ATTENDANT.

Take the advice of Doctor Segal
If accidentally spat upon
Be sure to use diluted phenol!

THIRD ATTENDANT.

Feeding time's a memorable scene!
Give the exhibits alcohol and nicotine!

FOURTH ATTENDANT.

Feed them with their favorite liquor!
They'll get gout and cirrhosis of the liver!

FIFTH ATTENDANT.

Give them nicotine in liberal doses!
A guarantee of arteriosclerosis!

SIXTH ATTENDANT.

Please give your ears the best protection.
These earphones filter every crude expression!

STEWARD [clearing a way to the rostrum]. The chairman of
the City Soviet and his closest colleagues have left their
highly important duties to attend our ceremony. Here they
come to the strains of our ancient national anthem. Let's
greet our dear comrades!

[All applaud. A group of PEOPLE with briefcases crosses the
stage. They bow stiffly and sing.]

PEOPLE.

The burdens of our office
Never tire or age us
There's a time for work
And a time for play
Greetings from the Soviet,
Workers of the Zoo!
We're the city fathers
And we're proud of you!

CHAIRMAN OF CITY SOVIET [mounts rostrum and waves a flag;
hushed silence]. Comrades, I declare the ceremony open.

The times in which we live are fraught with shocks and experiences of an internal nature. External occurrences are rare. Exhausted by the events of an earlier age, mankind is glad of this relative peace. All the same, we never deny ourselves a spectacle, which, however extravagant it may be in appearance, conceals a profound scientific meaning under its multicolored plumage. The unfortunate incidents which have taken place in our city were the result of the incautious admittance in our midst of two parasites. Through my efforts, as well as through the efforts of world medicine, these incidents have been eradicated. However, these incidents, stirring a distant memory of the past, underscore the horrors of a bygone age and the difficulties of the world proletariat in its mighty struggle for culture. May the hearts and souls of our young people be steeled by these sinister examples! Before calling on him to speak, it is incumbent upon me to move a vote of thanks to the director of our zoo, who has deciphered the meaning of these strange occurrences and turned these ugly phenomena into a gay and edifying entertainment. Hip-hip . . . Hurray! Hip-hip . . . Hurray!

[*All cheer. The musicians play a fanfare as the* DIRECTOR *climbs to the rostrum. He bows on all sides.*]

DIRECTOR. Comrades! I am both delighted and embarrassed by your kind words. With all due consideration for my part in the matter, it is incumbent upon me to express thanks to the dedicated workers of the Union of Hunters, who are the real heroes of the capture, and also to our respected professor of the Institute of Resurrection, who vanquished death by defrigeration. However, I must point out that it was a mistake on the part of our respected professor that led directly to the misfortunes of which you are aware. Owing to certain mimetic characteristics, such as its calluses and clothing, our respected professor mistakenly classified the resurrected mammal not only as a representative of *homo sapiens*, but even as a member of the highest group of the species—the working class. I do not attribute my success entirely to my long experience of dealing with animals and to my understanding of their psychology. I was aided by chance. Prompted by a vague, subconscious hope I wrote and distributed an advertisement. Here is the text:

"In accordance with the principles of the Zoological Garden, I seek a live human body to be constantly bitten by a newly acquired insect, for the maintenance and development of the said insect in the normal conditions to which it is accustomed."

VOICE FROM THE CROWD. How horrible!

DIRECTOR. I know it's horrible . . . I was myself astonished by by own absurd idea . . . yet, suddenly, a creature presents itself! It looks almost human . . . well, just like you and me. . . .

CHAIRMAN OF CITY SOVIET [*ringing his bell*]. Comrade director! I must call you to order!

DIRECTOR. My apologies, my apologies! Of course, I immediately established from my knowledge of comparative bestiology and by means of an interrogation that I was dealing with an anthropoid simulator and that this was the most remarkable of parasites. I shall not go into details, particularly as you will see it all for yourselves in a moment, in this absolutely extraordinary cage. There are two of them: the famous *bedbugus normalis* and . . . er . . . *bourgeoisius vulgaris*. They are different in size, but identical in essence. Both of them have their habitat in the musty mattresses of time.

Bedbugus normalis, having gorged itself on the body of a single human, falls under the bed.

Bourgeoisius vulgaris, having gorged itself on the body of all mankind, falls onto the bed. That's the only difference!

While after the Revolution the proletariat was writhing and scratching itself to rid itself of filth, these parasites built their nests and made their homes in this dirt, beat their wives, swore by Bebel, and relaxed blissfully in the shade of their own jodhpurs. But of the two, *bourgeoisius vulgaris* is the more frightening. With his monstrous mimetic powers he lured his victims by posing as a twittering versifier or as a drooling bird. In those days even their clothing had a kind of protective coloration. They wore birdlike winged ties with tail coats and white starched breasts. These birds nested in theater loges, perched in flocks on oak trees at the opera to the tune of the *Internationale*, rubbed their legs together in the ballet, dressed up Tolstoy to look like Marx, hung upside down from the twigs of their verse, shrieked and howled to a disgusting degree, and—forgive the expression, but this is a scientific lecture—excreted on a scale far in excess of the normal small droppings of a bird. Comrades! But see for yourselves!

[*He gives a signal and the attendants unveil the cage. The glass case containing the bedbug is on a pedestal. Behind it, on a platform, is a double bed. On the bed, PRISYPKIN with his guitar. A lamp with a yellow shade hangs above the cage. Above PRISYPKIN'S head is a glittering halo composed of post cards arranged fanwise. Bottles lying on the floor and spittoons placed around the sides of the cage, which is also equipped with filters and air-conditioners. Notices saying: 1) Caution—it spits! 2) No unauthorized entry! 3) Watch your ears—it curses! Musicians play a fanfare. Bengal lights. The crowd first surges back and then approaches the cage, mute with delight.*]

PRISYPKIN.

> On Lunacharsky Street
> There's an old house I know
> With staircase broad and neat
> And a curtain at the window!

DIRECTOR. Comrades, come closer, don't be frightened—it's quite tame. Come, come, don't be alarmed. On the inside of the cage there are four filters to trap all the dirty words. Only very few words come out and they're quite decent. The filters are cleaned every day by a special squad of attendants in gas masks. Look, it's now going to have what they called "a smoke."

VOICE FROM CROWD. Oh, how horrible!

DIRECTOR. Don't be frightened. Now it's going to "have a swig," as they said. Skripkin, drink!

[*PRISYPKIN reaches for a bottle of vodka.*]

VOICE FROM CROWD. Oh, don't, don't! Don't torment the poor animal!

DIRECTOR. Comrades, there's nothing to worry about. It's tame! Look, I'm now going to bring it out of the cage. [*Goes to the cage, puts on gloves, checks his revolver, opens the door, brings out PRISYPKIN onto the platform, and turns him around to face the guests of honor in the grandstand.*] Now then, say a few words, show how well you can imitate the human language, voice, and expression.

[PRISYPKIN *stands obediently, clears his throat, raises his guitar, and suddenly turns around and looks at the audience. His expression changes, a look of delight comes over his face. He pushes the* DIRECTOR *aside, throws down his guitar, and shouts to the audience.*]

PRISYPKIN. Citizens! Brothers! My own people! Darlings! How did you get here? So many of you! When were you unfrozen? Why am I alone in the cage? Darlings, friends, come and join me! Why am I suffering? Citizens! . . .

VOICES OF GUESTS.

> The children! Remove the children!
> Muzzle it . . . muzzle it!
> Oh, how horrible!
> Professor, put a stop to it!
> Ah, but don't shoot it!

[*The* DIRECTOR, *holding an electric fan, runs onto the stage with the attendants. The attendants drag* PRISYPKIN *off. The* DIRECTOR *ventilates the platform. The musicians play a fanfare. The attendants cover the cage.*]

DIRECTOR. My apologies, comrades . . . my apologies. . . . The insect is tired. The noise and the bright lights gave it hallucinations. Please be calm. It's nothing at all. It will recover tomorrow. . . . Disperse quietly, citizens, until tomorrow. Music. Let's have a march!

THE WRITERS AND THEIR PLAYS

Where no translations are known to exist, the plays' original titles are used.

TURGENEV, IVAN SERGYEYEVICH—1818–83 (publication dates)

Asya, 1900; One May Spin a Thread Too Finely, a Comedy in One Act, 1909; The Lady From the Provinces (also known as A Provincial Lady), 1923; An Amicable Settlement, 1924; The Bachelor, 1924; Broke, 1924; Carelessness, 1924; A Conversation on the Highway, 1924; An Evening in Sorrento, 1924; The Family Charge, 1924; A Month in the Country, 1924; Poor Gentleman, 1934.

Opera: Pesn' torzestvajuscez ljubvi, 1881.

CHEKHOV, ANTON PAVLOVITCH—1860–1904 (publication dates)

That Worthless Fellow Platonov (unfinished), 1881; On the High Road, 1884; Ivanov, 1887; The Tragedian in Spite of Himself, 1888; The Bear (The Boor), 1888; The Wood Demon, 1889; Tatyana Riepin, 1889; The Swan Song, 1889; The Proposal, 1889; The Sea Gull, 1896; Uncle Vanya, 1897; The Three Sisters, 1900; The Jubilee, 1903; The Wedding, 1903; The Cherry Orchard, 1904.

GORKI, MAXIM—1868–1936 (publication dates)

The Middle Class, 1900; The Lower Depths, 1902; Summer Folk, 1903; Children of the Sun, 1905; Barbarians, 1905; Odd People, 1910; Children, 1910; The Meeting, 1910; The Zykovs, 1913; The Judge (The Old Man), 1915; Enemies, 1916; The Last Ones, 1918; Cain and Artema, 1921; The Counterfeit Coin, 1926; Igor Bulichev and Others, 1932.

MAYAKOVSKY, VLADIMIR VLADIMIROVICH—1893–1930 (publication dates, except as noted)

Mystery Bouffe, 1921; The Earth Prancing, 1923; The Bedbug, 1929 (production); The Bathhouse, 1930 (production).

SELECTED BIBLIOGRAPHY

BAKSHY, ALEXANDER. *The Path of The Modern Russian Stage*, Boston, 1918.

GORCHAKOV, NIKOLAI. *The Theatre in Soviet Russia*, New York, 1957.

NEMIROVITCH-DANCHENKO, VLADIMIR. *My Life in the Russian Theatre* (Tr. by John Cournos), London, 1937.

SLONIM, MARC. *Russian Theatre: From the Empire to the Soviets*, New York, 1961.

STANISLAVSKY, KONSTANTIN. *My Life in Art* (Tr. by J. J. Robbins), Boston, 1924.

VARNEKE, B. V. *A History of the Russian Theatre*, New York, 1951.

Turgenev

BENTLEY, ERIC. *What Is Theatre*, New York, 1956.

SCHECHNER, RICHARD. "Introduction," to *A Month in the Country*, Chandler Editions in Drama, San Francisco, 1962.

Turgenev's Literary Reminiscences, with Essays on Turgenev by David Magarshack and Edmund Wilson, New York, 1958.

YARMOLINSKY, AVRAHM. *Turgenev: The Man, His Art, and His Age*, New York, 1959.

Chekhov

BRUSTEIN, ROBERT. *The Theatre of Revolt*, Boston, 1964.

CORRIGAN, ROBERT W. "Introduction," *Chekhov: Six Plays*, New York, 1962.

HINGLEY, RONALD. *Chekhov*, London, 1950.

MAGARSHACK, DAVID. *Chekhov: A Life*, New York, 1953.

———. *Chekhov the Dramatist*, London, 1952.

MANN, THOMAS. *Last Essays*, New York, 1958.

SIMMONS, ERNEST J. *Chekhov*, New York, 1962.

Gorky

BAKSHY, ALEXANDER. *The Path of the Modern Russian Stage*, Boston, 1918.

GORKY, MAXIM. *Reminiscences of Tolstoy, Chekhov, and Andreyev*, New York, 1921.

GOURFINKEL, NINA. *Gorky* (Tr. by Ann Feshbach), New York, 1960.

KANN, ALEXANDER. *Maxim Gorky and His Russia*, New York, 1931.

Mayakovsky

BLAKE, PATRICIA. "Introduction," *The Bedbug and Selected Poetry of Mayakovsky.* New York, 1960.

BLOK, ALEXANDER. *The Spirit of Music*, London, 1946.

BOWRA, C. M. *The Creative Experiment*, New York, 1948.

GORELIK, MORDECAI. *New Theatres for Old*, New York, 1940.

PASTERNAK, BORIS. *An Essay in Autobiography*, London, 1959.